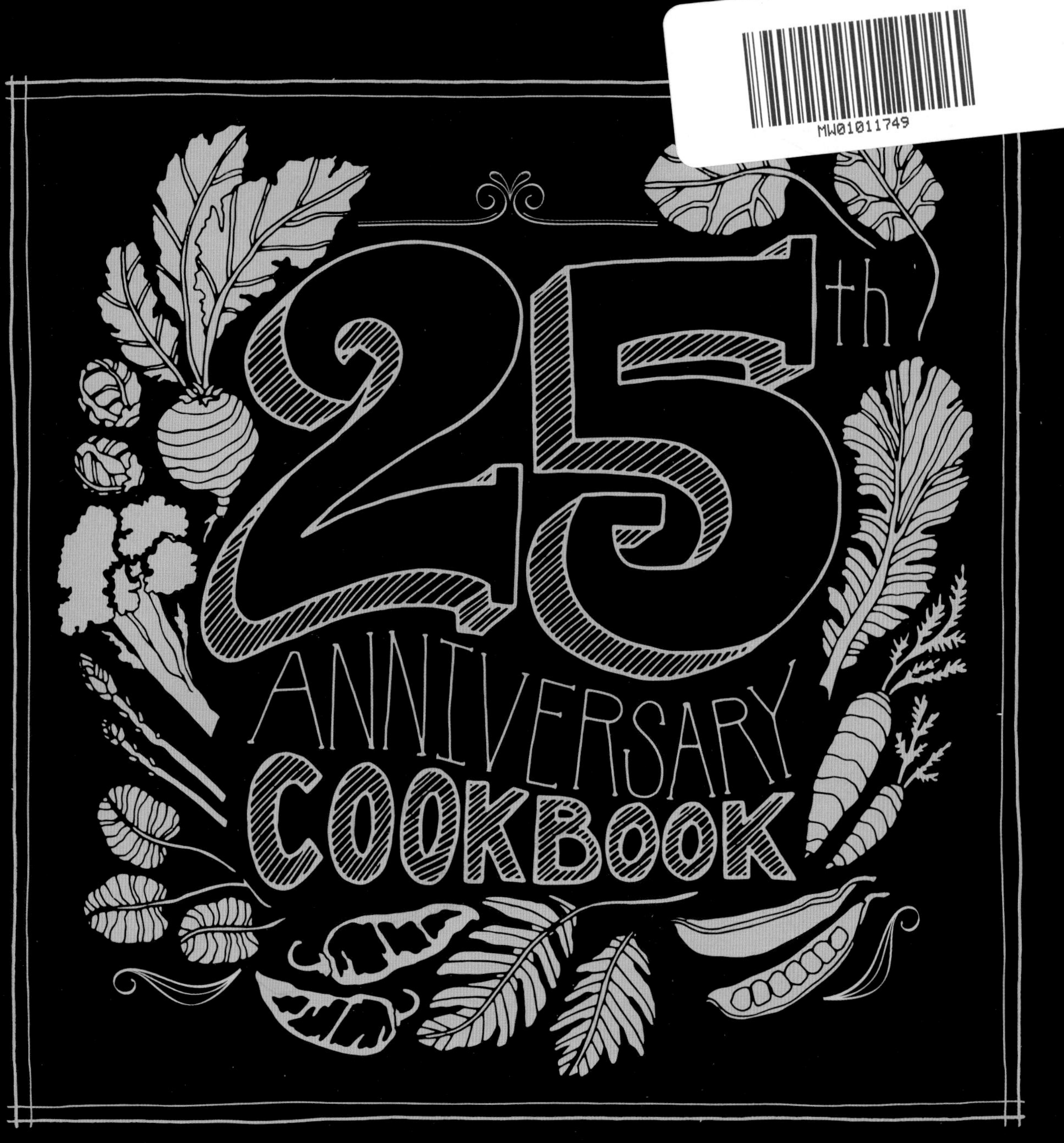

TASTE OF HOME BOOKS • RDA ENTHUSIAST BRANDS, LLC • MILWAUKEE, WI

Taste of Home

Pictured on cover: Best-Ever Fried Chicken, p. 394;
Mashed Potatoes, p. 395; Southern Buttermilk Biscuits, p. 396

Illustration on cover: Shawna Kirsch

Illustrations throughout book: Shutterstock A.U Design; Wiktoria Matynia

Pictured on back cover: Buffalo Chicken Lasagna, p. 126,
Juicy Watermelon Salad, p. 294; Sandy's Chocolate Cake, p. 39

1610 N. 2nd St., Suite 102, Milwaukee WI 53212-3906

International Standard Book Number: 978-1-61765-762-7
Library of Congress Control Number: 2018935816

Printed in China
1 3 5 7 9 10 8 6 4 2

Taste of Home

FAVORITES

DELICIOUS RECIPES SHARED ACROSS GENERATIONS

CONTENTS

P. 334
P. 95
P. 67

EMPTY PLATES. FULL HEARTS.

I've always been a lover of food. But after years of dining at buzzy, of-the-moment restaurants, exploring cities and cultures through their signature dishes while on assignment, and writing about my culinary adventures for magazines and websites, that passion became more of a job.

Thank goodness for *Taste of Home*.

Taking the position as Chief Content Officer meant digging into the history of *Taste of Home* and learning about the brand's genesis. It meant getting to know the community of Field Editors and the spirit of sharing that is at the heart of *Taste of Home*. And it offered an opportunity to work with a wonderful, dedicated and warm group of editors, art directors, photographers and Test Kitchen cooks and food stylists.

It meant a love of food was rekindled. And a purpose revealed.

Taste of Home celebrates the joy of a home-cooked meal. Of beloved recipes handed down through generations and shared generously among a community of individuals who love to cook for their families and friends. In essence, *Taste of Home* is real food. Real ingredients. Real human connection. And real love.

Since joining *Taste of Home*, I find myself often thinking about my beloved grandma. Grandma and I were particularly close, and I'd become positively giddy whenever my dad would tell me of one of her upcoming visits. You see, Mom was busy dealing with five rambunctious kids, all while maintaining a household—cleaning and ironing and darning and packing lunches. And in those days, men in the kitchen were practically unheard of... besides, Dad juggled three jobs to make ends meet.

So when Grandma came to town, we kids would anxiously wait for her undivided attention—and her mystical, magical, mythical recipe box. For it was this small box—and her culinary skills—that gave us her famous sauerbraten and German potato salad, which had us greedily asking for seconds and thirds. And when we thought we were full, we'd still dig in to Grandma's homemade chocolate cake as if we hadn't eaten in months. She even made spaghetti sauce from scratch, which was mind-boggling to us and my mother, whose time-starved method was opening a can of the packaged stuff.

TAKE A LOOK AT HOW WE'VE EVOLVED!

Taste of Home
The magazine edited by a thousand country cooks!
1990s

Taste of Home
2000s

To say that Grandma was an amazing cook is an understatement. But back then, it never crossed my mind to ask her for her recipes. And when Grandma passed away, my parents never thought to look for that magical recipe box when settling her estate.

Had Grandma been alive when *Taste of Home* launched back in 1993, I'm sure she would have been an original subscriber. And I'm sure those delicious dishes from my childhood would be in our expansive recipe database, which clearly holds so much love and history from readers.

Now, to me, food is about people. Sharing. Togetherness. Love. Joy. It's about honoring traditions. Appreciating the wonders of a hot-from-the-oven meal. The incredible aroma that permeates a home when there's a roast roasting, and the promise of laughter and smiles from the first bite to the last...when plates are empty and hearts are full.

That's *Taste of Home*—a bright beacon that points to those we love. And it's changed the way I think about food. *Taste of Home* now means family dinners at home with my husband and daughter. It means cooking tasty dishes together, setting aside smartphones and sitting down to good food and good conversation that makes time stop.

So in the spirit of the passion shown by our current and original 1,000 home cooks, we share this cookbook. Each chapter is filled with your best recipes of the past two and a half decades, as well as the stories that bring them to life. Thank you, *Taste of Home* readers, for sharing this part of your world with us—and for helping to create a world of love through down-home and delicious foods. We're truly honored.

Beth Tomkiw
Chief Content Officer
Taste of Home

MORE WAYS TO CONNECT WITH US:

LIKE US
facebook.com/tasteofhome

PIN US
pinterest.com/taste_of_home

FOLLOW US
@tasteofhome

TWEET US
twitter.com/tasteofhome

tasteofhome

2010s

2013

Taste of Home

25 YEARS: A LOOK BACK AT OUR HISTORY

Sometimes a secret is too good—too tantalizing, too delicious—to keep to yourself.

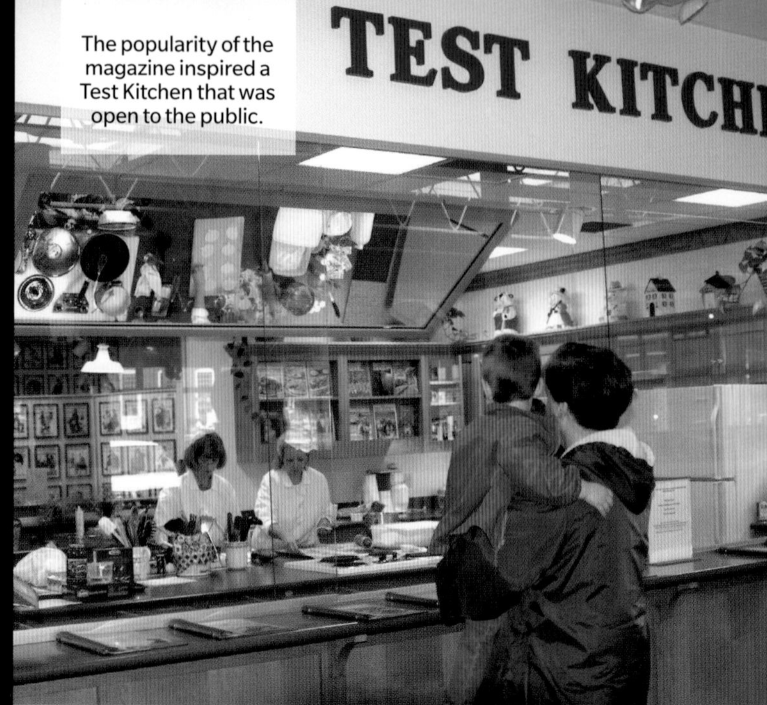

The popularity of the magazine inspired a Test Kitchen that was open to the public.

Sometimes a dish is just too tasty not to share. It was this idea that became the premise behind *Taste of Home* back in 1992, when editors and staff of what was then Reiman Publications met to brainstorm potential new offerings. The company already had successfully mined rural markets with titles like *Country Woman*. Devoted to farm life and all things that would appeal to rural female readers, *Country Woman* also featured a heaping helping of features on cooking. And people couldn't get enough.

"At that time, people wanted more (recipes) than we could allot in our magazines," says Mary Beth Jung, the founding food editor of *Taste of Home*. "I went to my boss and said we should do a food magazine...because it was a natural (extension)."

And that's where the secret-sharing began. Seems that the readers of the various publications loved to exchange their family recipes and submitted them in droves. And this sparked an idea.

The premiere issue in 1993.

The first issue offered farmhouse favorites.

MORE THAN RECIPES

In his business memoir, *I Could Write a Book...*, company founder Roy Reiman envisioned something special for his newest magazine.

"We decided this new one would be more than just a food magazine; it would be a people magazine as well," he wrote. "Instead of simply running a series of recipes, like most other food magazines do, we would give the story behind each recipe; we would tell how 'This recipe came from my Aunt Helen, who made it every time I visited her house, and Helen in turn got it from her mother, who lived on a ranch in Montana.' ...This would add meaning and appeal to each recipe; we'd make these recipes come alive by explaining their roots."

The staff decided to use only recipes and stories from readers—practically inventing the publishing world's concept of user-generated content.

And so the notion of sharing secrets—those closely kept family recipes that were handed down from generation to generation—became a driving force for the new publication, *Taste of Home*, while shining a spotlight on the cooks themselves and the stories they had to tell. Editors sat down to plot out the editorial calendar, aiming for a 1993 launch and tapping the unpublished recipes already submitted by readers for the first issue. To differentiate it from other magazines, the staff decided to use only recipes and stories from readers—practically inventing the publishing world's concept of user-generated content. Likewise, the magazine would also use Field Editors from across the country for submissions.

WHAT'S IN A NAME?

The staff batted around a number of ideas for titles, all focused on the "country" theme. Eventually they opened up a contest to a coterie of cooks who would become the magazine's Field Editors.

Ironically, it wasn't actually a country cook who named the magazine, but an East Coast resident, Janet Siciak of Bernardston, Massachusetts. She thought the country-oriented names were a bit too limiting—discounting all of those passionate cooks who lived outside rural areas—and instead created a title that evoked the feeling of the comforting home cooking that everyone enjoys. The focus shifted from country cooks to home cooks, and *Taste of Home* was born.

TASTE OF HOME, BY THE NUMBERS

It takes a lot of resources to produce the world's #1 food and entertaining brand. Over the years, those numbers add up. Here are just a few:

229,000

The number of recipes collected over the years in the *Taste of Home* database. If we wrote each recipe on a 3x5-inch index card and laid them end to end, they'd cover **318 football fields.**

3,000

The number of **recipes published per year** on various *Taste of Home* platforms.

PICTURE THIS

Taste of Home shoots more than **5,000 images** for its various platforms each year.

P. 33

P. 221

WHEN LIFE GIVES YOU...

Taste of Home uses **294 lemons** per year.

MMM, BACON

The team cooks **98 pounds** of bacon per year for various recipes.

3.6 TONS

That's the amount of flour *Taste of Home* Test Kitchen staff members use in a year—about **600 pounds** per month.

Grace Sheldon, a current *Taste of Home* photographer and stylist, was a freelance photographer at the time. Grace was contacted to shoot the first cover. The concept? A lineup of staffers in a "cookie kitchen," proudly showcasing sweet treats.

"It was funny because I had just met [the publisher]...I didn't know him at all," she says. "He was standing next to me and every time he wanted me to shoot, he'd lightly punch me in the arm. 'OK...now!' he'd say and punch me. 'OK...*now*!' when he wanted another shot. *Punch.* So I kind of moved away from him to compose the shots." And not get punched in the arm.

The first issue made its debut in January 1993—a time when the only food magazines catered to gourmet cooks and featured elaborate recipes. *Taste of Home's* user-generated approach to sharing content, and its practical, almost-heirloom recipes, stood out as revolutionary and were welcomed by readers from coast to coast.

BY LEAPS & BOUNDS

"It was a tremendous success from the get-go," Jung says. "I remember checking our early circulation numbers against a magazine like *Bon Appetit* that had been around forever. Almost out of the gate, we were larger." By the third issue, circulation surpassed 500,000, and by the fifth issue, *Taste of Home* had even more subscribers than *Bon Appetit*.

Over the years, and through a timely acquisition by Trusted Media Brands, *Taste of Home* continued to grow and shape the culinary landscape. In the early days, it featured a cooking school to teach home cooks various recipes and techniques; in recent years, that concept was adapted for Taste of Home Live!, a cross-country tour with interactive events that showcased recipes and kitchen tips. The staff also leveraged the success of the user-generated content to produce a wide variety of cookbooks,

P.292

as well as newsstand specials that focus on specific food topics and trends to augment the company's other newsstand publications. Now, under the Trusted Media Brands banner, *Taste of Home* has an audience of more than 12 million, making it the leading multiplatform producer of food content.

THE NEXT WAVE

As the world has become increasingly digitally focused, *Taste of Home* has adapted, building a robust web presence and social media arm to attract the next generation of cooks.

"I think millennials will be the next wave of great cooks," says Sarah Farmer, *Taste of Home* culinary director. "We definitely want to become multigenerational and to include millennials more. We are going to find additional recipe submissions from them, and the recipe development we do here is beginning to reflect what younger folks are preparing and eating."

One thing that won't change: the impetus for sharing those secret family recipes. "To share a recipe is like sharing a piece of you...and sharing your story," Farmer says. "It comes from a place of kindness and love—and wanting to make people happy." And that's a very fitting sentiment for the next 25 years of *Taste of Home*.

CRYING FOR YOU

We use, on average, **441 onions** per year; since the average 3-inch onion weighs 7 ounces, that's **192 pounds** of onions. And that's a lot of tears, what with all that chopping, dicing, slicing and cutting!

BETTER WITH BUTTER

Here's a fun fact: On the opening day of the Minnesota State Fair, an artist sculpts the likeness of a State Fair princess out of 90 pounds of butter. But that fair has nothing on us: We use more than **382 pounds of butter** per year.

TESTING, TESTING

The *Taste of Home* team tests more than **1,500** recipes submitted by readers per year.

Taste of Home *has an audience of more than 12 million, making it the leading multiplatform producer of food content.*

ILLUSTRATIONS BY NOUN PROJECT

MEET A FEW TASTE OF HOME FIELD EDITORS

The magazine once "edited by 1,000 country cooks" still turns to a group of super fans.

When *Taste of Home* launched, it relied on 1,000 Field Editors (or "country cooks") to supply recipes when the magazine needed particular dishes not sent by readers. While the Field Editors now number a more manageable 200, they are just as much a part of the brand as ever.

"Today, our volunteer Field Editors are our super fans," says Susan Stetzel, *Taste of Home* engagement editor. "We turn to them to research vintage recipes, find timesavers and try new ingredients for us." Some of the Field Editors have been with *Taste of Home* for decades; others are new cooks. Below are just a few of their stories.

SUE GRONHOLZ

I'm one of the original "1,000 country cooks" chosen to be a Field Editor when the magazine launched in 1993. I was excited because *Taste of Home*'s magazines and cookbooks felt like a big friendly recipe swap, and now I was part of that. The recipes come from real home cooks, prepared with love, and that quality shines through. When I make a *Taste of Home* dish, I know it's going to turn out perfect every time.

• *Try Sue's luscious Layered Mocha Cheesecake on page 378.*

COURTNEY STULTZ

When I was growing up, my mom instilled a love of cooking in me. I remember seeing *Taste of Home* everywhere—from relatives' homes to the doctor's office. I was drawn to the stories about the recipes as well as the fact that the dishes were easy to prepare. My love for *Taste of Home* stayed with me, so I became a Field Editor. When a new issue arrives, my daughter marks the recipes she likes. Then we make them together—just like Mom and I did.

• *Don't miss the Egg Roll Noodle Bowl on page 184. It's Courtney's go-to dish.*

ANGELA LIVELY

An old roommate had a subscription to *Taste of Home*, and I really enjoyed it. That was about 20 years ago, and I have just loved the magazine since. As a Field Editor, I meet so many wonderful readers in person and online. It's rewarding to learn how much people enjoy your recipes, tips and ideas. *Taste of Home* created a great group of family cooks, and I'm happy to be an active member of that community.

• *Turn to page 374 for a dessert Angela grew up on, Grandma's Strawberry Shortcake.*

JOAN HALLFORD

I became a *Taste of Home* Field Editor about 20 years ago, and I've cherished every minute of it. It's allowed me the chance to do food demos on local television, preparing my recipes for the viewers. I adore sharing recipes with others in the hope that my dishes will become favorites with their families, too. I fell in love with the magazine the first time I saw it. It just had a neighborly feel to it, and I loved it. I still do.

• *Check out Joan's Pork & Asparagus Sheet Pan Dinner on page 130.*

JENNIFER STOWELL

Becoming a Field Editor was a dream come true. I grew up looking through issues of the magazine with my grandma, and the Field Editors listed in the back were like celebrities to me. Grandma, now in her 90s, still loves getting *Taste of Home*, especially since she can read her granddaughter's name in the back of each issue. She is one of my favorite people and *Taste of Home* will always remind me of her.

• *See page 207 for Jennifer's appetizer, Slow Cooker Spinach & Artichoke Dip.*

Are you interested in becoming a volunteer Field Editor? Email FieldEditors@TasteofHome.com today!

FOLLOW THE JOURNEY OF A TASTE OF HOME RECIPE

FROM PLANNING TO PUBLICATION, OUR DISHES GO THROUGH SEVERAL STEPS BEFORE BECOMING DINNERTIME ALL-STARS.

Today's family cooks sharing their most-requested recipes—that's the hallmark of every *Taste of Home* product. Each year the *Taste of Home* **Test Kitchen receives more than 2,000 recipes.** Many of those are entries for contests and others are submitted for particular magazine features. Most, however, are simply shared by home cooks for the enjoyment of others.

What happens to those family favorites after they're received at the *Taste of Home* Test Kitchen? Let's consider the steps a dish goes through once it arrives in our mailbox. In this instance, we'll look at the history of the recipe **Grandma's Apple Cake**—an entry in the **Homemade Harvest Contest.**

Nearly 500 recipes were submitted for this contest, leaving a lot for the *Taste of Home* food editors and culinary assistants to review. They check to see which entries fit the contest criteria and whether submissions make sense for the *Taste of Home* family of recipes (easy to prepare, common ingredients, etc.). They also look to be sure *Taste of Home* hasn't published a similar recipe in the past.

Grandma's Apple Cake met all the editors' criteria, made all the cuts, and was scheduled for taste testing by the contest judges. In this process, a panel of test cooks and editors sample contest entries over a period of six tasting sessions. They rate each dish before sharing their results and opinions with one another.

Grandma's Apple Cake received 85 out of 100 points to win the Grand Prize! The winner was contacted, the cash prize was sent and the recipe was scheduled for photography at the *Taste of Home* photo studio.

The recipe was published in the **September/October 2017** edition of *Taste of Home* magazine and was later posted to **TasteofHome.com** as well as several social media sites.

Once a Grand Prize winner is published in the flagship magazine, we're eager to share it in our other products as well. For instance, **Grandma's Apple Cake** was published in two newsstand specials over the course of the following year as well as three cookbooks, including this one! **Be sure to turn to page 363** and bake up this award-winning treat!

Share your all-time favorite recipes at TasteofHome.com today.

25 GRAND PRIZE WINNERS

WHETHER ENTERING A RECIPE CONTEST OR SIMPLY MAKING THE WINNING DISHES FOR THEIR FAMILIES, TASTE OF HOME READERS CAN'T GET ENOUGH BLUE-RIBBON FAVORITES. HERE, WE'VE ASSEMBLED A DELICIOUS COLLECTION OF GRAND PRIZE WINNERS FROM EACH OF THE PAST 25 YEARS.

2017

BUTTERNUT SQUASH CHILI

BUTTERNUT SQUASH CHILI

I won the Fresh & Easy Weeknight Recipe Contest by adding cubes of butternut squash to chili. I hope your family enjoys this dish as much as mine does.

—Jeanne Larson, Rancho Santa Margarita, CA

Prep: 20 min. • **Cook:** 30 min.
Makes: 8 servings (2 qt.)

- 1 lb. ground beef or turkey
- ¾ cup chopped red onion
- 5 garlic cloves, minced
- 3 Tbsp. tomato paste
- 1 Tbsp. chili powder
- 1 tsp. ground cumin
- ½ to 1 tsp. salt
- 1¾ to 2 cups water
- 1 can (15 oz.) black beans, rinsed and drained
- 1 can (15 oz.) pinto beans, rinsed and drained
- 1 can (14½ oz.) diced tomatoes
- 1 can (14½ to 15 oz.) tomato sauce
- 3 cups peeled butternut squash, cut into ½-in. cubes
- 2 Tbsp. cider vinegar
- Chopped avocado, plain Greek yogurt and shredded mozzarella cheese, optional

1. In a Dutch oven over medium heat, cook beef and onion until beef is no longer pink and onion is tender, 6-8 minutes.
2. Add next five ingredients; cook 1 minute longer. Stir in water, both types of beans, diced tomatoes and tomato sauce. Bring to a boil; reduce heat. Stir in squash; simmer, covered, until squash is tender, 20-25 minutes. Stir in vinegar.
3. If desired, serve with optional ingredients.

Per cup: 261 cal., 8g fat (3g sat. fat), 35mg chol., 704mg sod., 32g carb. (6g sugars, 8g fiber), 18g pro. **Diabetic exchanges:** 2 starch, 2 lean meat.

PICKLED PEPPERONCINI DEVILED EGGS

It's hard to resist these adorable deviled trees on our buffet table. I think that's why they won the Holiday Appetizer Contest.

—Carmell Childs, Clawson, UT

Takes: 30 min. • **Makes:** 1 dozen

- 6 hard-boiled large eggs
- 1 jar (16 oz.) garlic and dill pepperoncini
- 1 medium ripe avocado, peeled and pitted
- 1 Tbsp. minced fresh cilantro, divided
- ¼ tsp. salt
- ⅛ tsp. pepper
- 1 Tbsp. minced sweet red pepper
- ¼ tsp. chili powder

1. Cut eggs lengthwise in half. Remove yolks, reserving whites. Mash yolks. Stir in 1 tsp. minced garlic from the pepperoncini jar and 2 tsp. pepperoncini juice. Add 3 Tbsp. minced pepperoncini and the avocado; mash with a fork until smooth. Stir in 2 tsp. cilantro, salt and pepper.
2. Cut a small hole in the tip of a pastry bag or in a corner of a food-safe plastic bag; insert a medium star tip. Transfer avocado mixture to bag. Pipe into egg whites, swirling mixture upward to resemble Christmas trees. Sprinkle the trees with minced red pepper, chili powder and remaining cilantro.
3. Cut open and seed one larger pepperoncini; slice into 12 small diamond shapes to top Christmas trees. Refrigerate, covered, until serving.

Per stuffed egg half: 59 cal., 4g fat (1g sat. fat), 93mg chol., 125mg sod., 1g carb. (0 sugars, 1g fiber), 3g pro.

PICKLED PEPPERONCINI DEVILED EGGS

2016

PEACH CREAM PUFFS

On a sizzling day, we crave light, airy treats. Nothing says summer like cream puffs stuffed with peaches, so I entered these in the Summer Desserts Contest. They won!
—Angela Benedict, Dunbar, WV

Prep: 55 min. + cooling
Bake: 25 min. + cooling
Makes: 16 servings

- 1 cup water
- ½ cup butter, cubed
- ⅛ tsp. salt
- 1 cup all-purpose flour
- 4 large eggs

FILLING

- 4 medium peaches, peeled and cubed (about 3 cups)
- ½ cup sugar
- ½ cup water
- ½ cup peach schnapps liqueur or peach nectar
- ½ tsp. ground cinnamon
- ¼ tsp. ground nutmeg

WHIPPED CREAM

- 2 cups heavy whipping cream
- ½ cup confectioners' sugar
- 3 Tbsp. peach schnapps liqueur, optional
- Additional confectioners' sugar

1. Preheat oven to 400°. In a large saucepan, bring water, butter and salt to a rolling boil. Add flour all at once and beat until blended. Cook over medium heat, stirring vigorously until mixture pulls away from sides of pan and forms a ball. Transfer dough to a large bowl; let stand 5 minutes.

2. Add eggs, one at a time, beating well after each addition until smooth. Continue beating until mixture is smooth and shiny.

3. Cut a ½-in. hole in tip of a pastry bag or in a corner of a food-safe plastic bag. Transfer dough to bag; pipe sixteen 2-in. mounds about 3 in. apart onto parchment paper-lined baking sheets.

4. Bake on a lower oven rack 25-30 minutes or until puffed, very firm and golden brown. Pierce side of each puff with tip of a knife to allow steam to escape. Cool completely on wire racks.

5. Meanwhile, in a large saucepan, combine filling ingredients; bring to a boil, stirring occasionally. Reduce heat; simmer, uncovered, 25-30 minutes or until slightly thickened and peaches are tender. Cool completely.

6. In a bowl, beat cream until it begins to thicken. Add confectioners' sugar and, if desired, peach schnapps; beat until soft peaks form.

7. Cut top third off each cream puff. Pull out and discard soft dough from inside tops and bottoms.

8. To serve, spoon 2 tablespoons whipped cream into each bottom shell; top with roughly 2 tablespoons of the filling and 2 tablespoons additional whipped cream. Replace the tops. Dust with additional confectioners' sugar.

Per cream puff with ¼ cup whipped cream and 2 Tbsp. filling: 256 cal., 18g fat (11g sat. fat), 103mg chol., 94mg sod., 21g carb. (14g sugars, 1g fiber), 3g pro.

CRANBERRY COOKIES WITH BROWNED BUTTER GLAZE

I won the Christmas Cookie Contest with these chunky cookies that are so easy to make, even novice bakers can pull them off. *—Laurie Cornett, Charlevoix, MI*

Prep: 40 min. • **Bake:** 10 min./batch + cooling • **Makes:** about 4½ dozen

- ½ cup butter, softened
- 1 cup sugar
- ¾ cup packed brown sugar
- 1 large egg
- 2 Tbsp. orange juice
- 3 cups all-purpose flour
- 1 tsp. baking powder
- ½ tsp. salt
- ¼ tsp. baking soda
- ¼ cup 2% milk
- 2½ cups coarsely chopped fresh cranberries
- 1 cup white baking chips
- 1 cup chopped pecans or walnuts

GLAZE

- ⅓ cup butter, cubed
- 2 cups confectioners' sugar
- 1½ tsp. vanilla extract
- 3 to 4 Tbsp. water

1. Preheat oven to 375°. In a large bowl, cream butter and sugars until light and fluffy. Beat in egg and orange juice. In another bowl, whisk flour, baking powder, salt and baking soda; add to creamed mixture alternately with milk. Stir in cranberries, baking chips and pecans.

2. Drop dough by level tablespoonfuls 1 in. apart onto greased baking sheets. Bake 10-12 minutes or until light brown. Remove from pans to wire racks to cool completely.

3. For glaze, in a small heavy saucepan, melt butter over medium heat. Heat 5-7 minutes or until golden brown, stirring constantly. Remove from heat. Stir in confectioners' sugar, vanilla and enough water to reach a drizzling consistency. Drizzle over cookies. Let stand until set.

Per cookie: 130 cal., 5g fat (3g sat. fat), 12mg chol., 66mg sod., 19g carb. (13g sugars, 1g fiber), 1g pro.

CRANBERRY COOKIES WITH BROWNED BUTTER GLAZE

2013

CHICKEN POT PIE SOUP

CHICKEN POT PIE SOUP

My grandmother hand-wrote a cookbook, featuring this amazing pie crust. I added a delicious soup to it for this specialty.
—Karen LeMay, Seabrook, TX

Prep: 20 min. + chilling • **Cook:** 20 min.
Makes: 6 servings

- 2 cups all-purpose flour
- 1¼ tsp. salt
- ⅔ cup shortening
- 5 to 6 Tbsp. 2% milk

SOUP

- 2 Tbsp. butter
- 1 cup cubed peeled potatoes
- 1 cup chopped sweet onion
- 2 celery ribs, chopped
- 2 medium carrots, chopped
- ½ cup all-purpose flour
- ½ tsp. salt
- ¼ tsp. pepper
- 3 cans (14½ oz. each) chicken broth
- 2 cups shredded cooked chicken
- 1 cup frozen petite peas
- 1 cup frozen corn

1. In a large bowl, mix flour and salt; cut in shortening until crumbly. Gradually add milk, tossing with a fork until dough holds together when pressed. Shape into a disk; wrap in plastic. Refrigerate for 30 minutes or overnight.

2. On a lightly floured surface, roll dough to ⅛-in. thickness. Using a floured 2½-in. heart-shaped or round cutter, cut out 18 shapes. Place 1 in. apart on ungreased baking sheets. Bake at 425° until golden brown, 8-11 minutes. Cool on a wire rack.

3. For soup, heat butter in a Dutch oven over medium-high heat. Add the potatoes, onion, celery and carrots; cook and stir for 5-7 minutes or until onion is tender.

4. Stir in flour, salt and pepper until blended; gradually whisk in broth. Bring to a boil over medium-high heat, stirring occasionally. Reduce heat; simmer, uncovered, until potatoes are tender, 8-10 minutes. Stir in remaining ingredients; heat through. Serve with pastries.

Per 1½ cups soup with 3 pastries: 614 cal., 30g fat (9g sat. fat), 57mg chol., 1706mg sod., 60g carb. (7g sugars, 5g fiber), 23g pro.

BUBBLY & GOLDEN MEXICAN BEEF COBBLER

BUBBLY & GOLDEN MEXICAN BEEF COBBLER

Add whatever you like to this Mexican beef cobbler to make it yours—black beans, sour cream, even guacamole!

—Mary Brooks, Clay, MI

Prep: 20 min. • **Bake:** 35 min.
Makes: 6 servings

- 1 lb. ground beef
- 1 envelope reduced-sodium taco seasoning
- ¾ cup water
- 1 jar (16 oz.) salsa
- 1 can (8¾ oz.) whole kernel corn, drained
- 2 cups shredded sharp cheddar cheese
- 3⅓ cups biscuit/baking mix
- 1⅓ cups 2% milk
- ⅛ tsp. pepper

1. In a large skillet, cook beef over medium heat for 6-8 minutes or until no longer pink, breaking into crumbles; drain. Stir in taco seasoning and water. Bring to a boil; cook until liquid is evaporated. Transfer to an 11x7-in. baking dish; layer with salsa, corn and cheese.

2. In a large bowl, mix biscuit mix and milk just until blended; drop by tablespoonfuls over cheese. Sprinkle with pepper.

3. Bake, uncovered, at 350° for 35-45 minutes or until bubbly and topping is golden brown.

Per serving: 646 cal., 31g fat (14g sat. fat), 90mg chol., 1877mg sod., 59g carb. (11g sugars, 3g fiber), 30g pro.

TERRIFIC TURKEY ENCHILADAS

This is a tasty take on a classic Southwestern dish, so I entered it in the New Southwest Recipe Contest.

—Jenn Tidwell, Fair Oaks, CA

Prep: 35 min. • **Bake:** 35 min.
Makes: 3 servings

- 1¼ cups frozen corn, thawed
- 1 can (4 oz.) chopped green chilies
- 1 cup fresh cilantro leaves
- ⅓ cup heavy whipping cream
- ¼ tsp. salt
- ¼ tsp. pepper

ENCHILADAS

- ¾ lb. ground turkey
- ⅓ cup chopped onion
- 1 garlic clove, minced
- 1 Tbsp. olive oil
- ¾ cup salsa
- 1 Tbsp. cornmeal
- 2 tsp. chili powder
- 1½ tsp. ground cumin
- 1 tsp. dried oregano
- ⅛ tsp. salt
- ⅛ tsp. pepper
- 6 flour tortillas (8 in.), warmed
- 1¼ cups shredded Mexican cheese blend, divided
- ¼ cup sliced ripe olives

1. Preheat oven to 350°. Place first six ingredients in a food processor; cover and pulse until blended.

2. In a large skillet, cook turkey, onion and garlic in oil over medium heat until meat is no longer pink. Remove from heat; stir in salsa, cornmeal and seasonings.

3. Spoon ⅓ cup turkey mixture down the center of each tortilla; top with 2 Tbsp. cheese. Roll up and place seam side down in a greased 11x7-in. baking dish. Spoon corn mixture over top; sprinkle with olives and remaining cheese.

4. Cover and bake 30 minutes. Uncover; bake 5-10 minutes or until heated through.

Per 2 enchiladas: 968 cal., 55g fat (23g sat. fat), 155mg chol., 1766mg sod., 81g carb. (4g sugars, 5g fiber), 41g pro.

TERRIFIC TURKEY ENCHILADAS

2010

CHICKEN FLORENTINE MEATBALLS

CHICKEN FLORENTINE MEATBALLS

Served over spaghetti squash and chunky mushroom-tomato sauce, these prize-winning meatballs are tops when it comes to great flavor.

—Diane Nemitz, Ludington, MI

Prep: 40 min. • **Cook:** 20 min.
Makes: 6 servings

- 2 large eggs, lightly beaten
- 1 pkg. (10 oz.) frozen chopped spinach, thawed and squeezed dry
- ½ cup dry bread crumbs
- ¼ cup grated Parmesan cheese
- 1 Tbsp. dried minced onion
- 1 garlic clove, minced
- ¼ tsp. salt
- ⅛ tsp. pepper
- 1 lb. ground chicken
- 1 medium spaghetti squash

SAUCE

- ½ lb. sliced fresh mushrooms
- 2 tsp. olive oil
- 1 can (14½ oz.) diced tomatoes, undrained
- 1 can (8 oz.) tomato sauce
- 2 Tbsp. minced fresh parsley
- 1 garlic clove, minced
- 1 tsp. dried oregano
- 1 tsp. dried basil

1. In a large bowl, combine the first eight ingredients. Crumble chicken over mixture and mix well. Shape into 1½-in. balls.

2. Place meatballs on a rack in a shallow baking pan. Bake, uncovered, at 400° for 20-25 minutes or until no longer pink. Meanwhile, cut squash in half lengthwise; discard seeds. Place squash cut side down on a microwave-safe plate. Microwave, uncovered, on high for 15-18 minutes or until tender.

3. For sauce, in a large nonstick skillet, saute mushrooms in oil until tender. Stir in the remaining ingredients. Bring to a boil. Reduce heat; simmer, uncovered, until slightly thickened, 8-10 minutes. Add meatballs and heat through.

SOUTH-OF-THE-BORDER CAPRESE SALAD

4. When squash is cool enough to handle, use a fork to separate strands. Serve with meatballs and sauce.

Per serving: 303 cal., 12g fat (3g sat. fat), 123mg chol., 617mg sod., 31g carb. (4g sugars, 7g fiber), 22g pro. **Diabetic exchanges:** 3 lean meat, 2 starch, ½ fat.

SOUTH-OF-THE-BORDER CAPRESE SALAD

Plump heirloom tomatoes highlight this garden-fresh showpiece that won the Seeing Red Recipe Contest. With a sweet-tart dressing and a sprinkle of cheese, it's perfect for an outdoor party. Best of all, it's so easy to make!

—Kathleen Merkley, Layton, UT

Takes: 30 min.
Makes: 6 servings (1 cup dressing)

CILANTRO VINAIGRETTE

- ⅓ cup white wine vinegar
- ½ cup fresh cilantro leaves
- 3 Tbsp. sugar
- 1 jalapeno pepper, seeded and chopped
- 1 garlic clove, peeled and quartered
- ¾ tsp. salt
- ⅔ cup olive oil

SALAD

- 4 cups torn mixed salad greens
- 3 large heirloom or other tomatoes, sliced
- ½ cup crumbled queso fresco or diced part-skim mozzarella cheese
- ¼ tsp. salt
- ⅛ tsp. pepper
- 1½ tsp. fresh cilantro leaves

1. In a blender, combine the first six ingredients. While processing, gradually add oil in a steady stream.

2. Arrange greens on a serving platter; top with tomatoes. Sprinkle with cheese, salt and pepper.

3. Just before serving, drizzle salad with ½ cup dressing; garnish with cilantro leaves. Refrigerate leftover dressing.

Note Wear disposable gloves when cutting hot peppers; the oils can burn skin. Avoid touching your face.

Per serving: 168 cal., 14g fat (3g sat. fat), 7mg chol., 286mg sod., 8g carb. (5g sugars, 2g fiber), 4g pro.

PUMPKIN SCONES WITH BERRY BUTTER

PUMPKIN SCONES WITH BERRY BUTTER

These scones are perfect on a cold winter day with a hot cup of coffee. In fact, they won the Great Pumpkin Recipe Contest.
—Judy Wilson, Sun City West, AZ

Prep: 25 min. + chilling • **Bake:** 15 min.
Makes: 8 scones (about ½ cup butter)

- 2 Tbsp. dried cranberries
- ½ cup boiling water
- ½ cup butter, softened
- 3 Tbsp. confectioners' sugar

DOUGH

- 2¼ cups all-purpose flour
- ¼ cup packed brown sugar
- 2 tsp. baking powder
- 1½ tsp. pumpkin pie spice
- ¼ tsp. salt
- ¼ tsp. baking soda
- ½ cup cold butter, cubed
- 1 large egg
- ½ cup canned pumpkin
- ⅓ cup 2% milk
- 2 Tbsp. chopped pecans, optional

1. Place cranberries in a small bowl; add boiling water. Let stand for 5 minutes; drain and chop. In a small bowl, beat butter until light and fluffy. Add confectioners' sugar and cranberries; mix well. Cover and refrigerate butter for at least 1 hour.

2. In a large bowl, combine the flour, brown sugar, baking powder, pie spice, salt and baking soda. Cut in butter until mixture resembles coarse crumbs. In a small bowl, whisk the egg, pumpkin and milk; add to crumb mixture just until moistened. Stir in pecans if desired.

3. Turn dough onto a floured surface; knead 10 times. Pat into an 8-in. circle. Cut into eight wedges; separate wedges and place on a greased baking sheet.

4. Bake at 400° for 12-15 minutes or until golden brown. Serve warm with the berry butter.

Per scone: 392 cal., 24g fat (15g sat. fat), 88mg chol., 391mg sod., 40g carb. (12g sugars, 2g fiber), 5g pro.

EDITOR'S CHOICE

RUSTIC NUT BARS

My friends love crunching into the crust—it tastes like shortbread—and wildly nutty topping on these chewy, gooey bars.
—Barbara Driscoll, West Allis, WI

Prep: 20 min.
Bake: 35 min. + cooling
Makes: about 3 dozen

- 1 Tbsp. plus ¾ cup cold butter, divided
- 2⅓ cups all-purpose flour
- ½ cup sugar
- ½ tsp. baking powder
- ½ tsp. salt
- 1 large egg, lightly beaten

TOPPING

- ⅔ cup honey
- ½ cup packed brown sugar
- ¼ tsp. salt
- 6 Tbsp. butter, cubed
- 2 Tbsp. heavy whipping cream
- 1 cup chopped hazelnuts, toasted
- 1 cup salted cashews
- 1 cup pistachios
- 1 cup salted roasted almonds

1. Preheat oven to 375°. Line a 13x9-in. baking pan with foil, letting ends extend over sides by 1 in. Grease foil with 1 Tbsp. butter.

2. In a large bowl, whisk flour, sugar, baking powder and salt. Cut in remaining butter until mixture resembles coarse crumbs. Stir in egg until blended (mixture will be dry). Press firmly onto bottom of prepared pan.

3. Bake 18-20 minutes or until edges are golden brown. Cool on a wire rack.

4. In a large heavy saucepan, combine honey, brown sugar and salt; bring to a boil over medium heat, stirring frequently to dissolve sugar. Boil 2 minutes, without stirring. Stir in butter and cream; return to a boil. Cook and stir 1 minute or until smooth. Remove from heat; stir in nuts. Spread over the crust.

5. Bake 15-20 minutes or until topping is bubbly. Cool completely in pan on a wire rack. Lifting with foil, remove from pan. Discard foil; cut into bars.

Note To toast nuts, bake in a shallow pan in a 350° oven for 5-10 minutes or cook in a skillet over low heat until lightly browned, stirring occasionally.

Per bar: 199 cal., 13g fat (4g sat. fat), 21mg chol., 157mg sod., 18g carb. (10g sugars, 1g fiber), 4g pro.

2006

RHUBARB SWIRL CHEESECAKE

RHUBARB SWIRL CHEESECAKE

Rhubarb complements the white chocolate in this cheesecake so well, I had to enter it in the Ready for Rhubarb Contest. What a great surprise to learn that it won!

—Carol Wit, Tinley Park, IL

Prep: 40 min. • **Bake:** 1 hour + chilling
Makes: 14 servings

- 2½ cups thinly sliced fresh or frozen rhubarb
- ⅓ cup plus ½ cup sugar, divided
- 2 Tbsp. orange juice
- 1¼ cups graham cracker crumbs
- ¼ cup butter, melted
- 3 pkg. (8 oz. each) cream cheese, softened
- 2 cups sour cream
- 8 oz. white baking chocolate, melted
- 1 Tbsp. cornstarch
- 2 tsp. vanilla extract
- ½ tsp. salt
- 3 large eggs, lightly beaten

1. In a large saucepan, bring rhubarb, ⅓ cup sugar and orange juice to a boil. Reduce heat; cook and stir until thickened and rhubarb is tender. Set aside.

2. In a small bowl, combine the cracker crumbs and butter. Press onto the bottom of a greased 9-in. springform pan. Place on a baking sheet. Bake at 350° until lightly browned, 7-9 minutes. Cool the crust on a wire rack.

3. In a large bowl, beat cream cheese and remaining sugar until smooth. Beat in the sour cream, white chocolate, cornstarch, vanilla and salt until smooth. Add eggs; beat just until combined.

4. Pour half of the filling into crust. Top with half of the rhubarb sauce; cut through batter with a knife to gently swirl rhubarb. Layer with remaining filling and rhubarb sauce; cut through top layers with a knife to gently swirl rhubarb.

5. Place pan on a double thickness of heavy-duty foil (about 18 in. square). Securely wrap foil around pan. Place in a large baking pan; add 1 in. of hot water to larger pan. Bake at 350° for 60-70 minutes or until center is almost set.

6. Cool on a wire rack for 10 minutes. Carefully run a knife around edge of pan to loosen; cool 1 hour longer. Cover and chill overnight. Refrigerate leftovers.

Note If using frozen rhubarb, measure while still frozen, then thaw completely. Drain in a colander, but do not press liquid out.

Per slice: 264 cal., 17g fat (10g sat. fat), 94mg chol., 244mg sod., 22g carb. (16g sugars, 1g fiber), 5g pro.

2005

MEXICAN SHRIMP BISQUE

MEXICAN SHRIMP BISQUE

I enjoy both Cajun and Mexican cuisine, and this rich, elegant soup combines the best of both worlds.

—Karen Harris, Littleton, CO

Takes: 30 min. • **Makes:** 3 servings

- 1 small onion, chopped
- 1 Tbsp. olive oil
- 2 garlic cloves, minced
- 1 Tbsp. all-purpose flour
- 1 cup water
- ½ cup heavy whipping cream
- 2 tsp. chicken bouillon granules
- 1 Tbsp. chili powder
- ½ tsp. ground cumin
- ½ tsp. ground coriander
- ½ lb. uncooked medium shrimp, peeled and deveined
- ½ cup sour cream
- Chopped fresh cilantro and sliced avocado, optional

1. In a small saucepan, saute onion in oil until tender. Add garlic; cook 1 minute longer. Stir in flour until blended. Stir in the water, cream, bouillon and seasonings; bring to a boil. Reduce heat; cover and simmer for 5 minutes.

2. Cut shrimp into bite-sized pieces if desired; add shrimp to soup. Simmer 5-10 minutes longer or until shrimp turn pink. Place sour cream in a small bowl; gradually stir in ½ cup hot soup. Return all to the pan, stirring constantly. Heat through (do not boil). Top with cilantro and avocado if desired.

Per cup: 357 cal., 28g fat (15g sat. fat), 173mg chol., 706mg sod., 10g carb. (3g sugars, 2g fiber), 16g pro.

CHUNKY BLUE CHEESE DIP

Every time I make this quick dip, someone asks for the recipe, so I decided to submit it to the 30-Minute Appetizer Contest. Try it with Gorgonzola cheese and pecans, too.
—Sandy Schneider, Naperville, IL

Takes: 15 min.
Makes: 12 servings

- 1 pkg. (8 oz.) cream cheese, softened
- ⅓ cup sour cream
- ½ tsp. white pepper
- ¼ to ½ tsp. salt
- 1 cup crumbled blue cheese
- ⅓ cup minced fresh chives
- Toasted chopped pecans, optional
- Apple and pear slices

Beat first four ingredients until blended; gently stir in blue cheese and chives. Transfer to a serving bowl. If desired, sprinkle with pecans. Serve with apple and pear slices.

Per 2 Tbsp.: 112 cal., 10g fat (6g sat. fat), 32mg chol., 229mg sod., 1g carb. (1g sugars, 0 fiber), 3g pro.

ONION BEEF AU JUS

When I read about the recipe contest for onion-and-garlic dishes, I instantly thought of these delicious beef sandwiches. We just love the tasty, rich broth for dipping. Once you try it, you'll find all sorts of ways to serve the tender beef.
—Blake Brown, West Union, IA

Prep: 20 min.
Bake: 2½ hours + standing
Makes: 12 servings

- 1 beef rump roast or bottom round roast (4 lbs.)
- 2 Tbsp. canola oil
- 2 large sweet onions, cut into ¼-in. slices
- 6 Tbsp. butter, softened, divided
- 5 cups water
- ½ cup reduced-sodium soy sauce
- 1 envelope onion soup mix
- 1 garlic clove, minced
- 1 tsp. browning sauce, optional
- 1 loaf (1 lb.) French bread
- 1 cup shredded Swiss cheese

1. In a Dutch oven over medium-high heat, brown roast on all sides in oil; drain. In a large skillet, saute onions in 2 Tbsp. of butter until tender. Add the water, soy sauce, soup mix, garlic and, if desired, browning sauce. Pour over roast.

2. Cover and bake at 325° for 2½ hours or until meat is tender.

3. Let the meat stand for 10 minutes, then thinly slice. Return meat to pan juices. Split bread lengthwise; cut into 3-in. sections. Spread with remaining butter. Place on a baking sheet.

4. Broil the bread 4-6 in. from the heat until golden brown, 2-3 minutes. Top with beef and onions; sprinkle with cheese. Broil until cheese is melted, 1-2 minutes. Serve with pan juices.

Per open-faced sandwich: 422 cal., 19g fat (8g sat. fat), 114mg chol., 1179mg sod., 24g carb. (2g sugars, 2g fiber), 38g pro.

ALMOND BEAR CLAWS

These bear claws are absolutely melt-in-your-mouth delicious! It's impossible to resist the delicate pastry, rich almond filling and pretty fanned tops sprinkled with sugar and almonds. I made yummy treats like this when I worked in a bakery years ago.

—Aneta Kish, La Crosse, WI

Prep: 45 min. + chilling
Bake: 15 min.
Makes: 1½ dozen

- 1½ cups cold butter, cut into ½-in. pieces
- 5 cups all-purpose flour, divided
- 1 pkg. (¼ oz.) active dry yeast
- 1¼ cups half-and-half cream
- ¼ cup granulated sugar
- ¼ tsp. salt
- 2 large eggs, divided use
- 1 large egg white
- ¾ cup confectioners' sugar
- ½ cup almond paste, cubed
- 1 Tbsp. water
- Coarse or granulated sugar
- Sliced almonds

1. In a bowl, toss butter with 3 cups flour until well coated; refrigerate. In a large bowl, combine yeast and remaining flour.
2. In a saucepan, heat cream, sugar and salt to 120°-130°. Add to yeast mixture with 1 egg. Beat until smooth. Stir in butter mixture just until moistened.
3. Place dough onto a well-floured surface; roll into a 21x12-in. rectangle. Starting at a short side, fold dough in thirds, forming a 12x7-in. rectangle. Give dough a quarter turn; roll into a 21x12-in. rectangle. Fold into thirds, starting with a short side. Repeat, flouring surface as needed. (Do not chill dough between each rolling and folding.) Cover and chill dough for 4 to 24 hours or until firm.
4. For filling, in a bowl, beat egg white until foamy. Gradually add confectioners' sugar and almond paste; beat until smooth. Cut the dough in half widthwise. Roll each portion into a 12-in. square; cut each square into three 12x4-in. strips. Spread about 2 Tbsp. filling down the center of each strip. Fold long edges together over filling; seal edges and ends. Cut into three pieces.
5. Place on parchment paper-lined baking sheets with folded edge facing away from you. With scissors, cut strips four times to within ½ in. of folded edge; separate slightly. Repeat with remaining dough and filling. Cover and let rise in a warm place until doubled, about 1 hour.
6. Lightly beat water and remaining egg; brush over dough. Sprinkle with sugar and almonds. Bake at 375° for 15 minutes or until golden brown. Remove from pans to wire racks to cool.

Per pastry: 352 cal., 19g fat (11g sat. fat), 73mg chol., 207mg sod., 38g carb. (10g sugars, 1g fiber), 6g pro.

ALMOND BEAR CLAWS

2001

S'MORE SANDWICH COOKIES

S'MORE SANDWICH COOKIES

Capture the taste of campfire s'mores in your kitchen. Graham cracker crumbs added to chocolate chip cookie dough bring out the flavor of the fireside favorite. Melting the cookies' marshmallow centers in the microwave makes them so simple to assemble, anyone can do it!

—Abby Metzger, Larchwood, IA

Prep: 25 min. • **Bake:** 10 min. + cooling
Makes: about 2 dozen

- ¾ cup butter, softened
- ½ cup sugar
- ½ cup packed brown sugar
- 1 large egg
- 2 Tbsp. whole milk
- 1 tsp. vanilla extract
- 1¼ cups all-purpose flour
- 1¼ cups graham cracker crumbs (about 20 squares)
- ½ tsp. baking soda
- ¼ tsp. salt
- ⅛ tsp. ground cinnamon
- 2 cups (12 oz.) semisweet chocolate chips
- 24 to 28 large marshmallows

1. In a bowl, cream butter and sugars until light and fluffy. Beat in the egg, milk and vanilla. Combine the flour, graham cracker crumbs, baking soda, salt and cinnamon; gradually add to creamed mixture and mix well. Stir in chocolate chips.

2. Drop by tablespoonfuls 2 in. apart onto ungreased baking sheets. Bake at 375° until golden brown, 8-10 minutes. Remove to wire racks to cool.

3. Place four cookies, bottom side up, on a microwave-safe plate; top each with a marshmallow. Microwave, uncovered, on high for 10-15 seconds or until the marshmallows begin to puff (do not overcook). Top each with another cookie. Repeat.

Per cookie: 221 cal., 11g fat (6g sat. fat), 24mg chol., 145mg sod., 32g carb. (22g sugars, 1g fiber), 2g pro.

TRADITIONAL LASAGNA

This rich entree is a holiday tradition at our home—and a favorite meal throughout the year. A friend shared the recipe with me, and I just had to send it into the Luscious Lasagna Contest. It won the Grand Prize! It's requested often by my sister's Italian in-laws. I consider that the highest compliment of all.

—Lorri Foockle, Granville, IL

Prep: 30 min. + simmering
Bake: 70 min. + standing
Makes: 12 servings

- 1 lb. ground beef
- ¾ lb. bulk pork sausage
- 3 cans (8 oz. each) tomato sauce
- 2 cans (6 oz. each) tomato paste
- 2 garlic cloves, minced
- 2 tsp. sugar
- 1 tsp. Italian seasoning
- ½ to 1 tsp. salt
- ¼ to ½ tsp. pepper
- 3 large eggs
- 3 Tbsp. minced fresh parsley
- 3 cups 4% small-curd cottage cheese
- 1 carton (8 oz.) ricotta cheese
- ½ cup grated Parmesan cheese
- 9 lasagna noodles, cooked and drained
- 6 slices provolone cheese (about 6 oz.)
- 3 cups shredded part-skim mozzarella cheese, divided

1. In a large skillet over medium heat, cook and crumble beef and sausage until no longer pink; drain. Add next seven ingredients. Bring to a boil. Reduce heat; simmer, uncovered, 1 hour, stirring occasionally. Adjust seasoning with additional salt and pepper, if desired.

2. Meanwhile, in a large bowl, lightly beat eggs. Add parsley; stir in cottage cheese, ricotta and Parmesan cheese.

3. Preheat oven to 375°. Spread 1 cup meat sauce in an ungreased 13x9-in. baking dish. Layer with three noodles, the provolone cheese, 2 cups cottage cheese mixture, 1 cup mozzarella, three noodles, 2 cups meat sauce, remaining cottage cheese mixture and 1 cup mozzarella. Top with remaining noodles, meat sauce and mozzarella (dish will be full).

4. Cover; bake 50 minutes. Uncover; bake until heated through, 20 minutes. Let stand 15 minutes before cutting.

Per serving: 503 cal., 27g fat (13g sat. fat), 136mg chol., 1208mg sod., 30g carb. (9g sugars, 2g fiber), 36g pro.

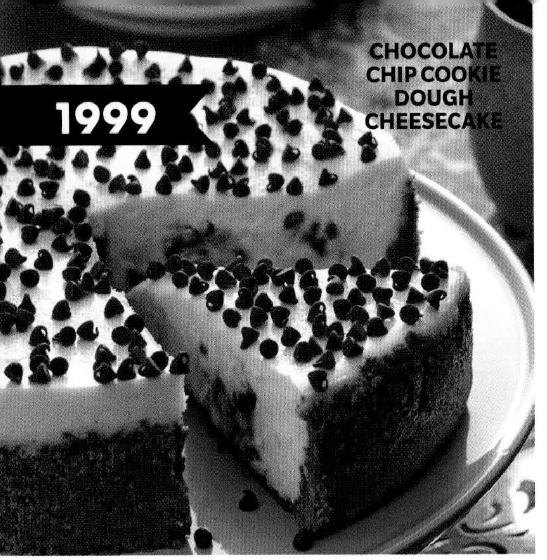

CHOCOLATE CHIP COOKIE DOUGH CHEESECAKE

I created this recipe to combine two of my all-time favorites: cheesecake for the grown-up in me and chocolate chip cookie dough for the little girl in me.

—Julie Craig, Kewaskum, WI

Prep: 25 min. • **Bake:** 45 min. + chilling
Makes: 14 servings

- 1¾ cups crushed chocolate chip cookies or chocolate wafer crumbs
- ¼ cup sugar
- ⅓ cup butter, melted

FILLING

- 3 pkg. (8 oz. each) cream cheese, softened
- 1 cup sugar
- 1 cup sour cream
- ½ tsp. vanilla extract
- 3 large eggs, lightly beaten

COOKIE DOUGH

- ¼ cup butter, softened
- ¼ cup sugar
- ¼ cup packed brown sugar
- 1 Tbsp. water
- 1 tsp. vanilla extract
- ½ cup all-purpose flour
- 1½ cups miniature semisweet chocolate chips, divided

1. In a small bowl, combine cookie crumbs and sugar; stir in butter. Press onto the bottom and 1 in. up the sides of a greased 9-in. springform pan. Place pan on a baking sheet; set aside.
2. In a large bowl, beat cream cheese and sugar until smooth. Beat in sour cream and vanilla. Add eggs; beat on low speed just until combined. Pour over crust; set aside.
3. In another bowl, cream butter and sugars until light and fluffy. Add water and vanilla. Gradually add flour and mix well. Stir in 1 cup chocolate chips.
4. Drop dough by teaspoonfuls over filling, gently pushing dough below surface (dough should be completely covered by filling). Place pan on a baking sheet.
5. Bake at 350° for 45-55 minutes or until center is almost set. Cool on a wire rack for 10 minutes. Carefully run a knife around edge of pan to loosen; cool 1 hour longer. Refrigerate overnight.
6. Remove sides of pan. Sprinkle with remaining chips. Refrigerate leftovers.

Per slice: 551 cal., 36g fat (22g sat. fat), 131mg chol., 328mg sod., 52g carb. (37g sugars, 2g fiber), 8g pro.

SURPRISE SAUSAGE BUNDLES

Kielbasa and sauerkraut star in a tasty filling for these scrumptious stuffed rolls, which won the Sizzling Sausage Contest. Try them for a quick lunch or alongside soup or salad.

—Barb Ruis, Grandville, MI

Prep: 45 min. + rising • **Bake:** 20 min.
Makes: 16 servings

- 6 bacon strips, diced
- 1 cup chopped onion
- 1 can (16 oz.) sauerkraut, rinsed and well drained
- ½ lb. smoked kielbasa or Polish sausage, coarsely chopped
- 2 Tbsp. brown sugar
- ½ tsp. garlic salt
- ¼ tsp. caraway seeds
- ⅛ tsp. pepper
- 1 pkg. (16 oz.) hot roll mix
- 2 large eggs
- 1 cup warm water (120° to 130°)
- 2 Tbsp. butter, softened
- Poppy seeds

1. In a large skillet, cook bacon until crisp; remove to paper towels. Reserve 2 Tbsp. drippings. Saute onion in drippings until tender. Stir in the sauerkraut, sausage, brown sugar, garlic salt, caraway and pepper. Cook and stir for 5 minutes. Remove from the heat; add bacon. Set aside to cool.
2. In a large bowl, combine contents of the roll mix and its yeast packet. Stir in one egg, water and butter to form a soft dough. Turn onto a floured surface; knead until smooth and elastic, about 5 minutes. Cover dough with a large bowl; let stand for 5 minutes.
3. Divide dough into 16 pieces. On a floured surface, roll out each piece into a 4-in. circle. Top each with ¼ cup filling. Fold dough around filling, forming a ball; pinch edges to seal. Place seam side down on greased baking sheets. Cover loosely with plastic wrap that has been coated with cooking spray. Let rise in a warm place for 15 minutes.
4. Beat remaining egg; brush over bundles. Sprinkle with poppy seeds. Bake at 350° for 16-17 minutes or until golden brown. Serve bundles warm.

Freeze option Freeze cooled bundles in a freezer container, separating layers with waxed paper. To use, reheat bundles on a greased baking sheet in a preheated 325° oven until heated through.

Per bundle: 233 cal., 12g fat (4g sat. fat), 46mg chol., 671mg sod., 24g carb. (5g sugars, 2g fiber), 7g pro.

CHICKEN & DUMPLING CASSEROLE

This casserole is one of my husband's favorites, so he agreed it would have a chance at winning the Comforting Casseroles Contest. He was right! Basil adds just the right touch of flavor and makes the whole house smell so good while dinner is cooking.

—Sue Mackey, Jackson, WI

Prep: 30 min.
Bake: 40 min.
Makes: 8 servings

- ½ cup chopped onion
- ½ cup chopped celery
- ¼ cup butter, cubed
- 2 garlic cloves, minced
- ½ cup all-purpose flour
- 2 tsp. sugar
- 1 tsp. salt
- 1 tsp. dried basil
- ½ tsp. pepper
- 4 cups chicken broth
- 1 pkg. (10 oz.) frozen green peas
- 4 cups cubed cooked chicken

DUMPLINGS

- 2 cups biscuit/baking mix
- 2 tsp. dried basil
- ⅔ cup 2% milk

1. Preheat oven to 350°. In a large saucepan, saute onion and celery in butter until tender. Add garlic; cook 1 minute longer. Stir in flour, sugar, salt, basil and pepper until blended. Gradually add broth; bring to a boil. Cook and stir 1 minute or until thickened; reduce heat. Add peas and cook 5 minutes, stirring constantly. Stir in chicken. Pour into a greased 13x9-in. baking dish.

2. For dumplings, in a small bowl, combine baking mix and basil. Stir in milk with a fork until moistened. Drop by tablespoonfuls into 12 mounds over chicken mixture.

3. Bake, uncovered, 30 minutes. Cover and bake 10 minutes longer or until a toothpick inserted in a dumpling comes out clean.

Per serving: 393 cal., 17g fat (7g sat. fat), 80mg chol., 1313mg sod., 33g carb. (6g sugars, 3g fiber), 27g pro.

SPINACH-TOPPED TOMATOES

I never dreamed my colorful side dish would win the very first *Taste of Home* recipe contest. The category was tomatoes, and this spinach-Parmesan filling seemed to win over the judges.

—Ila Mae Alderman, Galax, VA

Prep: 20 min. • **Bake:** 15 min.
Makes: 6 servings

- 1 pkg. (10 oz.) frozen chopped spinach
- 2 chicken bouillon cubes
- Salt
- 3 large tomatoes, halved
- 1 cup soft bread crumbs
- ½ cup grated Parmesan cheese
- ½ cup chopped onion
- ½ cup butter, melted
- 1 large egg, lightly beaten
- 1 garlic clove, minced
- ¼ tsp. pepper
- ⅛ tsp. cayenne pepper
- Shredded Parmesan cheese, optional

1. In a large saucepan, cook spinach according to package directions with bouillon; drain well. Cool slightly; press out excess liquid.

2. Lightly salt tomato halves; place with cut side down on a paper towel for 15 minutes to absorb excess moisture.

3. In a small bowl, combine the spinach, bread crumbs, cheese, onion, butter, egg, garlic, pepper and cayenne pepper.

4. Place tomato halves, cut side up, in a shallow baking dish. Divide the spinach mixture over tomatoes. Sprinkle with shredded cheese if desired. Bake at 350° for about 15 minutes or until heated through.

Per serving: 236 cal., 19g fat (11g sat. fat), 78mg chol., 649mg sod., 12g carb. (4g sugars, 3g fiber), 7g pro.

25 MOST POPULAR RECIPES

THIS COOKBOOK WOULDN'T BE COMPLETE WITHOUT A LIST OF OUR TOP 25 MOST-LOVED RECIPES! OUR EDITORS FOUND THE DISHES THAT RECEIVED THE MOST VIEWS AND THE BEST REVIEWS ON TASTEOFHOME.COM FOR THIS MOUTHWATERING CHAPTER.

EDITOR'S CHOICE

SANDY'S CHOCOLATE CAKE

I drove 4½ hours to a cake contest, holding my entry on my lap. One bite and you'll see why this beauty won first prize.

—Sandy Johnson, Tioga, PA

Prep: 30 min.
Bake: 30 min. + cooling
Makes: 16 servings

- 1 cup butter, softened
- 3 cups packed brown sugar
- 4 large eggs
- 2 tsp. vanilla extract
- 2⅔ cups all-purpose flour
- ¾ cup baking cocoa
- 3 tsp. baking soda
- ½ tsp. salt
- 1⅓ cups sour cream
- 1⅓ cups boiling water

FROSTING

- ½ cup butter, cubed
- 3 oz. unsweetened chocolate, chopped
- 3 oz. semisweet chocolate, chopped
- 5 cups confectioners' sugar
- 1 cup (8 oz.) sour cream
- 2 tsp. vanilla extract

1. Preheat oven to 350°. Grease and flour three 9-in. round baking pans.
2. In a large bowl, cream butter and brown sugar until light and fluffy. Add eggs, one at a time, beating well after each addition. Beat in vanilla.
3. In another bowl, whisk flour, cocoa, baking soda and salt; add to creamed mixture alternately with sour cream, beating well after each addition. Stir in water until blended. Transfer to pans. Bake until a toothpick comes out clean, 30-35 minutes. Cool in pans 10 minutes; remove to wire racks to cool completely. For the frosting, in a metal bowl over simmering water, melt the butter and chocolates; stir until smooth. Cool slightly.
4. In a large bowl, combine confectioners' sugar, sour cream and vanilla. Add chocolate mixture; beat until smooth. Spread frosting between layers and over top and sides of cake. Refrigerate leftovers.

Per slice: 685 cal., 29g fat (18g sat. fat), 115mg chol., 505mg sod., 102g carb. (81g sugars, 3g fiber), 7g pro.

MADE WITH LOVE

A friend asked for chocolate cake for his birthday. I chose this one because it received such great reviews. It truly is the absolute best chocolate cake I've ever had.

DANA MEREDITH
TASTE OF HOME MAGAZINE

FIESTA PINWHEELS

Whenever I serve these make-ahead appetizers, they disappear fast.

—Diane Martin, Brown Deer, WI

Prep: 15 min. + chilling
Makes: about 5 dozen

- 1 pkg. (8 oz.) cream cheese, softened
- ½ cup sour cream
- ¼ cup picante sauce
- 2 Tbsp. taco seasoning
- Dash garlic powder
- 1 can (4½ oz.) chopped ripe olives, drained
- 1 can (4 oz.) chopped green chilies
- 1 cup finely shredded cheddar cheese
- ½ cup thinly sliced green onions
- 8 flour tortillas (10 in.)
- Salsa

1. In a small bowl, beat cream cheese, sour cream, picante sauce, taco seasoning and garlic powder until smooth. Stir in olives, chilies, cheese and onions. Spread about ½ cup on each tortilla.
2. Roll up jelly-roll style; wrap in plastic. Refrigerate for 2 hours or overnight. Slice into 1-in. pieces. Serve with salsa.

Per 3 appetizers: 170 cal., 9g fat (5g sat. fat), 22mg chol., 402mg sod., 15g carb. (1g sugars, 3g fiber), 5g pro.

AMISH SUGAR COOKIES

AMISH SUGAR COOKIES

I've passed this recipe around to many friends. After I gave it to my sister, she entered the cookies in a local fair and won the best of show prize!

—Sylvia Ford, Kennett, MO

Prep: 10 min. • **Bake:** 10 min./batch
Makes: about 5 dozen

- 1 cup butter, softened
- 1 cup vegetable oil
- 1 cup sugar
- 1 cup confectioners' sugar
- 2 large eggs
- 1 tsp. vanilla extract
- 4½ cups all-purpose flour
- 1 tsp. baking soda
- 1 tsp. cream of tartar

1. In a large bowl, beat the butter, oil and sugars. Beat in eggs until well blended. Beat in vanilla. Combine the flour, baking soda and cream of tartar; gradually add to creamed mixture.

2. Drop dough by small teaspoonfuls onto ungreased baking sheets. Bake at 375° until lightly browned, 8-10 minutes. Remove to wire racks to cool.

Per 2 cookies: 233 cal., 14g fat (5g sat. fat), 31mg chol., 108mg sod., 25g carb. (11g sugars, 1g fiber), 2g pro.

EASY CHICKEN ENCHILADAS

A must for any Mexican meal at my house, these enchiladas can be served as a main dish or included as part of a buffet.

—Cheryl Pomrenke, Coffeyville, KS

Prep: 15 min. • **Bake:** 25 min. + standing
Makes: 10 servings

- 3 cups shredded cheddar cheese, divided
- 2 cups shredded Monterey Jack cheese
- 2 cups chopped cooked chicken
- 2 cups (16 oz.) sour cream
- 1 can (10¾ oz.) condensed cream of chicken soup, undiluted
- 1 can (4 oz.) chopped green chilies
- 2 Tbsp. finely chopped onion
- ¼ tsp. pepper
- ⅛ tsp. salt
- 10 flour tortillas (8 in.), warmed
- Pico de gallo, optional

1. In a large bowl, combine 2 cups cheddar cheese, Monterey Jack cheese, chicken, sour cream, soup, chilies, onion, pepper and salt. Spoon about ½ cup off center on each tortilla; roll up. Place seam side down in a greased 13x9-in. baking dish.

2. Cover and bake at 350° for 20 minutes. Uncover; sprinkle with remaining cheddar cheese. Bake 5 minutes longer or until cheese is melted. Let stand for 10 minutes before serving. If desired, serve with pico de gallo.

Per enchilada: 663 cal., 39g fat (23g sat. fat), 144mg chol., 1160mg sod., 39g carb. (3g sugars, 1g fiber), 35g pro.

MADE WITH LOVE

I have made this recipe quite a few times both for family and friends. It is delicious!

MEGNICHOLL TASTEOFHOME.COM

CHEESEBURGER SOUP

A local restaurant serves a similar soup but wouldn't share its recipe with me. I decided to develop my own, modifying a recipe for potato soup. I was really pleased at the way this all-American dish turned out.

—Joanie Shawhan, Madison, WI

Prep: 45 min. • **Cook:** 10 min.
Makes: 8 servings (2¼ qt.)

- ½ lb. ground beef
- 4 Tbsp. butter, divided
- ¾ cup chopped onion
- ¾ cup shredded carrots
- ¾ cup diced celery
- 1 tsp. dried basil
- 1 tsp. dried parsley flakes
- 1¾ lbs. (about 4 cups) cubed peeled potatoes
- 3 cups chicken broth
- ¼ cup all-purpose flour
- 2 to 4 cups shredded Velveeta process cheese
- 1½ cups whole milk
- ¾ tsp. salt
- ¼ to ½ tsp. pepper
- ¼ cup sour cream

1. In a large saucepan over medium heat, cook and crumble beef until no longer pink; drain and set aside. In same saucepan, melt 1 Tbsp. butter over medium heat. Saute onion, carrots, celery, basil and parsley until vegetables are tender, about 10 minutes. Add potatoes, ground beef and broth; bring to a boil. Reduce heat; simmer, covered, until potatoes are tender, 10-12 minutes.

2. Meanwhile, in a small skillet, melt the remaining butter. Add flour; cook and stir until bubbly, 3-5 minutes. Add to soup; bring to a boil. Cook and stir 2 minutes. Reduce heat to low. Stir in cheese, milk, salt and pepper; cook until cheese melts. Remove from heat; blend in sour cream.

Per cup: 450 cal., 27g fat (15g sat. fat), 100mg chol., 1421mg sod., 33g carb. (8g sugars, 3g fiber), 19g pro.

CHEESEBURGER SOUP

BACON MACARONI SALAD

This pleasing pasta salad is like eating a BLT in a bowl. It's a real crowd-pleaser!
—Norene Wright, Manilla, IN

Prep: 20 min. + chilling
Makes: 12 servings

- 2 cups uncooked elbow macaroni
- 1 large tomato, finely chopped
- 2 celery ribs, finely chopped
- 5 green onions, finely chopped
- 1¼ cups mayonnaise
- 5 tsp. white vinegar
- ¼ tsp. salt
- ⅛ to ¼ tsp. pepper
- 1 lb. bacon strips, cooked and crumbled

1. Cook macaroni according to package directions; drain and rinse in cold water. Transfer to a large bowl; stir in tomato, celery and green onions.
2. In a small bowl, whisk mayonnaise, vinegar, salt and pepper. Pour over macaroni mixture and toss to coat. Refrigerate, covered, at least 2 hours. Just before serving, stir in bacon.
Per ¾ cup: 290 cal., 25g fat (5g sat. fat), 19mg chol., 387mg sod., 11g carb. (1g sugars, 1g fiber), 6g pro.

HEARTY VEGETABLE SOUP

A friend gave me the idea to use V8 juice in veggie soup because it provides more flavor. This recipe has stood the test of time!
—Janice Steinmetz, Somers, CT

Prep: 25 min. • **Cook:** 1 hour 20 min.
Makes: 16 servings (4 qt.)

- 1 Tbsp. olive oil
- 8 medium carrots, sliced
- 2 large onions, chopped
- 4 celery ribs, chopped
- 1 large green pepper, seeded and chopped
- 1 garlic clove, minced
- 2 cups chopped cabbage
- 2 cups frozen cut green beans (about 8 oz.)
- 2 cups frozen peas (about 8 oz.)
- 1 cup frozen corn (about 5 oz.)
- 1 can (15 oz.) garbanzo beans or chickpeas, rinsed and drained
- 1 bay leaf
- 2 tsp. chicken bouillon granules
- 1½ tsp. dried parsley flakes
- 1 tsp. salt
- 1 tsp. dried marjoram
- 1 tsp. dried thyme
- ½ tsp. dried basil
- ¼ tsp. pepper
- 4 cups water
- 1 can (28 oz.) diced tomatoes, undrained
- 2 cups V8 juice

1. In a stockpot, heat oil over medium-high heat; saute carrots, onions, celery and green pepper until crisp-tender. Add garlic; cook and stir 1 minute. Stir in remaining ingredients; bring to a boil.
2. Reduce heat; simmer, covered, until vegetables are tender, 1-1½ hours. Remove bay leaf.
Per cup: 105 cal., 2g fat (0 sat. fat), 0 chol., 488mg sod., 20g carb. (9g sugars, 5g fiber), 4g pro. **Diabetic exchanges:** 1 starch.

FLAVORFUL CHICKEN FAJITAS

My chicken fajitas are in our rotation of favorite weeknight dinners. The marinated chicken in these popular wraps is just so incredible. The dish goes together in a snap and always get raves!

—Julie Sterchi, Campbellsvlle, KY

Prep: 20 min. + marinating • **Cook:** 5 min.
Makes: 6 servings

- 4 Tbsp. canola oil, divided
- 2 Tbsp. lemon juice
- 1½ tsp. seasoned salt
- 1½ tsp. dried oregano
- 1½ tsp. ground cumin
- 1 tsp. garlic powder
- ½ tsp. chili powder
- ½ tsp. paprika
- ½ tsp. crushed red pepper flakes, optional
- 1½ lbs. boneless skinless chicken breast, cut into thin strips
- ½ medium sweet red pepper, julienned
- ½ medium green pepper, julienned
- 4 green onions, thinly sliced
- ½ cup chopped onion
- 6 flour tortillas (8 in.), warmed
- Shredded cheddar cheese, taco sauce, salsa, guacamole and sour cream

1. In a large resealable plastic bag, combine 2 Tbsp. oil, lemon juice and seasonings; add the chicken. Seal and turn to coat; refrigerate for 1-4 hours.
2. In a large skillet, saute peppers and onions in remaining oil until crisp-tender. Remove and keep warm.
3. Discard marinade. In the same skillet, cook chicken over medium-high heat for 5-6 minutes or until no longer pink. Return pepper mixture to pan; heat through.
4. Spoon filling down the center of tortillas; fold in half. Serve with cheese, taco sauce, salsa, guacamole and sour cream.
Per fajita: 369 cal., 15g fat (2g sat. fat), 63mg chol., 689mg sod., 30g carb. (2g sugars, 1g fiber), 28g pro.

APPLE PIE

APPLE PIE

If you want to learn how to bake homemade apple pie, this is the recipe you need.

—Maggie Greene, Granite Falls, WA

Prep: 20 min.
Bake: 45 min.
Makes: 8 servings

- ½ cup sugar
- ½ cup packed brown sugar
- 3 Tbsp. all-purpose flour
- 1 tsp. ground cinnamon
- ¼ tsp. ground ginger
- ¼ tsp. ground nutmeg
- 6 to 7 cups thinly sliced peeled tart apples
- 1 Tbsp. lemon juice
- Pastry for double-crust pie (9 in.)
- 1 Tbsp. butter
- 1 large egg white
- Additional sugar

1. In a small bowl, combine the sugars, flour and spices; set aside. In a large bowl, toss apples with lemon juice. Add sugar mixture; toss to coat.
2. Line a 9-in. pie plate with bottom crust; trim pastry even with edge. Fill with apple mixture; dot with butter. Roll out remaining pastry to fit top of pie. Place over filling. Trim, seal and flute edges. Using a sharp paring knife, cut slits in top of pastry.
3. Beat egg white until foamy; brush over pastry. Sprinkle with sugar. Cover edges loosely with foil.
4. Bake at 375° for 25 minutes. Remove foil and bake 20-25 minutes longer or until crust is golden brown and filling is bubbly. Cool on a wire rack.
Per slice: 414 cal., 16g fat (7g sat. fat), 14mg chol., 227mg sod., 67g carb. (38g sugars, 2g fiber), 3g pro.

MADE WITH LOVE

I remember coming home sullen one day because we lost a softball game. Grandma suggested, "Maybe a slice of my homemade apple pie will make you feel better." She was always right. It's still making me feel better today.

MAGGIE GREENE GRANITE FALLS, WA

BUFFALO CHICKEN DIP

BUFFALO CHICKEN DIP

Buffalo wing sauce, cream cheese and ranch or blue cheese dressing make a great party dip. Everywhere I take it, people want this 30-minute recipe.

—Belinda Gibson, Dry Ridge, KY

Takes: 30 min.
Makes: about 2 cups

- 1 pkg. (8 oz.) cream cheese, softened
- 1 cup cooked chicken breast
- ½ cup Buffalo wing sauce
- ½ cup ranch or blue cheese salad dressing
- 2 cups shredded Colby-Monterey Jack cheese
- French bread baguette slices, celery ribs or tortilla chips

1. Preheat oven to 350°. Spread cream cheese into an ungreased shallow 1-qt. baking dish. Layer with chicken, wing sauce and salad dressing. Sprinkle with cheese.

2. Bake, uncovered, 20-25 minutes or until cheese is melted. Serve with baguette slices.

Per 2 Tbsp.: 156 cal., 13g fat (7g sat. fat), 38mg chol., 484mg sod., 2g carb. (1g sugars, 0 fiber), 7g pro.

BASIC HOMEMADE BREAD

If you'd like to learn how to make bread, here's a wonderful place to start. This recipe couldn't be easier. There's nothing like the comforting aroma wafting through my kitchen as it bakes.

—Sandra Anderson, New York, NY

Prep: 20 min. + rising
Bake: 30 min. + cooling
Makes: 2 loaves (16 slices each)

- 1 pkg. (¼ oz.) active dry yeast
- 2¼ cups warm water (110° to 115°)
- 3 Tbsp. sugar
- 1 Tbsp. salt
- 2 Tbsp. canola oil
- 6¼ to 6¾ cups all-purpose flour

1. In a large bowl, dissolve yeast in warm water. Add the sugar, salt, oil and 3 cups flour. Beat until smooth. Stir in enough remaining flour, ½ cup at a time, to form a soft dough.

2. Turn onto a floured surface; knead until smooth and elastic, 8-10 minutes. Place in a greased bowl, turning once to grease the top. Cover and let rise in a warm place until doubled, about 1½ hours.

3. Punch dough down. Turn onto a lightly floured surface; divide dough in half. Shape each into a loaf. Place in two greased 9x5-in. loaf pans. Cover and let rise until doubled, 30-45 minutes.

4. Bake at 375° for 30-35 minutes or until golden brown and bread sounds hollow when tapped. Remove from pans to wire racks to cool.

Per slice: 102 cal., 1g fat (0 sat. fat), 0 chol., 222mg sod., 20g carb. (1g sugars, 1g fiber), 3g pro.

CLASSIC BEEF STEW

Here's a good old-fashioned stew with lots of veggies in a rich beef gravy. It's the perfect dish for a cool day.

—Alberta McKay, Bartlesville, OK

Prep: 15 min. • **Bake:** 2½ hours
Makes: 6-8 servings

- 2 lbs. beef stew meat, cut into 1-in. cubes
- 1 to 2 Tbsp. canola oil
- 1½ cups chopped onions
- 1 can (14½ oz.) diced tomatoes, undrained
- 1 can (10½ oz.) condensed beef broth, undiluted
- 3 Tbsp. quick-cooking tapioca
- 1 garlic clove, minced
- 1 Tbsp. dried parsley flakes
- 1 tsp. salt
- ¼ tsp. pepper
- 1 bay leaf
- 6 medium carrots, cut into 2-in. pieces
- 3 medium potatoes, peeled and cut into 2-in. pieces
- 1 cup sliced celery (1-in. lengths)

1. In an oven-safe Dutch oven, brown beef in batchesin oil; drain. Return all meat to the pan. Add onions, tomatoes, broth, tapioca, garlic, parsley, salt, pepper and bay leaf. Bring to a boil.

2. Cover stew and bake at 350° for 1 hour. Stir in carrots, potatoes and celery. Bake, covered, 1 hour longer or until meat and vegetables are tender. Discard bay leaf.

Per cup: 245 cal., 10g fat (3g sat. fat), 71mg chol., 751mg sod., 14g carb. (6g sugars, 3g fiber), 24g pro.

I loved it! This stew is delicious and turns out perfect. I made it four times in two months.

DAWN537464 TASTEOFHOME.COM

CLASSIC BEEF STEW

SLOW COOKER POT ROAST

SLOW COOKER POT ROAST

I work full time, so this pot roast from a slow cooker is my go-to when I want a hearty, home-cooked meal. It's a comfort to walk in and smell this fall-apart tender roast.
—Gina Jackson, Ogdensburg, NY

Prep: 15 min.
Cook: 6 hours
Makes: 6 servings

- 1 cup warm water
- 1 Tbsp. beef base
- ½ lb. sliced fresh mushrooms
- 1 large onion, coarsely chopped
- 3 garlic cloves, minced
- 1 boneless beef chuck roast (3 lbs.)
- ½ tsp. pepper
- 1 Tbsp. Worcestershire sauce
- ¼ cup butter, cubed
- ⅓ cup all-purpose flour
- ¼ tsp. salt

1. In a 5- or 6-qt. slow cooker, whisk water and beef base; add mushrooms, onion and garlic. Sprinkle roast with pepper; transfer to slow cooker. Drizzle with Worcestershire sauce. Cook, covered, on low 6-8 hours or until meat is tender.

2. Remove roast to a serving platter; tent with foil. Strain cooking juices, reserving vegetables. Skim fat from cooking juices. In a large saucepan, melt butter over medium heat. Stir in flour and salt until smooth; gradually whisk in cooking juices. Bring to a boil, stirring constantly; cook and stir 1-2 minutes or until thickened. Stir in cooked vegetables. Serve with roast.

Note Look for beef base near the broth and bouillon.

Per serving: 507 cal., 30g fat (13g sat. fat), 168mg chol., 623mg sod., 11g carb. (3g sugars, 1g fiber), 47g pro.

EASY VANILLA BUTTERCREAM FROSTING

My simple buttercream recipe offers unbeatable homemade taste. It's easy to tweak, too. Try using peppermint or almond extract instead of vanilla, or substitute your own favorite flavors.
—Diana Wilson, Denver, CO

Takes: 10 min. • **Makes:** About 3 cups

- ½ cup butter, softened
- 4½ cups confectioners' sugar
- 1½ tsp. vanilla extract
- 5 to 6 Tbsp. 2% milk

In a large bowl, beat butter until creamy. Beat in the confectioners' sugar, vanilla and enough milk to achieve desired consistency.

Per 2 Tbsp.: 124 cal., 4g fat (2g sat. fat), 11mg chol., 40mg sod., 23g carb. (21g sugars, 0 fiber), 0 pro.

STRAWBERRY PRETZEL DESSERT

Need to bring a dish to pass this weekend? This make-ahead strawberry pretzel salad will disappear quickly at any potluck.
—Aldene Belch, Flint, MI

Prep: 20 min.
Bake: 10 min. + chilling
Makes: 16 servings

- 2 cups crushed pretzels (about 8 oz.)
- ¾ cup butter, melted
- 3 Tbsp. sugar

FILLING

- 2 cups whipped topping
- 1 pkg. (8 oz.) cream cheese, softened
- 1 cup sugar

TOPPING

- 2 pkg. (3 oz. each) strawberry gelatin
- 2 cups boiling water
- 2 pkg. (16 oz. each) frozen sweetened sliced strawberries, thawed
- Additional whipped topping and pretzels, optional

1. In a large bowl, combine the crushed pretzels, butter and sugar. Press mixture into an ungreased 13x9-in. baking dish. Bake crust at 350° for 10 minutes. Cool on a wire rack.

2. For filling, in a small bowl, beat whipped topping, cream cheese and sugar until smooth. Spread over pretzel crust. Refrigerate until chilled.

3. For topping, dissolve gelatin in boiling water in a large bowl. Stir in strawberries with syrup; chill until partially set. Carefully spoon over filling. Chill for 4-6 hours or until firm. Cut into squares; serve with whipped topping if desired.

Per piece: 295 cal., 15g fat (10g sat. fat), 39mg chol., 305mg sod., 38g carb. (27g sugars, 1g fiber), 3g pro.

STRAWBERRY PRETZEL DESSERT

BACON CHEESEBURGER SLIDER BAKE

These have been popular for a long time! I created the dish to fill two pans because the sliders disappear fast. Just cut the recipe in half if you only need one batch.

—Nick Iverson, Denver, CO

Prep: 20 min. • **Bake:** 25 min.
Makes: 2 dozen

- 2 pkg. (12 oz. each) Hawaiian sweet rolls
- 4 cups shredded cheddar cheese, divided
- 2 lbs. ground beef
- 1 cup chopped onion
- 1 can (14½ oz.) diced tomatoes with garlic and onion, drained
- 1 Tbsp. Dijon mustard
- 1 Tbsp. Worcestershire sauce
- ¾ tsp. salt
- ¾ tsp. pepper
- 24 bacon strips, cooked and crumbled

GLAZE

- 1 cup butter, cubed
- ¼ cup packed brown sugar
- 4 tsp. Worcestershire sauce
- 2 Tbsp. Dijon mustard
- 2 Tbsp. sesame seeds

1. Preheat oven to 350°. Without separating rolls, cut each package of rolls horizontally in half; arrange bottom halves in two greased 13x9-in. baking pans. Sprinkle each pan of rolls with 1 cup cheese. Bake until cheese is melted, 3-5 minutes.

2. In a large skillet, cook beef and onion over medium heat 6-8 minutes or until beef is no longer pink and onion is tender, breaking up beef into crumbles; drain. Stir in tomatoes, mustard, Worcestershire sauce, salt and pepper. Cook and stir until combined, 1-2 minutes.

3. Spoon beef mixture evenly over rolls; sprinkle with remaining cheese. Top with bacon. Replace tops. For glaze, in a microwave-safe bowl, combine butter, brown sugar, Worcestershire sauce and mustard. Microwave, covered, on high until butter is melted, stirring occasionally. Pour over rolls; sprinkle with sesame seeds. Bake, uncovered, until golden brown and heated through, 20-25 minutes.

Freeze option Cover and freeze unbaked sandwiches; prepare and freeze glaze. To use, partially thaw in refrigerator overnight. Remove from refrigerator 30 minutes before baking. Preheat oven to 350°. Pour glaze over buns and sprinkle with sesame seeds. Bake sandwiches as directed, increasing time by 10-15 minutes or until cheese is melted and a thermometer inserted in center reads 165°.

Per slider: 380 cal., 24g fat (13g sat. fat), 86mg chol., 628mg sod., 21g carb. (9g sugars, 2g fiber), 18g pro.

TRUE BELGIAN WAFFLES

It was on a visit to my husband's relatives in Europe that I was given this Belgian waffle recipe, and I've used it ever since.

—Rose Delemeester, St. Charles, MI

Takes: 20 min.
Makes: 10 waffles (about 4½ in.)

- 2 cups all-purpose flour
- ¾ cup sugar
- 3½ tsp. baking powder
- 2 large eggs, separated
- 1½ cups whole milk
- 1 cup butter, melted
- 1 tsp. vanilla extract
- Sliced fresh strawberries or syrup

1. In a bowl, combine flour, sugar and baking powder. In another bowl, lightly beat egg yolks. Add milk, butter and vanilla; mix well. Stir into dry ingredients just until combined. Beat egg whites until stiff peaks form; fold into batter.

2. Bake in a preheated waffle iron according to manufacturer's directions until golden brown. Serve with strawberries or syrup.

Per 2 waffles: 696 cal., 41g fat (25g sat. fat), 193mg chol., 712mg sod., 72g carb. (34g sugars, 1g fiber), 10g pro.

FAVORITE BANANA CREAM PIE

Homemade banana cream pie is my mom's specialty. This dreamy dessert has a yummy banana flavor and is easy to cut, too.
—Jodi Grable, Springfield, MO

Prep: 10 min. • **Cook:** 15 min. + chilling
Makes: 8 servings

- 1 cup sugar
- ¼ cup cornstarch
- ½ tsp. salt
- 3 cups 2% milk
- 2 large eggs, lightly beaten
- 3 Tbsp. butter
- 1½ tsp. vanilla extract
- 1 pie crust (9 in.), baked
- 2 large firm bananas
- 1 cup heavy whipping cream, whipped

1. In a large saucepan, combine sugar, cornstarch, salt and milk until smooth. Cook and stir over medium-high heat until thickened and bubbly. Reduce heat; cook and stir 2 minutes longer. Remove from heat. Stir a small amount of hot filling into eggs; return all to pan. Bring to a gentle boil; cook and stir 2 minutes longer.
2. Remove from heat. Gently stir in the butter and vanilla. Press plastic wrap onto surface of custard; refrigerate, covered, 30 minutes.
3. Spread half of the custard into crust. Slice bananas; arrange over filling. Pour remaining custard over bananas. Spread with whipped cream. Refrigerate 6 hours or overnight.
Per slice: 472 cal., 26g fat (14g sat. fat), 117mg chol., 353mg sod., 55g carb. (35g sugars, 1g fiber), 7g pro.

This is requested regularly at holiday meals, and my boyfriend prefers it over cake for his birthday.

13EGGSLATER TASTEOFHOME.COM

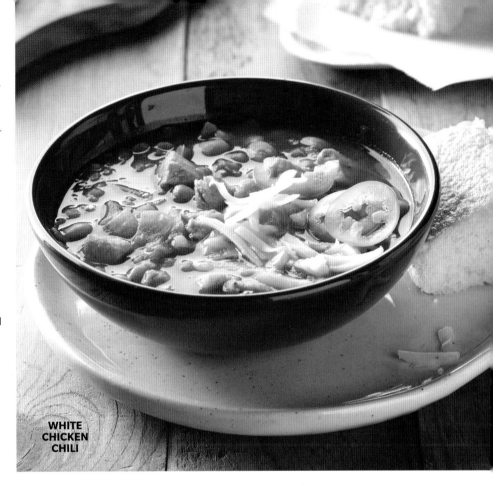

WHITE CHICKEN CHILI

WHITE CHICKEN CHILI

Folks will enjoy this variation on traditional chili with tender chicken and zippy peppers.
—Taste of Home *Test Kitchen*

Prep: 15 min. • **Cook:** 25 min.
Makes: 10 servings (2½ qt.)

- 1 lb. boneless skinless chicken breasts, chopped
- 1 medium onion, chopped
- 1 Tbsp. olive oil
- 2 garlic cloves, minced
- 2 cans (14 oz. each) chicken broth
- 1 can (4 oz.) chopped green chilies
- 2 tsp. ground cumin
- 2 tsp. dried oregano
- 1½ tsp. cayenne pepper
- 3 cans (14½ oz. each) great northern beans, drained, divided
- 1 cup shredded Monterey Jack cheese
- Sliced jalapeno pepper, optional

1. In a Dutch oven over medium heat, cook chicken and onion in oil until lightly browned. Add garlic; cook 1 minute longer. Stir in the broth, chilies, cumin, oregano and cayenne; bring to a boil.
2. Reduce heat to low. With a potato masher, mash one can of beans until smooth. Add to saucepan. Add remaining beans to saucepan. Simmer until the chicken is no longer pink and onion is tender, 20-30 minutes.
3. Top each serving with cheese and, if desired, jalapeno pepper.
Per cup: 219 cal., 7g fat (3g sat. fat), 37mg chol., 644mg sod., 21g carb. (1g sugars, 7g fiber), 19g pro.

ITALIAN BRUNCH TORTE

ITALIAN BRUNCH TORTE

We pair this impressive layered breakfast bake with a simple salad of mixed greens and tomato wedges. Served warm or cold, it's one of our most requested dishes.
—Danny Diamond, Farmington Hills, MI

Prep: 50 min. • **Bake:** 1 hour + standing
Makes: 12 servings

- 2 tubes (8 oz. each) refrigerated crescent rolls, divided
- 1 tsp. olive oil
- 1 pkg. (6 oz.) fresh baby spinach
- 1 cup sliced fresh mushrooms
- 7 large eggs
- 1 cup grated Parmesan cheese
- 2 tsp. Italian seasoning
- ⅛ tsp. pepper
- ½ lb. thinly sliced deli ham
- ½ lb. thinly sliced hard salami
- ½ lb. sliced provolone cheese
- 2 jars (12 oz. each) roasted sweet red peppers, drained, sliced and patted dry

1. Preheat oven to 350°. Place a greased 9-in. springform pan on a double thickness of heavy-duty foil (about 18 in. square). Securely wrap foil around pan. Unroll one tube of crescent dough and separate into triangles. Press onto bottom of prepared pan to form a crust, sealing seams well. Bake 10-15 minutes or until set.
2. Meanwhile, in a large skillet, heat oil over medium-high heat. Add spinach and mushrooms; cook and stir until mushrooms are tender. Drain on several layers of paper towels, blotting well. In a large bowl, whisk six of the eggs, Parmesan cheese, Italian seasoning and pepper.
3. Layer crust with half of each of the following: ham, salami, provolone cheese, red peppers and spinach mixture. Pour half of the egg mixture over top. Repeat layers; top with remaining egg mixture.
4. On a work surface, unroll and separate remaining crescent dough into triangles. Press together to form a circle and seal seams; place over filling. Whisk remaining egg; brush over dough.
5. Bake, uncovered, 1-1¼ hours or until a thermometer reads 160°, covering loosely with foil if needed to prevent overbrowning. Carefully loosen sides from pan with a knife; remove rim from pan. Let stand 20 minutes.
Per slice: 403 cal., 24g fat (10g sat. fat), 167mg chol., 1360mg sod., 19g carb. (5g sugars, 0 fiber), 23g pro.

SIMPLE TACO SOUP

We first sampled this chili-like soup at a church dinner. It's a warming dish on a cold day. And since it uses packaged seasonings and several cans of vegetables, it's a simple dinner to prepare.
—Glenda Taylor, Sand Springs, OK

Takes: 25 min.
Makes: 6-8 servings (about 2 qt.)

- 2 lbs. ground beef
- 1 envelope taco seasoning
- 1½ cups water
- 1 can (16 oz.) mild chili beans, undrained
- 1 can (15¼ oz.) whole kernel corn, drained
- 1 can (15 oz.) pinto beans, rinsed and drained
- 1 can (14½ oz.) stewed tomatoes
- 1 can (10 oz.) diced tomato with green chilies
- 1 can (4 oz.) chopped green chilies, optional
- 1 envelope ranch salad dressing mix

In a Dutch oven, cook beef over medium heat until no longer pink; drain. Add the taco seasoning and mix well. Stir in the remaining ingredients. Bring to a boil. Reduce heat; simmer, uncovered, for 15 minutes or until heated through, stirring occasionally.
Per cup: 370 cal., 14g fat (5g sat. fat), 70mg chol., 1369mg sod., 35g carb. (7g sugars, 7g fiber), 27g pro.

FAVORITE CHICKEN POTPIE

With plenty of chicken, potatoes, peas and corn, this all-time favorite makes two golden pies, so you can serve one at supper and save the other for a busy night. I'm sure this will become a staple at your home.

—Karen Johnson, Bakersfield, CA

Prep: 40 min. • **Bake:** 35 min. + standing
Makes: 2 potpies (8 servings each)

- 2 cups diced peeled potatoes
- 1¾ cups sliced carrots
- 1 cup butter, cubed
- ⅔ cup chopped onion
- 1 cup all-purpose flour
- 1¾ tsp. salt
- 1 tsp. dried thyme
- ¾ tsp. pepper
- 3 cups chicken broth
- 1½ cups whole milk
- 4 cups cubed cooked chicken
- 1 cup frozen peas
- 1 cup frozen corn
- 4 sheets refrigerated pie crust

1. Preheat oven to 425°. Place potatoes and carrots in a large saucepan; add water to cover. Bring to a boil. Reduce heat; cook, covered, 8-10 minutes or until vegetables are crisp-tender; drain.

2. In a large skillet, heat butter over medium-high heat. Add onion; cook and stir until tender. Stir in flour and seasonings until blended. Gradually stir in broth and milk. Bring to a boil, stirring constantly; cook and stir 2 minutes or until thickened. Stir in chicken, peas, corn and potato mixture; remove from heat.

3. Unroll one pie crust into each of two 9-in. pie plates; trim even with rims. Add chicken mixture. Unroll remaining crusts; place over filling. Trim, seal and flute edges. Cut slits in tops.

4. Bake until crusts are lightly browned, 35-40 minutes. Let stand 15 minutes before cutting.

Freeze option Cover and freeze unbaked potpies. To use, remove from freezer 30 minutes before baking (do not thaw). Preheat oven to 425°. Place pies on baking sheets; cover edges loosely with foil. Bake 30 minutes. Reduce oven setting to 350°; bake 70-80 minutes longer or until crust is golden brown and a thermometer inserted in center reads 165°.

Per serving: 475 cal., 28g fat (14g sat. fat), 74mg chol., 768mg sod., 41g carb. (5g sugars, 2g fiber), 15g pro.

FAVORITE CHICKEN POTPIE

COCONUT-PECAN GERMAN CHOCOLATE PIE

This recipe combines a few popular desserts into one sensational pie. It's so silky and smooth, you won't be able to put your fork down.

—Anna Jones, Coppell, TX

Prep: 50 min. + chilling
Bake: 35 min. + chilling • **Makes:** 8 servings

- 1¼ cups all-purpose flour
- ¼ tsp. salt
- 6 Tbsp. cold lard
- 3 to 4 Tbsp. ice water

FILLING

- 4 oz. German sweet chocolate, chopped
- 2 oz. unsweetened chocolate, chopped
- 1 can (14 oz.) sweetened condensed milk
- 4 large egg yolks
- 1 tsp. vanilla extract
- 1 cup chopped pecans

TOPPING

- ½ cup packed brown sugar
- ½ cup heavy whipping cream
- ¼ cup butter, cubed
- 2 large egg yolks
- 1 cup sweetened shredded coconut
- 1 tsp. vanilla extract
- ¼ cup chopped pecans

1. In a bowl, mix flour and salt; cut in lard until crumbly. Slowly add ice water, tossing with a fork until dough holds together when pressed. Shape into a disk; wrap in plastic. Refrigerate 30 minutes or overnight.

2. Preheat oven to 400°. On a lightly floured surface, roll dough to a ⅛-in.-thick circle; transfer to a 9-in. pie plate. Trim pastry to ½ in. beyond rim of plate; flute edge. Line unpricked pastry with a double thickness of foil. Fill with pie weights, dried beans or uncooked rice.

3. Bake 11-13 minutes or until bottom is lightly browned. Remove foil and weights; bake 6-8 minutes longer or until light brown. Cool on a wire rack. Reduce oven setting to 350°.

4. In a microwave, melt chocolates in a large bowl; stir until smooth. Cool slightly. Whisk in milk, egg yolks and vanilla; stir in pecans. Pour into crust. Bake 16-19 minutes or until set. Cool 1 hour on a wire rack.

5. Meanwhile, in a small heavy saucepan, combine brown sugar, cream and butter. Bring to a boil over medium heat, stirring to dissolve sugar. Remove from heat.

6. In a small bowl, whisk a small amount of hot mixture into egg yolks; return all to pan, whisking constantly. Cook 2-3 minutes or until mixture thickens and a thermometer reads 160°, stirring constantly. Remove from heat. Stir in coconut and vanilla; cool 10 minutes.

7. Pour over filling; sprinkle with pecans. Refrigerate 4 hours or until cold.

Per slice: 801 cal., 54g fat (24g sat. fat), 215mg chol., 227mg sod., 75g carb. (53g sugars, 5g fiber), 12g pro.

CREAMY COLESLAW

This is the best coleslaw recipe because the package of shredded cabbage really cuts down on prep time. I use it for potlucks as well as weeknight menus.

—Renee Endress, Galva, IL

Takes: 10 min. • **Makes:** 6 servings

- 1 pkg. (14 oz.) coleslaw mix
- ¾ cup mayonnaise
- ⅓ cup sour cream
- ¼ cup sugar
- ¾ tsp. seasoned salt
- ½ tsp. ground mustard
- ¼ tsp. celery salt

Place coleslaw mix in a large bowl. In a small bowl, combine the remaining ingredients; stir until blended. Pour over coleslaw mix and toss to coat. Refrigerate until serving.

Per ¾ cup: 283 cal., 24g fat (5g sat. fat), 19mg chol., 431mg sod., 13g carb. (11g sugars, 2g fiber), 1g pro.

MOM'S MEAT LOAF

Mom made the best meat loaf, and now I do, too. When I first met my husband, he didn't care for meat loaf recipes, but this version won him over.
—Michelle Beran, Claflin, KS

Prep: 15 min. • **Bake:** 1 hour + standing
Makes: 6 servings

- 2 large eggs, lightly beaten
- ¾ cup 2% milk
- ⅔ cup finely crushed saltines
- ½ cup chopped onion
- 1 tsp. salt
- ½ tsp. rubbed sage
- Dash pepper
- 1½ lbs. lean ground beef (90% lean)
- 1 cup ketchup
- ½ cup packed brown sugar
- 1 tsp. Worcestershire sauce

1. Preheat oven to 350°. In a large bowl, combine the first seven ingredients. Add beef; mix lightly but thoroughly. Shape into an 8x4-in. loaf in an ungreased 15x10x1-in. baking pan.
2. In a small bowl, combine remaining ingredients, stirring to dissolve sugar; remove ½ cup for sauce. Spread remaining mixture over meat loaf.
3. Bake 60-65 minutes or until a thermometer reads 160°. Let loaf stand 10 minutes before slicing. Serve with reserved sauce.
Per slice: 366 cal., 12g fat (5g sat. fat), 135mg chol., 1092mg sod., 38g carb. (31g sugars, 0 fiber), 26g pro.

While this savory dinner was an instant hit when it was published in Taste of Home *in 1997, the way we garnish platters has changed a lot since then!*

5-INGREDIENT FAVORITES

SATISFYING MAINS, SNACKS, COCKTAILS AND DESSERTS COME TOGETHER IN A SNAP WITH JUST A HANDFUL OF INGREDIENTS. EACH OF THESE FAST-TO-FIX RECIPES IS MADE WITH FIVE ITEMS OR FEWER (EXCLUDING WATER, SALT, PEPPER AND OIL).

CUCUMBER CANAPES

(PICTURED ON P.54)

One of our favorite culinary words, *canape*, is French for "sofa." In this classic recipe, fresh cucumber slices sit atop savory pillows of a garden vegetable spread.

—Taste of Home *Test Kitchen*

Prep: 20 min. + chilling • **Makes:** 2 dozen

- 1 loaf (1 lb.) white or rye bread
- 1 cup mayonnaise (no substitutes)
- 3 oz. spreadable garden vegetable cream cheese
- 2 medium cucumbers, scored and thinly sliced
- Diced pimientos and dill weed, optional

Using a 2½-in. biscuit cutter, cut out circles from bread slices. Mix mayonnaise and cream cheese; spread over each circle. Top with cucumber slices. If desired, garnish with pimientos and dill weed.

Per canape: 120 cal., 9g fat (2g sat. fat), 7mg chol., 134mg sod., 8g carb. (1g sugars, 1g fiber), 2g pro.

TOASTED RAVIOLI PUFFS

Toasted ravioli is such a fan favorite, it disappears faster than you can make it.

—*Kathy Morgan, Temecula, CA*

Takes: 30 min. • **Makes:** 2 dozen

- 24 refrigerated cheese ravioli
- 1 Tbsp. reduced-fat Italian salad dressing
- 1 Tbsp. Italian-style panko (Japanese) bread crumbs
- 1 Tbsp. grated Parmesan cheese
- Warm marinara sauce

1. Preheat oven to 400°. Cook ravioli according to package directions; drain. Transfer to a greased baking sheet. Brush with salad dressing. In a small bowl, mix bread crumbs and cheese; sprinkle over the ravioli.

2. Bake 12-15 minutes or until golden brown. Serve with marinara sauce.

Per ravioli: 21 cal., 1g fat (0 sat. fat), 3mg chol., 43mg sod., 3g carb. (0 sugars, 0 fiber), 1g pro.

LIKE 'EM HOT WINGS

These spicy Buffalo-style chicken wings are finger-licking good. They're an easy crowd-pleasing snack. If you like them hotter, just add more hot sauce.

—*Myra Innes, Auburn, KS*

Prep: 10 min. • **Bake:** 30 min.
Makes: about 2 dozen

- 2½ lbs. chicken wings
- 1 bottle (2 oz.) hot pepper sauce (about ¼ cup)
- 1 to 2 garlic cloves, minced
- 1½ tsp. dried rosemary, crushed
- 1 tsp. dried thyme
- ¼ tsp. salt
- ¼ tsp. pepper
- Celery sticks, carrot sticks and blue cheese salad dressing, optional

1. Cut chicken wings into three sections; discard wing tips. In a large resealable plastic bag, combine the hot pepper sauce, garlic and seasonings. Add wings; toss to evenly coat. Transfer to a well-greased 13x9-in. baking dish.

2. Bake, uncovered, at 425° for 30-40 minutes or until chicken juices run clear, turning every 10 minutes. Serve with celery, carrots and blue cheese dressing if desired.

Note Uncooked chicken wing sections (wingettes) may be substituted for whole chicken wings.

Per piece: 43 cal., 3g fat (1g sat. fat), 12mg chol., 51mg sod., 0 carb. (0 sugars, 0 fiber), 4g pro.

LIKE 'EM HOT WINGS

CHAMPION CHICKEN PUFFS

CHAMPION CHICKEN PUFFS

My guests peeled rubber getting to the table to munch on these chicken puffs. The tender bites are made with hassle-free refrigerated crescent rolls and a flavorful chicken and cream cheese filling.

—Amber Kimmich, Powhatan, VA

Takes: 30 min. • **Makes:** 32 appetizers

- 4 oz. cream cheese, softened
- ½ tsp. garlic powder
- ½ cup shredded cooked chicken
- 2 tubes (8 oz. each) refrigerated crescent rolls

1. In a small bowl, beat cream cheese and garlic powder until smooth. Stir in chicken.

2. Unroll the crescent dough; separate dough into 16 triangles. Cut each triangle in half lengthwise, forming two triangles. Place 1 tsp. of chicken mixture in the center of each. Fold short side over filling; press sides to seal and roll up.

3. Place 1 in. apart on greased baking sheets. Bake at 375° for 12-14 minutes or until golden brown. Serve warm.

Per 2 puffs: 135 cal., 8g fat (2g sat. fat), 11mg chol., 239mg sod., 13g carb. (3g sugars, 0 fiber), 4g pro.

TEST KITCHEN TIP

To make this recipe even faster, use pre-shredded rotisserie chicken from your grocer's deli.

CAPRESE SALAD KABOBS

Trade in the usual veggie party platter for these fun kabobs. I often make them as a healthy snack for my family to munch on, and it's a great recipe for kids to help with.
—Christine Mitchell, Glendora, CA

Takes: 10 min. • **Makes:** 12 kabobs

- 24 grape tomatoes
- 12 cherry-size fresh mozzarella cheese balls
- 24 fresh basil leaves
- 2 Tbsp. olive oil
- 2 tsp. balsamic vinegar

On each of 12 appetizer skewers, alternately thread two tomatoes, one cheese ball and two basil leaves. To serve, whisk together oil and vinegar; drizzle over kabobs.
Per kabob: 44 cal., 4g fat (1g sat. fat), 5mg chol., 10mg sod., 2g carb. (1g sugars, 0 fiber), 1g pro. **Diabetic exchanges:** 1 fat.

CRABBIE PHYLLO CUPS

I like a little extra chili sauce on top of these cute cups. If you don't have crab on hand, water-packed tuna works well, too.
—Johnna Johnson, Scottsdale, AZ

Takes: 20 min. • **Makes:** 2½ dozen

- ½ cup reduced-fat spreadable garden vegetable cream cheese
- ½ tsp. seafood seasoning
- ¾ cup lump crabmeat, drained
- 2 pkg. (1.9 oz. each) frozen miniature phyllo tart shells
- 5 Tbsp. chili sauce

In a small bowl, mix the cream cheese and seafood seasoning; gently stir in crab. Spoon 2 tsp. crab mixture into each tart shell; top with chili sauce.
Per phyllo cup: 34 cal., 2g fat (0 sat. fat), 5mg chol., 103mg sod., 3g carb. (1g sugars, 0 fiber), 1g pro.

CAPRESE SALAD KABOBS

CHEWY CARAMEL-COATED POPCORN

PARTY PESTO PINWHEELS

I took a couple of my favorite recipes and combined them to make these delicious and impressive hors d'oeuvres.
—Kathleen Farrell, Rochester, NY

Takes: 30 min. • **Makes:** 20 pinwheels

- 1 tube (8 oz.) refrigerated crescent rolls
- ⅓ cup prepared pesto sauce
- ¼ cup roasted sweet red peppers, drained and chopped
- ¼ cup grated Parmesan cheese
- 1 cup pizza sauce, warmed

1. Unroll crescent dough into two long rectangles; seal seams and perforations. Spread each with pesto; sprinkle with red peppers and cheese.
2. Roll each up jelly-roll style, starting with a short side. With a sharp knife, cut each roll into 10 slices. Place cut side down 2 in. apart on two ungreased baking sheets.
3. Bake at 400° for 8-10 minutes or until golden brown. Serve warm with pizza sauce.
Per pinwheel: 76 cal., 5g fat (1g sat. fat), 2mg chol., 201mg sod., 6g carb. (2g sugars, 0 fiber), 2g pro.

CHEWY CARAMEL-COATED POPCORN

My mom made this popcorn often when I was a kid. I've adapted it to make it more chewy and gooey than her crunchy, nut-loaded version. I get requests to make this for every event that I host, and have never had any leftovers!
—Shannon Dobos, Calgary, AB

Takes: 25 min. • **Makes:** about 6 qt.

- 1½ cups butter, cubed
- 2⅔ cups packed light brown sugar
- 1 cup golden syrup
- 1 tsp. vanilla extract
- 24 cups popped popcorn

1. Line two 15x10x1-in. pans with parchment paper. In a large heavy saucepan, melt butter over medium-high heat. Add brown sugar and syrup, stirring to dissolve brown sugar. Bring to a full rolling boil. Boil and stir 1 minute. Remove from heat and quickly stir in vanilla.
2. Pour caramel mixture over popcorn; stir lightly to coat. Using a rubber spatula, press popcorn into prepared pans. Cool. Pull apart into pieces. Store in airtight containers.
Per cup: 303 cal., 16g fat (8g sat. fat), 31mg chol., 216mg sod., 40g carb. (35g sugars, 1g fiber), 1g pro.

CREAMY GREEN ONION SPREAD

You need only a few basic ingredients to make this guaranteed party hit.
—Sue Seymour, Valatie, NY

Takes: 5 min. • **Makes:** 1 cup

- 1 pkg. (8 oz.) cream cheese, softened
- 2 Tbsp. whole milk
- 2 green onions with tops, chopped
- ¼ cup crushed pineapple, drained, optional
- Crackers

In a small bowl, beat cream cheese and milk until smooth. Stir in onions and, if desired, pineapple. Serve with crackers.
Per 2 Tbsp.: 102 cal., 10g fat (6g sat. fat), 32mg chol., 86mg sod., 1g carb. (1g sugars, 0 fiber), 2g pro.

CHICKEN CHILI WONTON BITES

Everyone needs a surefire grab-and-go tailgate or picnic recipe. Wonton wrappers filled with chicken and spices make these bites a winner every time.

—Heidi Jobe, Carrollton, GA

Takes: 30 min. • **Makes:** 3 dozen

- 36 wonton wrappers
- ½ cup buttermilk ranch salad dressing
- 1 envelope reduced-sodium chili seasoning mix
- 1½ cups shredded rotisserie chicken
- 1 cup shredded sharp cheddar cheese
- Sour cream and sliced green onions, optional

1. Preheat the oven to 350°. Press each wonton wrapper into a greased miniature muffin cup. Bake until lightly browned, 4-6 minutes.

2. In a small bowl, mix salad dressing and seasoning mix; add chicken and toss to coat. Spoon 1 Tbsp. filling into each wonton cup. Sprinkle with cheese.

3. Bake 8-10 minutes longer or until heated through and wrappers are golden brown. Serve warm. If desired, top with sour cream and green onions before serving.

Per appetizer: 67 cal., 3g fat (1g sat. fat), 10mg chol., 126mg sod., 6g carb. (0 sugars, 0 fiber), 3g pro.

TEST KITCHEN TIP

If you don't have chili seasoning on hand, use taco seasoning instead. For a milder flavor and a little extra heartiness, increase the shredded chicken to 2 cups.

CHICKEN CHILI WONTON BITES

ROSEMARY WALNUTS

ROSEMARY WALNUTS

My Aunt Mary started making this recipe years ago, and each time we visited her she would have a batch ready for us. Cayenne adds an unexpected zing to the savory combo of rosemary and walnuts.

—Renee Ciancio, New Bern, NC

Takes: 20 min. • **Makes:** 2 cups

- 2 cups walnut halves
- Cooking spray
- 2 tsp. dried rosemary, crushed
- ½ tsp. kosher salt
- ¼ to ½ tsp. cayenne pepper

1. Place walnuts in a small bowl. Spritz with cooking spray. Add the seasonings; toss to coat. Place in a single layer on a baking sheet.

2. Bake at 350° for 10 minutes. Serve warm, or cool completely and store in an airtight container.

Per ¼ cup: 166 cal., 17g fat (2g sat. fat), 0 chol., 118mg sod., 4g carb. (1g sugars, 2g fiber), 4g pro. **Diabetic exchanges:** 3 fat.

SEAFOOD CHEESE DIP

This cheesy recipe has a nice combination of seafood flavors and clings beautifully to slices of bread.

—Michelle Domm, Atlanta, NY

Prep: 15 min. • **Cook:** 1½ hours
Makes: 5 cups

- 1 pkg. (32 oz.) process cheese (Velveeta), cubed
- 2 cans (6 oz. each) lump crabmeat, drained
- 1 can (10 oz.) diced tomatoes and green chilies, undrained
- 1 cup frozen cooked salad shrimp, thawed
- French bread baguettes, toasted

In a greased 3-qt. slow cooker, combine the cheese, crab, tomatoes and shrimp. Cover and cook on low for 1½-2 hours or until cheese is melted, stirring occasionally. Serve with baguette slices.

Per ¼ cup: 172 cal., 12g fat (7g sat. fat), 77mg chol., 791mg sod., 4g carb. (3g sugars, 0 fiber), 12g pro.

APPETIZER BLUE CHEESE LOGS

(PICTURED ON P.55)

Three kinds of cheese make this cheese log a little more lively than most. Swipe it on your favorite cracker with a drizzle of honey for a sensational snack.

—Ethel Johnson, North Saanich, BC

Prep: 15 min. • **Cook:** 5 min. + chilling
Makes: 2 cheese logs

- 1 pkg. (8 oz.) cream cheese, softened
- 1 cup shredded sharp cheddar cheese
- ½ cup crumbled blue cheese
- 1 Tbsp. butter
- 1½ tsp. curry powder, optional
- ½ cup finely chopped pecans
- 2 Tbsp. minced fresh parsley, optional

1. Beat cream cheese until smooth. Fold in cheddar and blue cheeses. Refrigerate, covered, at least 2 hours.

2. In a small skillet, heat the butter over medium heat. If desired, add curry powder; saute 1-2 minutes. Stir in pecans; cook and stir 1 minute. If desired, stir in parsley. Cool slightly. Roll cheese mixture into two logs, each 5 in. long. Roll in pecans; refrigerate.

Per 2 Tbsp.: 196 cal., 19g fat (9g sat. fat), 45mg chol., 243mg sod., 2g carb. (1g sugar, 1g fiber), 6g pro.

CUCUMBER GIN SMASH

SOUR CHERRY SHANDY

GOLD RUSH

SPARKLING SANGRIA

SWEDISH ROSE SPRITZ

SOUR CHERRY SHANDY

A shandy is beer mixed with a nonalcoholic drink like fruit juice or lemonade.

—Taste of Home *Test Kitchen*

Takes: 5 min. • **Makes:** 1 serving

- ½ cup tart cherry juice
- 2 Tbsp. simple syrup
- 1½ cups beer, chilled

Combine cherry juice and simple syrup in a chilled pint glass; stir until blended. Top with chilled beer.

Per serving: 327 cal., 0 fat (0 sat. fat), 0 chol., 17mg sod., 57g carb. (53g sugars, 0 fiber), 1g pro.

CUCUMBER GIN SMASH

A smash is muddled fruit and/or herbs mixed with liquor, crushed ice, and seltzer water or soda.

—Taste of Home *Test Kitchen*

Takes: 5 min. • **Makes:** 1 serving

- 1 tsp. sugar
- 2 slices cucumber
- 4 basil sprigs
- 2 oz. gin
- Club soda

Muddle sugar, cucumber and basil sprigs in an old-fashioned glass. Add gin and crushed ice. Top with club soda and stir.

Per serving: 146 cal., 0 fat (0 sat. fat), 0 chol., 1mg sod., 5g carb. (4g sugars, 0 fiber), 0 pro.

GOLD RUSH

A Gold Rush is a sweet-tart version of a sour, a cocktail made with spirits and citrus juices.

—Taste of Home *Test Kitchen*

Takes: 5 min. • **Makes:** 1 serving

- 1½ oz. whiskey
- ¾ oz. fresh lemon juice
- 1 oz. honey liqueur
- Ginger beer

Combine whiskey, lemon juice and honey liqueur in an ice-filled cocktail shaker. Shake vigorously. Strain into a cocktail glass; top with a splash of ginger beer.

Per serving: 220 cal., 0 fat (0 sat. fat), 0 chol., 4mg sod., 17g carb. (15g sugars, 0 fiber), 0 pro.

SPARKLING SANGRIA

Sangria is a Spanish drink of wine mixed with sugar and fruit. Recipes can vary, and some call for sherry or brandy in addition to the wine. This recipe is delicious with fresh raspberries, strawberries and blueberries.

—Taste of Home *Test Kitchen*

Prep: 10 min. + chilling
Makes: 10 servings (about 2 qt.)

- 4 cups red wine, chilled
- ½ lb. fresh berries
- ¼ cup sugar
- 2 cups club soda, chilled
- 2 cups champagne
- 1 sliced orange, optional

In a pitcher, combine wine, berries and sugar until sugar is dissolved. Refrigerate for at least 1 hour. Just before serving, stir in club soda and champagne. Add orange slices if desired.

Per ¾ cup: 146 cal., 0 fat (0 sat. fat), 0 chol., 1mg sod., 5g carb. (4g sugars, 0 fiber), 0 pro.

SWEDISH ROSÉ SPRITZ

A spritz is a still or sparkling wine-based cocktail served with a small amount of liqueur and a splash of seltzer or soda.

—Taste of Home *Test Kitchen*

Takes: 5 min. • **Makes:** 1 serving

- 3 oz. dry rosé wine
- 1 oz. elderflower liqueur
- Lemon seltzer water

Fill a wine glass or tumbler three-fourths full of ice. Add wine and elderflower liqueur. Top with a splash of lemon seltzer; stir gently.

Per serving: 189 cal., 0 fat (0 sat. fat), 0 chol., 7mg sod., 19g carb. (14g sugars, 0 fiber), 0 pro.

ROAST PORK WITH APPLES & ONIONS

ROAST PORK WITH APPLES & ONIONS

With its crisp skin and melt-in-your-mouth flavor, this sweet and savory pork is one of my family's favorite dinners.

—Lily Julow, Lawrenceville, GA

Prep: 30 min. • **Bake:** 45 min. + standing
Makes: 8 servings

- **1 boneless pork loin roast (2 lbs.)**
- **¼ tsp. salt**
- **¼ tsp. pepper**
- **1 Tbsp. olive oil**
- **3 large Golden Delicious apples, cut into 1-in. wedges**
- **2 large onions, cut into ¾-in. wedges**
- **5 garlic cloves, peeled**
- **1 Tbsp. minced fresh rosemary or 1 tsp. dried rosemary, crushed**

1. Preheat oven to 350°. Sprinkle roast with salt and pepper. In a large nonstick skillet, heat oil over medium heat; brown roast on all sides. Transfer to a roasting pan coated with cooking spray. Place apples, onions and garlic around roast; sprinkle with rosemary.

2. Roast until a thermometer inserted in pork reads 145°, 45-55 minutes, turning apples, onion and garlic once. Remove from oven; tent with foil. Let stand 10 minutes before slicing roast. Serve with apple mixture.

Per serving: 210 cal., 7g fat (2g sat. fat), 57mg chol., 109mg sod., 14g carb. (9g sugars, 2g fiber), 23g pro.

SHRIMP FRIED RICE

This delectable shrimp dish is filled with color and a taste that makes it vanish fast. Bacon adds crispness and a hint of smoky heartiness. Consider it when you need a different main dish or brunch item.

—Sandra Thompson, White Hall, AR

Takes: 20 min. • **Makes:** 8 servings

- **4 Tbsp. butter, divided**
- **4 large eggs, lightly beaten**
- **3 cups cold cooked rice**
- **1 pkg. (16 oz.) frozen mixed vegetables**
- **1 lb. uncooked medium shrimp, peeled and deveined**
- **½ tsp. salt**
- **¼ tsp. pepper**
- **8 bacon strips, cooked and crumbled, optional**

1. In a large skillet, melt 1 Tbsp. butter over medium-high heat. Pour eggs into skillet. As eggs set, lift edges, letting uncooked portion flow underneath. Remove eggs and keep warm.

2. Melt remaining butter in the skillet. Add the rice, vegetables and shrimp; cook and stir for 5 minutes or until shrimp turn pink. Meanwhile, chop eggs into small pieces. Return eggs to the pan; sprinkle with salt and pepper. Cook until heated through, stirring occasionally. Sprinkle with bacon if desired.

Per cup: 241 cal., 9g fat (4g sat. fat), 206mg chol., 354mg sod., 24g carb. (2g sugars, 3g fiber), 15g pro.

SAUSAGE MANICOTTI

This classic Italian entree comes together in a snap but tastes as if it took hours. It's so delicious and comforting. My family can't get enough.

—Carolyn Henderson, Maple Plain, MN

Prep: 15 min. • **Bake:** 65 min.
Makes: 7 servings

- 1 lb. uncooked bulk pork sausage
- 2 cups 4% cottage cheese
- 1 pkg. (8 oz.) manicotti shells
- 1 jar (24 oz.) marinara sauce
- 1 cup shredded part-skim mozzarella cheese

1. In a large bowl, combine the sausage and cottage cheese. Stuff into uncooked manicotti shells. Place in a greased 13x9-in. baking dish. Top with marinara sauce.
2. Cover and bake at 350° for 55-60 minutes or until a thermometer inserted into the center of a shell reads 160°.
3. Uncover; sprinkle with mozzarella cheese. Bake 8-10 minutes longer or until cheese is melted. Let stand for 5 minutes before serving.

Freeze option Transfer individual portions of cooled manicotti to freezer containers; freeze. To use, partially thaw in refrigerator overnight. Transfer pasta to a microwave-safe dish and microwave on high, stirring occasionally and adding a little spaghetti sauce if necessary.

Per 2 filled manicotti shells: 489 cal., 24g fat (10g sat. fat), 59mg chol., 1232mg sod., 41g carb. (12g sugars, 3g fiber), 27g pro.

SAUSAGE MANICOTTI

ROASTED CHICKEN

ROASTED CHICKEN

A simple blend of seasonings makes this moist and tender roast chicken a snap to prepare. It smells heavenly as it roasts.
—Marian Platt, Sequim, WA

Prep: 10 min. • **Bake:** 1¼ hours + standing
Makes: 12 servings

- ¾ tsp. onion salt
- ¾ tsp. celery salt
- ¾ tsp. seasoned salt
- ½ tsp. pepper
- 2 broiler/fryer chickens (3 to 4 lbs. each)

1. Preheat oven to 400°. Mix seasonings.
2. Place chickens on a rack in a roasting pan, breast side up. Rub seasonings over outside and inside of chickens. Tuck under wings; tie together drumsticks. Roast until a thermometer inserted in thickest part of thigh reads 170°-175°, 1¼-1½ hours. (Cover loosely with foil if chickens brown too quickly.)
3. Remove from oven; tent with foil. Let stand 15 minutes before carving.
Per serving: 293 cal., 17g fat (5g sat. fat), 104mg chol., 370mg sod., 0 carb. (0 sugars, 0 fiber), 33g pro.

SPAGHETTI WITH BACON

As children, we always requested this dish for our birthday dinners. Our mother got the recipe from her grandmother. Now I pass on our cherished recipe.
—Ruth Keogh, North St. Paul, MN

Prep: 20 min. • **Bake:** 40 min.
Makes: 4 servings

- 8 oz. uncooked spaghetti
- ½ lb. bacon strips, chopped
- 1 medium onion, chopped
- 1 can (14½ oz.) diced tomatoes, undrained
- 1 can (8 oz.) tomato sauce

1. Preheat oven to 350°. Cook spaghetti according to the package directions for al dente.
2. In a large skillet, cook bacon and onion over medium heat until bacon is crisp, stirring occasionally; drain. Stir in tomatoes and tomato sauce; bring to a boil.
3. Drain spaghetti; transfer to a greased 11x7-in. baking dish. Spread sauce over top. Bake, covered, 40-45 minutes or until bubbly.
Per serving: 159 cal., 6g fat (2g sat. fat), 11mg chol., 498mg sod., 18g carb. (4g sugars, 2g fiber), 7g pro.

LASAGNA ROLLS

My Italian roll-ups are not complicated; they require only basic ingredients to assemble. Prepared spaghetti sauce helps me save time and get dinner on the table sooner.

—Mary Lee Thomas, Logansport, IN

Prep: 25 min. • **Bake:** 10 min.
Makes: 6 servings

- 6 lasagna noodles
- 1 lb. ground beef
- 1 jar (14 oz.) spaghetti sauce
- 1 tsp. fennel seed, optional
- 2 cups shredded part-skim mozzarella cheese, divided

1. Cook lasagna noodles according to package directions. Meanwhile, in a large skillet, cook beef over medium heat until no longer pink; drain. Stir in spaghetti sauce and, if desired, fennel seed; heat through.
2. Drain noodles. Spread ¼ cup meat sauce over each noodle; sprinkle with 2 Tbsp. cheese. Carefully roll up noodles and place seam side down in an 8-in. square baking dish. Top with remaining sauce and cheese.
3. Bake, uncovered, at 400° until heated through and cheese is melted, 10-15 minutes.
Per roll: 377 cal., 18g fat (8g sat. fat), 70mg chol., 549mg sod., 26g carb. (6g sugars, 2g fiber), 28g pro.

GRILLED RIBEYE WITH GARLIC BLUE CHEESE MUSTARD SAUCE

This simple steak gets a big flavor boost from two of my favorites: mustard and blue cheese. My husband and I make this recipe to celebrate our anniversary each year.

—Ashley Lecker, Green Bay, WI

Prep: 20 min. • **Grill:** 10 min. + standing
Makes: 4 servings

- 1 cup half-and-half cream
- ½ cup Dijon mustard
- ¼ cup plus 2 tsp. crumbled blue cheese, divided
- 1 garlic clove, minced
- 2 beef ribeye steaks (1½ in. thick and 12 oz. each)
- 1 Tbsp. olive oil
- ¼ tsp. salt
- ¼ tsp. pepper

1. In a small saucepan over medium heat, whisk together cream, mustard, ¼ cup blue cheese and garlic. Bring to a simmer. Reduce heat to low; whisk occasionally.
2. Meanwhile, rub meat with olive oil; sprinkle with salt and pepper. Grill steaks, covered, on a greased rack over high direct heat for 4-6 minutes on each side until meat reaches desired doneness (for medium-rare, a thermometer should read 135°; medium, 140°; medium-well, 145°). Remove from grill; let stand 10 minutes while sauce finishes cooking. When sauce is reduced by half, pour over steaks; top with remaining blue cheese.
Per ½ steak with 3 Tbsp. sauce: 547 cal., 39g fat (17g sat. fat), 138mg chol., 1088mg sod., 3g carb. (2g sugars, 0 fiber), 34g pro.

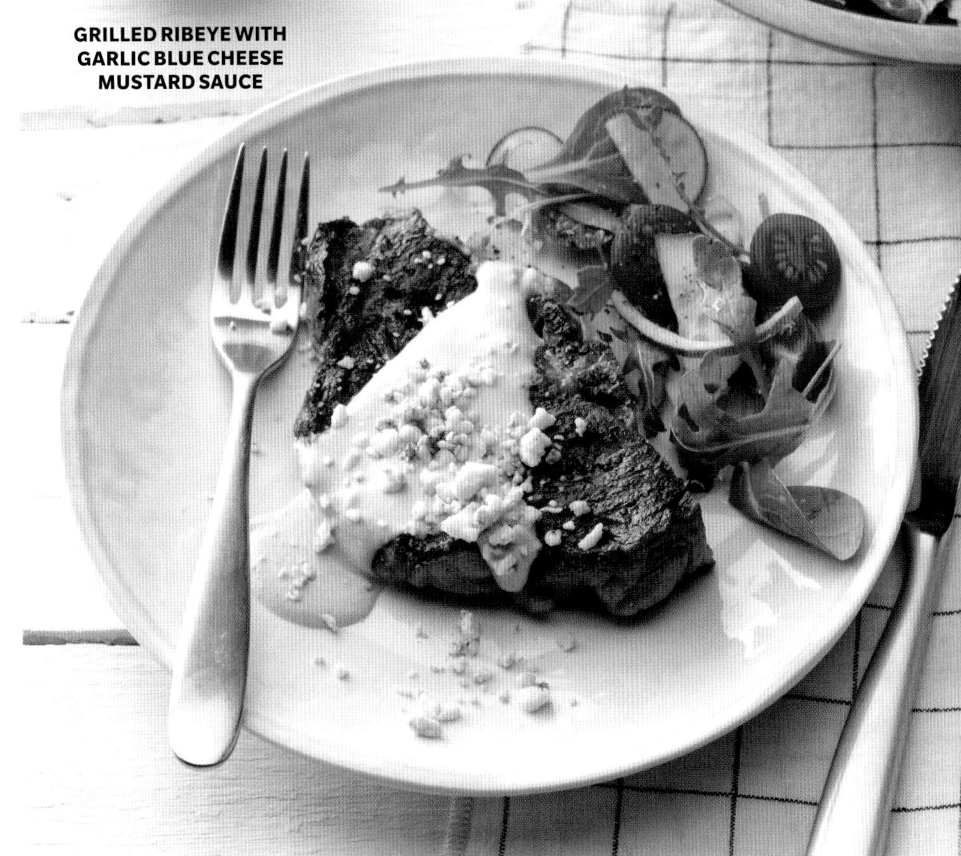

GRILLED RIBEYE WITH GARLIC BLUE CHEESE MUSTARD SAUCE

HAWAIIAN PORK ROAST

Bananas, liquid smoke and soy sauce flavor this tender pork roast. It's just like the kind I enjoyed at the luaus I went to in Hawaii.
—Mary Gaylord, Balsam Lake, WI

Prep: 10 min. + marinating • **Bake:** 4½ hours
Makes: 10 servings

- 1 boneless pork shoulder butt roast (3 to 4 lbs.)
- 4 tsp. liquid smoke
- 4 tsp. soy sauce
- 2 unpeeled ripe bananas
- ½ cup water

1. Place the roast on a 22x18-in. piece of heavy-duty foil; sprinkle with liquid smoke and soy sauce. Wash bananas and place at the base of each side of roast. Pull sides of foil up round meat; add water. Seal foil tightly; wrap again with another large piece of foil. Place in a shallow baking pan; refrigerate overnight, turning several times.
2. Place foil-wrapped meat in a roasting pan. Bake at 400° for 1 hour. Reduce heat to 325°; continue baking for 3½ hours. Drain; discard bananas and liquid. Shred meat with a fork.

Freeze option Freeze cooled meat with some of the juices in freezer containers. To use, partially thaw in refrigerator overnight. Heat pork through in a saucepan, stirring occasionally and adding a little water if necessary.

Per 3 oz.: 222 cal., 14g fat (5g sat. fat), 81mg chol., 207mg sod., 0 carb. (0 sugars, 0 fiber), 23g pro.

HAWAIIAN PORK ROAST

BARBECUED RIBS WITH BEER

These ribs are so simple to make, you will want to make them often. They always are juicy and have a wonderful taste.
—Catherine Santich, Alamo, CA

Prep: 2¼ hours • **Grill:** 10 min.
Makes: 3 servings

- 1 tsp. salt
- 1 tsp. Italian seasoning
- ½ tsp. pepper
- 1 rack pork spareribs (3 to 4 lbs.)
- 1 bottle (12 oz.) beer
- ⅔ cup barbecue sauce

1. Rub the salt, Italian seasoning and pepper over ribs and place in a shallow roasting pan; add beer. Cover and bake at 325° for 2 hours or until tender.
2. Drain ribs. Spoon some of the sauce over ribs. Using long-handled tongs, moisten a paper towel with cooking oil and lightly coat the grill rack. Grill, covered, over medium heat for 8-10 minutes or until browned, turning occasionally and basting with sauce.

Per serving: 935 cal., 65g fat (24g sat. fat), 255mg chol., 1494mg sod., 12g carb. (11g sugars, 1g fiber), 63g pro.

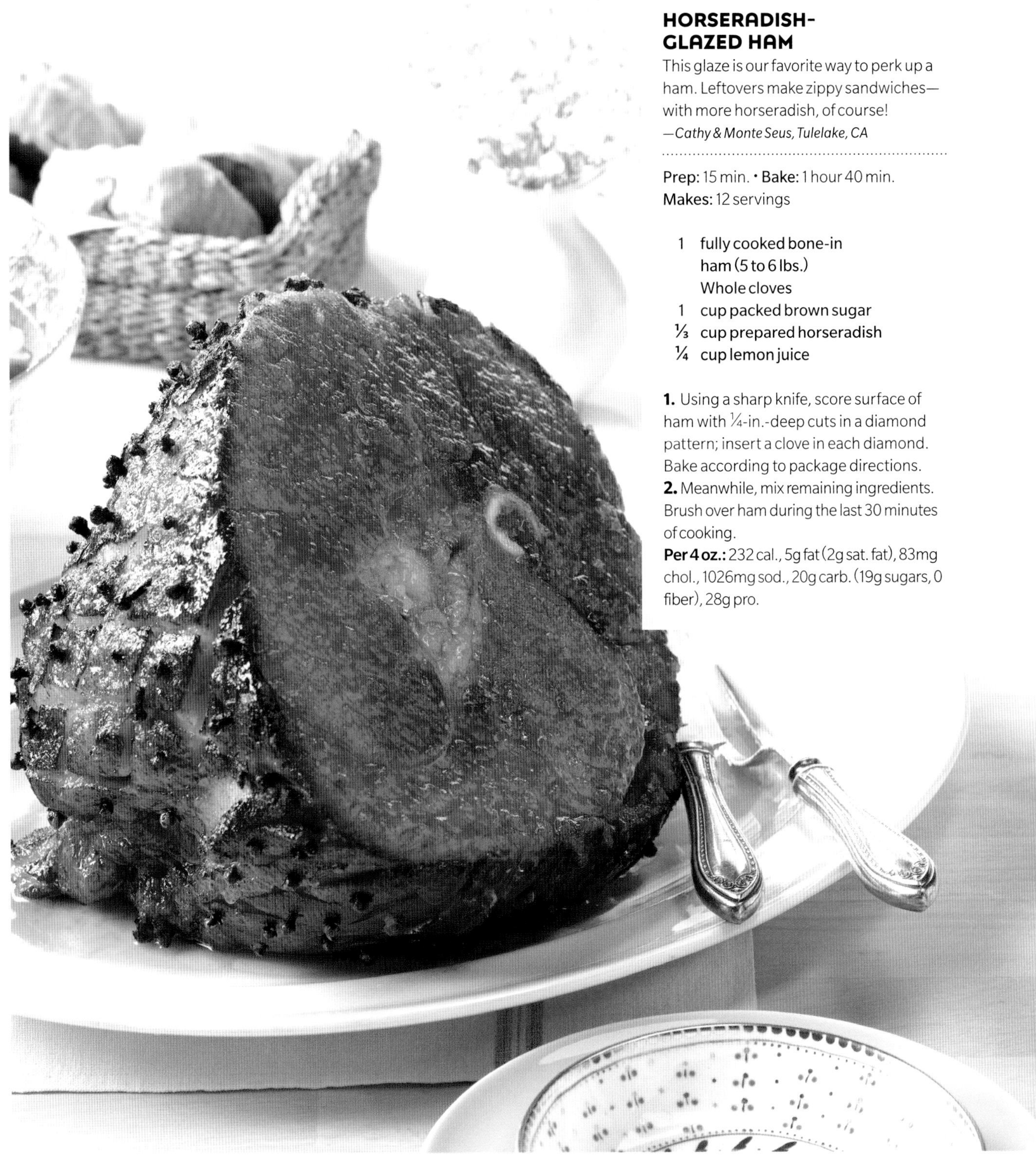

HORSERADISH-GLAZED HAM

This glaze is our favorite way to perk up a ham. Leftovers make zippy sandwiches—with more horseradish, of course!

—Cathy & Monte Seus, Tulelake, CA

Prep: 15 min. • **Bake:** 1 hour 40 min.
Makes: 12 servings

- 1 fully cooked bone-in ham (5 to 6 lbs.)
- Whole cloves
- 1 cup packed brown sugar
- ⅓ cup prepared horseradish
- ¼ cup lemon juice

1. Using a sharp knife, score surface of ham with ¼-in.-deep cuts in a diamond pattern; insert a clove in each diamond. Bake according to package directions.

2. Meanwhile, mix remaining ingredients. Brush over ham during the last 30 minutes of cooking.

Per 4 oz.: 232 cal., 5g fat (2g sat. fat), 83mg chol., 1026mg sod., 20g carb. (19g sugars, 0 fiber), 28g pro.

GRILLED TENDER FLANK STEAK

This marinated steak is so moist that it will become one of your favorite ways to serve beef. You can even prepare it on the grill. It can be easily cut into thin slices.

—Heather Ahrens, Columbus, OH

Prep: 10 min. + marinating • **Cook:** 20 min.
Makes: 6 servings

- 1 cup reduced-sodium soy sauce
- ¼ cup lemon juice
- ¼ cup honey
- 6 garlic cloves, minced
- 1 beef flank steak (1½ lbs.)

1. In a large resealable plastic bag, combine the soy sauce, lemon juice, honey and garlic; add steak. Seal bag and turn to coat; refrigerate for 6-8 hours.

2. Drain and discard marinade. Broil 4-6 in. from the heat or grill over medium heat for 8-10 minutes on each side or until meat reaches desired doneness (for medium-rare, a thermometer should read 135°; medium, 140°; medium-well, 145°). Thinly slice steak across the grain.

Per 3 oz.: 186 cal., 8g fat (4g sat. fat), 54mg chol., 471mg sod., 4g carb. (3g sugars, 0 fiber), 23g pro. **Diabetic exchanges:** 3 lean meat.

PIZZA CHICKEN ROLL-UPS

PIZZA CHICKEN ROLL-UPS

I love the chicken roll-ups my mom made, filled with spinach and cream cheese. My kids won't eat those, so I came up with pizza-flavored ones the whole family enjoys.
—Tanja Penquite, Oregon, OH

Prep: 10 min. • **Bake:** 40 min.
Makes: 4 servings

- 4 boneless skinless chicken breast halves (4 oz. each)
- 12 pepperoni slices
- 8 slices part-skim mozzarella cheese
- 1 can (15 oz.) pizza sauce

1. Flatten chicken to ¼-in. thickness. Place three slices of pepperoni and one slice of cheese on each. Roll up tightly; secure with toothpicks. Place in a greased 11x7-in. baking dish. Spoon pizza sauce over top.

2. Cover and bake at 350° for 35-40 minutes or until chicken is no longer pink. Uncover; top with remaining cheese. Bake 5 minutes longer or until cheese is melted. If desired, broil a minute or two to brown cheese slightly.

Per roll-up: 344 cal., 18g fat (9g sat. fat), 112mg chol., 673mg sod., 8g carb. (4g sugars, 2g fiber), 37g pro.

Flattening chicken breasts helps them cook quickly and evenly. Place chicken breasts between two pieces of waxed paper or plastic wrap or in a resealable plastic bag. Starting in the center and working out to edges, pound lightly with the flat side of a meat mallet until the chicken is even in thickness.

DEVILED CHICKEN

DEVILED CHICKEN

My family has always loved this flavorful golden brown chicken. I watch for the frequent sales on leg quarters to keep the cost per serving low.

—Linda Trammell, Kingston, MO

Prep: 10 min. • **Bake:** 50 min.
Makes: 6 servings

- 6 chicken leg quarters
- ¼ cup butter, melted
- 1 Tbsp. lemon juice
- 1 Tbsp. prepared mustard
- 1 tsp. salt
- 1 tsp. paprika
- ¼ tsp. pepper

1. Preheat oven to 375°. Place chicken in a 15x10x1-in. baking pan. In a small bowl, combine remaining ingredients. Pour over chicken.
2. Bake, uncovered, 50-60 minutes or until a thermometer reads 180°, basting occasionally with pan juices.
3. Serve immediately; or, before baking, cover tightly and freeze up to 3 months.
Freeze option Thaw in the refrigerator overnight. Remove from the refrigerator 30 minutes before reheating. Bake according to directions.
Per serving: 345 cal., 24g fat (9g sat. fat), 125mg chol., 567mg sod., 1g carb. (0 sugars, 0 fiber), 30g pro.

SPICY FRENCH DIP

SPICY FRENCH DIP

If I'm cooking for a family get-together or a party, I can put this beef in the slow cooker in the morning and then concentrate on other preparations. It's a time-saver that never fails to get rave reviews.

—Ginny Koeppen, Winnfield, LA

Prep: 10 min. • **Cook:** 8 hours
Makes: 12 servings

- 1 beef sirloin tip roast (3 lbs.), cut in half
- ½ cup water
- 1 can (4 oz.) diced jalapeno peppers, drained
- 1 envelope Italian salad dressing mix
- 12 crusty rolls (5 in.)

1. Place beef in a 5-qt. slow cooker. In a small bowl, combine the water, jalapenos and dressing mix; pour over beef. Cover and cook on low for 8-10 hours or until meat is tender.
2. Remove beef and shred with two forks. Skim fat from cooking juices. Serve beef on rolls with juice.
Per sandwich: 315 cal., 8g fat (2g sat. fat), 72mg chol., 582mg sod., 31g carb. (2 sugars, 1g fiber), 28g pro. **Diabetic exchanges:** 3 lean meat, 2 starch.

CLASSIC BEEF WELLINGTONS

EDITOR'S CHOICE

CLASSIC BEEF WELLINGTONS

This impressive entree is easy and perfect for the holidays. Find ready-made puff pastry sheets in the frozen food section.
—Kerry Dingwall, Wilmington, NC

Prep: 20 min. + chilling
Bake: 25 min. • **Makes:** 4 servings

- 4 beef tenderloin steaks (6 oz. each)
- ¾ tsp. salt, divided
- ½ tsp. pepper, divided
- 2 Tbsp. olive oil, divided
- 1¾ cups sliced fresh mushrooms
- 1 medium onion, chopped
- 1 pkg. (17.3 oz.) frozen puff pastry, thawed
- 1 large egg, lightly beaten

1. Sprinkle steaks with ½ tsp. salt and ¼ tsp. pepper. In a large skillet, brown steaks in 1 Tbsp. oil for 2-3 minutes on each side. Remove from skillet and refrigerate until chilled.
2. In the same skillet, saute mushrooms and onion in remaining oil until tender. Stir in remaining salt and pepper; cool to room temperature.
3. Preheat oven to 425°. On a lightly floured surface, roll each puff pastry sheet into a 14x9½-in. rectangle. Cut into two 7-in. squares (use scraps to make decorative cutouts if desired). Place a steak in the center of each square; top with mushroom mixture. Lightly brush pastry edges with water. Bring opposite corners of pastry over steak; pinch seams to seal tightly.
4. Place in a greased 15x10x1-in. baking pan. Cut four small slits in top of pastry. Arrange cutouts over top if desired. Brush with egg.
5. Bake 25-30 minutes or until pastry is golden brown and meat reaches desired doneness (for medium-rare, a thermometer should read 135°; medium, 140°; medium-well, 145°).

Per serving: 945 cal., 51g fat (13g sat. fat), 127mg chol., 866mg sod., 74g carb. (3g sugars, 10g fiber), 48g pro.

ZESTY GRILLED HAM

If ham is on the menu, you can bet my kids will eat it. They like this kicked-up grilled version the best. Even the little ones eat big portions, so be sure to make plenty.

—Mary Ann Lien, Tyler, TX

Takes: 15 min. • **Makes:** 4 servings

- ⅓ cup packed brown sugar
- 2 Tbsp. prepared horseradish
- 4 tsp. lemon juice
- 1 fully cooked bone-in ham steak (1 lb.)

1. Place brown sugar, horseradish and lemon juice in a small saucepan; bring to a boil, stirring constantly. Brush over both sides of ham.

2. Place ham on an oiled grill rack over medium heat. Grill, covered, until glazed and heated through, 7-10 minutes, turning occasionally.

Per serving: 180 cal., 5g fat (2g sat. fat), 44mg chol., 845mg sod., 20g carb. (19g sugars, 0 fiber), 14g pro.

Loved this recipe! Delicious! My 5-year-old and 3-year-old gave me a thumbs-up and asked me if I can make this again next time.

SGALLIRN TASTEOFHOME.COM

ZESTY GRILLED HAM

GARLIC HERBED BEEF TENDERLOIN

GARLIC HERBED BEEF TENDERLOIN

The mild blend of rosemary, basil and garlic adds just the right amount of seasoning to this beef roast.

—Ruth Andrewson, Leavenworth, WA

Prep: 5 min. • **Bake:** 40 min. + standing
Makes: 12 servings

- 1 beef tenderloin roast (3 lbs.)
- 2 tsp. olive oil
- 2 garlic cloves, minced
- 1½ tsp. dried basil
- 1½ tsp. dried rosemary, crushed
- 1 tsp. salt
- 1 tsp. pepper

1. Preheat oven to 425°. Tie tenderloin at 2-in. intervals with kitchen string. Combine oil and garlic; brush over meat. Combine the basil, rosemary, salt and pepper; sprinkle evenly over meat. Place on a rack in a shallow roasting pan.
2. Bake, uncovered, for 40-50 minutes or until meat reaches desired doneness (for medium-rare, a thermometer should read 135°; medium, 140°; medium-well, 145°). Let stand for 10 minutes before slicing.
Per 3 oz. cooked beef: 198 cal., 10g fat (4g sat. fat), 78mg chol., 249mg sod., 1g carb. (0 sugars, 0 fiber), 25g pro. **Diabetic exchanges:** 3 lean meat.

SPICY PLUM SALMON

I created this recipe after being challenged to use healthier ingredients. The fresh plum sauce complements the smoky grilled fish.

—Cheryl Hochstettler, Richmond, TX

Prep: 25 min. • **Grill:** 10 min.
Makes: 6 servings

- 5 medium plums, divided
- ½ cup water
- 2 Tbsp. ketchup
- 1 chipotle pepper in adobo sauce, finely chopped
- 1 Tbsp. sugar
- 1 Tbsp. olive oil
- 6 salmon fillets (6 oz. each)
- ¾ tsp. salt

1. Coarsely chop two plums; place in a small saucepan. Add water; bring to a boil. Reduce heat; simmer, uncovered, 10-15 minutes or until plums are softened and liquid is almost evaporated. Cool slightly. Transfer to a food processor; add ketchup, chipotle, sugar and oil. Process until pureed. Reserve ¾ cup sauce for serving.
2. Sprinkle salmon with salt; place on a greased grill rack, skin side up. Grill, covered, over medium heat until fish just begins to flake easily with a fork, about 10 minutes. Brush with remaining sauce during last 3 minutes. Slice remaining plums. Serve salmon with plums and reserved sauce.
Per 1 fillet with ½ plum and 2 Tbsp. sauce: 325 cal., 18g fat (3g sat. fat), 85mg chol., 460mg sod., 10g carb. (9g sugars, 1g fiber), 29g pro. **Diabetic exchanges:** 5 lean meat, 1 fruit, ½ fat.

SPICY PLUM SALMON

QUICK CHERRY TURNOVERS

QUICK CHERRY TURNOVERS

Refrigerated crescent rolls let you make these fruit-filled pastries in a hurry. Feel free to experiment with other pie fillings as well.
—Elleen Oberrueter, Danbury, IA

Takes: 20 min. • **Makes:** 4 servings

- 1 tube (8 oz.) refrigerated crescent rolls
- 1 cup cherry pie filling
- ½ cup confectioners' sugar
- 1 to 2 Tbsp. milk

1. Preheat oven to 375°. Unroll crescent dough and separate into four rectangles; place on an ungreased baking sheet. Press perforations to seal. Place ¼ cup pie filling on one half of each rectangle. Fold dough over filling; pinch edges to seal. Bake for 10-12 minutes or until golden.
2. Place the confectioners' sugar in a small bowl; stir in enough milk to achieve a drizzling consistency. Drizzle over turnovers. Serve warm.

Per turnover: 359 cal., 12g fat (3g sat. fat), 1mg chol., 459mg sod., 56g carb. (34g sugars, 0 fiber), 4g pro.

MADE WITH LOVE

Very good and simple. I used apple pie filling and they were a hit!

CINDIAK TASTEOFHOME.COM

CHOCOLATE & PEANUT BUTTER CRISPY BARS

EDITOR'S CHOICE

CHOCOLATE & PEANUT BUTTER CRISPY BARS

I was in need of a dairy-free dessert, so I came up with these yummy bars. My kids and their friends gobble them up. I talk about it on my blog, *joyfulscribblings.com*.
—Dawn Pasco, Overland Park, KS

Prep: 15 min. • **Bake:** 25 min. + chilling
Makes: 2 dozen

- 1 pkg. fudge brownie mix (13x9-in. pan size)
- 1½ cups chunky peanut butter
- 2 cups (12 oz.) semisweet chocolate chips
- 1 cup creamy peanut butter
- 3 cups Rice Krispies

1. Line a 13x9-in. baking pan with parchment paper, letting ends extend up sides. Prepare and bake brownie mix according to package directions, using prepared pan. Cool brownies on a wire rack 30 minutes. Refrigerate until cold.

2. Spread chunky peanut butter over brownies. Place chocolate chips and creamy peanut butter in a large microwave-safe bowl. Microwave in 30-second intervals until melted; stir until smooth. Stir in Rice Krispies; spread over chunky peanut butter layer. Refrigerate, covered, at least 30 minutes or until set.

3. Lifting with parchment paper, remove brownies from pan. Cut into bars. Store in an airtight container in the refrigerator.

Per bar: 390 cal., 27g fat (6g sat. fat), 16mg chol., 234mg sod., 35g carb. (21g sugars, 3g fiber), 9g pro.

LAYERED LEMON PIE

My pie is a refreshing ending to any meal. The creamy lemon filling is always a hit with my husband.

—Elizabeth Yoder, Belcourt, ND

Prep: 20 min. + chilling • **Makes:** 8 servings

- 1 pkg. (8 oz.) cream cheese, softened
- ½ cup sugar
- 1 can (15¾ oz.) lemon pie filling, divided
- 1 carton (8 oz.) frozen whipped topping, thawed
- 1 graham cracker crust (9 in.)

In a bowl, beat cream cheese and sugar until smooth. Beat in half of the pie filling. Fold in whipped topping. Spoon into crust. Spread remaining pie filling over cream cheese layer. Refrigerate at least 15 minutes before serving.

Per piece: 526 cal., 24g fat (13g sat. fat), 104mg chol., 251mg sod., 72g carb. (61g sugars, 1g fiber), 6g pro.

LAYERED LEMON PIE

BERRY PINEAPPLE PARFAITS

Here's a fruity treat that's bound to satisfy everyone's tastes.

—Ruth Andrewson, Leavenworth, WA

Takes: 20 min. • **Makes:** 6 servings

- 3 cups whole fresh strawberries
- 3 to 4 Tbsp. sugar
- 12 scoops vanilla ice cream
- 1 can (8 oz.) crushed pineapple, drained
- Whipped topping

1. Set aside six strawberries for garnish. Slice the remaining strawberries and toss with sugar; let stand for 10 minutes.

2. Spoon half of the sliced berries into six parfait glasses. Top with half of the ice cream and half of the pineapple. Repeat layers. Top with whipped topping and reserved berries.

Per parfait: 334 cal., 15g fat (9g sat. fat), 58mg chol., 107mg sod., 48g carb. (37g sugars, 2g fiber), 5g pro.

BUTTERSCOTCH FRUIT DIP

If you like the sweetness of butterscotch chips, you'll enjoy this warm rum-flavored fruit dip. I serve it with apple and pear wedges. It holds up for up to two hours in the slow cooker.

—Jeaune Hadl Van Meter, Lexington, KY

Prep: 5 min. • **Cook:** 45 min.
Makes: about 3 cups

- 2 pkg. (10 to 11 oz. each) butterscotch chips
- ⅔ cup evaporated milk
- ⅔ cup chopped pecans
- 1 Tbsp. rum extract
- Apple and pear wedges

In a 1½-qt. slow cooker, combine the butterscotch chips and milk. Cover and cook on low for 45-50 minutes or until chips are softened; stir until smooth. Stir in pecans and extract. Serve warm with fruit.

Per ¼ cup: 197 cal., 13g fat (7g sat. fat), 6mg chol., 32mg sod., 17g carb. (16g sugars, 1g fiber), 2g pro.

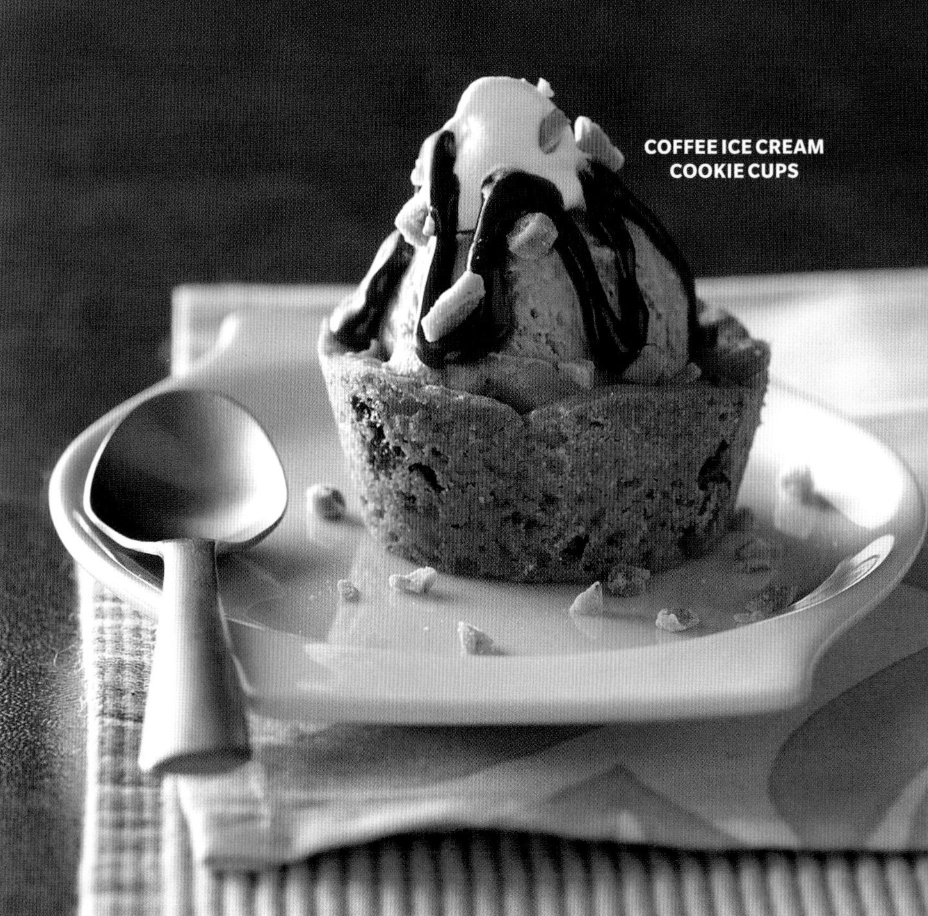

COFFEE ICE CREAM COOKIE CUPS

COFFEE ICE CREAM COOKIE CUPS

I'm a teen who has been blessed with a big family. I have six brothers and sisters, and we're always looking for new recipes to try with our favorite flavors of ice cream. I came up with this special dessert for my sister's birthday party, and everyone wanted more. I've also tried it with peanut butter cookie dough and other flavors of ice cream, but I like coffee the best.

—Marcus Dooley, Red Oak, TX

Prep: 30 min. • **Bake:** 15 min. + freezing
Makes: 12 servings

- 1 tube (16½ oz.) refrigerated chocolate chip cookie dough
- 2 cups coffee ice cream
- Whipped cream and chocolate syrup
- ⅓ cup English toffee bits or almond brickle chips

1. Preheat oven to 350°. Let dough stand at room temperature 5-10 minutes to soften. Cut into 12 slices; press onto bottoms and up the sides of greased muffin cups.

2. Bake 12-14 minutes or until golden brown. Cool slightly on a wire rack. Spoon ice cream into each cup. Cover and freeze 1-2 hours or until firm.

3. Remove cups from pan. Garnish with whipped cream and chocolate syrup. Sprinkle with toffee bits.

Per cookie cup: 255 cal., 13g fat (5g sat. fat), 20mg chol., 131mg sod., 33g carb. (24g sugars, 1g fiber), 2g pro.

CINNAMON FRUIT BISCUITS

CINNAMON FRUIT BISCUITS

Because these sweet treats are so easy, I'm almost embarrassed when people ask me for the recipe. They're a snap to make with refrigerated buttermilk biscuits, sugar, cinnamon and your favorite fruit preserves.
—Ione Burham, Washington, IA

Prep: 15 min. • **Bake:** 15 min. + cooling
Makes: 10 servings

- ½ cup sugar
- ½ tsp. ground cinnamon
- 1 tube (12 oz.) refrigerated buttermilk biscuits, separated into 10 biscuits
- ¼ cup butter, melted
- 10 tsp. strawberry preserves

1. In a small bowl, combine sugar and cinnamon. Dip top and sides of biscuits in butter, then in cinnamon-sugar.
2. Place on ungreased baking sheets. With the end of a wooden spoon handle, make a deep indentation in the center of each biscuit; fill with 1 tsp. preserves.
3. Bake at 375° for 15-18 minutes or until golden brown. Cool for 15 minutes before serving (preserves will be hot).
Per biscuit: 178 cal., 5g fat (3g sat. fat), 12mg chol., 323mg sod., 31g carb. (14g sugars, 0 fiber), 3g pro. **Diabetic exchanges:** 2 starch, 1 fat.

TEST KITCHEN TIP

You can find bottles of prepared cinnamon-sugar in the spice aisle of your grocery store. Or make your own by combining ½ cup sugar and 1 Tbsp. ground cinnamon. Store in an airtight container to use in a variety of recipes or to sprinkle over buttered toast at breakfast.

PEANUT BUTTER FUDGE

PEANUT BUTTER FUDGE

This fudge is a favorite no-fail recipe.
—Eleanore Peterson, Fort Atkinson, WI

Prep: 10 min. + chilling • **Makes:** 1¾ lbs.

- 1 lb. white candy coating
- 1 cup creamy peanut butter
- 1 cup coarsely chopped walnuts

Melt coating in a saucepan over medium-low heat, stirring constantly until smooth. Remove from heat; stir in peanut butter and walnuts. Spread into a greased 8-in. square pan. Chill until firm. Cut into 1-in. squares.
Per 2 pieces: 147 cal., 10g fat (5g sat. fat), 0 chol., 37mg sod., 12g carb. (10g sugars, 1g fiber), 3g pro.

LEMON MERINGUE FLOATS

I dreamed of this float idea one night, and woke up knowing I needed to make it!
—Cindy Reams, Philipsburg, PA

Takes: 5 min. • **Makes:** 6 servings

- 3 cups vanilla ice cream, softened if necessary
- 18 miniature meringue cookies
- 6 cups cold pink lemonade

Place ½ cup ice cream and three cookies in each of six tall glasses. Top with lemonade. Serve immediately.
Per 1½ cups with 3 cookies: 282 cal., 7g fat (4g sat. fat), 29mg chol., 77mg sod., 51g carb. (48g sugars, 0 fiber), 3g pro.

AUNT ROSE'S FANTASTIC BUTTER TOFFEE

I may not live there, but I love everything about country life—especially good old-fashioned home cooking. Every year, you'll find me at our county fair, entering a different recipe contest. This toffee has been a family favorite since I was a little girl.
—Kathy Dorman, Snover, MI

Prep: 25 min. • **Cook:** 15 min.
Makes: about 2 lbs.

- 2 cups unblanched whole almonds
- 11 oz. milk chocolate, chopped
- 1 cup butter, cubed
- 1 cup sugar
- 3 Tbsp. cold water

1. Preheat oven to 350°. In a shallow baking pan, toast almonds until golden brown, 5-10 minutes, stirring occasionally. Cool. Pulse chocolate in a food processor until finely ground (do not overprocess); transfer to a bowl. Pulse almonds in food processor until coarsely chopped. Sprinkle 1 cup almonds over bottom of a greased 15x10x1-in. pan. Sprinkle with 1 cup chocolate.
2. In a heavy saucepan, combine butter, sugar and water. Cook over medium heat until a candy thermometer reads 290° (soft-crack stage), stirring occasionally.
3. Immediately pour mixture over almonds and chocolate in pan. Sprinkle with remaining chocolate and almonds. Refrigerate until set; break into pieces.
Note We recommend that you test your candy thermometer before each use by bringing water to a boil; the thermometer should read 212°. Adjust your recipe temperature up or down based on your test.
Per 1 oz.: 177 cal., 13g fat (6g sat. fat), 17mg chol., 51mg sod., 14g carb. (12g sugars, 1g fiber), 3g pro.

AUNT ROSE'S FANTASTIC BUTTER TOFFEE

BAKED CUSTARD WITH CINNAMON

My mom made this comforting custard when I was growing up on our farm. It was a beloved treat after doing chores.
—Mary Kay Morris, Cokato, MN

Prep: 10 min.
Bake: 50 min. + cooling
Makes: 4 servings

- 2 large eggs
- 2 cups milk
- ⅓ cup sugar
- ¼ tsp. salt
- Dash ground cinnamon
- Dash ground nutmeg

1. In a small bowl, whisk the eggs, milk, sugar and salt. Pour into four ungreased 8-oz. custard cups; sprinkle with cinnamon and nutmeg.
2. Place cups in a 13x9-in. baking pan; pour hot water in pan to a depth of ¾ in. Bake, uncovered, at 350° for 50-55 minutes or until a knife inserted in the center comes out clean. Remove cups to a wire rack to cool. Serve warm or chilled. Store in the refrigerator.
Per serving: 177 cal., 7g fat (3g sat. fat), 123mg chol., 239mg sod., 23g carb. (22g sugars, 0 fiber), 7g pro.

SHORTBREAD

I live in Missouri, but many of my family recipes come from New Zealand, where I was born. These special-occasion cookies bring back warm memories of childhood, and I'm going to make sure they're passed on to the next generation in my family—no matter where they live!

—Allen Swenson, Camdenton, MO

Prep: 15 min. + chilling • **Bake:** 10 min./batch
Makes: 5 dozen

- 1 cup butter, softened
- ½ cup sugar
- ½ cup confectioners' sugar
- 2 cups all-purpose flour
- ½ cup cornstarch
- ½ tsp. salt

1. In large bowl, cream butter and sugars until light and fluffy. Combine flour, cornstarch and salt; gradually add to creamed mixture and mix well. Roll dough into a 15x2x1-in. rectangle; chill.

2. Preheat oven to 325°. Cut into ¼-in. slices; place 2 in. apart on ungreased baking sheets. Prick with a fork. Bake 10-12 minutes or until set. Remove to wire racks to cool.

Per cookie: 57 cal., 3g fat (2g sat. fat), 8mg chol., 44mg sod., 7g carb. (3g sugars, 0 fiber), 0 pro.

This recipe is fantastic! I ended up making shortbread jam cookies, and my mother, who doesn't like overly sweet things, said that this was the perfect recipe.

USAGITAN TASTEOFHOME.COM

SHORTBREAD

EDITOR'S CHOICE

HEAVENLY FILLED STRAWBERRIES

These luscious cream cheese-filled berries are the perfect bite-sized dessert.

—Stephen Munro, Beaverbank, NS

Takes: 20 min. • **Makes:** 3 dozen

- 3 dozen large fresh strawberries
- 11 oz. cream cheese, softened
- ½ cup confectioners' sugar
- ¼ tsp. almond extract
- Grated chocolate, optional

1. Remove stems from berries. Cut a deep "X" in each berry tip; gently spread open.
2. In a small bowl, beat the cream cheese, confectioners' sugar and extract until light and fluffy. Pipe or spoon about 2 tsp. into each berry; if desired, sprinkle with grated chocolate. Chill until serving.
Per strawberry: 41 cal., 3g fat (2g sat. fat), 10mg chol., 26mg sod., 3g carb. (2g sugars, 0 fiber), 1g pro.

MOCHA TRUFFLES

Nothing compares to the melt-in-your-mouth flavor of these truffles...or to the simplicity of the recipe. Whenever I make them for my family or friends, they're quickly devoured. No one has to know how easy they are to prepare!

—Stacy Abell, Olathe, KS

Prep: 25 min. + chilling
Makes: about 5½ dozen

- 2 pkg. (12 oz. each) semisweet chocolate chips
- 1 pkg. (8 oz.) cream cheese, softened
- 3 Tbsp. instant coffee granules
- 2 tsp. water
- 1 lb. dark chocolate candy coating, coarsely chopped
- White candy coating, optional

1. In a microwave-safe bowl, melt chocolate chips; stir until smooth. Beat in the cream cheese. Dissolve coffee in water; add to cream cheese and beat until smooth.
2. Chill until the chocolate mixture is firm enough to shape. Shape into 1-in. balls and place on waxed paper-lined baking sheet. Chill until firm, 1-2 hours.
3. In a microwave, melt chocolate coating; stir until smooth. Dip balls in chocolate; allow excess to drip off. Place on waxed paper; let stand until set. Melt white coating and drizzle over truffles if desired.
Per truffle: 73 cal., 5g fat (3g sat. fat), 4mg chol., 11mg sod., 8g carb. (7g sugars, 0 fiber), 1g pro.

SEMISWEET CHOCOLATE MOUSSE

A friend shared this rich, velvety mousse recipe with me. I love to cook and have tons of recipes, but this one is a favorite. Best of all, it's easy to make.

—Judy Spencer, San Diego, CA

Prep: 20 min. + chilling • **Makes:** 2 servings

- ¼ cup semisweet chocolate chips
- 1 Tbsp. water
- 1 large egg yolk, lightly beaten
- 1½ tsp. vanilla extract
- ½ cup heavy whipping cream
- 1 Tbsp. sugar
- Whipped cream and raspberries, optional

1. In a small saucepan, melt chocolate chips with water; stir until smooth. Stir a small amount of hot chocolate mixture into egg yolk; return all to pan, stirring constantly. Cook and stir for 2 minutes or until slightly thickened. Remove from the heat; stir in vanilla. Cool, stirring several times.
2. In a small bowl, beat whipping cream until it begins to thicken. Add sugar; beat until soft peaks form. Fold in cooled chocolate mixture. Cover and refrigerate for at least 2 hours. Garnish with whipped cream and raspberries if desired.
Per cup: 367 cal., 31g fat (18g sat. fat), 188mg chol., 29mg sod., 21g carb. (20g sugars, 1g fiber), 3g pro.

BREADED PORK CHOPS

These traditional pork chops have a delicious home-cooked flavor just like the ones my mom used to make. The breading makes them crispy outside and tender and juicy inside.
—Deborah Amrine, Fort Myers, FL

Takes: 20 min. • **Makes:** 6 servings

- 1 large egg, lightly beaten
- ½ cup 2% milk
- 1½ cups crushed saltine crackers
- 6 boneless pork loin chops (1 in. thick)
- ¼ cup canola oil

1. In a shallow bowl, combine egg and milk. Place cracker crumbs in another shallow bowl. Dip each pork chop in egg mixture, then coat with cracker crumbs, patting to make a thick coating.
2. In a large skillet, cook the chops in oil for 4-5 minutes on each side or until a thermometer reads 145°. Let meat stand for 5 minutes before serving.
Per serving: 329 cal., 18g fat (4g sat. fat), 87mg chol., 218mg sod., 14g carb. (1g sugars, 0 fiber), 25g pro.

"More pork chops, m'lady? How about more grapes?" Apparently we were in a Renaissance mood when we first shot this dish in 1993.

FAST-FIX STAPLES

NOTHING BEATS FOOD YOU CAN GET ON THE TABLE FAST. TIME-PRESSED COOKS WILL LOVE THIS GOLD MINE OF SIMPLE SNACKS THAT CAN BE PREPPED IN UNDER 15 MINUTES AND BUSY-DAY DINNERS THAT GO FROM KITCHEN TO TABLE IN 30 MINUTES OR LESS.

PINA COLADA FRUIT DIP

PINA COLADA FRUIT DIP

A taste of the tropics is always welcome and refreshing. This cool and creamy appetizer dip is also terrific to munch on after dinner.
—Shelly L. Bevington, Hermiston, OR

Takes: 15 min. • **Makes:** 2½ cups

- 1 pkg. (8 oz.) cream cheese, softened
- 1 jar (7 oz.) marshmallow creme
- 1 can (8 oz.) crushed pineapple, drained
- ½ cup sweetened shredded coconut
- Assorted fresh fruit and/or cubed pound cake

In a small bowl, beat the cream cheese and marshmallow creme until fluffy. Fold in the pineapple and coconut. Cover and chill until serving. Serve with fruit, pound cake or both.
Per ¼ cup: 186 cal., 10g fat (6g sat. fat), 25mg chol., 96mg sod., 24g carb. (19g sugars, 0 fiber), 2g pro.

EDITOR'S CHOICE

PARMESAN-COATED BRIE

A golden Parmesan-crusted exterior gives way to warm, melty cheese, making this perfect for sliced French bread or crackers.
—Karen Grant, Tulare, CA

Takes: 10 min. • **Makes:** 8 servings

- 1 large egg
- 1 Tbsp. water
- ½ cup seasoned bread crumbs
- ¼ cup grated Parmesan cheese
- 1 round (8 oz.) Brie cheese or Brie cheese with herbs
- ¼ cup canola oil
- Assorted crackers and/or fresh fruit

1. In a shallow bowl, combine egg and water. In another bowl, combine bread crumbs and Parmesan cheese. Dip Brie in egg mixture, turning to coat all sides; coat with crumb mixture. Repeat.
2. In a small skillet, cook Brie in oil over medium heat for 2 minutes on each side or until golden brown. Serve with crackers, fresh fruit or both.
Per 2 Tbsp.: 202 cal., 16g fat (6g sat. fat), 57mg chol., 333mg sod., 5g carb. (0 sugars, 0 fiber), 9g pro.

Brie is a soft cows' milk cheese, named after the French region of Brie, that is pale in color with a grayish white edible rind. The interior has a soft, spreadable consistency when served at room temperature. Perfect for use on cheese trays or melted in sandwiches, soups and fondues.

SPICY CRAB DIP

SPICY CRAB DIP

White wine and a generous helping of crabmeat makes this dip feel special, yet it only takes minutes to prepare. Add the cayenne pepper and hot sauce if you want to amp up the heat.

—Carol Forcum, Marion, IL

Takes: 15 min. • **Makes:** 4 cups

- ⅓ cup mayonnaise
- 2 Tbsp. dried minced onion
- 2 Tbsp. lemon juice
- 2 Tbsp. white wine or white grape juice
- 1 Tbsp. minced garlic
- ½ tsp. cayenne pepper, optional
- ½ tsp. hot pepper sauce, optional
- 2 pkg. (8 oz. each) cream cheese, cubed
- 1 lb. imitation crabmeat, chopped
- Assorted crackers or fresh vegetables

1. In a food processor, combine the first eight ingredients. Cover and process until smooth. Transfer to a large microwave-safe bowl. Stir in crab; mix well.

2. Cover and microwave mixture on high for 2-3 minutes or until bubbly. Serve warm with crackers or vegetables.

Per 2 Tbsp.: 82 cal., 7g fat (3g sat. fat), 18mg chol., 133mg sod., 3g carb. (0 sugars, 0 fiber), 2g pro.

LAYERED HUMMUS DIP

My love for Greece inspired this fast-to-fix Mediterranean dip. It's great for parties and a delicious way to include garden-fresh veggies on your menu.

—Cheryl Snavely, Hagerstown, MD

Takes: 15 min. • **Makes:** 12 servings

- 1 carton (10 oz.) hummus
- ¼ cup finely chopped red onion
- ½ cup Greek olives, chopped
- 2 medium tomatoes, seeded and chopped
- 1 large English cucumber, chopped
- 1 cup crumbled feta cheese
- Baked pita chips

Spread hummus into a shallow 10-in. round dish. Layer with onion, olives, tomatoes, cucumber and cheese. Refrigerate until serving. Serve with chips.

Per serving: 88 cal., 5g fat (2g sat. fat), 5mg chol., 275mg sod., 6g carb. (1g sugars, 2g fiber), 4g pro. **Diabetic exchanges:** 1 fat, ½ starch.

QUICK AMBROSIA FRUIT SALAD

I mix in a little coconut and just enough marshmallows so this salad tastes like the creamy ambrosia I grew up with.

—Trisha Kruse, Eagle, ID

Takes: 10 min. • **Makes:** 6 servings

- 1 can (8¼ oz.) fruit cocktail, drained
- 1 can (8 oz.) unsweetened pineapple chunks, drained
- 1 cup green grapes
- 1 cup seedless red grapes
- 1 cup miniature marshmallows
- 1 medium banana, sliced
- ¾ cup vanilla yogurt
- ½ cup sweetened shredded coconut

In a large bowl, combine all ingredients. Chill until serving.

Per ¾ cup: 191 cal., 4g fat (3g sat. fat), 2mg chol., 48mg sod., 40g carb. (34g sugars, 2g fiber), 3g pro.

LAYERED HUMMUS DIP

HOMEMADE PEANUT BUTTER

HOMEMADE PEANUT BUTTER

We eat a lot of peanut butter, so I decided to make my own. When I compared the cost of my own to store-bought, homemade was much cheaper—and tastier!
—Marge Austin, North Pole, AK

Takes: 15 min. • **Makes:** about 1 cup

- 2 cups unsalted dry roasted peanuts
- ½ tsp. salt
- 1 Tbsp. honey

Process peanuts and salt in a food processor until desired consistency, about 5 minutes, scraping down sides as needed. Add honey; process just until blended. Store in an airtight container in refrigerator.

Per 1 Tbsp: 111 cal., 9g fat (1g sat. fat), 0 chol., 75mg sod., 5g carb. (2g sugars, 2g fibers), 4g pro.

TEX-MEX POPCORN

Spicy Southwest seasoning makes this snackin' good popcorn ideal for any fiesta.
—Katie Rose, Pewaukee, WI

Takes: 15 min. • **Makes:** 4 qt.

- ½ cup popcorn kernels
- 3 Tbsp. canola oil
- ½ tsp. cumin seeds
- Refrigerated butter-flavored spray
- ¼ cup minced fresh cilantro
- 1 tsp. salt
- 1 tsp. chili powder
- ½ tsp. garlic powder
- ⅛ tsp. smoked paprika

1. In a Dutch oven over medium heat, cook the popcorn kernels, oil and cumin seeds until the oil begins to sizzle. Cover and shake for 2-3 minutes or until popcorn stops popping.
2. Transfer to a large bowl; spritz with butter-flavored spray. Add remaining ingredients and toss to coat. Continue spritzing and tossing until popcorn is coated.

Per cup: 44 cal., 3g fat (0 sat. fat), 0 chol., 150mg sod., 5g carb. (0 sugars, 1g fiber), 1g pro. **Diabetic exchanges:** ½ starch, ½ fat.

CREAMY EGG SALAD

I love this egg salad's versatility—serve it on a nest of mixed greens, tucked into a sandwich or with your favorite crackers.
—Cynthia Kolberg, Syracuse, IN

Takes: 10 min. • **Makes:** 3 cups

- 3 oz. cream cheese, softened
- ¼ cup mayonnaise
- ½ tsp. salt
- ⅛ tsp. pepper
- ¼ cup finely chopped green or sweet red pepper
- ¼ cup finely chopped celery
- ¼ cup sweet pickle relish
- 2 Tbsp. minced fresh parsley
- 8 hard-boiled large eggs, chopped

In a bowl, mix cream cheese, mayonnaise, salt and pepper until smooth. Stir in green pepper, celery, relish and parsley. Fold in eggs. Refrigerate, covered, until serving.

Per ½ cup: 234 cal., 19g fat (6g sat. fat), 268mg chol., 466mg sod., 5g carb. (4g sugars, 0 fiber), 9g pro.

TEST KITCHEN TIP

Sub a 4-oz. jar of pimientos for the finely chopped pepper, and add ½ cup of finely grated sharp cheddar cheese for a heartier take on this Southern classic. Freshen this recipe from your summer garden by using dill instead of (or in addition to) the parsley. Dill packs quite a punch, so 2 tsp. instead of 2 Tbsp. should do it.

COBB SALAD SUB

COBB SALAD SUB

When we need a quick bite, we turn Cobb salad into a sandwich masterpiece.
—Kimberly Grusendorf, Medina, OH

Takes: 15 min. • **Makes:** 12 servings

- 1 loaf (1 lb.) unsliced Italian bread
- ½ cup balsamic vinaigrette or dressing of your choice
- 5 oz. fresh baby spinach (about 6 cups)
- 1½ lbs. sliced deli ham
- 4 hard-boiled large eggs, finely chopped
- 8 bacon strips, cooked and crumbled
- ½ cup crumbled Gorgonzola cheese
- 1 cup cherry tomatoes, chopped

Cut loaf of bread in half; hollow out top and bottom, leaving a ¾-in. shell (discard removed bread or save for another use). Brush vinaigrette over bread halves. Layer spinach, ham, eggs, bacon, cheese and tomatoes on bread bottom. Replace top. Cut in half lengthwise; cut crosswise five times to make 12 total pieces.
Per piece: 233 cal., 10g fat (3g sat. fat), 97mg chol., 982mg sod., 17g carb. (3g sugars, 1g fiber), 18g pro.

SPARKLING CRANBERRY KISS

Cranberry and orange juices are a terrific pairing with ginger ale in this party punch. We use cranberry juice cocktail, but blends like cranberry-apple also sparkle.
—Shannon Copley, Upper Arlington, OH

Takes: 5 min. • **Makes:** 14 servings

- 6 cups cranberry juice
- 1½ cups orange juice
- 3 cups ginger ale
- Ice cubes
- Orange slices, optional

Combine cranberry juice and orange juice. Just before serving, stir in ginger ale; serve over ice. If desired, serve with orange slices.
Per ¾ cup: 81 cal., 0 fat (0 sat. fat), 0 chol., 9mg sod., 21g carb. (20g sugars, 0 fiber), 1g pro.

MEXICAN CHOCOLATE DIP

MEXICAN CHOCOLATE DIP

Chocolate, cinnamon and a touch of heat are a classic Mexican trio. Any fruit goes well with this dip...or try it with churros!
—Taste of Home *Test Kitchen*

Takes: 10 min. • **Makes:** ½ cup

- ¾ cup semisweet chocolate chips
- ⅓ cup heavy whipping cream
- ⅛ tsp. ground cinnamon
- ⅛ tsp. cayenne pepper
- Assorted fresh fruit

In a small heavy saucepan, combine the chocolate chips and cream. Using a whisk, heat and stir over medium-low heat for 4-5 minutes or until smooth. Remove from heat; stir in cinnamon and cayenne. Cool slightly. Dip will become firmer as it cools. If desired, warm gently in the microwave to soften. Serve with fruit.
Per 2 Tbsp.: 221 cal., 17g fat (10g sat. fat), 27mg chol., 11mg sod., 21g carb. (18g sugars, 2g fiber), 2g pro.

TROPICAL SWEET & SPICY PORK TENDERLOIN

TROPICAL SWEET & SPICY PORK TENDERLOIN

Every now and then we crave something sweet and spicy. Pork tenderloin cooked with chipotle peppers, barbecue sauce and pineapple always delivers.

—Cynthia Gerken, Naples, FL

Takes: 30 min. • **Makes:** 4 servings

- 1 pork tenderloin (1 lb.), cut into 1-in. cubes
- ¼ tsp. salt
- ¼ tsp. pepper
- 2 Tbsp. olive oil
- 1 medium onion, chopped
- 1 medium green pepper, chopped
- 3 garlic cloves, minced
- 1 cup chicken stock
- 1 can (20 oz.) pineapple tidbits, drained
- 1 cup honey barbecue sauce
- ½ cup packed brown sugar
- 2 finely chopped chipotle peppers plus 2 tsp. adobo sauce
- 2 Tbsp. reduced-sodium soy sauce
- Hot cooked rice

1. Sprinkle pork with salt and pepper. In a large skillet, heat oil over medium-high heat. Add the pork; cook until browned, 4-6 minutes. Remove.

2. In same skillet, cook onion and pepper until softened, 2-4 minutes. Add garlic; cook 1 minute. Return pork to pan; stir in chicken stock. Cook, covered, until pork is tender, about 5 minutes.

3. Stir in next five ingredients; simmer, uncovered, until sauce is thickened, about 5 minutes. Serve with rice.

Per 1½ cups: 539 cal., 11g fat (2g sat. fat), 64mg chol., 1374mg sod., 82g carb. (72g sugars, 2g fiber), 25g pro.

A chipotle pepper is a smoked and dried jalapeno originating from the area surrounding Mexico City. In the United States, they are often available canned in a chili sauce.

SPICY PEANUT CHICKEN & NOODLES

This simple recipe tastes like it took hours to make. Everybody says it has the perfect levels of heat and spice.

—Sharon Collison, Newark, DE

Takes: 30 min. • **Makes:** 4 servings

- 1 pkg. (10.8 oz.) frozen broccoli, carrot and sugar snap pea blend
- ¾ cup reduced-sodium chicken broth
- ⅓ cup creamy peanut butter
- ¼ cup teriyaki sauce
- ¼ tsp. pepper
- ¼ tsp. cayenne pepper
- 1 cup coarsely shredded rotisserie chicken
- 1 pkg. (8.8 oz.) thick rice noodles
- 3 green onions, thinly sliced on a diagonal
- Additional chicken broth, optional

1. Microwave frozen vegetables according to package directions.
2. Place the chicken broth, peanut butter, teriyaki sauce, pepper and cayenne in a large skillet; cook and stir over medium heat until blended. Stir in chicken; heat through. Stir in vegetables.
3. Prepare noodles according to package directions. Drain and immediately add to chicken mixture, tossing to combine. Sprinkle with green onions. If desired, moisten with additional chicken broth. Serve immediately.

Per serving: 489 cal., 14g fat (3g sat. fat), 31mg chol., 971mg sod., 68g carb. (8g sugars, 4g fiber), 22g pro.

SPICY PEANUT CHICKEN & NOODLES

GRANDMA'S SWEDISH MEATBALLS

GRANDMA'S SWEDISH MEATBALLS

My mother made these hearty meatballs when we were growing up, and now my kids love them, too. My daughter likes to help shake the meatballs in flour.

—Karin Ness, Big Lake, MN

Takes: 30 min. • **Makes:** 4 servings

- 1 large egg, lightly beaten
- ½ cup crushed saltines (about 10 crackers)
- ¼ tsp. seasoned salt
- ¼ tsp. pepper
- ½ lb. ground beef
- ½ lb. bulk pork sausage
- ¼ cup plus 2 Tbsp. all-purpose flour, divided
- 2½ cups reduced-sodium beef broth, divided
- Hot mashed potatoes
- Minced fresh parsley, optional

1. Mix first four ingredients. Add beef and sausage; mix lightly but thoroughly. Shape mixture into 1-in. balls; toss with ¼ cup flour, coating lightly.

2. In a large skillet, brown meatballs over medium-high heat. Add 2 cups beef broth; bring to a boil. Reduce heat and simmer, covered, until the meatballs are cooked through, 5-6 minutes.

3. Remove meatballs with a slotted spoon. Mix remaining flour and broth until smooth; add to pan. Bring to a boil; cook and stir until thickened, 1-2 minutes. Return the meatballs to pan; heat through. Serve with mashed potatoes. If desired, sprinkle with the parsley.

Per serving: 348 cal., 21g fat (7g sat. fat), 115mg chol., 846mg sod., 17g carb. (1g sugars, 1g fiber), 21g pro.

SMOKED MOZZARELLA CHICKEN WITH PASTA

EDITOR'S CHOICE

SMOKED MOZZARELLA CHICKEN WITH PASTA

Take an ordinary chicken breast into wow territory with this recipe. Try prosciutto instead of ham to make it extra impressive.

—Naylet LaRochelle, Miami, FL

Takes: 30 min. • **Makes:** 4 servings

- 8 oz. uncooked angel hair pasta or thin spaghetti
- 4 boneless skinless chicken breast halves (6 oz. each)
- ½ tsp. salt
- ¼ tsp. pepper
- ⅔ cup seasoned bread crumbs
- 2 Tbsp. olive oil
- 4 thin slices smoked deli ham
- 4 slices smoked mozzarella cheese
- ½ tsp. dried sage leaves
- ½ cup prepared pesto
- Grated Parmesan cheese, optional

1. Cook pasta according to package directions. Drain; transfer to a large bowl.

2. Meanwhile, pound chicken breasts with a meat mallet to ½-in. thickness; sprinkle with salt and pepper. Place bread crumbs in a shallow bowl. Dip the chicken in bread crumbs to coat both sides; shake off excess.

3. In a skillet, heat oil over medium-high heat. Add chicken; cook 4 minutes. Turn; cook 2 minutes longer. Top with ham and mozzarella; sprinkle with sage. Cook for 1-2 minutes or until a thermometer inserted in chicken reads 165°. Remove from heat.

4. Add pesto to pasta; toss to coat. Serve chicken with pasta. If desired, sprinkle with Parmesan cheese.

Per 1 chicken breast half with ¾ cup pasta: 694 cal., 28g fat (7g sat. fat), 122mg chol., 1184mg sod., 53g carb. (4g sugars, 3g fiber), 53g pro.

GRILLED ORANGE CHICKEN THIGHS

SALMON WITH CREAMY DILL SAUCE

There's nothing like fresh salmon, and my mom bakes it just right so it nearly melts in your mouth. The sour cream sauce is subtly seasoned with dill and horseradish so that it gives a welcome flavor boost without overpowering the delicate salmon flavor.

—Susan Emery, Everett, WA

Takes: 30 min. • **Makes:** 6 servings

- 1 salmon fillet (about 2 lbs.)
- 1 to 1½ tsp. lemon-pepper seasoning
- 1 tsp. onion salt
- 1 small onion, sliced and separated into rings
- 6 lemon slices
- ¼ cup butter, cubed

DILL SAUCE

- ⅓ cup sour cream
- ⅓ cup mayonnaise
- 1 Tbsp. finely chopped onion
- 1 tsp. lemon juice
- 1 tsp. prepared horseradish
- ¾ tsp. dill weed
- ¼ tsp. garlic salt
- Pepper to taste

1. Line a 15x10x1-in. baking pan with heavy-duty foil; grease lightly. Place the salmon skin side down on foil. Sprinkle with lemon pepper and onion salt. Top with the onion and lemon. Dot with butter. Fold foil around salmon; seal tightly.
2. Bake at 350° for 20 minutes. Open foil carefully, allowing steam to escape. Broil 4-6 in. from the heat for 8-12 minutes or until the fish flakes easily with a fork.
3. Combine the sauce ingredients until smooth. Serve with salmon.

Per 4 oz. cooked salmon with 2 Tbsp. sauce: 418 cal., 33g fat (11g sat. fat), 100mg chol., 643mg sod., 3g carb. (1g sugars, 0 fiber), 26g pro.

GRILLED ORANGE CHICKEN THIGHS

This was the first meal I served my then-future husband. He thought it was amazing and gobbled it up.

—Leah Harvath, Heber City, UT

Takes: 30 min. • **Makes:** 6 servings

- 1 cup orange juice
- ⅓ cup sugar
- ⅓ cup packed light brown sugar
- ¼ tsp. salt
- 1 Tbsp. Dijon mustard
- 2 tsp. grated orange zest

CHICKEN

- 6 boneless skinless chicken thighs (about 1½ lbs.)
- ½ tsp. lemon-pepper seasoning

1. In a small saucepan, combine juice, sugars and salt; bring to a boil, stirring to dissolve sugar. Cook, uncovered, for 10-15 minutes or until mixture reaches a glaze consistency. Remove from heat; stir in mustard and orange zest.
2. Sprinkle chicken with lemon pepper. On a lightly greased grill rack, grill chicken, covered, over medium heat 6-8 minutes on each side or until a thermometer reads 170°, brushing occasionally with some of the sauce during the last 5 minutes. Serve chicken with the remaining sauce.

Per chicken thigh with 1 Tbsp. sauce: 277 cal., 8g fat (2g sat. fat), 76mg chol., 256mg sod., 29g carb. (27g sugars, 0 fiber), 21g pro.

BEEFY TORTELLINI SKILLET

This tortellini skillet is a dish my family craves. From browning the beef to cooking the pasta and melting the cheese, everything happens in one pan. Add basil or chives for a fresh touch.
—Juli Meyers, Hinesville, GA

Takes: 20 min. • **Makes:** 4 servings

- 1 lb. ground beef
- ½ tsp. Montreal steak seasoning
- 1 cup water
- 1 tsp. beef bouillon granules
- 1 pkg. (19 oz.) frozen cheese tortellini
- 1 cup shredded Italian cheese blend

1. In a large skillet, cook beef over medium heat 5-6 minutes or until no longer pink, breaking into crumbles; drain. Stir in steak seasoning. Add water and bouillon; bring to a boil. Stir in tortellini; return to a boil. Reduce heat; simmer, covered, 3-4 minutes or until tortellini are tender.

2. Remove from the heat; sprinkle with cheese. Let stand, covered, until the cheese is melted.

Per 1½ cups: 566 cal., 28g fat (13g sat. fat), 111mg chol., 899mg sod., 37g carb. (2g sugars, 2g fiber), 39g pro.

CUBAN SLIDERS

EDITOR'S CHOICE

CUBAN SLIDERS

Bake these wonderful little rolls until they are lightly toasted and the cheese melts. Leftovers keep well in the fridge, and they make a lovely cold snack. So many people love these!

—Serene Herrera, Dallas, TX

Takes: 30 min. • **Makes:** 2 dozen

- 2 pkg. (12 oz. each) Hawaiian sweet rolls
- 1¼ lbs. thinly sliced deli ham
- 9 slices Swiss cheese (about 6 oz.)
- 24 dill pickle slices

TOPPING

- ½ cup butter, cubed
- 2 Tbsp. finely chopped onion
- 2 Tbsp. Dijon mustard

1. Preheat the oven to 350°. Without separating rolls, cut each package of rolls in half horizontally; arrange bottom halves in a greased 13x9-in. baking pan. Layer with ham, cheese and pickles; replace top halves of rolls.

2. In a microwave, melt butter; stir in the onion and mustard. Drizzle over rolls. Bake sliders, covered, 10 minutes. Uncover; bake until golden brown and heated through, 5-10 minutes longer.

Per slider: 191 cal., 10g fat (5g sat. fat), 42mg chol., 532mg sod., 17g carb. (6g sugars, 1g fiber), 10g pro.

CHEDDAR BEAN BURRITOS

My family goes meatless several nights a week, and this recipe is one of our very favorites. I usually puree a can or two of chipotles in adobo and freeze in ice cube trays so I can use a small amount when I need it.

—Amy Bravo, Ames, IA

Takes: 25 min. • **Makes:** 6 servings

- 2 tsp. canola oil
- 1 Tbsp. minced chipotle pepper in adobo sauce
- 2 garlic cloves, minced
- 2 tsp. chili powder
- 1 tsp. ground cumin
- ⅛ tsp. salt
- 2 cans (15 oz. each) black beans, rinsed and drained
- 2 Tbsp. water
- ½ cup pico de gallo
- 6 flour tortillas (8 in.), warmed
- 1 cup shredded cheddar or Monterey Jack cheese
- ½ cup sour cream
- Additional pico de gallo and sour cream, optional

1. In a large skillet, heat oil over medium heat; saute chipotle pepper, garlic and seasonings 2 minutes. Stir in beans and water; bring to a boil. Reduce heat; simmer, uncovered, until the flavors are blended, 5-7 minutes, stirring occasionally.

2. Coarsely mash bean mixture; stir in pico de gallo. Spoon onto the tortillas; top with cheese and sour cream and roll up. Serve with additional pico de gallo and sour cream if desired.

Freeze option Cool the filling before assembling the burritos. Individually wrap burritos in paper towels and foil; freeze in a resealable plastic freezer bag. To use, remove foil; place a paper towel-wrapped burrito on a plate and microwave on high until heated through, 4-6 minutes, turning once. Let stand 2 minutes.

Per burrito: 410 cal., 16g fat (7g sat. fat), 23mg chol., 726mg sod., 50g carb. (2g sugars, 8g fiber), 16g pro.

EDITOR'S CHOICE

WHITE CHEDDAR MAC & CHEESE

My macaroni and cheese is simple and gets lots of flavor from the cheeses and ground chipotle. I use conchiglie pasta because its shape allows more melted cheese to pool inside. Yum!

—Colleen Delawder, Herndon, VA

Takes: 25 min. • **Makes:** 8 servings

- 1 pkg. (16 oz.) small pasta shells
- ½ cup butter, cubed
- ½ cup all-purpose flour
- ½ tsp. onion powder
- ½ tsp. ground chipotle pepper
- ½ tsp. pepper
- ¼ tsp. salt
- 4 cups 2% milk
- 2 cups shredded sharp white cheddar cheese
- 2 cups shredded Manchego or additional white cheddar cheese

1. In a 6-qt. stockpot, cook pasta according to package directions. Drain; return to pot.

2. Meanwhile, in a large saucepan, melt butter over medium heat. Stir in flour and seasonings until smooth; gradually whisk in milk. Bring to a boil, stirring constantly; cook and stir until thickened, 6-8 minutes. Remove from heat; stir in cheeses until melted. Add to pasta; toss to coat.

Per cup: 650 cal., 35g fat (22g sat. fat), 101mg chol., 607mg sod., 55g carb. (8g sugars, 2g fiber), 27g pro.

WHITE CHEDDAR MAC & CHEESE

SPICY CHICKEN NUGGETS

SPICY CHICKEN NUGGETS

We devour these golden brown chicken nuggets at least once a week. Skip the chipotle pepper if you want to tone down the heat.

—Cheryl Cook, Palmyra, VA

Takes: 30 min. • **Makes:** 6 servings

- 1½ cups panko (Japanese) bread crumbs
- 1½ cups grated Parmesan cheese
- ½ tsp. ground chipotle pepper, optional
- ¼ cup butter, melted
- 1½ lbs. boneless skinless chicken thighs, cut into 1½-in. pieces

1. Preheat oven to 400°. In a shallow bowl, mix bread crumbs, cheese and, if desired, chipotle pepper. Place butter in a separate shallow bowl. Dip chicken pieces in butter, then in crumb mixture, patting to help coating adhere.

2. Place chicken on a greased 15x10x1-in. baking pan; sprinkle with remaining crumb mixture. Bake 20-25 minutes or until no longer pink.

Per serving: 371 cal., 22g fat (10g sat. fat), 113mg chol., 527mg sod., 13g carb. (1g sugars, 1g fiber), 29g pro.

FAJITA-STYLE SHRIMP & GRITS

I combined two favorite dishes—shrimp with cheesy grits, and fajitas—into this spicy one-dish meal. For more heat, use pepper jack instead of the cheese blend.

—Arlene Erlbach, Morton Grove, IL

Takes: 30 min. • **Makes:** 4 servings

- 1 lb. uncooked shrimp (16-20 per lb.), peeled and deveined
- 2 Tbsp. fajita seasoning mix
- 1 cup quick-cooking grits
- 4 cups boiling water
- 1½ cups shredded Mexican cheese blend
- 3 Tbsp. 2% milk
- 2 Tbsp. canola oil
- 3 medium sweet peppers, seeded and cut into 1-in. strips
- 1 medium sweet onion, cut into 1-in. strips
- 1 jar (15½ to 16 oz.) medium chunky salsa
- ¼ cup orange juice
- ¼ cup plus 1 Tbsp. fresh cilantro leaves, divided

1. Sprinkle shrimp with fajita seasoning; toss to coat. Set aside.

2. Slowly stir grits into boiling water. Reduce heat to medium; cook, covered, stirring occasionally, until thickened, 5-7 minutes. Remove from heat. Stir in the cheese blend until melted; stir in milk. Keep warm.

3. In a large skillet, heat oil over medium-high heat. Add peppers and onion; cook and stir until tender and pepper edges are slightly charred. Add salsa, orange juice and shrimp. Cook, stirring constantly, until shrimp turn pink, 4-6 minutes. Stir in ¼ cup cilantro. Remove from heat.

4. Spoon grits into serving bowls; top with shrimp mixture. Sprinkle dishes with the remaining cilantro.

Per serving: 561 cal., 23g fat (8g sat. fat), 176mg chol., 1324mg sod., 55g carb. (12g sugars, 4g fiber), 33g pro.

TEST KITCHEN TIP

This recipe is a great introduction to grits for people who haven't tried them before. Their creamy texture balances the rest of the ingredients and lets them shine. Even though it's a small amount, don't skip the orange juice—it adds a lot of flavor. Be sure to watch the shrimp while they're cooking and remove them from the heat as soon as they're done so they don't become tough and rubbery.

FAJITA-STYLE SHRIMP & GRITS

DILL PICKLE HAMBURGER PIZZA

My husband's favorite foods are pizza and cheeseburgers, so I combined the two in a pie with mayo and dill pickle juice topping. People who try it start laughing because it's such a fun, crazy mashup and so good!
—Angie Zimmerman, Eureka, IL

Takes: 30 min. • **Makes:** 6 servings

- ½ lb. ground beef
- 1 prebaked 12-in. pizza crust
- ½ cup ketchup
- ¼ cup prepared mustard
- 1½ cups shredded cheddar cheese
- 2 cups shredded lettuce
- ½ cup chopped dill pickle
- ¼ cup chopped onion
- ½ cup mayonnaise
- 2 to 3 Tbsp. dill pickle juice

1. Preheat oven to 425°. In a large skillet, cook and crumble beef over medium heat until no longer pink, 3-4 minutes; drain.
2. Meanwhile, place crust on an ungreased baking sheet or pizza pan. Mix ketchup and mustard; spread over crust. Add ground beef; bake 5 minutes. Sprinkle with cheese; bake until cheese is bubbly and crust is lightly browned, 8-10 minutes more.
3. Top with lettuce, pickle and onion. Whisk mayonnaise and enough pickle juice to reach desired consistency; pour over pizza.
Per slice: 521 cal., 32g fat (10g sat. fat), 59mg chol., 1192mg sod., 36g carb. (7g sugars, 2g fiber), 21g pro.

SPINACH & FETA STUFFED CHICKEN

My stuffed chicken bundles are simple and comforting. Serve them with wild rice and green beans for a complete meal.

—Jim Knepper, Mount Holly Springs, PA

Takes: 30 min. • Makes: 2 servings

- 8 oz. fresh spinach (about 10 cups)
- 1½ tsp. cider vinegar
- ½ tsp. sugar
- ⅛ tsp. pepper
- 2 boneless skinless chicken thighs
- ½ tsp. chicken seasoning
- 3 Tbsp. crumbled feta cheese
- 1 tsp. olive oil
- ¾ cup reduced-sodium chicken broth
- 1 tsp. butter

1. Preheat oven to 375°. In a large skillet, cook and stir spinach over medium-high heat until wilted. Stir in vinegar, sugar and pepper; cool slightly.

2. Pound chicken thighs with a meat mallet to flatten slightly; sprinkle with chicken seasoning. Top chicken with spinach mixture and cheese. Roll up chicken from a long side; tie securely with kitchen string.

3. In an ovenproof skillet, heat oil over medium-high heat; add the chicken and brown on all sides. Transfer to oven; roast until a thermometer inserted in chicken reads 170°, 13-15 minutes.

4. Remove chicken from pan; keep warm. On stovetop, add chicken broth and butter to skillet; bring to a boil, stirring to loosen browned bits from pan. Cook until slightly thickened, 3-5 minutes. Serve sauce with chicken roll-ups.

Per 1 chicken roll-up with 2 Tbsp. sauce: 253 cal., 14g fat (5g sat. fat), 86mg chol., 601mg sod., 5g carb. (2g sugars, 2g fiber), 26g pro. **Diabetic exchanges:** 3 lean meat, 2 vegetable, 1½ fat.

TANGY GLAZED MEATBALLS

SHRIMP SCAMPI

This shrimp scampi looks like you fussed, but it's easy to prepare. Lemon and herbs enhance the seafood, and bread crumbs add a nice crunch. Serve over pasta for a meal that's unforgettable.

—Lori Packer, Omaha, NE

Takes: 20 min. • **Makes:** 4 servings

- 3 to 4 garlic cloves, minced
- ¼ cup butter, cubed
- ¼ cup olive oil
- 1 lb. uncooked medium shrimp, peeled and deveined
- ¼ cup lemon juice
- ½ tsp. pepper
- ¼ tsp. dried oregano
- ½ cup grated Parmesan cheese
- ¼ cup dry bread crumbs
- ¼ cup minced fresh parsley
- Hot cooked angel hair pasta

1. In a 10-in. ovenproof skillet, saute garlic in butter and oil until fragrant. Add shrimp, lemon juice, pepper and oregano; cook and stir until the shrimp turn pink. Sprinkle with cheese, bread crumbs and minced parsley.

2. Broil 6 in. from the heat for 2-3 minutes or until topping is golden brown. Serve with angel hair pasta.

Per cup: 395 cal., 30g fat (11g sat. fat), 177mg chol., 420mg sod., 9g carb. (1g sugars, 1g fiber), 24g pro.

TANGY GLAZED MEATBALLS

(PICTURED ON P. 90)

The slightly sweet sauce in this recipe has such a great zing to it. These meatballs can be enjoyed as an appetizer or served over noodles or cooked rice for a main meal.

—John Slivon, Milton, FL

Takes: 25 min. • **Makes:** 5 dozen

- 1 jar (9 oz.) mango chutney
- ¾ cup A.1. steak sauce
- ½ cup chili sauce
- ½ cup ketchup
- 2 Tbsp. Worcestershire sauce
- 1 tsp. hot pepper sauce
- 1 pkg. (32 oz.) frozen fully cooked homestyle meatballs, thawed

In a large saucepan, combine the first six ingredients; cook and stir over medium heat until blended. Add meatballs; cook, covered, 15-20 minutes or until heated through, stirring occasionally.

Per meatball: 69 cal., 4g fat (2g sat. fat), 6mg chol., 266mg sod., 6g carb. (4g sugars, 0 fiber), 2g pro.

CHICKEN QUESADILLAS

Add some Southwestern flair to the dinner table with these scrumptious chicken quesadillas that are ready in 30 minutes.

—Linda Wetzel, Woodland Park, CO

Takes: 30 min. • **Makes:** 6 servings

- 2½ cups shredded cooked chicken
- ⅔ cup salsa
- ⅓ cup sliced green onions
- ¾ to 1 tsp. ground cumin
- ½ tsp. salt
- ½ tsp. dried oregano
- 6 flour tortillas (8 in.)
- ¼ cup butter, melted
- 2 cups shredded Monterey Jack cheese
- Sour cream and guacamole

1. In a large skillet, combine the first six ingredients. Cook, uncovered, over medium heat for 10 minutes or until heated through, stirring occasionally.
2. Brush one side of tortillas with butter; place buttered side down on a lightly greased baking sheet. Spoon ⅓ cup chicken mixture over half of each tortilla; sprinkle with ⅓ cup cheese.
3. Fold plain side of tortilla over cheese. Bake at 375° for 9-11 minutes or until crisp and golden brown. Cut into wedges; serve with sour cream and guacamole.

Per quesadilla: 477 cal., 26g fat (13g sat. fat), 106mg chol., 901mg sod., 27g carb. (1g sugars, 1g fiber), 31g pro.

We were all about kooky plates and bright colors when we originally published this recipe in 1999.

BEST OVEN RECIPES

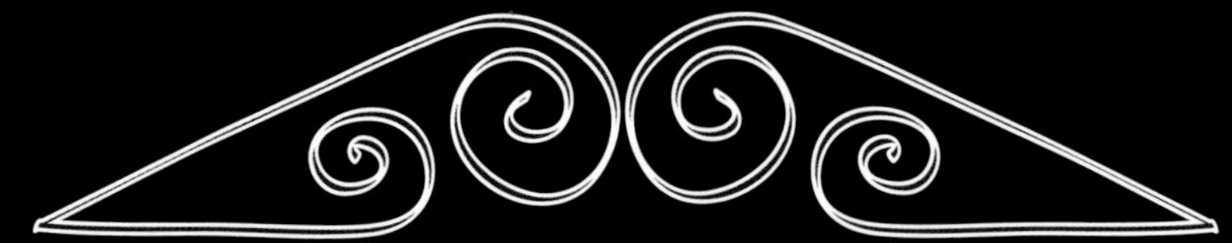

ALL HAIL THE KING OF KITCHEN APPLIANCES: THE OVEN. WHETHER IT'S ROASTING A MEAT-AND-POTATOES CLASSIC, BAKING BREAD OR SLOWLY SIMMERING A CASSEROLE, THIS MASTERPIECE OF A MACHINE ENSURES YOUR HEARTY ONE-DISH WONDER WILL BE A SUREFIRE SUCCESS!

2. In a small bowl, combine the cornstarch and milk until smooth; gradually add to the vegetable mixture. Bring to a boil; cook and stir for 2 minutes or until thickened. Remove from the heat; stir in cheese and mayonnaise until cheese is melted. Fold in noodles and tuna.

3. Pour into a greased 2½-qt. baking dish. In a small skillet, brown bread crumbs in butter; sprinkle over casserole. Bake, uncovered, at 350° for 25-30 minutes or until heated through.

Per serving: 343 cal., 15g fat (5g sat. fat), 57mg chol., 770mg sod., 27g carb. (7g sugars, 2g fiber), 24g pro.

TUNA MUSHROOM CASSEROLE

TUNA MUSHROOM CASSEROLE

The first time I made this dish, my uncle asked for seconds even though tuna casseroles don't top his list of favorites. The green beans add nice texture, color and flavor.

—Jone Furlong, Santa Rosa, CA

Prep: 30 min. • **Bake:** 25 min.
Makes: 4 servings

- ½ cup water
- 1 tsp. chicken bouillon granules
- 1 pkg. (9 oz.) frozen cut green beans
- 1 cup chopped onion
- 1 cup sliced fresh mushrooms
- ¼ cup chopped celery
- 1 garlic clove, minced
- ½ tsp. dill weed
- ½ tsp. salt
- ⅛ tsp. pepper
- 4 tsp. cornstarch
- 1½ cups cold whole milk
- ½ cup shredded Swiss cheese
- ¼ cup mayonnaise
- 2½ cups egg noodles, cooked and drained
- 1 can (12 oz.) light tuna in water, drained and flaked
- ⅓ cup dry bread crumbs
- 1 Tbsp. butter

1. In a large saucepan, bring water and bouillon to a boil; stir until bouillon is dissolved. Add the next eight ingredients; bring to a boil. Reduce heat; cover and simmer for 5 minutes or until vegetables are tender.

AMISH BREAKFAST CASSEROLE

We enjoyed hearty breakfast casseroles during a visit to an Amish inn. When I asked for a recipe, one of the women told me the ingredients right off the top of her head. I modified it to create this version my family loves. If you like, try breakfast sausage in place of the bacon.

—Beth Notaro, Kokomo, IN

Prep: 15 min. • **Bake:** 35 min. + standing
Makes: 12 servings

- 1 lb. sliced bacon, diced
- 1 medium sweet onion, chopped
- 6 large eggs, lightly beaten
- 4 cups frozen shredded hash brown potatoes, thawed
- 2 cups shredded cheddar cheese
- 1½ cups 4% cottage cheese
- 1¼ cups shredded Swiss cheese

1. Preheat oven to 350°. In a large skillet, cook bacon and onion over medium heat until bacon is crisp; drain. In a large bowl, combine remaining ingredients; stir in bacon mixture. Transfer to a greased 13x9-in. baking dish.

2. Bake, uncovered, 35-40 minutes or until a knife inserted in the center comes out clean. Let stand 10 minutes before cutting.

Per serving: 273 cal., 18g fat (10g sat. fat), 153mg chol., 477mg sod., 8g carb. (3g sugars, 1g fiber), 18g pro.

SPAGHETTI MEATBALL BAKE

SPAGHETTI MEATBALL BAKE

Some nights, we're in the mood for pasta—and nothing else will do! I came up with this saucy dish to satisfy our cravings.

—Kimberly Forni, Laconia, NH

Prep: 45 min. • **Bake:** 30 min.
Makes: 10 servings

- 1½ cups dry bread crumbs, divided
- 3 large eggs, lightly beaten
- 1½ cups cooked spaghetti (3 oz. uncooked), coarsely chopped
- 2 garlic cloves, minced
- 2 tsp. dried basil
- ¾ tsp. salt
- 1 tsp. dried oregano
- 1 tsp. pepper
- 2 lbs. ground beef

SAUCE

- 2 jars (24 oz. each) meatless pasta sauce
- 1 small onion, finely chopped
- 2 garlic cloves, minced
- 2 tsp. dried basil
- 1 tsp. dried oregano
- 2 cups shredded part-skim mozzarella cheese

1. Preheat oven to 375°. Place 1 cup bread crumbs in a shallow bowl. In a large bowl, combine eggs, chopped spaghetti, garlic, seasonings and remaining bread crumbs. Add beef; mix lightly but thoroughly. Shape into 1½-in. balls.

2. Roll meatballs in bread crumbs; place in a greased 13x9-in. baking dish. Bake for 15-20 minutes or until cooked through.

3. In a large saucepan, combine the pasta sauce, onion, garlic and seasonings. Bring to a boil over medium heat, occasionally stirring. Pour over meatballs; sprinkle with cheese. Bake 15-20 minutes longer or until cheese is lightly browned.

Per 4 meatballs with ½ cup sauce: 390 cal., 17g fat (7g sat. fat), 124mg chol., 1074mg sod., 29g carb. (10g sugars, 3g fiber), 29g pro.

EDITOR'S CHOICE

EASY ARROZ CON POLLO

My kids look forward to dinner when this is on the menu. I love that it's easy to make.
—Debbie Harris, Tucson, AZ

Prep: 10 min. • **Bake:** 1 hour
Makes: 6 servings

- 1¾ cups uncooked instant rice
- 6 boneless skinless chicken breast halves (4 oz. each)
- Garlic salt and pepper to taste
- 1 can (14½ oz.) chicken broth
- 1 cup picante sauce
- 1 can (8 oz.) tomato sauce
- ½ cup chopped onion
- ½ cup chopped green pepper
- ½ cup shredded Monterey Jack cheese
- ½ cup shredded cheddar cheese

1. Spread the rice in a greased 13x9-in. baking dish. Sprinkle both sides of chicken with garlic salt and pepper; place over rice. In a large bowl, combine the broth, picante sauce, tomato sauce, onion and green pepper; pour over the chicken.
2. Cover and bake at 350° for 55 minutes or until a thermometer reads 170°. Sprinkle with cheeses. Bake, uncovered, 5 minutes longer or until cheese is melted.
Per serving: 351 cal., 9g fat (5g sat. fat), 91mg chol., 791mg sod., 30g carb. (4g sugars, 1g fiber), 35g pro.

HAM & SWISS POTATO CASSEROLE

HAM & SWISS POTATO CASSEROLE

When I wanted to use up ingredients I had on hand, I started experimenting—and hit a home run! The classic trio of ham, Swiss cheese and potatoes comes together in this comforting bake, which is now one of my go-to recipes to feed a crowd.
—Sarah Wilham, Elkhart, IL

Prep: 25 min. • **Bake:** 20 min.
Makes: 8 servings

- 5 large potatoes (about 4 lbs.), peeled and cut into ¾-in. pieces
- ¼ cup butter, cubed
- 1 medium onion, chopped
- 1 garlic clove, minced
- ⅓ cup all-purpose flour
- 2 cups 2% milk
- 1⅓ cups roasted red pepper Alfredo sauce
- 1 tsp. dried basil
- ¼ tsp. salt
- ¼ tsp. dill weed
- ¼ tsp. pepper
- 2 cups cubed fully cooked ham
- 2 cups shredded Swiss cheese
- ¼ cup seasoned bread crumbs
- 1 Tbsp. butter, melted

1. Preheat oven to 375°. Place potatoes in a large saucepan; add water to cover. Bring to a boil. Reduce heat; simmer, covered, 8-10 minutes or until crisp-tender. Meanwhile, in a large skillet, heat butter over medium-high heat. Add onion; cook and stir 6-8 minutes or until tender. Add garlic; cook and stir 1 minute. Stir in flour until blended; gradually whisk in milk. Bring to a boil, stirring constantly; cook and stir for 1-2 minutes or until thickened. Stir in Alfredo sauce and seasonings; heat through.
2. Drain potatoes; transfer to a greased 13x9-in. baking dish. Layer with ham, cheese and sauce. In a small bowl, combine bread crumbs and butter. Sprinkle over top. Bake, uncovered, 18-22 minutes or until topping is golden brown and cheese is melted. Let stand 5 minutes before serving.
Per serving: 456 cal., 22g fat (13g sat. fat), 93mg chol., 897mg sod., 45g carb. (7g sugars, 3g fiber), 22g pro.

CRUSTLESS SPINACH QUICHE

I served this at a church lunch, and I had to laugh when one guy told me how much he doesn't like vegetables. He was among those surprised by how much they loved this veggie-filled crustless quiche recipe.
—Melinda Calverley, Janesville, WI

Prep: 25 min. • **Bake:** 40 min.
Makes: 8 servings

- 1 cup chopped onion
- 1 cup sliced fresh mushrooms
- 1 Tbsp. vegetable oil
- 1 pkg. (10 oz.) frozen chopped spinach, thawed and well drained
- ⅔ cup finely chopped fully cooked ham
- 5 large eggs
- 3 cups shredded Muenster or Monterey Jack cheese
- ⅛ tsp. pepper

In a large skillet, saute onion and mushrooms in oil until tender. Add spinach and ham; cook and stir mixture until the excess moisture is evaporated. Cool slightly. Beat eggs; add cheese and mix well. Stir in spinach mixture and pepper; blend well. Spread evenly into a greased 9-in. pie plate or quiche dish. Bake at 350° for 40-45 minutes or until a knife inserted in center comes out clean.
Per serving: 251 cal., 18g fat (10g sat. fat), 164mg chol., 480mg sod., 4g carb. (2g sugars, 1g fiber), 18g pro.

PUFF PASTRY CHICKEN POTPIE

When my wife is craving comfort food, I whip up my chicken potpie. It is easy to make and delivers soul-satisfying flavor.
—Nick Iverson, Denver, CO

Prep: 45 min. • **Bake:** 45 min. + standing
Makes: 8 servings

- 1 pkg. (17.3 oz.) frozen puff pastry, thawed
- 2 lbs. boneless skinless chicken breasts, cut into 1-in. pieces
- 1 tsp. salt, divided
- 1 tsp. pepper, divided
- 4 Tbsp. butter, divided
- 1 large onion, chopped
- 2 garlic cloves, minced
- 1 tsp. minced fresh thyme or ¼ tsp. dried thyme
- 1 tsp. minced fresh sage or ¼ tsp. rubbed sage
- ½ cup all-purpose flour
- 2 cups chicken broth
- 1 cup plus 1 Tbsp. half-and-half cream, divided
- 2 cups frozen mixed vegetables (about 10 oz.)
- 1 Tbsp. lemon juice
- 1 large egg yolk

1. Preheat oven to 400°. On a lightly floured surface, roll each puff pastry sheet into a 12x10-in. rectangle. Cut one pastry sheet crosswise into six 2-in. strips; cut remaining sheet lengthwise into five 2-in. strips. On a baking sheet, closely weave strips to make a 12x10-in. lattice. Place in the freezer.
2. Toss chicken with ½ tsp. each salt and pepper. In a large skillet, heat 1 Tbsp. butter over medium-high heat; saute chicken until browned, 5-7 minutes. Remove from pan.
3. In the same skillet, heat remaining butter over medium-high heat; saute onion until tender, 5-7 minutes. Stir in garlic and herbs; cook 1 minute. Stir in flour until blended; cook and stir 1 minute. Gradually stir in broth and 1 cup cream. Bring to a boil, stirring constantly; cook and stir until thickened, about 2 minutes.
4. Stir in vegetables, lemon juice, chicken and the remaining salt and pepper; return to a boil. Transfer chicken mixture to a greased 2-qt. oblong baking dish. Remove lattice from the freezer and place it on top of filling, trimming to fit.
5. Whisk together egg yolk and remaining cream; brush over pastry. Bake, uncovered, until bubbly and golden brown, 45-55 minutes. Let potpie stand for 15 minutes before serving.
Per serving: 523 cal., 25g fat (10g sat. fat), 118mg chol., 829mg sod., 42g carb. (4g sugars, 6 g fiber), 30 g pro.

PUFF PASTRY
CHICKEN POTPIE

BUTTERNUT SQUASH & SAUSAGE STUFFED SHELLS

BUTTERNUT SQUASH & SAUSAGE STUFFED SHELLS

It's a rare occurrence if I invite friends for dinner and no one requests this easy dish. The sweet squash complements the spicy sausage, and the creamy goat cheese makes it all just melt in your mouth. You can substitute manicotti or even rolled lasagna noodles for the shells. The stuffed shells and sauce can be prepared a day ahead and assembled just before baking.

—Taylor Hale, Sonoma, CA

Prep: 55 min. • **Bake:** 30 min. + standing
Makes: 10 servings

- 5 cups peeled butternut squash, cut into 1-in. cubes
- 3 Tbsp. extra virgin olive oil, divided
- 32 uncooked jumbo pasta shells
- ¾ lb. bulk hot Italian sausage
- 2 cups finely chopped sweet onion, divided
- 1 pkg. (5 oz.) baby kale salad blend, chopped
- 8 oz. crumbled goat cheese, divided
- 4 garlic cloves, minced
- 1 carton (26.46 oz.) chopped tomatoes, undrained
- 2 Tbsp. fresh sage
- 1 Tbsp. sugar
- ½ cup fat-free half-and-half

1. Preheat oven to 400°. On a foil-lined baking sheet, toss squash with 1 Tbsp. olive oil. Roast squash, stirring halfway through, until tender and starting to caramelize, about 40 minutes. Transfer to a large bowl; roughly mash. Reduce heat to 350°.
2. Cook pasta according to the package directions. Drain.
3. In a large nonstick skillet over medium-high heat, cook sausage and 1 cup onion, crumbling meat, until no longer pink. Add baby kale; cook until tender, 3-5 minutes. Mix with squash. Stir in 4 oz. goat cheese.
4. In same skillet, heat remaining olive oil. Add remaining onion; cook until softened, 3-5 minutes. Add garlic; cook, stirring, for 1 minute more. Add tomatoes, sage and sugar; bring to a boil. Reduce heat; simmer, stirring occasionally, until the sauce is thickened, about 15 minutes. Cool about 5 minutes. Pulse mixture in a blender until combined. Add half-and-half; pulse until smooth. Pour about half of the sauce into a greased 13x9-in. baking dish.
5. Stuff each shell with about 2 Tbsp. squash mixture; arrange in the baking dish. Pour remaining tomato sauce over shells; top with remaining goat cheese. Bake, covered, until casserole begins to bubble, 20 minutes. Remove cover; bake another 10 minutes. Let shells stand 10 minutes before serving.

Per serving: 379 cal., 18g fat (7g sat. fat), 47mg chol., 344mg sod., 43g carb. (9g sugars, 6g fiber), 15g pro.

EDITOR'S CHOICE

CHILI CHEESE DOG CASSEROLE

Kids and parents alike will dive into this hearty, comforting dish. With a crispy cheese topping on a warm cornbread crust, this recipe is a keeper.

—Taste of Home *Test Kitchen*

Prep: 20 min. • **Bake:** 30 min.
Makes: 6 servings

- 1 pkg. (8½ oz.) cornbread/muffin mix
- 1 cup chopped green pepper
- ½ cup chopped onion
- ½ cup chopped celery
- 1 Tbsp. olive oil
- 1 pkg. (1 lb.) hot dogs, halved lengthwise and cut into bite-sized pieces
- 1 can (15 oz.) chili with beans
- 2 Tbsp. brown sugar
- ½ tsp. garlic powder
- ½ tsp. chili powder
- 1 cup shredded cheddar cheese, divided

1. Prepare cornbread batter according to the package directions. Spread half the batter into a greased 8-in. square baking dish; set aside.
2. In a large skillet, saute the green pepper, onion and celery in oil until crisp-tender. Stir in hot dogs; saute 3-4 minutes longer or until lightly browned. Stir in the chili, brown sugar, garlic powder and chili powder; heat through. Stir in ¾ cup cheese.
3. Spoon over cornbread batter; top with remaining cornbread batter. Sprinkle remaining cheese over the top.
4. Bake, uncovered, at 350° for 28-32 minutes or until a toothpick inserted in the center comes out clean. Let stand for 5 minutes before serving.
Per serving: 615 cal., 37g fat (16g sat. fat), 115mg chol., 1585mg sod., 49g carb. (18g sugars, 4g fiber), 22g pro.

BROCCOLI HAM QUICHE

This rich quiche is featured in a family cookbook I put together. My husband is proof that quiche can satisfy even the heartiest of appetites.

—Marilyn Day, North Fort Myers, FL

Prep: 20 min. + cooling
Bake: 55 min. + standing
Makes: 8 servings

- 1 unbaked deep-dish pie crust (9 in.)
- 1 cup shredded Swiss cheese
- 1 cup shredded part-skim mozzarella cheese
- 2 Tbsp. all-purpose flour
- 4 large eggs, lightly beaten
- 1½ cups whole milk
- 2 Tbsp. chopped green onion
- ¼ tsp. salt
- ⅛ tsp. pepper
- ⅛ tsp. dried thyme
- ⅛ tsp. dried rosemary, crushed
- ½ cup diced fully cooked ham
- ½ cup chopped fresh broccoli

1. Line unpricked pie crust with a double thickness of heavy-duty foil. Bake at 450° for 8 minutes. Remove foil; bake 5 minutes longer. Cool crust on a wire rack while preparing filling.
2. Toss the cheeses with flour; set aside. In a large bowl, combine eggs, milk, onion and seasonings. Stir in ham, broccoli and the cheese mixture. Pour into crust.
3. Bake at 350° for 55-60 minutes or until set. Let stand 10 minutes before cutting.
Per serving: 269 cal., 17g fat (7g sat. fat), 140mg chol., 408mg sod., 16g carb. (3g sugars, 0 fiber), 14g pro.

BROCCOLI HAM QUICHE

CONTEST-WINNING REUBEN CASSEROLE

Sauerkraut, kielbasa and Swiss cheese combine for a creamy Reuben-style entree. I've had this recipe in my files for quite some time, and from the stains on it, you can tell it's been well-used.

—Sally Mangel, Bradford, PA

Takes: 30 min. • **Makes:** 2 servings

- 1½ cups uncooked egg noodles
- ⅔ cup condensed cream of mushroom soup, undiluted
- ⅓ cup 2% milk
- 2 Tbsp. chopped onion
- ¾ tsp. prepared mustard
- 1 can (8 oz.) sauerkraut, rinsed and well drained
- ⅓ lb. smoked kielbasa or Polish sausage, cut into ½-in. slices
- ½ cup shredded Swiss cheese
- 3 Tbsp. soft whole wheat bread crumbs
- 1½ tsp. butter, melted

1. Cook noodles according to package directions. Meanwhile, in a small bowl, combine the soup, milk, onion and mustard; set aside.

2. Spread sauerkraut into a 1-qt. baking dish coated with cooking spray. Drain noodles; place over sauerkraut. Layer with the soup mixture and kielbasa; sprinkle with cheese.

3. In a small bowl, combine bread crumbs and butter; sprinkle over casserole. Bake, uncovered, at 350° for 15-20 minutes or until bubbly.

Per 2 cups: 587 cal., 37g fat (15g sat. fat), 109mg chol., 2315mg sod., 40g carb. (7g sugars, 5g fiber), 26g pro.

TEXAS-STYLE LASAGNA

With its spicy flavor, this casserole stands apart from typical red sauce lasagnas. Serve with picante sauce, guacamole and tortilla chips.

—Effie Gish, Fort Worth, TX

Prep: 40 min. • **Bake:** 30 min. + standing
Makes: 12 servings

- 1½ lbs. ground beef
- 1 tsp. seasoned salt
- 1 pkg. (1¼ oz.) taco seasoning
- 1 can (14½ oz.) diced tomatoes, undrained
- 1 can (15 oz.) tomato sauce
- 1 can (4 oz.) chopped green chilies
- 2 cups 4% cottage cheese
- 2 large eggs, lightly beaten
- 12 corn tortillas (6 in.), torn
- 3½ to 4 cups shredded Monterey Jack cheese
- Optional toppings: crushed tortilla chips, salsa and cubed avocado

1. In a large skillet, cook beef over medium heat until no longer pink; drain. Add the seasoned salt, taco seasoning, tomatoes, tomato sauce and chilies. Reduce heat; simmer, uncovered, for 15-20 minutes. In a small bowl, combine the cottage cheese and eggs.

2. In a greased 13x9-in. baking dish, layer half of each of the following: meat sauce, tortillas, cottage cheese mixture and Monterey Jack cheese. Repeat layers.

3. Bake, uncovered, at 350° for 30 minutes or until bubbly. Let stand 10 minutes before serving. Garnish with toppings if desired.

Freeze option Before baking, cover and freeze lasagna up to 3 months. Thaw in the refrigerator overnight. Remove from refrigerator 30 minutes before baking. Bake as directed, increasing time as necessary for a thermometer to read 160°.

Per serving: 349 cal., 18g fat (10g sat. fat), 101mg chol., 1041mg sod., 20g carb. (3g sugars, 2g fiber), 26g pro.

CHICKEN TATER BAKE

You'll please everyone in the family with this inviting dish. It tastes like chicken potpie with a crispy Tater Tot crust.

—Fran Allen, St. Louis, MO

Prep: 20 min. • **Bake:** 35 min.
Makes: 2 casseroles (6 servings each)

- 2 cans (10¾ oz. each) condensed cream of chicken soup, undiluted
- ½ cup 2% milk
- ¼ cup butter, cubed
- 3 cups cubed cooked chicken
- 1 pkg. (16 oz.) frozen peas and carrots, thawed
- 1½ cups shredded cheddar cheese, divided
- 1 pkg. (32 oz.) frozen Tater Tots

1. In a large saucepan, combine the soup, milk and butter. Cook and stir over medium heat until heated through. Remove from the heat; stir in the chicken, peas and carrots, and 1 cup cheese.

2. Transfer to two greased 8-in. square baking dishes. Top with Tater Tots.

3. Cover and freeze one casserole for up to 3 months. Bake the remaining casserole at 400° until bubbling, for 25-30 minutes. Sprinkle with ¼ cup cheese; bake 5 minutes longer or until cheese is melted.

Freeze option Remove from the freezer 30 minutes before baking (do not thaw). Sprinkle with ¼ cup cheese. Cover and bake at 350° for 1½-1¾ hours or until heated through.

Per serving: 356 cal., 21g fat (9g sat. fat), 61mg chol., 844mg sod., 29g carb. (3g sugars, 4g fiber), 18g pro.

CHICKEN TATER BAKE

BUFFALO CHICKEN LASAGNA

BUFFALO CHICKEN LASAGNA

(PICTURED ON P. 114)

This recipe was inspired by my daughter's favorite food—Buffalo wings! It tastes as if it came from a restaurant.

—Melissa Millwood, Lyman, SC

Prep: 1 hour 40 min.
Bake: 40 min. + standing
Makes: 12 servings

- 1 Tbsp. canola oil
- 1½ lbs. ground chicken
- 1 small onion, chopped
- 1 celery rib, finely chopped
- 1 large carrot, grated
- 2 garlic cloves, minced
- 1 can (14½ oz.) diced tomatoes, drained
- 1 bottle (12 oz.) Buffalo wing sauce
- ½ cup water
- 1½ tsp. Italian seasoning
- ½ tsp. salt
- ¼ tsp. pepper
- 9 lasagna noodles
- 1 carton (15 oz.) ricotta cheese
- 1¾ cups crumbled blue cheese, divided
- ½ cup minced Italian flat-leaf parsley
- 1 large egg, lightly beaten
- 3 cups shredded part-skim mozzarella cheese
- 2 cups shredded white cheddar cheese

1. In a Dutch oven, heat oil over medium heat. Add chicken, onion, celery and carrot; cook and stir until meat is no longer pink and vegetables are tender. Add garlic; cook 2 minutes longer. Stir in tomatoes, wing sauce, water, Italian seasoning, salt and pepper; bring to a boil. Reduce heat; cover and simmer 1 hour.

2. Meanwhile, cook noodles according to package directions; drain. In a small bowl, mix the ricotta cheese, ¾ cup blue cheese, parsley and egg. Preheat oven to 350°.

3. Spread 1½ cups sauce into a greased 13x9-in. baking dish. Layer with three noodles, 1½ cups sauce, ⅔ cup ricotta mixture, 1 cup mozzarella cheese, ⅔ cup cheddar cheese and ⅓ cup blue cheese. Repeat layers twice.

4. Bake, covered, 20 minutes. Uncover; bake until bubbly and cheese is melted, 20-25 minutes. Let stand for 10 minutes before serving.

Per serving: 466 cal., 28g fat (15g sat. fat), 124mg chol., 1680mg sod., 22g carb. (6g sugars, 2g fiber), 33g pro.

CHEESY VEGETABLE EGG DISH

I'm a cook at a Bible camp, and this is one of my most popular recipes with the kids. I was touched when a 10-year-old boy asked me for the recipe so he could have his mother make it at home.

—Elsie Campbell, Dulzura, CA

Prep: 20 min. • **Bake:** 35 min.
Makes: 10 servings

- 1 medium zucchini, diced
- 1 medium onion, chopped
- 1 can (4 oz.) mushroom stems and pieces, drained
- ¼ cup chopped green pepper
- ½ cup butter, cubed
- ½ cup all-purpose flour
- 1 tsp. baking powder
- ½ tsp. salt
- 10 large eggs, lightly beaten
- 2 cups 4% cottage cheese
- 4 cups shredded Monterey Jack cheese

1. In a large skillet, saute the zucchini, onion, mushrooms and green pepper in butter until tender. Stir in the flour, baking powder and salt until blended.

2. In a large bowl, combine eggs and cottage cheese. Stir in vegetables and Monterey Jack cheese.

3. Transfer to a greased 2½-qt. baking dish. Bake, uncovered, at 350° for 35-45 minutes or until a thermometer reads 160°.

Per serving: 407 cal., 30g fat (17g sat. fat), 287mg chol., 759mg sod., 10g carb. (4g sugars, 1g fiber), 24g pro.

ITALIAN SAUSAGE EGG BAKE

This hearty entree warms up any breakfast or brunch menu with its herb-seasoned flavor. It's even terrific for dinner!

—Darlene Markham, Rochester, NY

Prep: 20 min. + chilling • **Bake:** 50 min.
Makes: 12 servings

- 8 slices white bread, cubed
- 1 lb. Italian sausage links, casings removed, sliced
- 2 cups shredded sharp cheddar cheese
- 2 cups shredded part-skim mozzarella cheese
- 9 large eggs, lightly beaten
- 3 cups 2% milk
- 1 tsp. dried basil
- 1 tsp. dried oregano
- 1 tsp. fennel seed, crushed

1. Place bread cubes in a greased 13x9-in. baking dish; set aside. In a large skillet, cook sausage over medium heat until no longer pink; drain. Spoon sausage over bread; sprinkle with cheeses.

2. In a large bowl, whisk the eggs, milk and seasonings; pour over casserole. Cover and refrigerate overnight.

3. Remove from the refrigerator 30 minutes before baking. Bake, uncovered, at 350° for 50-55 minutes or until a knife inserted in the center comes out clean. Let stand for 5 minutes before cutting.

Per serving: 316 cal., 20g fat (10g sat. fat), 214mg chol., 546mg sod., 13g carb. (5g sugars, 1g fiber), 21g pro.

ITALIAN SAUSAGE EGG BAKE

POTLUCK CORDON BLEU CASSEROLE

POTLUCK CORDON BLEU CASSEROLE

People ask me to bring this tempting casserole whenever I'm invited to a potluck. The turkey, ham and cheese are delectable combined with the crunchy topping. When I bake a turkey, I keep the leftovers for this dish, knowing I'll be making it again soon.
—Joyce Paul, Moose Jaw, SK

Prep: 25 min. • **Bake:** 30 min.
Makes: 10 servings

- 4 cups cubed cooked turkey
- 3 cups cubed fully cooked ham
- 1 cup shredded cheddar cheese
- 1 cup chopped onion
- ¼ cup butter, cubed
- ⅓ cup all-purpose flour
- 2 cups half-and-half cream
- 1 tsp. dill weed
- ⅛ tsp. ground mustard
- ⅛ tsp. ground nutmeg

TOPPING

- 1 cup dry bread crumbs
- 2 Tbsp. butter, melted
- ¼ tsp. dill weed
- ¼ cup shredded cheddar cheese
- ¼ cup chopped walnuts

1. In a large bowl, combine the turkey, ham and cheese; set aside. In a large saucepan, saute the onion in butter until tender. Add the flour; stir until blended. Gradually add the cream, stirring constantly. Bring to a boil; cook and stir for 1-2 minutes or until thickened. Stir in the dill, mustard and nutmeg. Remove from the heat and pour over meat mixture.

2. Spoon into a greased 13x9-in. baking dish. In a small bowl, combine the bread crumbs, butter and dill. Stir in cheese and walnuts. Sprinkle over casserole.

3. Bake, uncovered, at 350° for 30 minutes or until heated through.

Per serving: 421 cal., 24g fat (13g sat. fat), 122mg chol., 848mg sod., 16g carb. (3g sugars, 1g fiber), 32g pro.

FARMER'S CASSEROLE

Between family and friends, we average 375 visitors a year! This casserole is so handy—you can put it together the night before, let the flavors blend, then bake it in the morning.

—Nancy Schmidt, Center, CO

Prep: 10 min. + chilling • **Bake:** 55 min.
Makes: 6 servings

- 3 cups frozen shredded hash brown potatoes
- ¾ cup shredded Monterey Jack cheese
- 1 cup cubed fully cooked ham
- ¼ cup chopped green onions
- 4 large eggs
- 1 can (12 oz.) evaporated milk
- ¼ tsp. pepper
- ⅛ tsp. salt

1. Place potatoes in an 8-in. baking dish. Sprinkle with cheese, ham and onions. Whisk eggs, milk, pepper and salt; pour over all. Cover and refrigerate for several hours or overnight.
2. Remove from refrigerator 30 minutes before baking. Preheat oven to 350°. Bake, uncovered, 55-60 minutes or until a knife inserted in the center comes out clean.
Per serving: 252 cal., 14g fat (7g sat. fat), 187mg chol., 531mg sod., 14g carb. (7g sugars, 1g fiber), 17g pro.

CHICKEN ALFREDO LASAGNA

My family was growing tired of traditional red sauce lasagna, so I created this fun twist using a creamy homemade Alfredo sauce. Store-bought rotisserie chicken keeps prep simple and fast.

—Caitlin MacNeilly, Uncasville, CT

Prep: 35 min. • **Bake:** 45 min. + standing
Makes: 12 servings

- 4 oz. thinly sliced pancetta, cut into strips
- 3 oz. thinly sliced prosciutto or deli ham, cut into strips
- 3 cups shredded rotisserie chicken
- 5 Tbsp. unsalted butter, cubed
- ¼ cup all-purpose flour
- 4 cups whole milk
- 2 cups shredded Asiago cheese, divided
- 2 Tbsp. minced fresh parsley, divided
- ¼ tsp. coarsely ground pepper
- Pinch ground nutmeg
- 9 no-cook lasagna noodles
- 1½ cups shredded part-skim mozzarella cheese
- 1½ cups shredded Parmesan cheese

1. In a skillet, cook pancetta and prosciutto over medium heat until browned. Drain on paper towels. Transfer to a large bowl; add chicken and toss to combine.
2. For sauce, in a large saucepan, melt butter over medium heat. Stir in flour until smooth; gradually whisk in milk. Bring to a boil, stirring constantly; cook and stir 1-2 minutes or until thickened. Remove from heat; stir in ½ cup Asiago cheese, 1 Tbsp. parsley, pepper and nutmeg.
3. Preheat oven to 375°. Spread ½ cup sauce into a greased 13x9-in. baking dish. Layer with a third of each of the following: noodles, sauce, meat mixture, Asiago, mozzarella and Parmesan cheeses. Repeat layers twice.
4. Bake, covered, 30 minutes. Uncover; bake 15 minutes longer or until bubbly. Sprinkle with remaining parsley. Let stand 10 minutes before serving.
Per serving: 421 cal., 25g fat (13g sat. fat), 99mg chol., 688mg sod., 18g carb. (5g sugars, 1g fiber), 31g pro.

CHICKEN ALFREDO LASAGNA

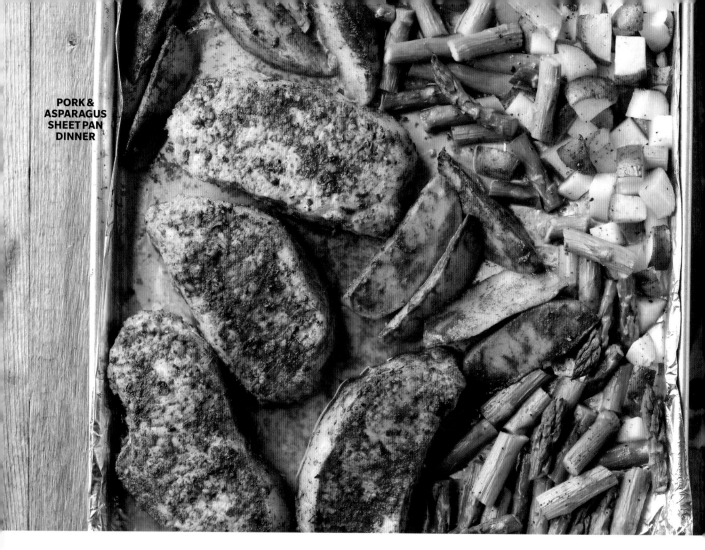

PORK & ASPARAGUS SHEET PAN DINNER

When time is of the essence, nothing is better than this sheet pan superstar. Not only is it delicious, but you can clean it up in a flash.

—Joan Hallford, North Richland Hills, TX

Prep: 20 min. • **Bake:** 20 min.
Makes: 4 servings

- ¼ cup olive oil, divided
- 3 cups diced new potatoes
- 3 cups fresh asparagus, cut into 1-in. pieces
- ¼ tsp. salt
- ¼ tsp. pepper
- 1 large Gala or Honeycrisp apple, peeled and cut into ½-in. slices
- 2 tsp. brown sugar
- 1 tsp. ground cinnamon
- ¼ tsp. ground ginger
- 4 boneless pork loin chops (1 in. thick and about 6 oz. each)
- 2 tsp. Southwest seasoning

1. Preheat oven to 425°. Line a 15x10x1-in. sheet pan with foil; brush pan with 2 tsp. olive oil.

2. In a large bowl, toss potatoes with 1 Tbsp. olive oil. Place in one section of prepared sheet pan. In same bowl, toss asparagus with 1 Tbsp. olive oil; place in another section of pan. Sprinkle salt and pepper over potatoes and asparagus.

3. In same bowl, toss apple with 1 tsp. olive oil. Mix brown sugar, cinnamon and ginger; sprinkle over apples and toss to coat. Transfer to a different section of pan.

4. Brush pork chops with remaining olive oil; sprinkle both sides with Southwest seasoning. Place chops in remaining section of pan. Bake until a thermometer inserted in pork reads 145° and potatoes and apples are tender, 20-25 minutes. Let stand 5 minutes.

Per serving: 486 cal., 23g fat (5g sat. fat), 82mg chol., 447mg sod., 32g carb. (10g sugars, 5g fiber), 37g pro.

SHEET PAN PINEAPPLE CHICKEN FAJITAS

I combined chicken and pineapple for a new fajita flavor. Just a little sweet, it's a sheet of happiness right out of the oven.
—Nancy Heishman, Las Vegas, NV

Prep: 20 min. • **Cook:** 20 min.
Makes: 6 servings

- 2 Tbsp. coconut oil, melted
- 3 tsp. chili powder
- 2 tsp. ground cumin
- 1 tsp. garlic powder
- ¾ tsp. kosher salt
- 1½ lbs. chicken tenderloins, halved lengthwise
- 1 large red or sweet onion, halved and sliced (about 2 cups)
- 1 large sweet red pepper, cut into ½-in. strips
- 1 large green pepper, cut into ½-in. strips
- 1 Tbsp. minced seeded jalapeno pepper
- 2 cans (8 oz. each) unsweetened pineapple tidbits, drained
- 2 Tbsp. honey
- 2 Tbsp. lime juice
- 12 corn tortillas (6 in.), warmed
- Optional toppings: pico de gallo, sour cream, shredded Mexican cheese blend and sliced avocado
- Lime wedges, optional

1. Preheat oven to 425°. In a large bowl, mix first five ingredients; stir in chicken. Add onion, peppers, pineapple, honey and lime juice; toss to combine. Spread evenly in two greased 15x10x1-in. pans.

2. Roast 10 minutes, rotating pans halfway through cooking. Remove pans from oven; preheat broiler.

3. Broil chicken mixture, one pan at a time, 3-4 in. from heat until vegetables are lightly browned and chicken is no longer pink, 3-5 minutes. Serve in tortillas, with toppings and lime wedges as desired.

Per 2 fajitas: 359 cal., 8g fat (4g sat. fat), 56mg chol., 372mg sod., 45g carb. (19g sugars, 6g fiber), 31g pro.

SHEET PAN PINEAPPLE CHICKEN FAJITAS

SHEET PAN CHICKEN PARMESAN

SHEET PAN CHICKEN PARMESAN

Saucy chicken, melty mozzarella and crisp-tender broccoli, all in one pan. Dinner is served.

—Becky Hardin, St. Peters, MO

Prep: 15 min. • **Bake:** 20 min. + broiling
Makes: 4 servings

- 1 large egg
- ½ cup panko (Japanese) bread crumbs
- ½ cup grated Parmesan cheese
- ½ tsp. salt
- 1 tsp. pepper
- 1 tsp. garlic powder
- 4 boneless skinless chicken breast halves (6 oz. each)
- Olive oil-flavored cooking spray
- 4 cups fresh or frozen broccoli florets (about 10 oz.)
- 1 cup marinara sauce
- 1 cup shredded mozzarella cheese
- ¼ cup minced fresh basil, optional

1. Preheat oven to 400°. Lightly coat a 15x10x1-in. sheet pan with cooking spray.
2. In a shallow bowl, whisk the egg. In a separate shallow bowl, stir together the next five ingredients. Dip chicken breast in egg; allow excess to drip off. Then dip in crumb mixture, patting to help coating adhere. Repeat with remaining chicken. Place chicken breasts in center third of baking sheet. Spritz with cooking spray.
3. Bake 10 minutes. Remove from oven. Spread broccoli in a single layer along both sides of sheet pan (if broccoli is frozen, break pieces apart). Return to oven; bake 10 minutes longer. Remove from oven.
4. Preheat broiler. Spread marinara sauce over chicken; top with shredded cheese. Broil chicken and broccoli 3-4 in. from heat until the cheese is golden brown and vegetables are tender, 3-5 minutes. If desired, sprinkle with basil.

Per serving: 504 cal., 17g fat (7g sat. fat), 147mg chol., 1151mg sod., 27g carb. (10g sugars, 8g fiber), 52g pro.

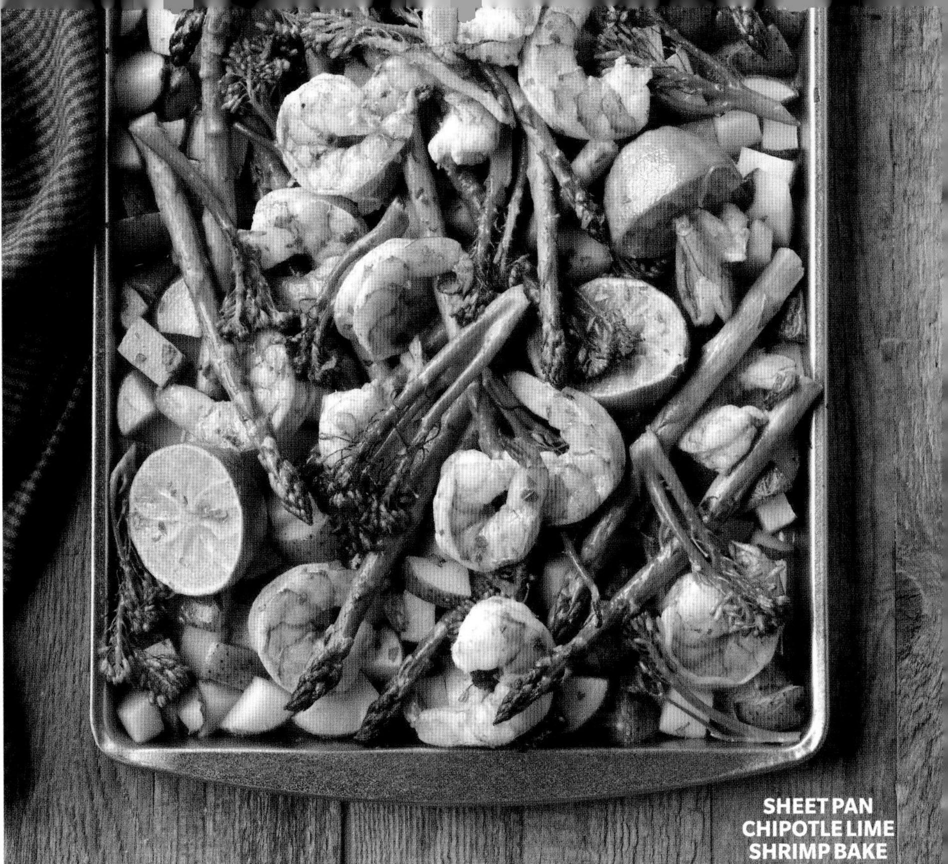

SHEET PAN CHIPOTLE LIME SHRIMP BAKE

SHEET PAN CHIPOTLE LIME SHRIMP BAKE

This seafood dinner for company tastes amazing but takes little effort to throw together. Use asparagus, Broccolini or a mix of the two. It is all about what is available for a decent price.

—Colleen Delawder, Herndon, VA

Prep: 10 min. • **Bake:** 45 min.
Makes: 4 servings

- 1½ lbs. baby red potatoes, cut into ¾-in. cubes
- 1 Tbsp. extra virgin olive oil
- ¾ tsp. sea salt, divided
- 3 medium limes
- ¼ cup unsalted butter, melted
- 1 tsp. ground chipotle pepper
- ½ lb. fresh asparagus, trimmed
- ½ lb. Broccolini or broccoli cut into small florets
- 1 lb. uncooked shrimp (16-20 per lb.), peeled and deveined
- 2 Tbsp. minced fresh cilantro

1. Preheat oven to 400°. Place potatoes in a greased 15x10x1-in. sheet pan; drizzle with olive oil. Sprinkle with ¼ tsp. sea salt; stir to combine. Bake for 30 minutes. Meanwhile, squeeze ⅓ cup juice from limes, reserving fruit. Combine lime juice, melted butter, chipotle and remaining sea salt.
2. Remove sheet pan from oven; stir the potatoes. Arrange asparagus, Broccolini, shrimp and reserved limes on top of potatoes. Pour lime juice mixture over vegetables and shrimp.
3. Bake until shrimp turn pink and vegetables are tender, about 10 minutes. Sprinkle with cilantro.

Per serving: 394 cal., 17g fat (8g sat. fat), 168mg chol., 535mg sod., 41g carb. (4g sugars, 6g fiber), 25g pro.

HOISIN SRIRACHA SHEET PAN CHICKEN

HOISIN SRIRACHA SHEET PAN CHICKEN

The convenience and simplicity of this chicken dinner make it extra awesome. Change up the veggies throughout the year—the sticky-spicy-sweet sauce is good on all of them!

—Julie Peterson, Crofton, MD

Prep: 20 min. • **Bake:** 40 min.
Makes: 4 servings

- ⅓ cup hoisin sauce
- ⅓ cup reduced-sodium soy sauce
- 2 Tbsp. maple syrup
- 2 Tbsp. Sriracha Asian hot chili sauce
- 1 Tbsp. rice vinegar
- 2 tsp. sesame oil
- 2 garlic cloves, minced
- ½ tsp. minced fresh gingerroot
- 4 bone-in chicken thighs (6 oz. each)
- ¼ tsp. salt
- ¼ tsp. pepper
- 1 medium sweet potato, cut into ¾-in. cubes
- 2 Tbsp. olive oil, divided
- 4 cups fresh cauliflowerets
- 1 medium sweet red pepper, cut into ¾-in. pieces
- Sesame seeds, optional

1. Preheat oven to 400°. Whisk together the first eight ingredients. Set aside.
2. Sprinkle chicken with salt and pepper. Place chicken and sweet potato cubes in a single layer in a foil-lined 15x10x1-in. sheet pan. Drizzle with 1 Tbsp. olive oil and a third of hoisin mixture; toss to coat.
3. Bake 15 minutes; turn the chicken and potatoes. Add cauliflower and red pepper; drizzle with another third of hoisin mixture and the remaining olive oil. Bake until a thermometer inserted in chicken reads 170°-175°, about 25 minutes longer. Drizzle with remaining sauce. If desired, sprinkle with sesame seeds.

Per serving: 504 cal., 17g fat (7g sat. fat), 147mg chol., 1151mg sod., 27g carb. (10g sugars, 8g fiber), 52g pro.

SAUSAGE & PEPPER SHEET PAN SANDWICHES

Sausage with peppers was a staple when I was growing up. Now I do it the easy way—just grab a sheet pan and the ingredients, then let my oven do the work.

—Debbie Glasscock, Conway, AR

Prep: 20 min. • **Bake:** 35 min.
Makes: 6 servings

- 1 lb. uncooked sweet Italian turkey sausage links, roughly chopped
- 3 medium sweet red peppers, seeded and sliced
- 1 large onion, halved and sliced
- 1 Tbsp. olive oil
- 6 hot dog buns, split
- 6 slices provolone cheese

1. Preheat oven to 375°. Place the sausage pieces in a 15x10x1-in. sheet pan, arranging the peppers and onions around sausage. Drizzle the olive oil over the sausage and vegetables; bake, stirring mixture after 15 minutes, until sausage is no longer pink and vegetables are tender, 30-35 minutes.
2. During last 5 minutes of baking, arrange buns cut side up in a second sheet pan; top each bun bottom with a cheese slice. Bake until buns are golden brown and cheese is melted. Spoon sausage and pepper mixture onto bun bottoms. Replace tops.

Per sandwich: 315 cal., 15g fat (5g sat. fat), 43mg chol., 672mg sod., 28g carb. (7g sugars, 2g fiber), 18g pro.

EDITOR'S CHOICE

SWEET & TANGY SALMON WITH GREEN BEANS

I'm always up for new ways to cook salmon. In this dish, a sweet sauce gives the fish and green beans some down-home barbecue tang. Even our kids love it.

—Aliesha Caldwell, Robersonville, NC

Prep: 20 min.
Bake: 15 min.
Makes: 4 servings

- 4 salmon fillets (6 oz. each)
- 1 Tbsp. butter
- 2 Tbsp. brown sugar
- 2 Tbsp. reduced-sodium soy sauce
- 2 Tbsp. Dijon mustard
- 1 Tbsp. olive oil
- ½ tsp. pepper
- ⅛ tsp. salt
- 1 lb. fresh green beans, trimmed

1. Preheat oven to 425°. Place fillets on a 15x10x1-in. baking pan coated with cooking spray. In a small skillet, melt butter; stir in the brown sugar, soy sauce, mustard, oil, pepper and salt. Brush half of the mixture over salmon.

2. Place green beans in a large bowl; drizzle with remaining brown sugar mixture and toss to coat. Arrange green beans around fillets. Roast 14-16 minutes or until fish just begins to flake easily with a fork and green beans are crisp-tender.

Per 1 fillet with ¾ cup green beans: 394 cal., 22g fat (5g sat. fat), 93mg chol., 661mg sod., 17g carb. (10g sugars, 4g fiber), 31g pro.

SWEET & TANGY SALMON WITH GREEN BEANS

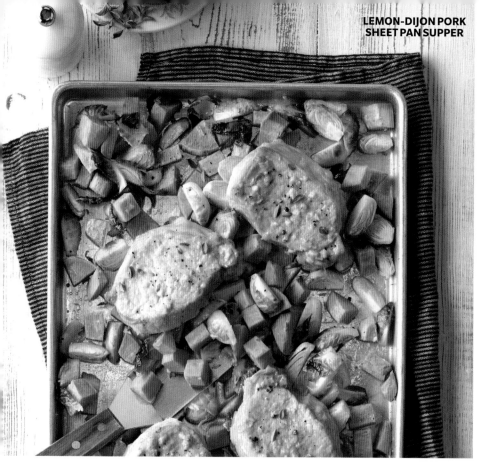

LEMON-DIJON PORK SHEET PAN SUPPER

SHEET PAN TILAPIA & VEGETABLE MEDLEY

Unlike some one-pan dinners that require precooking in a skillet or pot, this one, with fish and spring veggies, uses just the sheet pan, period. How sweet is that?

—Judy Batson, Tampa, FL

Prep: 10 min. • **Bake:** 20 min. + broiling
Makes: 2 servings

- 2 medium Yukon Gold potatoes, cut into wedges
- 3 large fresh Brussels sprouts, thinly sliced
- 3 large radishes, thinly sliced
- 1 cup fresh sugar snap peas, cut into ½-in. pieces
- 1 small carrot, thinly sliced
- 2 Tbsp. butter, melted
- ½ tsp. garlic salt
- ½ tsp. pepper
- 2 tilapia fillets (6 oz. each)
- 2 tsp. minced fresh tarragon or ½ tsp. dried tarragon
- ⅛ tsp. salt
- 1 Tbsp. butter, softened
- Lemon wedges and tartar sauce, optional

1. Preheat oven to 450°. Line a 15x10x1-in. sheet pan with foil; grease foil.
2. In a large bowl, combine the first five ingredients. Add melted butter, garlic salt and pepper; toss to coat. Place vegetables in a single layer in prepared pan; bake until potatoes are tender, about 20 minutes.
3. Remove from oven; preheat broiler. Arrange vegetables on one side of sheet pan. Add fish to other side. Sprinkle fillets with tarragon and salt; dot with softened butter. Broil 4-5 in. from heat until fish flakes easily with a fork, about 5 minutes. If desired, serve with lemon wedges and tartar sauce.

Per serving: 555 cal., 20g fat (12g sat. fat), 129mg chol., 892mg sod., 56g carb. (8g sugars, 8g fiber), 41g pro.

LEMON-DIJON PORK SHEET PAN SUPPER

Most nights, I need something on the table with minimal effort and maximum results. This sheet pan supper has become an all-time favorite, not only because of its bright flavors, but also because of its speedy clean-up time!

—Elisabeth Larsen, Pleasant Grove, UT

Takes: 30 min. • **Makes:** 4 servings

- 4 tsp. Dijon mustard
- 2 tsp. grated lemon zest
- 1 garlic clove, minced
- ½ tsp. salt
- 2 Tbsp. canola oil
- 1½ lbs. sweet potatoes (about 3 medium), cut into ½-in. cubes
- 1 lb. fresh Brussels sprouts (about 4 cups), quartered
- 4 boneless pork loin chops (6 oz. each)
- Coarsely ground pepper, optional

1. Preheat oven to 425°. In a large bowl, mix first four ingredients; gradually whisk in oil. Remove 1 Tbsp. mixture for brushing pork. Add vegetables to remaining mixture; toss to coat.
2. Place pork chops and vegetables in a 15x10x1-in. pan coated with cooking spray. Brush chops with the reserved mustard mixture. Roast 10 minutes.
3. Turn chops and stir vegetables; roast until a thermometer inserted in pork reads 145° and vegetables are tender, 10-15 minutes. If desired, sprinkle with pepper.

Per 1 pork chop with 1¼ cups vegetables: 516 cal., 17g fat (4g sat. fat), 82mg chol., 505mg sod., 51g carb. (19g sugars, 9g fiber), 39g pro. **Diabetic exchanges:** 5 lean meat, 3 starch, 1½ fat, 1 vegetable.

SHEET PAN TILAPIA & VEGETABLE MEDLEY

CREAMY HASH BROWN CASSEROLE

A creamy cheese sauce and crunchy cornflake topping make this versatile potato casserole a popular standby for family dinners and potlucks.

—Teresa Stutzman, Adair, OK

Prep: 10 min. • **Bake:** 50 min.
Makes: 8 servings

- 1 pkg. (32 oz.) frozen cubed hash brown potatoes, thawed
- 1 lb. process cheese (Velveeta), cubed
- 2 cups sour cream
- 1 can (10¾ oz.) condensed cream of chicken soup, undiluted
- ¾ cup butter, melted, divided
- 3 Tbsp. chopped onion
- ¼ tsp. paprika
- 2 cups cornflakes, lightly crushed
- Fresh savory, optional

In a large bowl, combine the hash browns, cheese, sour cream, soup, ½ cup butter and onion. Spread into a greased 13x9-in. baking dish. Sprinkle with paprika. Combine the cornflakes and remaining butter; sprinkle on top. Bake, covered, at 350° for 40-50 minutes or until heated through. Uncover, bake for 10 minutes longer or until top is golden brown. If desired, garnish with savory.

Freeze option Cover and freeze unbaked casserole. To use, partially thaw in the refrigerator overnight. Remove from refrigerator 30 minutes before baking. Preheat oven to 350°. Bake casserole as directed, increasing time as necessary to heat through and for a thermometer inserted in center to read 165°.

Per ¾ cup: 663 cal., 43g fat (27g sat. fat), 125mg chol., 1359mg sod., 49g carb. (9g sugars, 3g fiber), 19g pro.

BAKED GERMAN POTATO SALAD

What makes this German potato salad so different is that it's sweet instead of tangy. During the holidays, my family hosts an annual ham dinner, and this always makes a welcome appearance.

—Julie Myers, Lexington, OH

Prep: 50 min. • **Bake:** 30 min.
Makes: 10 servings

- 12 medium red potatoes (about 3 lbs.)
- 8 bacon strips
- 2 medium onions, chopped
- ¾ cup packed brown sugar
- ⅔ cup water, divided
- ⅓ cup white vinegar
- ⅓ cup sweet pickle juice
- 2 tsp. dried parsley flakes
- 1 tsp. salt
- ½ to ¾ tsp. celery seed
- 4½ tsp. all-purpose flour

1. In a saucepan, cook the potatoes until just tender; drain. Peel and slice into an ungreased 2-qt. baking dish; set aside.
2. In a skillet, cook bacon until crisp; drain, reserving 2 Tbsp. drippings. Crumble bacon and set aside. Saute onions in drippings until tender. Stir in the brown sugar, ½ cup water, vinegar, pickle juice, parsley, salt and celery seed. Simmer, uncovered, for 5-10 minutes.
3. Meanwhile, combine flour and remaining water until smooth; stir into onion mixture. Bring to a boil. Cook and stir for 2 minutes or until thickened. Pour over the potatoes. Add the bacon; gently stir to coat. Bake, uncovered, at 350° for 30 minutes or until heated through.
Per ¾ cup: 284 cal., 11g fat (4g sat. fat), 12mg chol., 434mg sod., 43g carb. (21g sugars, 3g fiber), 5g pro.

GARLIC-CHIVE BAKED FRIES

GARLIC-CHIVE BAKED FRIES

No one can resist golden brown fries seasoned with garlic and fresh chives. Their savory crunch pairs especially well with a juicy steak or grilled burger.

—Steve Westphal, Wind Lake, WI

Prep: 15 min. • **Bake:** 20 min.
Makes: 4 servings

- 4 medium russet potatoes
- 1 Tbsp. olive oil
- 4 tsp. dried minced chives
- ½ tsp. salt
- ½ tsp. garlic powder
- ¼ tsp. pepper

1. Preheat oven to 450°. Cut potatoes into ¼-in. julienne strips. Rinse well and pat dry.
2. Transfer potatoes to a large bowl. Drizzle with oil and sprinkle with the remaining ingredients. Toss to coat. Arrange in a single layer in two 15x10x1-in. baking pans coated with cooking spray.
3. Bake 20-25 minutes or until lightly browned, turning once.
Per serving: 200 cal., 4g fat (1g sat. fat), 0 chol., 308mg sod., 39g carb. (3g sugars, 4g fiber), 5g pro.

DOUBLE-BAKED MASHED POTATOES

DOUBLE-BAKED MASHED POTATOES

Dress up an all-time favorite with savory fixings. You can easily double or triple it to serve a crowd.

—Anna Mayer, Fort Branch, IN

Prep: 30 min. • **Bake:** 30 min.
Makes: 6 servings

- 2½ lbs. medium potatoes, peeled
- 1 cup sour cream
- ¼ cup whole milk
- 2 Tbsp. butter, melted
- 1½ cups shredded cheddar cheese, divided
- ½ cup chopped onion
- 5 bacon strips, cooked and crumbled
- ½ tsp. salt
- ⅛ tsp. pepper

1. Place potatoes in a large saucepan and cover with water. Bring to a boil over high heat. Reduce the heat to medium; cover and cook for 15-20 minutes or until the potatoes are tender. Drain.

2. In a large bowl, mash potatoes. Add the sour cream, milk, butter and 1 cup cheese. Stir in the onion, bacon, salt and pepper. Spoon into a greased 2-qt. baking dish. Sprinkle with remaining cheese.

3. Bake, uncovered, at 350° for 30-35 minutes or until heated though.

Per ¾ cup: 363 cal., 21g fat (14g sat. fat), 74mg chol., 537mg sod., 30g carb. (4g sugars, 2g fiber), 12g pro.

THREE-BEAN BAKED BEANS

I got this recipe from an aunt and made a couple of changes to suit our tastes. With ground beef and bacon mixed in, these satisfying beans are a big hit at backyard barbecues and church picnics.

—Julie Currington, Gahanna, OH

Prep: 20 min. • **Bake:** 1 hour
Makes: 12 servings

- ½ lb. ground beef
- 5 bacon strips, diced
- ½ cup chopped onion
- ⅓ cup packed brown sugar
- ¼ cup sugar
- ¼ cup ketchup
- ¼ cup barbecue sauce
- 2 Tbsp. molasses
- 2 Tbsp. prepared mustard
- ½ tsp. chili powder
- ½ tsp. salt
- 2 cans (16 oz. each) pork and beans, undrained
- 1 can (16 oz.) butter beans, rinsed and drained
- 1 can (16 oz.) kidney beans, rinsed and drained

1. Preheat oven to 350°. In a large skillet, cook and crumble beef with bacon and onion over medium heat until beef is no longer pink; drain.

2. Stir in sugars, ketchup, barbecue sauce, molasses, mustard, chili powder and salt until blended. Stir in beans. Transfer to a greased 2½-qt. baking dish. Bake, covered, until beans reach desired thickness, about 1 hour.

Freeze option Freeze cooled bean mixture in freezer containers. To use, partially thaw in refrigerator overnight. Heat through in a saucepan, stirring occasionally and adding a little water if necessary.

Per ¾ cup: 269 cal., 8g fat (2g sat. fat), 19mg chol., 708mg sod., 42g carb. (21g sugars, 7g fiber), 13g pro.

THREE-BEAN BAKED BEANS

CHEESY CORN
SPOON BREAD

CHEESY CORN SPOON BREAD

Homey and comforting, this moist side dish, almost like a souffle, is always a favorite. The jalapeno pepper adds just the right bite. Seconds helpings of this splendid casserole are common—leftovers aren't.
—Katherine Franklin, Carbondale, IL

Prep: 15 min. • **Bake:** 35 min.
Makes: 15 servings

- ¼ cup butter, cubed
- 1 medium onion, chopped
- 2 large eggs
- 2 cups sour cream
- 1 can (15¼ oz.) whole kernel corn, drained
- 1 can (14¾ oz.) cream-style corn
- ¼ tsp. salt
- ¼ tsp. pepper
- 1 pkg. (8½ oz.) cornbread/muffin mix
- 2 medium jalapeno peppers, divided
- 2 cups shredded cheddar cheese, divided

1. Preheat oven to 375°. In a large skillet, heat butter over medium-high heat. Add onion; saute until tender. Set aside.
2. Beat eggs; add sour cream, both cans of corn, salt and pepper. Stir in cornbread mix just until blended. Mince 1 jalapeno pepper; fold into corn mixture with the sauteed onion and 1½ cups of cheese.
3. Transfer to a greased shallow 3-qt. baking dish. Sprinkle with remaining cheese. Bake, uncovered, until a toothpick inserted in center comes out clean, 35-40 minutes; cool slightly. Slice the remaining jalapeno; sprinkle over dish.
Note Wear disposable gloves when cutting hot peppers; the oils can burn skin. Avoid touching your face.
Per serving: 266 cal., 17g fat (9g sat. fat), 56mg chol., 470mg sod., 21g carb. (7g sugars, 2g fiber), 8g pro.

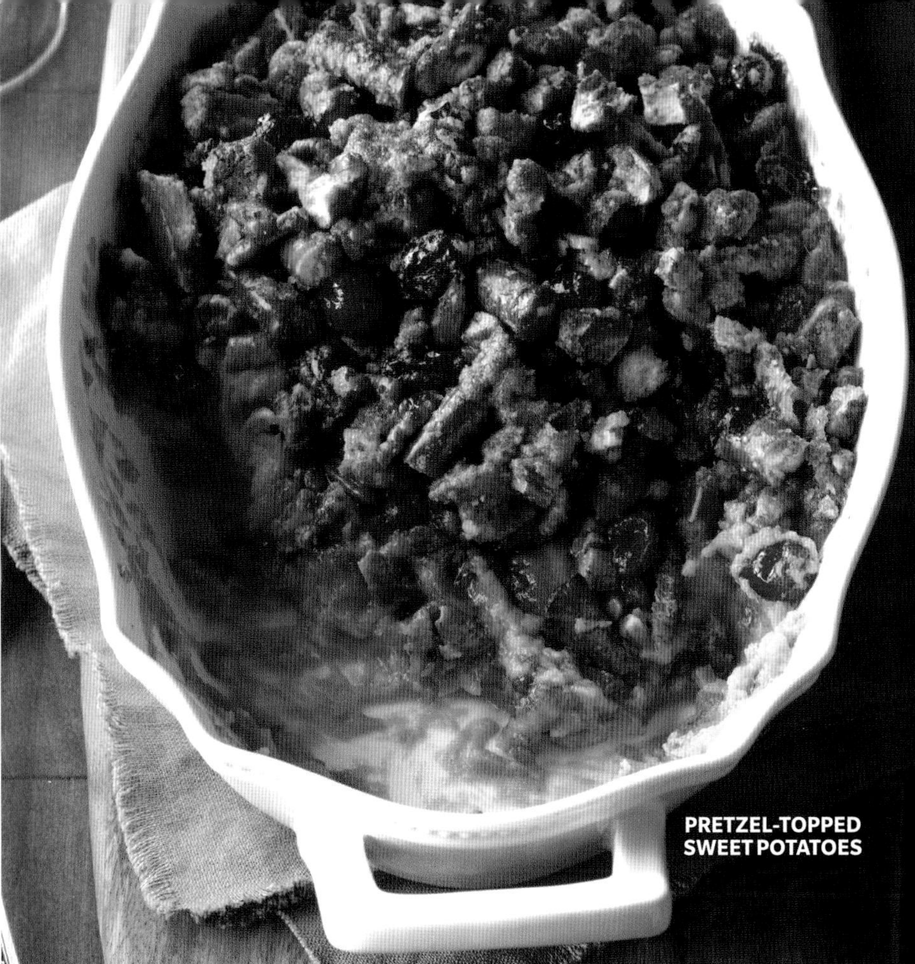

PRETZEL-TOPPED SWEET POTATOES

PRETZEL-TOPPED SWEET POTATOES

Everyone I've shared this recipe with says it's the tastiest way to serve sweet potatoes. I make it for special dinners and even for brunch as a colorful side dish. The sweet, tart and salty flavors are a delightful treat.
—Sue Mallory, Lancaster, PA

Prep: 20 min. • **Bake:** 25 min.
Makes: 12 servings

- 2 cups chopped pretzel rods (about 13)
- 1 cup chopped pecans
- 1 cup fresh or frozen cranberries
- 1 cup packed brown sugar
- 1 cup butter, melted, divided
- 1 can (2½ lbs.) sweet potatoes, drained
- 1 can (5 oz.) evaporated milk
- ½ cup sugar
- 1 tsp. vanilla extract

1. In a large bowl, combine the pretzels, pecans, cranberries, brown sugar and ½ cup butter; set aside.
2. In a large bowl, beat sweet potatoes until smooth. Add the milk, sugar, vanilla and remaining butter; beat until well blended.
3. Spoon into a greased shallow 2-qt. baking dish; sprinkle with pretzel mixture. Bake, uncovered, at 350° for 25-30 minutes or until the edges are bubbly.
Per ¾ cup: 484 cal., 24g fat (11g sat. fat), 44mg chol., 606mg sod., 66g carb. (43g sugars, 4g fiber), 5g pro.

NEVER-FAIL SCALLOPED POTATOES

NEVER-FAIL SCALLOPED POTATOES

Take the chill off a cold day with something special to accompany your favorite meaty entree. These creamy scalloped potatoes are sure to be a winner.

—Agnes Ward, Stratford, ON

Prep: 25 min. • **Bake:** 1 hour
Makes: 6 servings

- 2 Tbsp. butter
- 3 Tbsp. all-purpose flour
- 1 tsp. salt
- ¼ tsp. pepper
- 1½ cups fat-free milk
- ½ cup shredded reduced-fat cheddar cheese
- 2 lbs. red potatoes, peeled and thinly sliced (about 4 cups)
- 1 cup thinly sliced onions, divided

1. Preheat oven to 350°. In a saucepan, melt butter; stir in flour, salt and pepper until smooth. Gradually whisk in milk. Bring to a boil, stirring constantly; cook and stir until thickened, about 2 minutes. Remove from heat; stir in cheese until melted.

2. Coat an 8-in. square baking dish with cooking spray. Place half of the potatoes in dish; layer with ½ cup onion and half of the cheese sauce. Repeat layers.

3. Bake, covered, 50 minutes. Uncover; bake until bubbly and potatoes are tender, 10-15 minutes.

Per ¾ cup: 215 cal., 6g fat (4g sat. fat), 18mg chol., 523mg sod., 32g carb. (5g sugars, 3g fiber), 8g pro. **Diabetic exchanges:** 2 starch, 1 fat.

CAULIFLOWER CASSEROLE

To dress up cauliflower, Mom liked to use a marvelous mixture of a cheesy sauce, bright red and green pepper pieces and crushed cornflakes.

—Linda McGinty, Parma, OH

Prep: 15 min. • **Bake:** 30 min.
Makes: 8 servings

- 1 medium head cauliflower, broken into florets
- 1 cup sour cream
- 1 cup shredded cheddar cheese
- ½ cup crushed cornflakes
- ¼ cup chopped green pepper
- ¼ cup chopped sweet red pepper
- 1 tsp. salt
- ¼ cup grated Parmesan cheese
- Paprika

1. Place 1 in. of water in a saucepan; add cauliflower. Bring to a boil. Reduce heat; cover and simmer for 5-10 minutes or until crisp-tender. Drain.

2. In a large bowl, combine the cauliflower, sour cream, cheddar cheese, cornflakes, peppers and salt; transfer to a greased 2-qt. baking dish. Sprinkle with Parmesan cheese and paprika.

3. Bake, uncovered, at 325° for 30-35 minutes or until heated through.

Per serving: 162 cal., 10g fat (7g sat. fat), 37mg chol., 503mg sod., 10g carb. (4g sugars, 2g fiber), 7g pro.

When purchasing fresh cauliflower, look for a head with compact florets that are free from yellow or brown spots. The leaves should be crisp and green, not withered or discolored. Tightly wrap an unwashed head of cauliflower and refrigerate for up to five days. Before using, wash and remove the leaves at the base and trim the stem.

CAULIFLOWER CASSEROLE

GARLIC-ROASTED BRUSSELS SPROUTS WITH MUSTARD SAUCE

Don't be afraid to bring out the Brussels sprouts. Mellowed by roasting and tossed with mustard sauce, they may just convert even the most skeptical folks.
—Becky Walch, Orland, CA

Takes: 20 min. • **Makes:** 6 servings

- 1½ lbs. fresh Brussels sprouts, halved
- 2 Tbsp. olive oil
- 3 garlic cloves, minced
- ½ cup heavy whipping cream
- 3 Tbsp. Dijon mustard
- ⅛ tsp. white pepper
- Dash salt

1. Place Brussels sprouts in an ungreased 15x10x1-in. baking pan. Combine oil and garlic; drizzle over Brussels sprouts and toss to coat.
2. Bake, uncovered, at 450° for 10-15 minutes or until sprouts are tender, stirring occasionally.
3. Meanwhile, in a small saucepan, combine the cream, mustard, pepper and salt. Bring to a gentle boil; cook for 1-2 minutes or until slightly thickened. Spoon over Brussels sprouts.

Per ¾ cup: 167 cal., 12g fat (5g sat. fat), 27mg chol., 241mg sod., 13g carb. (3g sugars, 4g fiber), 4g pro.

SIMPLE AU GRATIN POTATOES

These super cheesy potatoes are always welcome at our dinner table. A perfect complement to ham, this homey potato gratin also goes well with pork, chicken and other entrees.

—Cris O'Brien, Virginia Beach, VA

Prep: 20 min. • **Bake:** 1½ hours
Makes: 8 servings

- 3 Tbsp. butter
- 3 Tbsp. all-purpose flour
- 1½ tsp. salt
- ⅛ tsp. pepper
- 2 cups 2% milk
- 1 cup shredded cheddar cheese
- 5 cups thinly sliced peeled potatoes (about 6 medium)
- ½ cup chopped onion

1. Preheat oven to 350°. In a large saucepan, melt butter over low heat. Stir in flour, salt and pepper until smooth. Gradually add milk. Bring to a boil; cook and stir 2 minutes or until thickened. Remove from heat; stir in cheese until melted. Add potatoes and onion.
2. Transfer to a greased 2-qt. baking dish. Cover and bake 1 hour. Uncover; bake 30-40 minutes or until the potatoes are tender.
Per ¾ cup: 224 cal., 10g fat (7g sat. fat), 35mg chol., 605mg sod., 26g carb. (4g sugars, 2g fiber), 7g pro.

ROASTED GREEN VEGETABLE MEDLEY

ROASTED GREEN VEGETABLE MEDLEY

Roasting broccoli, green beans and Brussels sprouts makes for a lovely vegetable combo.

—Suzan Crouch, Grand Prairie, TX

Prep: 20 min. • **Bake:** 20 min.
Makes: 10 servings

- 1 lb. fresh green beans, trimmed and cut into 2-in. pieces
- 4 cups fresh broccoli florets
- 10 small fresh mushrooms, halved
- 8 fresh Brussels sprouts, halved
- 2 medium carrots, cut into ¼-in. slices
- 1 medium onion, halved and sliced
- 3 to 5 garlic cloves, thinly sliced
- 4 Tbsp. olive oil, divided
- ½ cup grated Parmesan cheese
- 3 Tbsp. julienned fresh basil leaves, optional
- 2 Tbsp. minced fresh parsley
- 1 Tbsp. grated lemon zest
- 2 Tbsp. lemon juice
- ¼ tsp. salt
- ¼ tsp. pepper

1. Preheat oven to 425°. Place first seven ingredients in a large bowl; toss mixture with 2 Tbsp. oil. Divide between two 15x10x1-in. pans coated with cooking spray.
2. Roast until tender, 20-25 minutes, stirring occasionally. Transfer to a large bowl. Mix remaining ingredients with remaining oil; toss with vegetables.
Per serving: 109 cal., 7g fat (1g sat. fat), 3mg chol., 96mg sod., 10g carb. (3g sugars, 3g fiber), 4g pro. **Diabetic exchanges:** 1 vegetable, 1 fat.

EDITOR'S CHOICE

CAULIFLOWER WITH ROASTED ALMOND & PEPPER DIP

Make cauliflower sing with this sauce, rich in both color and flavor. The sauce takes some time but is well worth it.
—Lauren Knoelke, Milwaukee, WI

Prep: 40 min. • **Bake:** 35 min.
Makes: 10 servings (2¼ cups dip)

- 10 cups water
- 1 cup olive oil, divided
- ¾ cup sherry or red wine vinegar, divided
- 3 Tbsp. salt
- 1 bay leaf
- 1 Tbsp. crushed red pepper flakes
- 1 large head cauliflower
- ½ cup whole almonds, toasted
- ½ cup soft whole wheat or white bread crumbs, toasted
- ½ cup fire-roasted crushed tomatoes
- 1 jar (8 oz.) roasted sweet red peppers, drained
- 2 Tbsp. minced fresh parsley
- 2 garlic cloves
- 1 tsp. sweet paprika
- ½ tsp. salt
- ¼ tsp. freshly ground pepper

1. In a 6-qt. stockpot, bring water, ½ cup oil, ½ cup sherry, salt, bay leaf and pepper flakes to a boil. Add cauliflower. Reduce heat; simmer, uncovered, until a knife easily inserts into center, 15-20 minutes, turning halfway through cooking. Remove with a slotted spoon; drain well on paper towels.
2. Preheat oven to 450°. Place cauliflower on a greased wire rack in a 15x10x1-in. baking pan. Bake on a lower oven rack until dark golden, 35-40 minutes.
3. Meanwhile, place almonds, bread crumbs, tomatoes, roasted peppers, parsley, garlic, paprika, salt and pepper in a food processor; pulse until finely chopped. Add remaining sherry; process until blended. Continue processing while gradually adding remaining oil in a steady stream. Serve with cauliflower.

Per serving: 194 cal., 16g fat (2g sat. fat), 0 chol., 470mg sod., 9g carb. (3g sugars, 3g fiber), 4g pro.

SPINACH-PARM CASSEROLE

Some people aren't fond of spinach, but when the healthy green is baked inside a warm casserole with garlicky butter and Parmesan, they quickly change their minds!
—Judy Batson, Tampa, FL

Takes: 25 min. • **Makes:** 6 servings

- 2 lbs. fresh baby spinach
- 5 Tbsp. butter
- 3 Tbsp. olive oil
- 3 garlic cloves, minced
- 1 Tbsp. Italian seasoning
- ¾ tsp. salt
- 1 cup grated Parmesan cheese

1. Preheat oven to 400°. In a stockpot, bring 5 cups water to a boil. Add spinach; cook, covered, 1 minute or just until wilted. Drain well.
2. In a small skillet, heat butter and oil over medium-low heat. Add the garlic, Italian seasoning and salt; cook and stir until garlic is tender, 1-2 minutes.
3. Spread spinach in a greased 8-in. square or 1½-qt. baking dish. Drizzle with butter mixture; sprinkle with the cheese. Bake, uncovered, until cheese is lightly browned, 10-15 minutes.

Per ⅔ cup: 239 cal., 21g fat (9g sat. fat), 37mg chol., 703mg sod., 7g carb. (1g sugars, 3g fiber), 10g pro.

SPINACH-PARM
CASSEROLE

SWEET POTATO CINNAMON BREAD

My family loves quick breads. This one is perfectly spicy for a cool autumn day, and it's one of our faves. If you don't have mini loaf pans, the recipe works just as well in regular-sized pans.

—Nancy Foust, Stoneboro, PA

Prep: 20 min. • **Bake:** 35 min. + cooling
Makes: 4 loaves (6 slices each)

- 3½ cups all-purpose flour
- 2⅔ cups sugar
- 2 tsp. baking soda
- 1 tsp. salt
- ½ tsp. baking powder
- 1½ tsp. ground cinnamon
- 1 tsp. ground ginger
- ½ tsp. ground cloves
- 4 large eggs
- 2 cups mashed sweet potatoes
- ⅔ cup canola oil
- ⅔ cup 2% milk
- 1½ cups raisins
- 1 cup chopped walnuts

1. Preheat oven to 350°. In a large bowl, whisk the first eight ingredients. In another bowl, whisk the eggs, sweet potatoes, oil and milk until blended. Add to the flour mixture; stir just until moistened. Fold in the raisins and walnuts.

2. Transfer to four greased 5¾x3x2-in. loaf pans. Bake 35-40 minutes or until a toothpick inserted in center comes out clean. Cool in pans 10 minutes before removing to wire racks to cool.

For larger loaves Prepare recipe as directed, using two greased 9x5-in. loaf pans. Bake in preheated 350° oven 55-60 minutes or until a toothpick comes out clean. Makes two loaves (12 slices each).

Per slice: 299 cal., 10g fat (1g sat. fat), 36mg chol., 236mg sod., 49g carb. (30g sugars, 2g fiber), 4g pro.

SWEET POTATO CINNAMON BREAD

ANGEL BISCUITS

Light, airy biscuits taste heavenly when served with butter and honey.
—Faye Hintz, Springfield, MO

Prep: 20 min. + rising
Bake: 10 min.
Makes: 2½ dozen

- 2 pkg. (¼ oz. each) active dry yeast
- ¼ cup warm water (110° to 115°)
- 2 cups warm buttermilk (110° to 115°)
- 5 to 5½ cups all-purpose flour
- ⅓ cup sugar
- 2 tsp. salt
- 2 tsp. baking powder
- 1 tsp. baking soda
- 1 cup shortening
- Melted butter

1. In a small bowl, dissolve yeast in warm water. Let stand 5 minutes. Stir in warm buttermilk; set aside.
2. In a large bowl, combine the flour, sugar, salt, baking powder and baking soda. Cut in shortening with a pastry blender until mixture resembles coarse crumbs. Stir in yeast mixture.
3. Turn onto a lightly floured surface; knead lightly 3-4 times. Roll out dough to ½-in. thickness; cut with a 2½-in. round biscuit cutter or pumpkin-shaped cookie cutter. Place 2 in. apart on lightly greased baking sheets. Cover with kitchen towels and let rise in a warm place until almost doubled, about 1 hour.
4. Bake at 450° for 8-10 minutes or until golden brown. Lightly brush tops with melted butter. Serve warm.

Per biscuit: 150 cal., 7g fat (2g sat. fat), 1mg chol., 244mg sod., 19g carb. (3g sugars, 1g fiber), 3g pro.

PERFECT PIZZA CRUST

I spent years trying different recipes and techniques to achieve the perfect pizza crust. I'm proud to say this is it. Here is a crust that my family prefers over the pizza parlor's!

—Lesli Dustin, Nibley, UT

Prep: 20 min. + rising • **Bake:** 20 min.
Makes: 8 servings

- 1 Tbsp. active dry yeast
- 1½ cups warm water (110° to 115°)
- 2 Tbsp. sugar
- ½ tsp. salt
- 2 cups bread flour
- 1½ cups whole wheat flour
- Cornmeal
- Pizza toppings of your choice

1. In a large bowl, dissolve yeast in warm water. Add sugar, salt, 1 cup bread flour and the whole wheat flour. Beat until smooth. Stir in enough remaining bread flour to form a soft dough (the dough will be sticky).

2. Turn onto a floured surface; knead until smooth and elastic, 6-8 minutes. Place in a greased bowl, turning once to grease the top. Cover and let rise in a warm place until doubled, about 1 hour.

3. Punch the dough down and roll into a 15-in. circle. Grease a 14-in. pizza pan and sprinkle with cornmeal. Transfer dough to prepared pan; build up edges slightly. Add toppings of your choice.

4. Bake at 425° for 20-25 minutes or until crust is golden brown and toppings are lightly browned and heated through.

Per slice: 193 cal., 0 fat (0 sat. fat), 0 chol., 149mg sod., 42g carb. (3g sugars, 4g fiber), 8g pro.

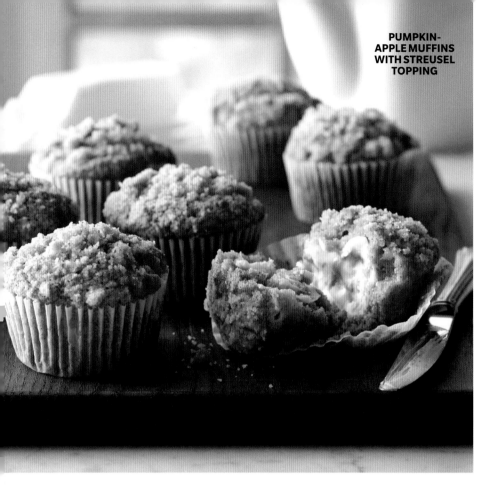

PUMPKIN-APPLE MUFFINS WITH STREUSEL TOPPING

My mother always made these muffins, fruity with pumpkin and apple, for family get-togethers. Now they're a favorite at my house, and my in-laws love them, too!

—Carolyn Riley, Carlisle, PA

Prep: 20 min. • **Bake:** 30 min. + cooling
Makes: 1½ dozen

- 2½ cups all-purpose flour
- 2 cups sugar
- 1 Tbsp. pumpkin pie spice
- 1 tsp. baking soda
- ½ tsp. salt
- 2 large eggs, lightly beaten
- 1 cup canned pumpkin
- ½ cup vegetable oil
- 2 cups finely chopped peeled apples

TOPPING
- ¼ cup sugar
- 2 Tbsp. all-purpose flour
- ½ tsp. ground cinnamon
- 1 Tbsp. butter or margarine

In a large bowl, combine the flour, sugar, pumpkin pie spice, baking soda and salt. Combine eggs, pumpkin and oil; stir into dry ingredients just until moistened. Fold in the apples. Fill 18 greased or paper-lined muffin cups three-fourths full. For topping, combine sugar, flour and cinnamon. Cut in butter until mixture resembles coarse crumbs; sprinkle 1 tsp. over each muffin. Bake at 350° until muffins test done, 30-35 minutes. Cool in pan 10 minutes before removing to a wire rack.

Per muffin: 243 cal., 8g fat (1g sat. fat), 25mg chol., 150mg sod., 42g carb. (27g sugars, 1g fiber), 3g pro.

LEMON BLUEBERRY BREAD

Of all the quick breads we had growing up, this beautifully glazed berry-studded loaf is the best! The lemon glaze adds a lustrous finish and locks in moisture.
—Julianne Johnson, Grove City, MN

Prep: 15 min. • **Bake:** 1 hour + cooling
Makes: 1 loaf (16 slices)

- ⅓ cup butter, melted
- 1 cup sugar
- 3 Tbsp. lemon juice
- 2 large eggs
- 1½ cups all-purpose flour
- 1 tsp. baking powder
- ½ tsp. salt
- ½ cup milk
- 1 cup fresh or frozen blueberries
- ½ cup chopped nuts
- 2 Tbsp. grated lemon zest

GLAZE

- 2 Tbsp. lemon juice
- ¼ cup sugar

1. In a large bowl, beat the butter, sugar, lemon juice and eggs. Combine the flour, baking powder and salt; stir into egg mixture alternately with milk, beating well after each addition. Fold in the blueberries, nuts and lemon zest.

2. Transfer to a greased 8x4-in. loaf pan. Bake at 350° for 60-70 minutes or until a toothpick inserted in the center comes out clean. Cool for 10 minutes before removing from pan to a wire rack.

3. Combine glaze ingredients; drizzle over warm bread. Cool completely.

Note If using frozen blueberries, use without thawing to avoid discoloring the batter while mixing.

Per slice: 181 cal., 7g fat (3g sat. fat), 38mg chol., 149mg sod., 27g carb. (17g sugars, 1g fiber), 3g pro.

LEMON BLUEBERRY BREAD

GIANT CINNAMON ROLL

GIANT CINNAMON ROLL

This must-try cinnamon roll is all about the pillowy texture, the sweet spices and the homemade caramel drizzle.
—Leah Rekau, Milwaukee, WI

Prep: 30 min. + rising • **Bake:** 30 min.
Makes: 12 servings

- 1 pkg. (¼ oz.) active dry yeast
- ½ cup warm water (110° to 115°)
- ½ cup heavy whipping cream, warmed (110° to 115°)
- ½ cup sugar
- ½ tsp. sea salt
- 3 to 4 cups all-purpose flour
- 1 large egg, beaten
- 3 Tbsp. butter, melted

FILLING

- ¼ cup butter, softened
- ¼ cup sugar
- 1 Tbsp. ground cinnamon

TOPPING

- 1 cup sugar
- 2 Tbsp. water
- 6 Tbsp. butter
- ½ cup heavy whipping cream
- 1 tsp. sea salt

1. Dissolve yeast in warm water and whipping cream until foamy. In another bowl, combine sugar and salt; add 3 cups flour, yeast mixture, egg and melted butter. Stir until moistened. Add enough of the remaining flour to form a soft dough.

2. Turn onto a lightly floured surface; knead until smooth and elastic, 3-4 minutes. Place in a greased bowl, turning once to grease top. Cover with plastic wrap; let rise in a warm place until doubled, 30 minutes.

3. Punch down dough. Turn onto a lightly floured surface; roll into a 15x12-in. rectangle. Spread softened butter over dough. Sprinkle with sugar and cinnamon. Using a pizza cutter, cut into 2-in.-wide strips. Roll up one strip and place in the center of a greased 9-in. deep-dish pie plate; wrap remaining strips around center to form one giant roll. Cover with greased plastic wrap; let rise until doubled, about 1 hour. Meanwhile, preheat oven to 350°.

4. Bake until golden brown, 30-40 minutes. If dough starts browning too quickly, cover loosely with foil. Cool on a wire rack.

5. To prepare topping, combine sugar and water in a small saucepan; cook over medium heat until it turns light amber. Add butter, stirring vigorously. Remove from heat; add cream while continuing to stir vigorously. Cool slightly. Pour ¾ cup sauce over warm roll; sprinkle with sea salt. Serve with the remaining sauce.

Per piece: 416 cal., 21g fat (13g sat. fat), 76mg chol., 354mg sod., 55g carb. (30g sugars, 1g fiber), 5g pro.

SOFT SESAME BREADSTICKS

SOFT SESAME BREADSTICKS

You can't beat the homemade goodness of soft and chewy breadsticks. For variety, skip the sesame seeds and sprinkle with a little garlic salt and Parmesan cheese.
—Nancy Johnson, Connersville, IN

Takes: 30 min. • **Makes:** 1 dozen

- 1¼ cups all-purpose flour
- 2 tsp. sugar
- 1½ tsp. baking powder
- ½ tsp. salt
- ⅔ cup milk
- 3 Tbsp. butter, melted
- 2 tsp. sesame seeds

1. Preheat oven to 450°. In a small bowl, combine flour, sugar, baking powder and salt. Gradually add milk and stir to form a soft dough. Turn onto a floured surface, knead gently 3-4 times. Roll dough into a 10x5x½-in. rectangle; cut rectangle into 12 breadsticks.

2. Place butter in a 13x9-in. baking pan. Place breadsticks in butter and turn to coat. Sprinkle with sesame seeds. Bake 14-18 minutes or until golden brown. Serve breadsticks warm.

Per 3 breadsticks: 257 cal., 11g fat (6g sat. fat), 29mg chol., 553mg sod., 34g carb. (5g sugars, 1g fiber), 6g pro.

DID YOU KNOW?

Sesame seeds are available as white or black seeds. They have a nutlike flavor and are sprinkled on breads, chicken, seafood and other dishes.

SALLY LUNN BATTER BREAD

The tantalizing aroma of this golden loaf baking in the oven draws people into my mother's kitchen. With its circular shape, it's pretty, too. I've never seen it last more than two days!

—Jeanne Voss, Anaheim Hills, CA

Prep: 15 min. + rising • **Bake:** 25 min.
Makes: 16 servings

- 1 pkg. (¼ oz.) active dry yeast
- ½ cup warm water (110° to 115°)
- 1 cup warm whole milk (110° to 115°)
- ½ cup butter, softened
- ¼ cup sugar
- 2 tsp. salt
- 3 large eggs
- 5½ to 6 cups all-purpose flour

HONEY BUTTER

- ½ cup butter, softened
- ½ cup honey

1. In a large bowl, dissolve yeast in warm water. Add the milk, butter, sugar, salt, eggs and 3 cups flour; beat until smooth. Stir in enough remaining flour to form a soft dough.

2. Do not knead. Place in a greased bowl, turning once to grease the top. Cover and let rise in a warm place until doubled, about 1 hour.

3. Stir the dough down. Spoon into a greased and floured 10-in. tube pan. Cover and let rise until doubled, about 1 hour.

4. Bake at 400° for 25-30 minutes or until golden brown. Remove from pan to a wire rack to cool.

5. Combine the honey butter ingredients until smooth. Serve with bread.

Per slice: 326 cal., 13g fat (8g sat. fat), 73mg chol., 431mg sod., 46g carb. (13g sugars, 1g fiber), 6g pro.

EDITOR'S CHOICE

ZUCCHINI MUFFINS

These muffins are studded with currants and walnuts and are an excellent way to use up a garden surplus of zucchini.

—Peg Gausz, Watchung, NJ

Prep: 20 min. • **Bake:** 25 min.
Makes: 6 muffins

- ¾ cup all-purpose flour
- ½ cup sugar
- ¼ tsp. baking powder
- ¼ tsp. baking soda
- ¼ tsp. salt
- ¼ tsp. ground cinnamon
- 1 large egg
- ¼ cup canola oil
- 1 cup finely shredded unpeeled zucchini
- ½ cup chopped walnuts
- ¼ cup dried currants or chopped raisins

1. In a large bowl, combine the first six ingredients. Combine the egg and oil; stir into dry ingredients just until moistened. Fold in the zucchini, walnuts and currants.

2. Coat muffin cups with cooking spray or use paper liners; fill three-fourths full with batter. Bake at 350° for 22-25 minutes or until a toothpick comes out clean. Cool for 5 minutes before removing from pan to a wire rack.

Per muffin: 318 cal., 16g fat (1g sat. fat), 35mg chol., 180mg sod., 40g carb. (25g sugars, 2g fiber), 6g pro.

TEST KITCHEN TIP

For a little extra pop of color, substitute shredded carrots for a small portion of the zucchini.

SUNFLOWER SEED & HONEY WHEAT BREAD

I've tried other bread recipes, but this one is keeper. I won $50 in a baking contest with a loaf that I had stored in the freezer.

—Mickey Turner, Grants Pass, OR

Prep: 40 min. + rising
Bake: 35 min. + cooling
Makes: 3 loaves (12 slices each)

- 2 pkg. (¼ oz. each) active dry yeast
- 3¼ cups warm water (110° to 115°)
- ¼ cup bread flour
- ⅓ cup canola oil
- ⅓ cup honey
- 3 tsp. salt
- 6½ to 7½ cups whole wheat flour
- ½ cup sunflower kernels
- 3 Tbsp. butter, melted

1. In a large bowl, dissolve yeast in warm water. Add the bread flour, oil, honey, salt and 4 cups whole wheat flour. Beat until smooth. Stir in the sunflower kernels and enough of the remaining flour to form a firm dough.

2. Turn onto a floured surface; knead until smooth and elastic, 6-8 minutes. Place in a greased bowl, turning once to grease the top. Cover and let rise in a warm place until doubled, about 1 hour.

3. Punch dough down; divide into three portions. Shape into loaves; place in three greased 8x4-in. loaf pans. Cover and let rise until doubled, about 30 minutes. Bake at 350° for 35-40 minutes or until golden brown. Brush with melted butter. Remove from pans to wire racks to cool.

Freeze option Securely wrap and freeze cooled loaves in foil, and place in resealable plastic freezer bags. To use, thaw at room temperature.

Per slice: 125 cal., 4g fat (1g sat. fat), 3mg chol., 212mg sod., 19g carb. (3g sugars, 3g fiber), 4g pro. **Diabetic exchanges:** 1 starch, 1 fat.

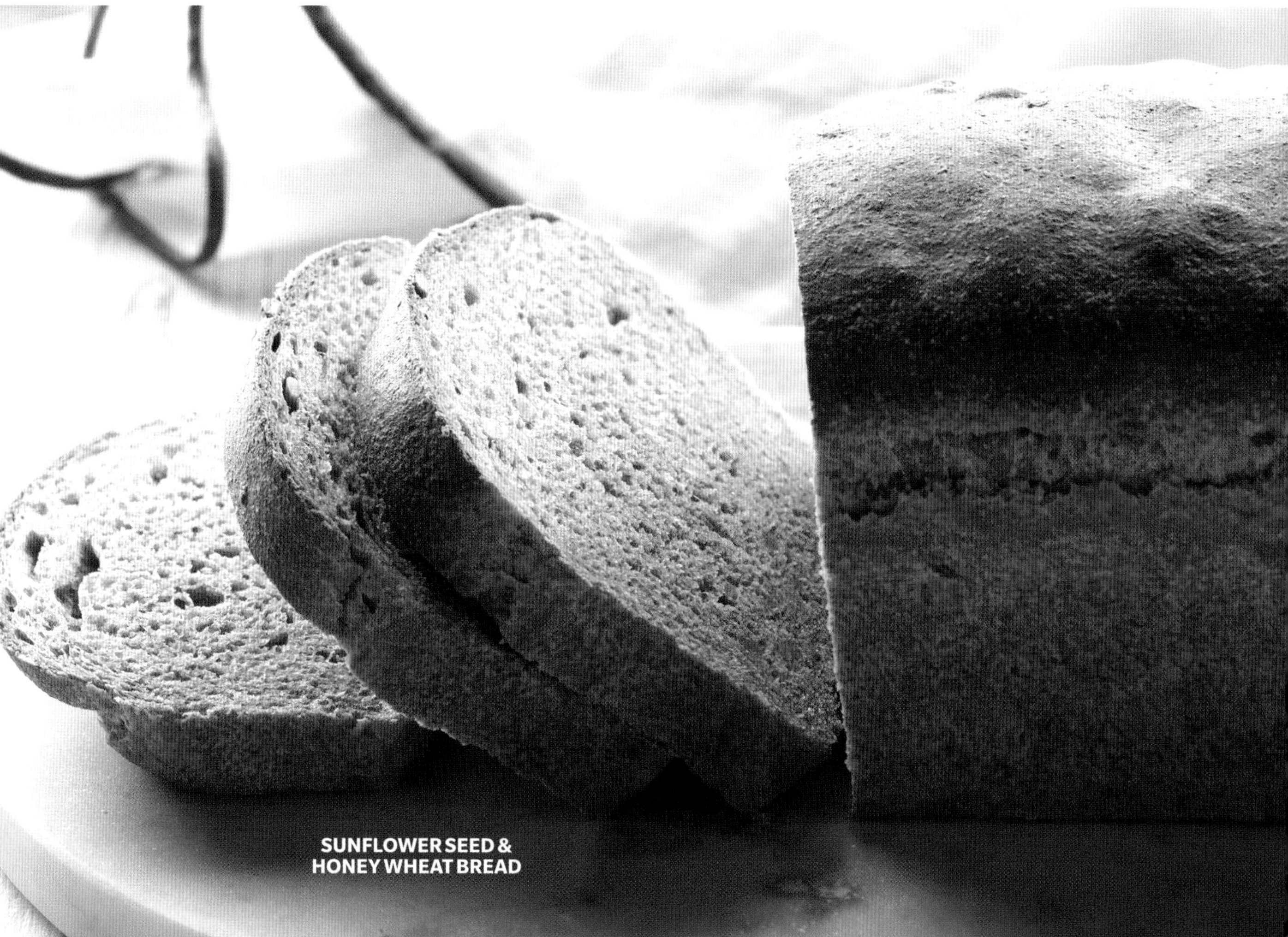

SUNFLOWER SEED & HONEY WHEAT BREAD

APPLE STREUSEL MUFFINS

APPLE STREUSEL MUFFINS

These muffins remind us of coffee cake, and my husband and kids love them as a quick breakfast or snack. A little drizzle of glaze makes them pretty enough for company.
—Dulcy Grace, Roaring Spring, PA

Prep: 20 min. • **Bake:** 15 min. + cooling
Makes: 1 dozen

- 2 cups all-purpose flour
- 1 cup sugar
- 1 tsp. baking powder
- ½ tsp. baking soda
- ½ tsp. salt
- 2 large eggs
- ½ cup butter, melted
- 1¼ tsp. vanilla extract
- 1½ cups peeled chopped tart apples

STREUSEL TOPPING

- ⅓ cup packed brown sugar
- 1 Tbsp. all-purpose flour
- ⅛ tsp. ground cinnamon
- 1 Tbsp. cold butter

GLAZE

- ¾ cup confectioners' sugar
- 2 to 3 tsp. 2% milk
- 1 tsp. butter, melted
- ⅛ tsp. vanilla extract
- Dash salt

1. Preheat oven to 375°. Whisk together first five ingredients. In another bowl, whisk together eggs, melted butter and vanilla; add to the flour mixture, stirring just until moistened (batter will be stiff). Fold the apples into the batter.

2. Fill 12 greased or paper-lined muffin cups three-fourths full. For topping, mix brown sugar, flour and cinnamon; cut in butter until crumbly. Sprinkle over batter.

3. Bake until a toothpick inserted in center comes out clean, 15-20 minutes. Cool for 5 minutes before removing from pan to a wire rack to cool. Mix glaze ingredients; drizzle over tops.

Per muffin: 295 cal., 10g fat (6g sat. fat), 55mg chol., 398mg sod., 49g carb. (32g sugars, 1g fiber), 3g pro.

RUSTIC RYE BREAD

RUSTIC RYE BREAD

This gorgeous rye bread has just a touch of sweetness and caraway—and holds up well for sandwiches.

—Holly Wade, Harrisonburg, VA

Prep: 25 min. + rising
Bake: 30 min. + cooling
Makes: 2 loaves (12 slices each)

- 1 pkg. (¼ oz.) active dry yeast
- 1¾ cups warm water (110° to 115°), divided
- ¼ cup packed brown sugar
- ¼ cup light molasses
- 3 Tbsp. caraway seeds
- 2 Tbsp. canola oil
- 1 Tbsp. salt
- 1¾ cups rye flour
- ¾ cup whole wheat flour
- 2½ to 3 cups all-purpose flour
- Egg white and caraway seeds, optional

1. In a large bowl, dissolve yeast in ¼ cup warm water. Stir in brown sugar, molasses, caraway seeds, oil, salt and remaining water. Add rye flour, whole wheat flour and 1 cup all-purpose flour; beat on medium speed until smooth. Stir in enough remaining flour to form a firm dough.

2. Turn dough onto a floured surface; knead until smooth and elastic, 6-8 minutes. Place in a greased bowl, turning once to grease the top. Cover and let rise in a warm place until doubled, about 1½ hours.

3. Punch down dough. Turn onto a lightly floured surface; divide in half. Shape each into a round loaf; place on a baking sheet coated with cooking spray. Cover with kitchen towels; let rise in a warm place until almost doubled, about 1½ hours. Preheat oven to 350°.

4. Bake until golden brown, 30-35 minutes. Remove from pan to wire racks to cool. For caraway topping, brush the loaves with an egg white beaten lightly with water before baking; sprinkle with caraway seeds.

Per slice: 118 cal., 2g fat (0 sat. fat), 0 chol., 298mg sod., 24g carb. (5g sugars, 2g fiber), 3g pro.

PERFECT DINNER ROLLS

JUDY'S CHOCOLATE CHIP BANANA BREAD

I received this recipe from my co-worker and dear friend, Judy, more than 30 years ago. When she gave it to me, she told me I would never need another banana bread recipe. She was almost right. I added lots of chocolate chips for the chocolate lovers in my family.

—Debra Keiser, St. Cloud, MN

Prep: 20 min. • **Bake:** 1 hour + cooling
Makes: 1 loaf (16 slices)

- ½ cup butter, softened
- 1¼ cups sugar
- 2 large eggs
- 1 cup mashed ripe bananas (about 2 medium)
- ¼ cup buttermilk
- 1 tsp. vanilla extract
- 2 cups all-purpose flour
- 1 tsp. baking powder
- ¾ tsp. baking soda
- ½ tsp. salt
- ¾ cup semisweet chocolate chips
- ¼ cup chopped walnuts, optional

1. Preheat oven to 350°. Line bottom of a greased 9x5-in. loaf pan with parchment paper; grease paper.

2. In a large bowl, beat butter and sugar until crumbly. Add eggs, one at a time, beating well after each addition. Beat in the bananas, buttermilk and vanilla. In another bowl, mix flour, baking powder, baking soda and salt; stir into creamed mixture. Fold in chocolate chips and, if desired, walnuts.

3. Transfer to prepared pan. Bake 60-65 minutes or until a toothpick inserted in center comes out clean. Cool 10 minutes before removing from pan to a wire rack; remove paper.

Per slice: 229 cal., 9g fat (5g sat. fat), 42mg chol., 212mg sod., 36g carb. (22g sugars, 1g fiber), 3g pro.

PERFECT DINNER ROLLS

My mom made these tender rolls when I was growing up. I carry on the tradition with my kids, so they can have the same happy memories of freshly baked bread.

—Gayleen Grote, Battleview, ND

Prep: 30 min. + rising • **Bake:** 15 min.
Makes: 2 dozen

- 1 Tbsp. active dry yeast
- 2¼ cups warm water (110° to 115°)
- ⅓ cup sugar
- ⅓ cup shortening
- ¼ cup powdered nondairy creamer
- 2¼ tsp. salt
- 6 to 7 cups bread flour

1. In a large bowl, dissolve yeast in warm water. Add the sugar, shortening, creamer, salt and 5 cups flour. Beat until smooth. Stir in enough remaining flour to form a soft dough (dough will be sticky).

2. Turn onto a floured surface; knead until smooth and elastic, about 6-8 minutes. Place in a bowl coated with cooking spray, turning once to coat the top. Cover and let rise in a warm place until doubled, about 1 hour.

3. Punch dough down. Turn onto a lightly floured surface; divide into 24 pieces. Shape each into a roll. Place each roll 2 in. apart on baking sheets coated with cooking spray. Cover and let rise until doubled, about 30 minutes.

4. Meanwhile, preheat oven to 350°. Bake 12-15 minutes or until lightly browned. Remove from pans to wire racks.

Per roll: 142 cal., 3g fat (1g sat. fat), 0 chol., 222mg sod., 25g carb. (3g sugars, 1g fiber), 4g pro. **Diabetic exchanges:** 1½ starch, ½ fat.

FRESH PEAR BREAD

When our tree branches are loaded with ripe, juicy pears, I treat my loved ones to loaves of this cinnamony bread. We love the crunch from walnuts. I always receive raves and requests for the recipe.
—Linda Patrick, Houston, TX

Prep: 15 min. • **Bake:** 55 min. + cooling
Makes: 2 loaves

- 3 large eggs
- 1½ cups sugar
- ¾ cup vegetable oil
- 1 tsp. vanilla extract
- 3 cups all-purpose flour
- 2 tsp. baking powder
- 2 tsp. ground cinnamon
- 1 tsp. baking soda
- 1 tsp. salt
- 4 cups finely chopped peeled ripe pears (about 4 medium)
- 1 tsp. lemon juice
- 1 cup chopped walnuts

1. In a bowl, combine the eggs, sugar, oil and vanilla; mix well. Combine flour, baking powder, cinnamon, baking soda and salt; stir dry ingredients into the egg mixture just until moistened. Toss pears with lemon juice. Stir pears and walnuts into batter (batter will be thick).

2. Spoon batter into two greased 9x5-in. loaf pans. Bake at 350° for 55-60 minutes or until a toothpick inserted in the center comes out clean. Cool loaves for 10 minutes before removing from pans to wire racks.

Per slice: 168 cal., 8g fat (1g sat. fat), 20mg chol., 144mg sod., 22g carb. (12g sugars, 1g fiber), 3g pro.

Nuts, pears and that odd little stuffed-fruit treat in the corner...they all disappeared when we reshot this photo from 1994.

STOVETOP
SENSATIONS

MEALS DON'T GET MUCH SIMPLER THAN A TASTY DISH WHIPPED UP ON THE STOVETOP. TURN TO THESE SIZZLING RECIPES FOR ALL YOUR WEEKNIGHT DINNER SOLUTIONS, AND BREAKFAST, TOO!

ZUCCHINI & GOUDA SKILLET FRITTATA

CHOCOLATE-FRUIT CREPES

These graceful dessert crepes are as simple to make as they are special. They would shine at a fancy brunch, too.

—Laura McDowell, Lake Villa, IL

Prep: 30 min. + chilling • **Cook:** 5 min./batch
Makes: 10 servings

- 1½ cups buttermilk
- 3 large eggs
- 3 Tbsp. butter, melted
- 1 cup all-purpose flour
- 2 Tbsp. sugar
- 2 Tbsp. baking cocoa

FILLING

- 1 can (21 oz.) cherry pie filling
- 1 can (8½ oz.) sliced peaches, drained and chopped
- ½ tsp. ground cinnamon
- ⅛ tsp. almond extract
- ⅓ cup hot fudge ice cream topping, warmed
- Whipped cream, optional

1. In a large bowl, combine the buttermilk, eggs and butter. Combine the flour, sugar and cocoa; add to buttermilk mixture and mix well. Cover and refrigerate for 1 hour.
2. Heat a lightly greased 8-in. nonstick skillet over medium heat; pour 2 Tbsp. batter into the center of skillet. Lift and tilt pan to coat bottom evenly. Cook until top appears dry; turn and cook 15-20 seconds longer. Remove to a wire rack. Repeat with remaining batter, greasing skillet as needed. When cool, stack crepes with waxed paper or paper towels in between.
3. In a microwave-safe bowl, combine the pie filling, peaches and cinnamon. Microwave, uncovered, on high for 3-4 minutes or until heated through, stirring once. Stir in extract. Spoon 2 Tbsp. filling down the center of each crepe. Fold sides of crepe over filling. Drizzle with ice cream topping and, if desired, garnish with whipped cream.
Per 2 crepes: 241 cal., 6g fat (3g sat. fat), 74mg chol., 109mg sod., 41g carb. (26g sugars, 1g fiber), 5g pro.

ZUCCHINI & GOUDA SKILLET FRITTATA

This is a version of a skillet dish that my mother-in-law, Millie, created to use up all that extra summer zucchini. The Gouda melts beautifully, but you can make it with Swiss or sharp cheddar, too.

—Susan Marshall, Colorado Springs, CO

Takes: 30 min. • **Makes:** 6 servings

- 6 large eggs
- 2 Tbsp. 2% milk
- 1 tsp. chopped fresh oregano
- ½ tsp. salt
- ⅛ tsp. pepper
- 2 Tbsp. butter
- 2 medium zucchini (7 to 8 oz. each), thinly sliced
- 1 medium onion, chopped
- 2 Tbsp. olive oil
- 1 medium tomato, diced
- 1 cup shredded Gouda cheese
- 2 Tbsp. minced fresh basil

1. Combine the first five ingredients; set aside. In a large nonstick skillet, melt butter over medium heat. Add zucchini and onion. Cook until tender, 6-8 minutes; remove.
2. In same skillet, heat oil over medium heat. Add egg mixture. Cook until set, gently lifting edges of cooked egg to allow liquid to run underneath. Top with zucchini mixture, diced tomato and cheese. Cover; cook until cheese is melted, 2-3 minutes. Sprinkle basil on top.
Per wedge: 238 cal., 19g fat (8g sat. fat), 218mg chol., 462mg sod., 6g carb. (4g sugars, 1g fiber), 12g pro.

MAPLE SAUSAGE PATTIES

MAPLE SAUSAGE PATTIES

Maple syrup, sage, thyme and a blend of other seasonings give delightful flavor to homemade sausage patties. They're a definite treat, especially alongside pancakes or waffles.

—Margaret Eid, Huron, SD

Prep: 15 min. + chilling • **Cook:** 10 min.
Makes: 8 servings

- 1 Tbsp. maple syrup
- ½ tsp. salt
- ½ tsp. onion powder
- ½ tsp. rubbed sage
- ½ tsp. dried thyme
- ½ tsp. poultry seasoning
- ½ tsp. ground nutmeg
- ¼ tsp. cayenne pepper
- 1 to 2 tsp. liquid smoke, optional
- 1 lb. ground pork

1. In a large bowl, mix maple syrup, salt, spices and, if desired, liquid smoke. Add pork; mix lightly but thoroughly. Shape into eight 2½-in. patties. Refrigerate, covered, at least 1 hour.

2. In a large nonstick skillet coated with cooking spray, cook patties over medium heat until a thermometer reads 160°, 4-6 minutes per side.

Per patty: 128 cal., 8g fat (3g sat. fat), 38mg chol., 177mg sod., 2g carb. (2g sugars, 0 fiber), 10g pro.

EGG BURRITOS

Zap one of these frozen burritos in the microwave and you'll stave off hunger all morning. This recipe is my family's favorite combo, but I sometimes use breakfast sausage instead of bacon.

—Audra Niederman, Aberdeen, SD

Takes: 25 min. • **Makes:** 10 burritos

- 12 bacon strips, chopped
- 12 large eggs
- ½ tsp. salt
- ¼ tsp. pepper
- 10 flour tortillas (8 in.), warmed
- 1½ cups shredded cheddar cheese
- 4 green onions, thinly sliced

1. In a large skillet, cook the bacon until crisp; drain on paper towels. Remove all but 1-2 Tbsp. drippings from pan.

2. Whisk together eggs, salt and pepper. Heat skillet over medium heat; pour in egg mixture. Cook and stir until the eggs are thickened and no liquid egg remains; remove from heat.

3. Spoon about ¼ cup egg mixture onto center of each tortilla; sprinkle with cheese, bacon and green onions. Roll into burritos.

Freeze option Cool eggs before making burritos. Individually wrap burritos in paper towels and foil; freeze in a resealable plastic freezer bag. To use, remove foil; place paper towel-wrapped burrito on a microwave-safe plate. Microwave burritos on high until heated through, turning once. Let stand 15 seconds.

Per burrito: 376 cal., 20g fat (8g sat. fat), 251mg chol., 726mg sod., 29g carb. (0 sugars, 2g fiber), 19g pro.

EGG BURRITOS

BISCUITS & SAUSAGE GRAVY

BISCUITS & SAUSAGE GRAVY

This is an old southern recipe that I've adapted. It's the kind of hearty breakfast that will warm you right up.

—Sue Baker, Jonesboro, AR

Takes: 15 min. • **Makes:** 2 servings

- ¼ lb. bulk pork sausage
- 2 Tbsp. butter
- 2 to 3 Tbsp. all-purpose flour
- ⅛ tsp. salt
- ⅛ tsp. pepper
- 1¼ to 1⅓ cups whole milk
- Warm biscuits

In a small skillet, cook sausage over medium heat until no longer pink; drain. Add butter and heat until melted. Add the flour, salt and pepper; cook and stir until blended. Gradually add the milk, stirring constantly. Bring to a boil; cook and stir for 2 minutes or until thickened. Serve with biscuits.

Per ¾ cup gravy: 337 cal., 27g fat (14g sat. fat), 72mg chol., 718mg sod., 14g carb. (8g sugars, 0 fiber), 10g pro.

GERMAN APPLE PANCAKE

If you're looking for a pretty dish to make when hosting guests for brunch, try this. Everyone I've served it to has enjoyed it —except for one time, that is, when my husband tried to make it following my recipe, which I'd written down incorrectly! If you don't leave out the flour, as I did, it will turn out terrific!

—Judi Van Beek, Lynden, WA

Prep: 15 min. • **Bake:** 20 min.
Makes: 6 servings

PANCAKE

- 3 large eggs
- 1 cup whole milk
- ¾ cup all-purpose flour
- ½ tsp. salt
- ⅛ tsp. ground nutmeg
- 3 Tbsp. butter

TOPPING

- 2 tart baking apples, peeled and sliced
- 3 to 4 Tbsp. butter
- 2 Tbsp. sugar
- Confectioners' sugar

1. Preheat a 10-in. cast-iron skillet in a 425° oven. Meanwhile, in a blender, combine the eggs, milk, flour, salt and nutmeg; cover and process until smooth.

2. Add butter to hot skillet; return to oven until butter bubbles. Pour batter into skillet. Bake, uncovered, for 20 minutes or until the pancake puffs and the edges are browned and crisp.

3. For topping, in a skillet, combine the apples, butter and sugar; cook and stir over medium heat until apples are tender. Spoon into baked pancake. Sprinkle with confectioners' sugar. Cut pancake and serve immediately.

Per serving: 192 cal., 12g fat (7g sat. fat), 107mg chol., 273mg sod., 18g carb. (8g sugars, 1g fiber), 5g pro.

GERMAN APPLE PANCAKE

MAKE-AHEAD BREAKFAST BURRITOS

MAKE-AHEAD BREAKFAST BURRITOS

Burritos for breakfast? These zesty little handfuls will wake up your taste buds and start your day with a smile. Make and freeze them ahead, then just pop them into the microwave for a quick meal.

—Linda Wells, St. Mary's, GA

Takes: 30 min. • **Makes:** 12 burritos

- 1 lb. bulk pork sausage
- 1½ cups frozen cubed hash brown potatoes
- ¼ cup diced onion
- ¼ cup diced green or red pepper
- 4 large eggs, lightly beaten
- 12 flour tortillas (8 in.), warmed
- ½ cup shredded cheddar cheese
- Picante sauce and sour cream, optional

1. In a large skillet, cook sausage over medium heat until no longer pink; drain. Add the potatoes, onion and pepper; cook and stir for 6-8 minutes or until tender. Add eggs; cook and stir until set.

2. Spoon filling off center on each tortilla. Sprinkle with cheese. Fold sides and ends over filling and roll up. Serve with picante sauce and sour cream if desired.

3. To freeze and reheat burritos: Wrap each burrito in waxed paper and foil. Freeze for up to 1 month. To use, remove the foil and waxed paper. Place one burrito on a microwave-safe plate. Microwave on high for 2-2¼ minutes or until a thermometer reads 165°, turning burrito over once. Let stand for 20 seconds.

Per burrito: 303 cal., 15g fat (5g sat. fat), 87mg chol., 521mg sod., 30g carb. (0 sugars, 2g fiber), 12g pro.

TEST KITCHEN TIP

To prevent tortillas from tearing while rolling them up, simply warm them slightly in a nonstick skillet before filling. The warm tortillas are more pliable.

AVOCADO SCRAMBLED EGGS

Bacon and avocado blend nicely in these eggs. They're easy perfection for breakfast, but I'll also whip them up after a church meeting or a football game—or any time friends drop by for coffee and a bite to eat.

—Sundra Hauck, Bogalusa, LA

Takes: 10 min. • **Makes:** 6 servings

- 8 large eggs
- ½ cup whole milk
- ½ tsp. salt
- ¼ tsp. pepper
- 1 medium ripe avocado, peeled and cubed
- 2 Tbsp. butter
- 6 bacon strips, cooked and crumbled

In a bowl, beat eggs. Add milk, salt and pepper; stir in avocado. In a skillet over medium heat, melt butter. Add the egg mixture; cook and stir gently until the eggs are completely set. Sprinkle with bacon.

Per serving: 233 cal., 19g fat (7g sat. fat), 302mg chol., 434mg sod., 4g carb. (2g sugars, 1g fiber), 12g pro.

BACON & EGG SANDWICHES

I came across this unique grilled combo when I was digging in my mom's recipe box. The crisp bacon, hard-cooked eggs and crunchy green onions make these cozy sandwiches look impressive.

—Ann Fuemmeler, Glasgow, MO

Takes: 20 min. • **Makes:** 4 servings

- ½ cup sour cream
- 8 slices bread
- 4 green onions, chopped
- 4 slices process American cheese
- 2 hard-boiled large eggs, cut into ¼-in. slices
- 8 cooked bacon strips
- 2 Tbsp. butter, softened

1. Spread sour cream over four bread slices; top with green onions, cheese, eggs, bacon and remaining bread. Spread outsides of sandwiches with butter.

2. Toast sandwiches until golden brown and cheese is melted, 2-3 minutes per side.

Per sandwich: 461 cal., 27g fat (13g sat. fat), 137mg chol., 887mg sod., 32g carb. (6g sugars, 2g fiber), 19g pro.

SAUSAGE, EGG & CHEDDAR FARMER'S BREAKFAST

This hearty combination of sausage, hash browns and eggs will warm you up and start your day off right.

—Bonnie Roberts, Newaygo, MI

Takes: 30 min. • **Makes:** 4 servings

- 6 large eggs
- ⅓ cup 2% milk
- ½ tsp. dried parsley flakes
- ¼ tsp. salt
- 6 oz. bulk pork sausage
- 1 Tbsp. butter
- 1½ cups frozen cubed hash brown potatoes, thawed
- ¼ cup chopped onion
- 1 cup shredded cheddar cheese

1. Whisk eggs, milk, parsley and salt; set aside. In a 9-in. cast-iron skillet, cook the sausage over medium heat until no longer pink; remove and drain. In same skillet, heat butter over medium heat. Add potatoes and onion; cook and stir for 5-7 minutes or until tender. Return sausage to the pan.

2. Add egg mixture; cook and stir until almost set. Sprinkle with cheese. Cover and cook for 1-2 minutes or until cheese is melted.

Per cup: 386 cal., 29g fat (13g sat. fat), 339mg chol., 736mg sod., 9g carb. (2g sugars, 0 fiber), 22g pro.

BACON & EGG SANDWICHES

BACON & ASPARAGUS FRITTATA

BACON & ASPARAGUS FRITTATA

My frittata makes a marvelous light meal. When I prepare this for guests, I also serve rice and bread. It's quick and easy, but it always wins compliments.

—Gwen Clemon, Soldier, IA

Prep: 10 min. • **Cook:** 25 min.
Makes: 6 servings

- 12 oz. bacon
- 2 cups sliced fresh asparagus (cut in ½-in. pieces)
- 1 cup chopped onion
- 2 garlic cloves, minced
- 10 large eggs, beaten
- ¼ cup minced parsley
- ½ tsp. seasoned salt
- ¼ tsp. pepper
- 1 large tomato, thinly sliced
- 1 cup shredded cheddar cheese

1. Cook bacon until crisp. Drain, reserving 1 Tbsp. drippings. In a 9- or 10-in. ovenproof skillet, heat the reserved drippings on medium-high. Add asparagus, onion and garlic; saute until onion is tender. Crumble bacon; set aside a third. In a large bowl, combine remaining bacon, eggs, parsley, salt and pepper.

2. Pour egg mixture into skillet; stir. Top with tomato, cheese and reserved bacon. Cover and cook over medium-low until eggs are nearly set, 10-15 minutes. Preheat broiler; place skillet 6 in. from heat. Broil until lightly browned, about 2 minutes. Serve frittata immediately.

Per serving: 344 cal., 24g fat (10g sat. fat), 351mg chol., 738mg sod., 7g carb. (3g sugars, 2g fiber), 23g pro.

HUEVOS RANCHEROS

I like to spice things up with tempting whole eggs poached in a zesty tomato sauce. This southwestern fare is perfect for brunch.

—Olga Koetting, Terre Haute, IN

Prep: 15 min. • **Cook:** 25 min.
Makes: 6 servings

- 1 small onion, finely chopped
- 1 medium green pepper, finely chopped
- 2 garlic cloves, minced
- 1 Tbsp. canola oil
- 2 cans (14½ oz. each) stewed tomatoes, undrained
- 2 to 4 tsp. seeded minced jalapeno pepper
- 2 tsp. dried oregano
- 1 tsp. chili powder
- ½ tsp. ground cumin
- ½ tsp. pepper
- 6 large eggs
- 1 cup shredded cheddar cheese
- Flour tortillas, warmed, optional

1. In a large skillet, saute onion, green pepper and garlic in oil until tender. Stir in tomatoes, jalapeno and seasonings; simmer, uncovered, for 15 minutes. Make six indentations in the tomato mixture with a spoon. Break eggs into indentations.

2. Cover and cook on low heat for 5 minutes or until the eggs are set. Sprinkle with the cheese; cover and cook until melted, about 1 minute. If desired, serve with tortillas.

Note Wear disposable gloves when cutting hot peppers; the oils can burn skin. Avoid touching your face.

Per serving: 197 cal., 13g fat (6g sat. fat), 233mg chol., 311mg sod., 10g carb. (5g sugars, 2g fiber), 11g pro.

APPLE PANCAKES WITH CIDER SYRUP

Tender pancakes are filled with minced apple and raisin, and drizzled with apple cider syrup. They're wonderful in the summer or on a cool fall morning.

—April Harmon, Greeneville, TN

Takes: 30 min.
Makes: 6 pancakes (⅔ cup syrup)

- ½ cup all-purpose flour
- ¼ cup whole wheat flour
- 2 tsp. sugar
- ¼ tsp. baking soda
- ¼ tsp. salt
- ¼ tsp. ground cinnamon
- ⅔ cup finely chopped peeled apple
- ¼ cup raisins
- ⅔ cup buttermilk
- 1 large egg, separated
- 2 tsp. butter, melted
- ¼ tsp. vanilla extract

SYRUP

- ¼ cup sugar
- 2 tsp. cornstarch
- ⅔ cup apple cider or juice
- 1 cinnamon stick (1½ in.)
- Dash ground nutmeg
- Additional butter, optional

1. In a small bowl, combine the first six ingredients; stir in apple and raisins. Combine the buttermilk, egg yolk, butter and vanilla; stir into dry ingredients. In a small bowl, beat egg white until soft peaks form; fold into batter.

2. Pour batter by heaping ¼ cupfuls onto a hot griddle coated with cooking spray; turn when bubbles form on top. Cook until the second side is lightly browned.

3. Meanwhile, in a small saucepan, combine the sugar, cornstarch and cider until smooth; add the cinnamon stick. Bring to a boil over medium heat; cook and stir for 2 minutes or until thickened. Discard cinnamon stick. Stir nutmeg into syrup. Serve pancakes with warm syrup and, if desired, additional butter.

Per 3 pancakes with ⅓ cup syrup: 492 cal., 6g fat (3g sat. fat), 116mg chol., 605mg sod., 101g carb. (58g sugars, 4g fiber), 12g pro.

SWEET POTATO PANCAKES WITH CINNAMON CREAM

SWEET POTATO PANCAKES WITH CINNAMON CREAM

Topped with a rich cinnamon cream, these pancakes are an ideal dish for celebrating the tastes and aromas of fall.

—Tammy Rex, New Tripoli, PA

Prep: 25 min. • **Cook:** 5 min./batch
Makes: 12 servings (1½ cups topping)

- 1 pkg. (8 oz.) cream cheese, softened
- ¼ cup packed brown sugar
- ½ tsp. ground cinnamon
- ½ cup sour cream

PANCAKES

- 6 large eggs
- ¾ cup all-purpose flour
- ½ tsp. ground nutmeg
- ½ tsp. salt
- ¼ tsp. pepper
- 6 cups shredded peeled sweet potatoes (about 3 large)
- 3 cups shredded peeled apples (about 3 large)
- ⅓ cup grated onion
- ½ cup canola oil

1. In a small bowl, beat the cream cheese, brown sugar and cinnamon until blended; beat in sour cream. Set aside.

2. In a large bowl, whisk the eggs, flour, nutmeg, salt and pepper. Add the sweet potatoes, apples and onion; toss to coat.

3. In a large nonstick skillet, heat about 2 Tbsp. oil over medium heat. Working in batches, drop sweet potato mixture by ⅓ cupfuls into oil; press slightly to flatten. Fry 2-3 minutes on each side until golden brown, using remaining oil as needed. Drain on paper towels. Serve with cinnamon topping.

Per 2 pancakes with 2 Tbsp. topping: 325 cal., 21g fat (7g sat. fat), 114mg chol., 203mg sod., 30g carb. (15g sugars, 3g fiber), 6g pro.

AMISH APPLE SCRAPPLE

The aroma of this when it's cooking at breakfast time takes me back to my days growing up in Pennsylvania. The recipe was a favorite at home and at church breakfasts.
—Marion Lowery, Medford, OR

Prep: 1 hour 20 min. + chilling
Cook: 10 min. • **Makes:** 8 servings

- ¾ lb. bulk pork sausage
- ½ cup finely chopped onion
- 4 Tbsp. butter, divided
- ½ cup diced apple, unpeeled
- ¾ tsp. dried thyme
- ½ tsp. ground sage
- ¼ tsp. pepper
- 3 cups water, divided
- ¾ cup cornmeal
- 1 tsp. salt
- 2 Tbsp. all-purpose flour
- Maple syrup

1. In a large skillet, cook sausage and onion over medium-high heat until sausage is no longer pink and onion is tender. Remove from skillet; set aside.
2. Discard all but 2 Tbsp. drippings. Add 2 Tbsp. butter, apple, thyme, sage and pepper to drippings; cook over low heat until apple is tender, about 5 minutes. Remove from heat; stir in sausage mixture. Set aside.
3. In a large heavy saucepan, bring 2 cups water to a boil. Combine cornmeal, salt and remaining water; slowly pour into boiling water, stirring constantly. Return to a boil. Reduce heat; simmer, covered, for 1 hour, stirring occasionally. Stir in the sausage mixture. Pour into a greased 8x4-in. loaf pan. Refrigerate, covered, for 8 hours or overnight.
4. Slice ½ in. thick. Sprinkle flour over both sides of each slice. In a large skillet, heat remaining butter over medium heat. Add slices; cook until both sides are browned. Serve with syrup.
Per piece: 251 cal., 18g fat (7g sat. fat), 44mg chol., 667mg sod., 16g carb. (1g sugars, 1g fiber), 7g pro.

COUNTRY-STYLE SCRAMBLED EGGS

COUNTRY-STYLE SCRAMBLED EGGS

I added extra colors and flavors to ordinary scrambled eggs with green pepper, onion and red potatoes.
—Joyce Platfoot, Wapakoneta, OH

Takes: 30 min. • **Makes:** 4 servings

- 8 bacon strips, diced
- 2 cups diced red potatoes
- ½ cup chopped onion
- ½ cup chopped green pepper
- 8 large eggs
- ¼ cup whole milk
- 1 tsp. salt
- ¼ tsp. pepper
- 1 cup shredded cheddar cheese

1. In a 9-in. cast-iron or other ovenproof skillet, cook bacon over medium heat until crisp. Using a slotted spoon, remove to paper towels to drain. Cook and stir potatoes in drippings over medium heat for 12 minutes or until tender. Add the onion and green pepper. Cook and stir for 3-4 minutes or until crisp-tender; drain. Stir in the bacon.
2. In a large bowl, whisk the eggs, milk, salt and pepper; add to skillet. Cook and stir until eggs are completely set. Sprinkle with cheese; stir it in or let stand until melted.
Per serving: 577 cal., 45g fat (19g sat. fat), 487mg chol., 1230mg sod., 18g carb. (4g sugars, 2g fiber), 25g pro.

LEMON CHICKEN & RICE

LEMON CHICKEN & RICE

We live on a busy ranch, so we need tasty meals that are quick. This all-in-one chicken dish—with its delicate lemon flavor—fits the bill and is inexpensive to boot.

—Kat Thompson, Prineville, OR

Takes: 30 min. • **Makes:** 4 servings

- 2 Tbsp. butter
- 1 lb. boneless skinless chicken breasts, cut into strips
- 1 medium onion, chopped
- 1 large carrot, thinly sliced
- 2 garlic cloves, minced
- 1 Tbsp. cornstarch
- 1 can (14½ oz.) chicken broth
- 2 Tbsp. lemon juice
- ½ tsp. salt
- 1 cup frozen peas
- 1½ cups uncooked instant rice

1. In a large skillet, heat the butter over medium-high heat; saute chicken, onion, carrot and garlic until chicken is no longer pink, 5-7 minutes.

2. In a small bowl, mix the cornstarch, broth, lemon juice and salt until smooth. Gradually add to skillet; bring to a boil. Cook and stir until thickened, 1-2 minutes.

3. Stir in peas; return to a boil. Stir in rice. Remove from the heat; let stand, covered, 5 minutes.

Per serving: 370 cal., 9g fat (4g sat. fat), 80mg chol., 893mg sod., 41g carb. (4g sugars, 3g fiber), 29g pro.

SKILLET SHEPHERD'S PIE

This is the best shepherd's pie I've ever tasted. It's very quick to make, and I usually have most—if not all—of the ingredients already on hand.

—Tirzah Sandt, San Diego, CA

Takes: 30 min. • **Makes:** 6 servings

- 1 lb. ground beef
- 1 cup chopped onion
- 2 cups frozen corn, thawed
- 2 cups frozen peas, thawed
- 2 Tbsp. ketchup
- 1 Tbsp. Worcestershire sauce
- 2 tsp. minced garlic
- 1 Tbsp. cornstarch
- 1 tsp. beef bouillon granules
- ½ cup cold water
- ½ cup sour cream
- 3½ cups mashed potatoes (prepared with milk and butter)
- ¾ cup shredded cheddar cheese

1. In a large skillet, cook beef and onion over medium heat until meat is no longer pink; drain. Stir in the corn, peas, ketchup, Worcestershire sauce and garlic. Reduce heat to medium-low; cover and cook for 5 minutes.

2. Combine the cornstarch, bouillon and water until well blended; stir into beef mixture. Bring to a boil over medium heat; cook and stir for 2 minutes or until thickened. Stir in sour cream and heat through (do not boil).

3. Spread mashed potatoes over the top; sprinkle with cheese. Cover and cook until potatoes are heated through and cheese is melted.

Freeze option Prepare beef mixture as directed but do not add sour cream. Freeze cooled meat mixture in a freezer container. To use, partially thaw in the refrigerator overnight. Heat through in a large skillet, stirring occasionally and adding a little water if necessary. Stir in sour cream and proceed as directed.

Per serving: 448 cal., 20g fat (12g sat. fat), 80mg chol., 781mg sod., 45g carb. (8g sugars, 7g fiber), 24g pro.

SKILLET SHEPHERD'S PIE

BARBECUE PORK & PENNE SKILLET

BARBECUE PORK & PENNE SKILLET

Because we're an active family with a schedule to match, I appreciate simple, tasty, quick meals. A hearty pasta dish is my go-to dinner after errands, school activities and soccer practice.

—Judy Armstrong, Prairieville, LA

Takes: 25 min. • **Makes:** 8 servings

- 1 pkg. (16 oz.) penne pasta
- 1 cup chopped sweet red pepper
- ¾ cup chopped onion
- 1 Tbsp. butter
- 1 Tbsp. olive oil
- 3 garlic cloves, minced
- 1 carton (16 oz.) refrigerated fully cooked barbecued shredded pork
- 1 can (14½ oz.) diced tomatoes with mild green chilies, undrained
- ½ cup beef broth
- 1 tsp. ground cumin
- 1 tsp. pepper
- ¼ tsp. salt
- 1¼ cups shredded cheddar cheese
- ¼ cup chopped green onions

1. Cook pasta according to package directions. Meanwhile, in a large skillet, saute red pepper and onion in butter and oil until tender. Add garlic; saute 1 minute longer. Stir in the pork, tomatoes, broth, cumin, pepper and salt; heat through.

2. Drain pasta. Add pasta and cheese to pork mixture; stir until blended. Sprinkle with green onions.

Freeze option Freeze cooled pasta mixture in freezer containers. To use, partially thaw in refrigerator overnight. Place in a shallow microwave-safe dish. Cover and microwave on high until heated through.

Per 1¼ cups: 428 cal., 11g fat (6g sat. fat), 40mg chol., 903mg sod., 61g carb. (16g sugars, 4g fiber), 20g pro.

EDITOR'S CHOICE

CRISPY TOFU WITH BLACK PEPPER SAUCE

Sometimes tofu can be boring and tasteless. Here, the crispy vegetarian bean curd is so loaded with flavor, you'll never shy away from tofu again.
—Nick Iverson, Denver, CO

Takes: 30 min. • **Makes:** 4 servings

- 2 Tbsp. reduced-sodium soy sauce
- 2 Tbsp. chili garlic sauce
- 1 Tbsp. packed brown sugar
- 1 Tbsp. rice vinegar
- 4 green onions
- 8 oz. extra-firm tofu, drained
- 3 Tbsp. cornstarch
- 6 Tbsp. canola oil, divided
- 8 oz. fresh sugar snap peas (about 2 cups), trimmed and thinly sliced
- 1 tsp. freshly ground pepper
- 3 garlic cloves, minced
- 2 tsp. grated fresh gingerroot

1. Mix the first four ingredients. Mince white parts of green onions; thinly slice green parts.
2. Cut tofu into ½-in. cubes; pat dry with paper towels. Toss tofu with cornstarch. In a large skillet, heat 4 Tbsp. oil over medium-high heat. Add tofu; cook until crisp and golden brown, 5-7 minutes, stirring occasionally. Remove from pan; drain on paper towels.
3. In the same pan, heat 1 Tbsp. oil over medium-high heat. Add the peas; stir-fry until crisp-tender, 2-3 minutes. Remove from the pan.
4. In the same pan, heat remaining oil over medium-high heat. Add the pepper; cook 30 seconds. Add garlic, ginger and minced green onions; stir-fry 30-45 seconds. Stir in soy sauce mixture; cook and stir until slightly thickened. Remove from heat; stir in tofu and peas. Sprinkle with sliced green onions.
Per cup: 316 cal., 24g fat (2g sat. fat), 0 chol., 583mg sod., 20g carb. (8g sugars, 2g fiber), 7g pro.

CRISPY TOFU WITH BLACK PEPPER SAUCE

SHRIMP WITH WARM GERMAN-STYLE COLESLAW

SHRIMP WITH WARM GERMAN-STYLE COLESLAW

We love anything that is tangy or has bacon. With fennel and tarragon, this is a savory dish that pleases all.

—Ann Sheehy, Lawrence, MA

Takes: 30 min. • **Makes:** 4 servings

- 6 bacon strips
- 2 Tbsp. canola oil, divided
- 3 cups finely shredded green cabbage
- ½ cup finely shredded carrot (1 medium carrot)
- 1 cup finely shredded red cabbage, optional
- ½ cup finely shredded fennel bulb, optional
- 6 green onions, trimmed and finely chopped
- 3 Tbsp. minced fresh parsley
- 2 Tbsp. minced fresh tarragon or 2 tsp. dried tarragon
- ¼ tsp. salt
- ⅛ tsp. pepper
- ¼ cup red wine vinegar
- 1 lb. uncooked shrimp (26-30 per lb.), peeled and deveined
- 3 cups hot cooked rice or multigrain medley

1. In a large skillet, cook bacon over medium heat until crisp. Remove to paper towels to drain. Pour off the drippings, discarding all but 2 Tbsp. Crumble bacon.

2. In same skillet, heat 1 Tbsp. drippings with 1 Tbsp. oil over medium heat. Add green cabbage and carrot and, if desired, red cabbage and fennel; cook and stir until vegetables are just tender, 1-2 minutes. Remove to a bowl. Stir in the green onions, parsley, tarragon, salt and pepper; toss with vinegar. Keep warm.

3. Add remaining drippings and remaining oil to skillet. Add shrimp; cook and stir over medium heat until shrimp turn pink, 2-3 minutes. Remove from heat.

4. To serve, spoon rice and coleslaw into soup bowls. Top with shrimp; sprinkle with the crumbled bacon.

Per serving: 472 cal., 20g fat (5g sat. fat), 156mg chol., 546mg sod., 44g carb. (2g sugars, 3g fiber), 28g pro.

RED BEANS & SAUSAGE

Turkey sausage makes a traditional dish a little more healthy, while a zesty blend of seasonings lets it keep its spark.

—Cathy Webster, Morris, IL

Takes: 25 min. • **Makes:** 6 servings

- 1 Tbsp. canola oil
- 1 medium green pepper, diced
- 1 medium onion, chopped
- 2 garlic cloves, minced
- 2 cans (16 oz. each) kidney beans, rinsed and drained
- ½ lb. smoked turkey sausage, sliced
- 1 tsp. Cajun seasoning
- ⅛ tsp. hot pepper sauce
- ¾ cup water
- Hot cooked rice, optional

1. In a large saucepan, heat the oil over medium heat; saute pepper and onion until tender. Add garlic; cook and stir 1 minute.

2. Stir in beans, sausage, Cajun seasoning, pepper sauce and water; bring to a boil. Reduce heat; simmer, uncovered, until heated through, 5-7 minutes. If desired, serve with rice.

Per ⅔ cup: 212 cal., 4g fat (1g sat. fat), 24mg chol., 706mg sod., 27g carb. (4g sugars, 8g fiber), 16g pro. **Diabetic exchanges:** 2 lean meat, 1½ starch, ½ fat.

JERK CHICKEN WITH TROPICAL COUSCOUS

Caribbean cuisine brightens up our weeknights thanks to its bold colors and flavors. Done in less than 30 minutes, this easy chicken is one of my go-to meals.
—Jeanne Holt, Mendota Heights, MN

Takes: 25 min. • **Makes:** 4 servings

- 1 can (15.25 oz.) mixed tropical fruit
- 1 lb. boneless skinless chicken breasts, cut into 2½-in. strips
- 3 tsp. Caribbean jerk seasoning
- 1 Tbsp. olive oil
- ½ cup chopped sweet red pepper
- 1 Tbsp. finely chopped seeded jalapeno pepper
- ⅓ cup thinly sliced green onions (green portion only)
- 1½ cups reduced-sodium chicken broth
- 3 Tbsp. chopped fresh cilantro, divided
- 1 Tbsp. lime juice
- ¼ tsp. salt
- 1 cup uncooked whole wheat couscous
- Lime wedges

1. Drain mixed fruit, reserving ¼ cup syrup. Chop fruit.
2. Toss chicken with seasoning. In a skillet, heat oil over medium-high heat; saute chicken until no longer pink, 4-5 minutes. Remove from pan, reserving drippings.
3. In same pan, saute peppers and green onions in drippings 2 minutes. Add broth, 1 Tbsp. cilantro, lime juice, salt, reserved syrup and chopped fruit; bring to a boil. Stir in couscous; reduce heat to low. Place the chicken on top; cook, covered, until liquid is absorbed and chicken is heated through, 3-4 minutes. Sprinkle with remaining cilantro. Serve with lime wedges.

Per 1½ cups: 411 cal., 7g fat (1g sat. fat), 63mg chol., 628mg sod., 57g carb. (19g sugars, 7g fiber), 31g pro.

JERK CHICKEN WITH TROPICAL COUSCOUS

SPINACH SKILLET BAKE

SPINACH SKILLET BAKE

Over the years, I've tried to instill a love of cooking in our children. We've enjoyed a variety of delicious recipes, including this savory, comforting stovetop entree.
—Nancy Robaidek, Krakow, WI

Prep: 30 min. • **Bake:** 20 min.
Makes: 6 servings

- 1 lb. ground beef
- 1 medium onion, chopped
- 1 pkg. (10 oz.) frozen chopped spinach, thawed and squeezed dry
- 1 can (4 oz.) mushroom stems and pieces, drained
- 1 tsp. garlic salt
- 1 tsp. dried basil
- ¼ cup butter
- ¼ cup all-purpose flour
- ½ tsp. salt
- 2 cups whole milk
- 1 cup shredded Monterey Jack cheese or part-skim mozzarella cheese
- Biscuits, optional

1. In a 10-in. cast-iron or other ovenproof skillet, cook beef and onion over medium heat until no longer pink; drain. Add the spinach, mushrooms, garlic salt and basil. Cover and cook for 5 minutes.

2. In a saucepan, melt butter over medium heat. Stir in the flour and salt until smooth. Gradually add milk. bring to a boil; cook and stir for 2 minutes or until thickened. Stir in cheese. Pour over meat mixture; mix well. Reduce heat; cook, covered, until heated through. If desired, serve with biscuits.

Per serving: 351 cal., 23g fat (13g sat. fat), 85mg chol., 872mg sod., 13g carb. (6g sugars, 2g fiber), 23g pro.

TURKEY CURRY

TURKEY CURRY

I'm always looking for new and interesting ways to use leftover turkey—especially around the holidays. This is a zesty entree you can make as spicy as you like by varying the amount of curry powder.

—Martha Balser, Cincinnati, OH

Takes: 20 min. • **Makes:** 4 servings

- 1 cup sliced celery
- ½ cup sliced carrots
- 1 cup fat-free milk
- 2 Tbsp. cornstarch
- ¾ cup reduced-sodium chicken broth
- 2 cups diced cooked turkey or chicken
- 2 Tbsp. dried minced onion
- ½ tsp. garlic powder
- 1 to 4 tsp. curry powder
- Hot cooked rice, optional

1. Lightly coat a skillet with cooking spray; saute celery and carrots until tender. In a bowl, mix ¼ cup milk and cornstarch until smooth. Add broth and remaining milk; mix until smooth.

2. Pour over vegetables in skillet. Bring to a boil; cook and stir for 2 minutes or until thickened. Add the turkey, onion, garlic powder and curry powder; heat through, stirring occasionally. Serve curry with hot cooked rice if desired.

Per cup: 172 cal., 3g fat (1g sat. fat), 72mg chol., 235mg sod., 12g carb. (5g sugars, 1g fiber), 24g pro. **Diabetic exchanges:** 1 starch, 3 lean meat.

EGG ROLL NOODLE BOWL

We love Asian egg rolls, but they can be challenging to make. Simplify everything with this deconstructed egg roll in a bowl made on the stovetop.

—Courtney Stultz, Weir, KS

Takes: 30 min. • **Makes:** 4 servings

- 1 Tbsp. sesame oil
- ½ lb. ground pork
- 1 Tbsp. soy sauce
- 1 garlic clove, minced
- 1 tsp. ground ginger
- ½ tsp. salt
- ¼ tsp. ground turmeric
- ¼ tsp. pepper
- 6 cups shredded cabbage (about 1 small head)
- 2 large carrots, shredded (about 2 cups)
- 4 oz. rice noodles
- 3 green onions, thinly sliced
- Additional soy sauce, optional

1. In a large skillet, heat oil over medium-high heat; cook and crumble pork until browned, 4-6 minutes. Stir in soy sauce, garlic and seasonings. Add cabbage and carrots; cook 4-6 minutes longer or until vegetables are tender, stirring occasionally.

2. Cook rice noodles according to package directions; drain. Immediately add to pork mixture; toss to combine. Sprinkle with green onions. If desired, serve with extra soy sauce.

Per 1½ cups: 302 cal., 12g fat (4g sat. fat), 38mg chol., 652mg sod., 33g carb. (2g sugars, 4g fiber), 14g pro.

EGG ROLL NOODLE BOWL

STOVETOP HAMBURGER CASSEROLE

This is quick comfort food at its best. Hearty and mildly seasoned, it's a fast supper that everyone will enjoy.

—Edith Landinger, Longview, TX

Takes: 25 min. • **Makes:** 6 servings

- 1 pkg. (7 oz.) small pasta shells
- 1½ lbs. ground beef
- 1 large onion, chopped
- 3 medium carrots, chopped
- 1 celery rib, chopped
- 3 garlic cloves, minced
- 3 cups cubed cooked red potatoes
- 1 can (15¼ oz.) whole kernel corn, drained
- 2 cans (8 oz. each) tomato sauce
- 1½ tsp. salt
- ½ tsp. pepper
- 1 cup shredded cheddar cheese

1. Cook pasta according to the package directions. Meanwhile, in a large skillet, cook beef and onion over medium heat until the meat is no longer pink; drain. Add the carrots and celery; cook and stir for 5 minutes or until vegetables are crisp-tender. Add garlic; cook 1 minute longer.
2. Stir in the potatoes, corn, tomato sauce, salt and pepper; heat through. Drain pasta and add to skillet; toss to coat. Sprinkle with cheddar cheese. Cover and cook until the cheese is melted.

Per cup: 508 cal., 17g fat (9g sat. fat), 76mg chol., 1172mg sod., 53g carb. (9g sugars, 5g fiber), 32g pro.

TEST KITCHEN TIP

Ground beef is often labeled using the cut of meat that it is ground from, such as ground chuck or ground round. (Ground beef comes from a combination of beef cuts.) Ground beef can also be labeled according to the fat content of the ground mixture or the percentage of lean meat to fat, such as 85% or 90% lean. The higher the percentage, the leaner the meat.

LEMON-PEPPER TILAPIA WITH MUSHROOMS

LEMON-PEPPER TILAPIA WITH MUSHROOMS

My husband and I are trying to add more fish and healthy entrees to our diet. This one comes together in less than 30 minutes, so it's perfect for hectic weeknights.

—Donna McDonald, Lake Elsinore, CA

Takes: 25 min. • **Makes:** 4 servings

- 2 Tbsp. butter
- ½ lb. sliced fresh mushrooms
- ¾ tsp. lemon-pepper seasoning, divided
- 3 garlic cloves, minced
- 4 tilapia fillets (6 oz. each)
- ¼ tsp. paprika
- ⅛ tsp. cayenne pepper
- 1 medium tomato, chopped
- 3 green onions, thinly sliced

1. In a 12-in. skillet, heat the butter over medium heat. Add mushrooms and ¼ tsp. lemon pepper; cook and stir 3-5 minutes or until tender. Add garlic; cook 30 seconds.
2. Place fillets over mushrooms; sprinkle with paprika, cayenne and the remaining lemon pepper. Cook, covered, 5-7 minutes or until fish just begins to flake easily with a fork. Top with tomato and green onions.

Per fillet: 216 cal., 8g fat (4g sat. fat), 98mg chol., 173mg sod., 5g carb. (2g sugars, 1g fiber), 34g pro. **Diabetic exchanges:** 4 lean meat, 1½ fat.

BISTRO CHICKEN FETTUCINE

BISTRO CHICKEN FETTUCCINE

This is one of my go-to weeknight meals made from pantry ingredients. Every bite makes me think of France.

—Devon Delaney, Westport, CT

Prep: 20 min. • **Cook:** 15 min.
Makes: 4 servings

- ½ lb. uncooked spinach fettuccine
- 2 Tbsp. extra virgin olive oil, divided
- 1 lb. boneless skinless chicken breasts, cut into ½-in. strips
- ¼ tsp. salt
- ¼ tsp. pepper
- 2 plum tomatoes, chopped
- ¼ lb. prosciutto, julienned
- 1 shallot, minced (about 2 Tbsp.)
- 2 Tbsp. finely chopped dried apricots
- ⅛ tsp. crushed red pepper flakes
- ¼ cup white wine or chicken broth
- 1 Tbsp. Dijon mustard
- ½ cup crumbled goat cheese
- ¼ tsp. dried tarragon or ½ tsp. minced fresh tarragon
- ¼ cup chopped walnuts, toasted

1. Cook fettuccine according to package directions for al dente; drain, reserving ½ cup pasta water. Transfer to a serving platter; keep warm.

2. In a large skillet, heat 1 Tbsp. oil over medium heat. Sprinkle chicken with salt and pepper. Add to skillet; cook and stir until no longer pink, 4-6 minutes. Remove chicken. Add remaining oil to the skillet; stir in the next five ingredients, and saute 4-6 minutes. Return chicken to skillet.

3. Stir in wine and mustard. Bring to a boil; cook until liquid is reduced slightly, about 2-4 minutes. Pour chicken mixture over fettuccine; add cheese and tarragon. Toss to combine, adding enough reserved pasta water to moisten pasta. Top with walnuts.

Note To toast nuts, bake in a shallow pan in a 350° oven for 5-10 minutes or cook in a skillet over low heat until lightly browned, stirring occasionally.

Per 1½ cup: 561 cal., 22g fat (6g sat. fat), 116mg chol., 942mg sod., 45g carb. (4g sugars, 4g fiber), 42g pro.

BEST SPAGHETTI & MEATBALLS

BEST SPAGHETTI & MEATBALLS

We had unexpected company one evening, so I pulled some of these meatballs from my freezer for a quick appetizer. Everyone raved! This classic recipe makes a big batch and is perfect for entertaining.

—Mary Lou Koskella, Prescott, AZ

Prep: 30 min. • **Cook:** 2 hours
Makes: 16 servings

- 2 Tbsp. olive oil
- 1½ cups chopped onions
- 3 garlic cloves, minced
- 2 cans (12 oz. each) tomato paste
- 3 cups water
- 1 can (29 oz.) tomato sauce
- ⅓ cup minced fresh parsley
- 1 Tbsp. dried basil
- 2 tsp. salt
- ½ tsp. pepper

MEATBALLS

- 4 large eggs, lightly beaten
- 2 cups soft bread cubes (cut into ¼-in. pieces)
- 1½ cups whole milk
- 1 cup grated Parmesan cheese
- 3 garlic cloves, minced
- 2 tsp. salt
- ½ tsp. pepper
- 3 lbs. ground beef
- 2 Tbsp. canola oil
- 2 lbs. spaghetti, cooked

1. In a Dutch oven, heat the olive oil over medium heat. Add the onions; saute until softened. Add garlic; cook 1 minute longer. Stir in tomato paste; cook 3-5 minutes. Add next six ingredients. Bring to a boil. Reduce heat; simmer, covered, for 50 minutes.

2. Combine the first seven meatball ingredients. Add beef; mix lightly but thoroughly. Shape into 1½-in. balls.

3. In a large skillet, heat canola oil over medium heat. Add meatballs; brown in batches until no longer pink. Drain. Add to sauce; bring to a boil. Reduce heat; simmer, covered, until flavors are blended, about 1 hour, stirring occasionally. Serve with hot cooked spaghetti.

Per serving: 519 cal., 18g fat (6g sat. fat), 106mg chol., 1043mg sod., 59g carb. (8g sugars, 4g fiber), 30g pro.

PASTA WITH ASPARAGUS

SAUCY SPROUTS & ORANGES

Expect compliments when you serve this mouthwatering recipe for Brussels sprouts. Citrus and mustard flavor the tasty sauce.
—Carolyn Hannay, Antioch, TN

Takes: 30 min. • **Makes:** 6 servings

- 3 medium navel oranges
- 1 lb. fresh Brussels sprouts, trimmed and halved
- 1 Tbsp. butter
- 2 tsp. cornstarch
- 2 Tbsp. honey mustard
- ¼ tsp. Chinese five-spice powder
- 2 Tbsp. slivered almonds, toasted

1. Finely grate zest of one orange; set zest aside. Cut that orange in half; squeeze juice into a 1-cup measuring cup. Add enough water to measure ½ cup; set aside. Peel and discard white membranes from remaining oranges; section them and set aside.
2. In a large saucepan, bring 1 in. of water and Brussels sprouts to a boil. Cover and cook for 8-10 minutes or until crisp-tender.
3. Meanwhile, in a small saucepan, melt butter. Whisk cornstarch and reserved orange juice mixture until smooth; add to the butter. Stir in mustard and five-spice powder. Bring to a boil over medium heat; cook and stir for 1-2 minutes or until thickened and bubbly.
4. Drain sprouts; gently stir in orange sections. Transfer to a serving bowl; drizzle with sauce. Sprinkle with almonds and grated orange zest.

Per ¾ cup: 97 cal., 4g fat (1g sat. fat), 5mg chol., 81mg sod., 15g carb. (8g sugars, 3g fiber), 4g pro. **Diabetic exchanges:** 1 vegetable, 1 fat, ½ fruit.

PASTA WITH ASPARAGUS

The garlic, asparagus, Parmesan cheese and red pepper flakes create an irresistible taste combination in this recipe.
—Jean Fisher, Redlands, CA

Takes: 20 min. • **Makes:** 6 servings

- 5 garlic cloves, minced
- ¼ to ½ tsp. crushed red pepper flakes
- 2 to 3 dashes hot pepper sauce
- ¼ cup olive oil
- 1 Tbsp. butter
- 1 lb. fresh asparagus, cut into 1½-in. pieces
- Salt to taste
- ¼ tsp. pepper
- ¼ cup shredded Parmesan cheese
- ½ lb. mostaccioli or elbow macaroni, cooked and drained

In a large skillet, cook the garlic, red pepper flakes and hot pepper sauce in oil and butter for 1 minute. Add the asparagus, salt and pepper; saute until asparagus is crisp-tender, about 8-10 minutes. Stir in cheese. Pour over hot pasta and toss to coat. Serve immediately.

Per serving: 259 cal., 13g fat (3g sat. fat), 8mg chol., 83mg sod., 30g carb. (2g sugars, 2g fiber), 7g pro.

SAUCY SPROUTS
& ORANGES

CHEESY ZUCCHINI SAUTE

CHEESY ZUCCHINI SAUTE

Although I no longer have a garden of my own, friend and neighbors keep me amply supplied with squash. To thank them, I pass along the recipe for this refreshing zucchini saute. It's quick, easy and tasty!
—Doris Biggs, Felton, DE

Takes: 20 min. • **Makes:** 6 servings

- ½ cup chopped onion
- ¼ cup butter, cubed
- 3 cups coarsely shredded zucchini
- 2 tsp. minced fresh basil or ½ tsp. dried basil
- ½ tsp. salt
- ⅛ tsp. garlic powder
- 1 cup shredded cheddar cheese
- 1 cup diced fresh tomato
- 2 Tbsp. sliced ripe olives

1. In a large skillet, saute onion in butter until crisp-tender. Stir in the zucchini, basil, salt and garlic powder. Cook and stir for 4-5 minutes or until zucchini is crisp-tender. Sprinkle with the cheese, tomato and olives.
2. Cover and cook for 4-5 minutes or until cheese is melted. Serve immediately.
Per cup: 157 cal., 13g fat (9g sat. fat), 40mg chol., 416mg sod., 5g carb. (3g sugars, 1g fiber), 5g pro.

SALSA CORN CAKES

This recipe is super with fresh or canned corn. I whip up these patties to serve alongside nachos or tacos on hot summer evenings. The salsa is subtle but adds flavor.
—Lisa Boettcher, Rosebush, MI

Takes: 20 min. • **Makes:** 8 servings

- 6 oz. cream cheese, softened
- ¼ cup butter, melted
- 6 large eggs
- 1 cup whole milk
- 1½ cups all-purpose flour
- ½ cup cornmeal
- 1 tsp. baking powder
- 1 tsp. salt
- 1 can (15¼ oz.) whole kernel corn, drained
- ½ cup salsa, drained
- ¼ cup minced green onions
- Sour cream and additional salsa

1. In a large bowl, beat cream cheese and butter until smooth; add the eggs and mix well. Beat in milk until smooth. Combine the flour, cornmeal, baking powder and salt just until moistened. Fold in the corn, salsa and onions.
2. Pour batter by ¼ cupfuls onto a greased hot griddle. Turn when bubbles form on top; cook until the second side is golden brown. Serve with sour cream and salsa.
Per serving: 324 cal., 15g fat (8g sat. fat), 191mg chol., 715mg sod., 34g carb. (5g sugars, 3g fiber), 11g pro.

DID YOU KNOW?

Cornmeal can be white, yellow or blue depending on which strain of corn is used. Traditionally, white cornmeal is more popular in the South and yellow is preferred in the North. Blue cornmeal can be found in specialty stores. All three types can be used interchangeably in recipes.

LEMON RICE PILAF

No need to buy premade pilaf mix when you can easily make your own in 20 minutes. The lemon zest adds a welcome tang to this recipe.

—Taste of Home *Test Kitchen*

Takes: 20 min. • **Makes:** 6 servings

- 1 cup uncooked jasmine or long grain white rice
- 2 Tbsp. butter
- 1 cup sliced celery
- 1 cup thinly sliced green onions
- 1 Tbsp. grated lemon zest
- 1 tsp. salt
- ¼ tsp. pepper

Cook rice according to package directions. Meanwhile, in a skillet, heat butter over medium heat. Add celery and onions; cook until tender. Add rice, lemon zest, salt and pepper; toss lightly. Cook until warm.

Per ¾ cup: 155 cal., 4g fat (2g sat. fat), 10mg chol., 454mg sod., 27g carb. (1g sugars, 1g fiber), 3g pro.

LEMON RICE PILAF

HONEY-LEMON ASPARAGUS

HARVARD BEETS

The bright citrusy flavors make these beets an ideal companion for down-to-earth entrees. Even non-beet lovers enjoy them.

—Jean Ann Perkins, Newburyport, MD

Takes: 15 min. • **Makes:** 4-6 servings

- 1 **can (16 oz.) sliced beets**
- ¼ **cup sugar**
- 1½ **tsp. cornstarch**
- 2 **Tbsp. vinegar**
- 2 **Tbsp. orange juice**
- 1 **Tbsp. grated orange zest**

Drain beets, reserving 2 Tbsp. juice; set beets and juice aside. In a saucepan, combine sugar and cornstarch. Add vinegar, orange juice and beet juice; bring to a boil. Reduce heat and simmer for 3-4 minutes or until thickened. Add the beets and orange zest; heat through.

Per serving: 61 cal., 0 fat (0 sat. fat), 0 chol., 147mg sod., 15g carb. (12g sugars, 1g fiber), 1g pro.

HONEY-LEMON ASPARAGUS

Everyone who tastes my asparagus takes a second helping, so I double the recipe. The honey-lemon glaze also works splendidly on root veggies like turnips and parsnips.

—Lorraine Caland, Shuniah, ON

Takes: 15 min. • **Makes:** 8 servings

- 2 **lbs. fresh asparagus, trimmed**
- ¼ **cup honey**
- 2 **Tbsp. butter**
- 2 **Tbsp. lemon juice**
- 1 **tsp. sea salt**
- 1 **tsp. balsamic vinegar**
- 1 **tsp. Worcestershire sauce**

1. In a large saucepan, bring 8 cups water to a boil. Add asparagus in batches; cook, uncovered, 1-2 minutes or just until crisp-tender. Drain asparagus and pat dry.
2. Meanwhile, in a small saucepan, combine the remaining ingredients. Bring to a boil. Reduce heat; simmer, uncovered, 2 minutes or until slightly thickened.
3. Transfer asparagus to a large bowl; drizzle with glaze and toss gently to coat.

Per serving: 73 cal., 3g fat (2g sat. fat), 8mg chol., 276mg sod., 12g carb. (10g sugars, 1g fiber), 2g pro. **Diabetic exchanges:** 1 vegetable, ½ starch, ½ fat.

NEW ENGLAND BAKED BEANS

You can't beat this classic picnic side that starts with a pound of dried beans. It's a little sweet from maple syrup and molasses.
—Pat Medeiros, Tiverton, RI

Prep: 1½ hours + soaking • **Bake:** 2½ hours
Makes: 12 servings (⅔ cup each)

- 1 lb. dried great northern beans
- ½ lb. thick-sliced bacon strips, chopped
- 2 large onions, chopped
- 3 garlic cloves, minced
- 2 cups ketchup
- 1½ cups packed dark brown sugar
- ⅓ cup molasses
- ⅓ cup maple syrup
- ¼ cup Worcestershire sauce
- ½ tsp. salt
- ¼ tsp. coarsely ground pepper

1. Sort beans and rinse with cold water. Place beans in a Dutch oven; add enough water to cover by 2 in. Bring to a boil; boil for 2 minutes. Remove from the heat; cover and let stand for 1 hour or until the beans are softened.
2. Drain and rinse beans, discarding liquid. Return beans to Dutch oven; add 6 cups water. Bring to a boil. Reduce heat; cover and simmer for 1 hour or until beans are almost tender.
3. In a large skillet, cook the bacon over medium heat until crisp. Remove to paper towels with a slotted spoon; drain, reserving 2 Tbsp. drippings. Saute onions in drippings until tender. Add garlic; cook 1 minute longer. Stir in the ketchup, brown sugar, molasses, syrup, Worcestershire sauce, salt and pepper.
4. Drain beans, reserving cooking liquid; place in an ungreased 3-qt. baking dish. Stir in onion mixture and bacon. Cover and bake at 300° for 2½ hours or until beans are tender and reach desired consistency, stirring every 30 minutes. Add reserved cooking liquid as needed.
Per ⅔ cup: 385 cal., 5g fat (2g sat. fat), 7mg chol., 810mg sod., 77g carb. (50g sugars, 8g fiber), 11g pro.

NEW ENGLAND BAKED BEANS

RED CABBAGE WITH BACON

Red cabbage is often braised, marinated or served raw, but I recommend this steamed version. Toss it with bacon and a tangy sauce for a pretty side dish.
—Sherri Melotik, Oak Creek, WI

Takes: 25 min. • **Makes:** 6 servings

- 1 medium head red cabbage (about 2 lbs.), shredded
- 8 bacon strips, chopped
- 1 small onion, quartered and thinly sliced
- 2 Tbsp. all-purpose flour
- ¼ cup packed brown sugar
- ½ cup water
- ¼ cup cider vinegar
- 1 tsp. salt
- ⅛ tsp. pepper

1. In a large saucepan, place steamer basket over 1 in. of water. Place cabbage in basket. Bring water to a boil. Reduce heat to maintain a simmer; steam, covered, 6-8 minutes or just until tender.
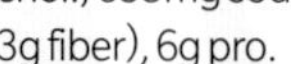
2. Meanwhile, in a skillet, cook bacon over medium heat until crisp, stirring occasionally. Remove with a slotted spoon; drain on paper towels. Discard drippings, reserving 2 Tbsp. in pan.
3. Add onion to drippings; cook and stir over medium-high heat 4-6 minutes or until tender. Stir in flour and brown sugar until blended. Gradually stir in water and vinegar. Bring to a boil, stirring constantly; cook and stir 1-2 minutes or until thickened. Stir in cabbage, bacon, salt and pepper.
Per ¾ cup: 188 cal., 9g fat (3g sat. fat), 15mg chol., 635mg sod., 23g carb. (15g sugars, 3g fiber), 6g pro.

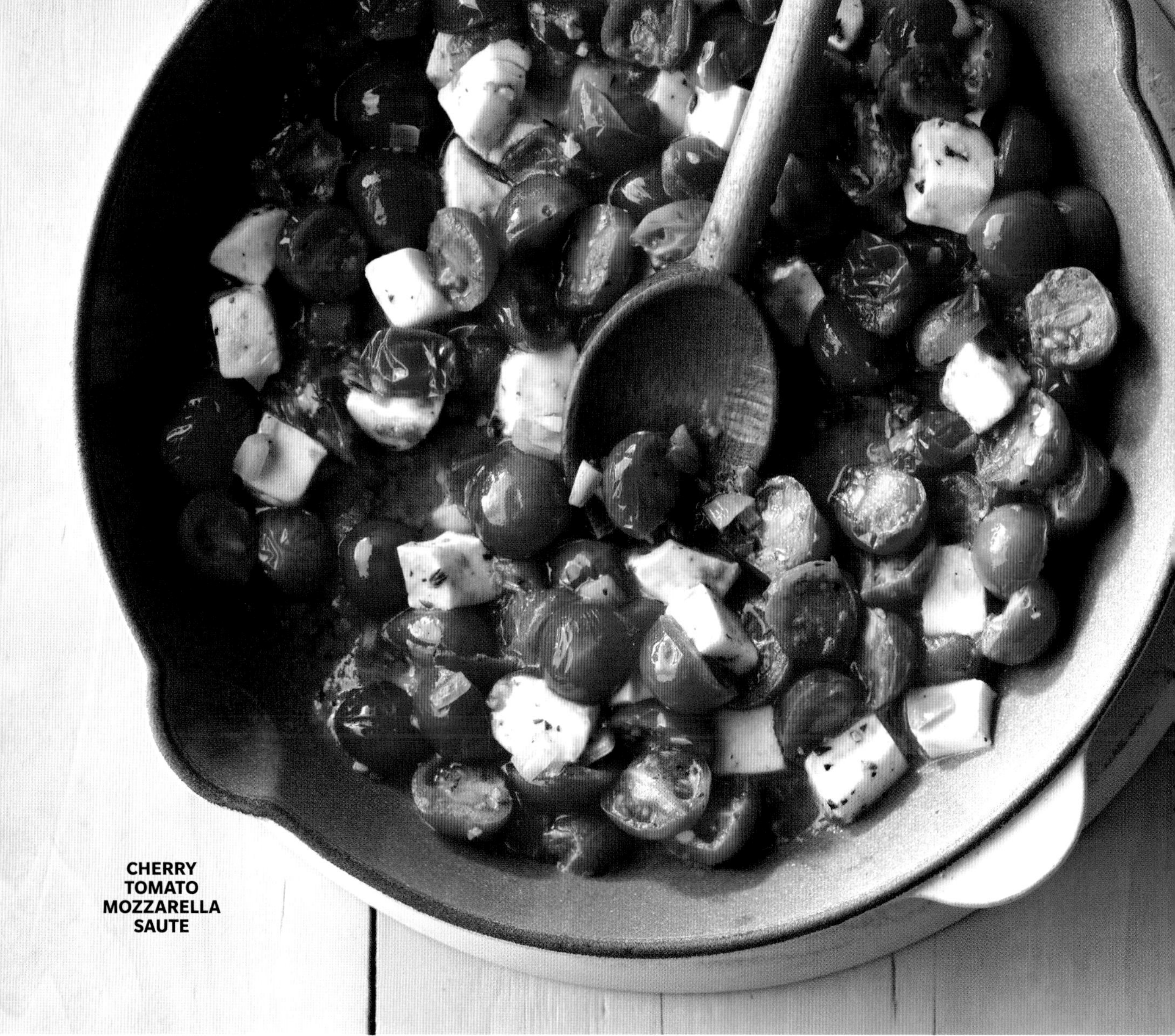

CHERRY TOMATO MOZZARELLA SAUTE

CHERRY TOMATO MOZZARELLA SAUTE

My tomato dish is fast to fix and full of flavor. The mix of cherry tomatoes and mozzarella makes it the perfect accompaniment for almost any main dish.

—Summer Jones, Pleasant Grove, UT

Takes: 25 min. • **Makes:** 4 servings

- 2 tsp. olive oil
- ¼ cup chopped shallots
- 1 tsp. minced fresh thyme
- 1 garlic clove, minced
- 2½ cups cherry tomatoes, halved
- ¼ tsp. salt
- ¼ tsp. pepper
- 4 oz. fresh mozzarella cheese cut into ½-in. cubes

In a large skillet, heat oil over medium-high heat; saute shallots with thyme until tender. Add garlic; cook and stir 1 minute. Stir in tomatoes, salt and pepper; heat through. Remove from heat; stir in cheese.

Per ⅔ cup: 127 cal., 9g fat (4g sat. fat), 22mg chol., 194mg sod., 6g carb. (4g sugars, 2g fiber), 6g pro.

ORANGE-GLAZED CARROTS, ONIONS & RADISHES

ORANGE-GLAZED CARROTS, ONIONS & RADISHES

Carrots and radishes give color and crunch to this sweet, spicy side. We never have leftovers. If you make it ahead, reheat it and add the walnuts just before serving.
—Thomas Faglon, Somerset, NJ

Prep: 15 min. • **Cook:** 20 min.
Makes: 8 servings

- 1 lb. fresh pearl onions
- ¼ cup butter, cubed
- 2 lbs. medium carrots, thinly sliced
- 12 radishes, thinly sliced
- ½ cup dark brown sugar
- 4 tsp. grated orange zest
- ½ cup orange juice
- 1 cup chopped walnuts, toasted

1. In a large saucepan, bring 4 cups water to a boil. Add pearl onions; boil 3 minutes. Drain and rinse with cold water. Peel.
2. In a large skillet, heat butter over medium heat. Add carrots, pearl onions, radishes, brown sugar, orange zest and juice; cook, covered, 10-15 minutes or until vegetables are tender, stirring occasionally. Cook, uncovered, 5-7 minutes longer or until slightly thickened. Sprinkle vegetables with toasted walnuts.
Note To toast nuts, bake in a shallow pan in a 350° oven for 5-10 minutes or cook in a skillet over low heat until lightly browned, stirring occasionally.
Per ¾ cup: 277 cal., 16g fat (5g sat. fat), 15mg chol., 141mg sod., 34g carb. (23g sugars, 5g fiber), 4g pro.

SUGAR SNAP PEA STIR-FRY

SUGAR SNAP PEA STIR-FRY

Fresh ginger, balsamic vinegar, soy sauce and sesame oil provide a nice blend of flavors in this Asian-inspired recipe for fresh sugar snap peas. The recipe is easy to double when serving a crowd.
—Taste of Home *Test Kitchen*

Takes: 20 min. • **Makes:** 6 servings

- 1 lb. fresh sugar snap peas
- 2 tsp. canola oil
- 1 garlic clove, minced
- 2 tsp. minced fresh gingerroot
- 1½ tsp. balsamic vinegar
- 1½ tsp. reduced-sodium soy sauce
- 1 tsp. sesame oil
- Dash cayenne pepper
- 1 Tbsp. minced fresh basil or 1 tsp. dried basil
- 2 tsp. sesame seeds, toasted

In a large nonstick skillet or wok, saute the peas in canola oil until crisp-tender. Add the garlic, ginger, vinegar, soy sauce, sesame oil and cayenne; saute 1 minute longer. Add basil; toss to combine. Sprinkle with the sesame seeds.
Per ½ cup: 60 cal., 3g fat (0 sat. fat), 0 chol., 59mg sod., 6g carb. (3g sugars, 2g fiber), 3g pro. **Diabetic exchanges:** 1 vegetable, ½ fat.

WILD RICE & SQUASH PILAF

WILD RICE & SQUASH PILAF

This pilaf is fantastic with fish or poultry. We especially love it with turkey. I love the color it adds to a holiday spread.

—Erica Ollmann, San Diego, CA

Prep: 15 min. • **Cook:** 20 min.
Makes: 10 servings

- 1½ cups sliced fresh mushrooms
- 1½ cups finely chopped peeled winter squash
- 2 medium onions, finely chopped
- 1 small green pepper, chopped
- 2 Tbsp. olive oil
- 2 to 3 garlic cloves, minced
- 3 cups cooked wild rice
- ½ cup chicken broth or vegetable broth
- 1 Tbsp. reduced-sodium soy sauce
- ½ tsp. dried savory
- ¼ cup sliced almonds, toasted

1. In a large saucepan, saute mushrooms, squash, onions and green pepper in oil until crisp-tender. Add the minced garlic; saute 1 minute longer.
2. Stir in the rice, broth, soy sauce and savory. Cover and cook over medium-low heat for 13-15 minutes or until squash is tender. Stir in almonds.

Per ½ cup: 118 cal., 4g fat (1g sat. fat), 0 chol., 114mg sod., 18g carb. (3g sugars, 3g fiber), 4g pro. **Diabetic exchanges:** 1 starch, 1 fat.

AU GRATIN PEAS & POTATOES

While this delicious potato skillet is a wonderful side dish, it's satisfying enough to be a main course, too. The skillet prep takes less time than it does to bake an au gratin casserole or scalloped potatoes—but it's still good, old-fashioned comfort food at its best!

—Marie Peterson, DeForest, WI

Takes: 30 min. • **Makes:** 4 servings

- 6 bacon strips, diced
- 1 medium onion, chopped
- 4 cups sliced peeled cooked potatoes
- ½ tsp. salt
- 1 pkg. (10 oz.) frozen peas, cooked and drained
- 2 cups shredded sharp cheddar cheese, divided
- ½ cup mayonnaise
- ½ cup whole milk

1. In a large skillet, cook bacon until crisp. Remove with a slotted spoon to paper towels. Drain, reserving 1 Tbsp. drippings. In the drippings, saute onion until tender.
2. Layer skillet with potatoes, salt, peas, 1 cup cheese and the bacon. Reduce heat; cover and simmer for 10 minutes or until heated through.
3. Combine mayonnaise and milk until smooth; pour over bacon. Sprinkle with the remaining cheese. Remove from the heat; let stand for 5 minutes before serving.

Per serving: 679 cal., 44g fat (17g sat. fat), 82mg chol., 1038mg sod., 48g carb. (9g sugars, 7g fiber), 23g pro.

VEGETABLE FRITTATA

When you're looking for something healthy in a hurry, you can't beat this veggie-filled frittata cooked in a cast-iron skillet.

—Janet Eckhoff, Woodland, CA

Takes: 30 min. • **Makes:** 6 servings

- ½ cup chopped onion
- ½ cup chopped green pepper
- ½ cup chopped sweet red pepper
- 1 garlic clove, minced
- 3 Tbsp. olive oil, divided
- 2 medium red potatoes, cooked and cubed
- 1 small zucchini, cubed
- 6 large eggs
- ½ tsp. salt
- Pinch pepper

1. In a 10-in. cast-iron or ovenproof skillet, saute onion, peppers and garlic in 2 Tbsp. oil until the vegetables are tender. Remove vegetables with a slotted spoon; set aside.
2. In the same skillet over medium heat, lightly brown potatoes in remaining oil. Add vegetable mixture and zucchini; simmer for 4 minutes.
3. In a bowl, beat eggs, salt and pepper; pour over vegetables. Cover and cook for 8-10 minutes or until eggs are nearly set. Broil 6 in. from the heat for 2 minutes or until eggs are set on top. Cut into wedges.

Per wedge: 177 cal., 12g fat (2g sat. fat), 213mg chol., 264mg sod., 10g carb. (3g sugars, 2g fiber), 8g pro.

Frittatas are just as popular today as they were when this recipe first published in 1995.

SLOW-COOKED WONDERS

SLOW-COOKED RECIPES HAVE ALWAYS BEEN FAVORITES WITH OUR READERS. HERE ARE 50 OF OUR ALL-TIME BEST.

SLOW COOKER CHEDDAR BACON BEER DIP

SLOW COOKER CHEDDAR BACON BEER DIP

My tangy, smoky dip won the top prize at our office party recipe contest.
—Ashley Lecker, Green Bay, WI

Prep: 15 min. • **Cook:** 3 hours
Makes: 4½ cups

- 18 oz. cream cheese, softened
- ¼ cup sour cream
- 1½ Tbsp. Dijon mustard
- 1 tsp. garlic powder
- 1 cup amber beer or nonalcoholic beer
- 2 cups shredded cheddar cheese
- 1 lb. bacon strips, cooked and crumbled, divided
- ¼ cup heavy whipping cream
- 1 green onion, thinly sliced
- Soft pretzel bites

1. In a greased 3-qt. slow cooker, combine cream cheese, sour cream, mustard and garlic powder until smooth. Stir in beer, cheese and all but 2 Tbsp. bacon. Cook, covered, on low, stirring occasionally, until heated through, 3-4 hours.
2. In last 30 minutes, stir in heavy cream. Top with onion and remaining bacon. Serve with soft pretzel bites.
Per ¼ cup dip: 213 cal., 19g fat (10g sat. fat), 60mg chol., 378mg sod., 2g carb. (1g sugars, 0 fiber), 8g pro.

CHEESE-TRIO ARTICHOKE & SPINACH DIP

No appetizer array is complete without at least one amazing dip, and this is it! Creamy, cheesy and chock-full of veggies, it will quickly become your new go-to appetizer.
—Diane Speare, Kissimmee, FL

Prep: 20 min. • **Cook:** 2 hours
Makes: 4 cups

- 1 cup chopped fresh mushrooms
- 1 Tbsp. butter
- 2 garlic cloves, minced
- 1½ cups mayonnaise
- 1 pkg. (8 oz.) cream cheese, softened
- 1 cup plus 2 Tbsp. grated Parmesan cheese, divided
- 1 cup shredded part-skim mozzarella cheese, divided
- 1 can (14 oz.) water-packed artichoke hearts, rinsed, drained and chopped
- 1 pkg. (10 oz.) frozen chopped spinach, thawed and squeezed dry
- ¼ cup chopped sweet red pepper
- Toasted French bread baguette slices

1. In a large skillet, saute mushrooms in butter until tender. Add garlic; cook 1 minute longer.
2. In a large bowl, combine mayonnaise, cream cheese, 1 cup Parmesan cheese and ¾ cup mozzarella cheese. Add the mushroom mixture, artichokes, spinach and red pepper.
3. Transfer to a 3-qt slow cooker. Sprinkle with remaining cheeses. Cover and cook on low 2-3 hours or until heated through. Serve with baguette slices.
Per ¼ cup dip: 264 cal., 25g fat (8g sat. fat), 34mg chol., 354mg sod., 4g carb. (0 sugars, 1g fiber), 6g pro.

SLOW COOKER CRAB & GREEN ONION DIP

BBQ CHICKEN SLIDERS

Brining the chicken overnight helps it taste exceptionally delicious. The chicken is so tender it almost melts in your mouth.

—Rachel Kunkel, Schell City, MO

Prep: 25 min. + brining • **Cook:** 4 hours
Makes: 8 servings (2 sliders each)

BRINE

- 1½ qt. water
- ¼ cup packed brown sugar
- 2 Tbsp. salt
- 1 Tbsp. liquid smoke
- 2 garlic cloves, minced
- ½ tsp. dried thyme

CHICKEN

- 2 lbs. boneless skinless chicken breasts
- ⅓ cup liquid smoke
- 1½ cups hickory smoke-flavored barbecue sauce
- 16 slider buns or dinner rolls, split and warmed

1. In a large bowl, mix brine ingredients, stirring to dissolve brown sugar. Reserve 1 cup brine for cooking chicken; cover and refrigerate.
2. Place chicken in a large resealable bag; add remaining brine. Seal bag, pressing out as much air as possible; turn to coat the chicken. Place in a large bowl; refrigerate 18-24 hours, turning occasionally.
3. Remove chicken from brine and transfer to a 3-qt. slow cooker; discard brine in bag. Add reserved 1 cup brine and ⅓ cup liquid smoke to chicken. Cook, covered, on low 4-5 hours or until chicken is tender.
4. Remove chicken; cool slightly. Discard cooking juices. Shred chicken with two forks and return to slow cooker. Stir in the barbecue sauce; heat through. Serve on buns.

Per 2 sliders: 376 cal., 8g fat (2g sat. fat), 98mg chol., 883mg sod., 43g carb. (9g sugars, 3g fiber), 30g pro.

SLOW COOKER CRAB & GREEN ONION DIP

This creamy dip reminds me of my dad, who took us crabbing as kids. Our fingers were tired after those excursions, but eating the fresh crab was always worth it.

—Nancy Zimmerman, Cape May Court House, NJ

Prep: 10 min. • **Cook:** 3 hours
Makes: 16 servings (¼ cup each)

- 3 pkg. (8 oz. each) cream cheese, cubed
- 2 cans (6 oz. each) lump crabmeat, drained
- 4 green onions, chopped
- ¼ cup 2% milk
- 2 tsp. prepared horseradish
- 2 tsp. Worcestershire sauce
- ¼ tsp. salt
- Baked pita chips or assorted fresh vegetables

In a greased 3-qt. slow cooker, combine the first seven ingredients. Cook, covered, on low 3-4 hours or until heated through, stirring occasionally. Serve with chips.

Per ¼ cup dip: 167 cal., 15g fat (8g sat. fat), 68mg chol., 324mg sod., 2g carb. (2g sugars, 0 fiber), 7g pro.

BBQ CHICKEN SLIDERS

TANGY BARBECUE WINGS

TANGY BARBECUE WINGS

I took these slow-cooked wings to work, and they vanished before I even got a bite! The simple sauce is lip-smacking good.

—Sherry Pitzer, Troy, MO

Prep: 1 hour • **Cook:** 3 hours
Makes: 2 dozen wings (2 sections each)

- 5 lbs. chicken wings
- 2½ cups ketchup
- ⅔ cup white vinegar
- ⅔ cup honey
- ½ cup molasses
- 2 to 3 Tbsp. hot pepper sauce
- 1 tsp. salt
- 1 tsp. Worcestershire sauce
- ½ tsp. onion powder
- ½ tsp. chili powder
- ½ to 1 tsp. liquid smoke, optional

1. Preheat oven to 375°. Using a sharp knife, cut through the two wing joints; discard wing tips. Arrange remaining wing pieces in two greased 15x10x1-in. baking pans. Bake 30 minutes; drain. Turn wings; bake 20-25 minutes longer or until juices run clear.

2. Meanwhile, in a large saucepan, combine the remaining ingredients; bring to a boil. Reduce the heat; simmer, uncovered, for 30 minutes, stirring occasionally.

3. Drain wings. Place one-third of the chicken in a 5-qt. slow cooker; top with one-third of the sauce. Repeat layers twice. Cook, covered, on low 3-4 hours. Stir before serving.

Note Chicken wing sections (wingettes) may be substituted for whole chicken wings.

Per wing (2 sections): 178 cal., 7g fat (2g sat. fat), 30mg chol., 458mg sod., 19g carb. (19g sugars, 0 fiber), 10g pro.

SLOW COOKER SPINACH & ARTICHOKE DIP

With this creamy dip, I can get my daughters to eat spinach and artichokes. We serve it with chips, toasted pita bread or fresh veggies.

—Jennifer Stowell, Deep River, IA

Prep: 10 min. • **Cook:** 2 hours
Makes: 8 cups

- 2 cans (14 oz. each) water-packed artichoke hearts, drained and chopped
- 2 pkg. (10 oz. each) frozen chopped spinach, thawed and squeezed dry
- 1 jar (15 oz.) Alfredo sauce
- 1 pkg. (8 oz.) cream cheese, cubed
- 2 cups shredded Italian cheese blend
- 1 cup shredded part-skim mozzarella cheese
- 1 cup shredded Parmesan cheese
- 1 cup 2% milk
- 2 garlic cloves, minced
- Assorted crackers and/or cucumber slices

In a greased 4-qt. slow cooker, combine the first nine ingredients. Cook, covered, on low 2-3 hours or until heated through. Serve with crackers and/or cucumber slices.

Per ¼ cup dip: 105 cal., 7g fat (4g sat. fat), 21mg chol., 276mg sod., 5g carb. (1g sugars, 1g fiber), 6g pro.

MADE WITH LOVE

I make this dip for potlucks. It's delicious and so easy to make. Definitely going in the recipe box!

EJSHELLABARGER
TASTEOFHOME.COM

SLOW COOKER SPINACH & ARTICHOKE DIP

TACO JOE DIP

TACO JOE DIP

My daughter was the first to try this recipe. She thought it was so good she passed it on to me, and my husband and I think it's terrific. Because it's made in a slow cooker, it's meant for parties or busy days.

—Lang Secrest, Sierra Vista, AZ

Prep: 5 min.
Cook: 5 hours
Makes: about 7 cups

- 1 can (16 oz.) kidney beans, rinsed and drained
- 1 can (15¼ oz.) whole kernel corn, drained
- 1 can (15 oz.) black beans, rinsed and drained
- 1 can (14½ oz.) stewed tomatoes, undrained
- 1 can (8 oz.) tomato sauce
- 1 can (4 oz.) chopped green chilies, drained
- 1 envelope taco seasoning
- ½ cup chopped onion
- Tortilla chips

In a 5-qt. slow cooker, combine the first eight ingredients. Cover and cook on low for 5-6 hours. Serve with tortilla chips.

Per ¼ cup dip: 49 cal., 0 fat (0 sat. fat), 0 chol., 291mg sod., 9g carb. (2g sugars, 2g fiber), 2g pro.

PADDY'S REUBEN DIP

This slow-cooked spread tastes just like the popular Reuben sandwich. Even when I double the recipe, I end up with an empty dish. Don't wait until March to make it!
—Mary Jane Kimmes, Hastings, MN

Prep: 5 min.
Cook: 2 hours
Makes: about 4 cups

- 4 pkg. (2 oz. each) thinly sliced deli corned beef, finely chopped
- 1 pkg. (8 oz.) cream cheese, cubed
- 1 can (8 oz.) sauerkraut, rinsed and drained
- 1 cup (8 oz.) sour cream
- 1 cup shredded Swiss cheese
- Rye bread or crackers

In a 1½-qt. slow cooker, combine the first five ingredients. Cover and cook on low for 2 hours or until cheese is melted; stir until blended. Serve warm with bread or crackers.

Per 2 Tbsp. dip: 58 cal., 5g fat (3g sat. fat), 18mg chol., 126mg sod., 1g carb. (1g sugars, 0 fiber), 2g pro.

PADDY'S REUBEN DIP

BUTTER CHICKEN MEATBALLS

My husband and I love meatballs, and we love butter chicken. We had the idea to combine the two for our contribution to an appetizer party. The bites got rave reviews! Want them as a main dish? Just serve with basmati rice.

—Shannon Dobos, Calgary, AB

Prep: 30 min. • **Cook:** 3 hours
Makes: about 3 dozen

- 1½ lbs. ground chicken or turkey
- 1 large egg, lightly beaten
- ½ cup soft bread crumbs
- 1 tsp. garam masala
- ½ tsp. tandoori masala seasoning
- ½ tsp. salt
- ¼ tsp. cayenne pepper
- 3 Tbsp. minced fresh cilantro, divided
- 1 jar (14.1 oz.) butter chicken sauce

Combine the first seven ingredients plus 2 Tbsp. cilantro; mix lightly but thoroughly. With wet hands, shape into 1-in. balls. Place meatballs in a 3-qt. slow cooker coated with cooking spray. Pour butter sauce over the meatballs. Cook, covered, on low until meatballs are cooked through, 3-4 hours. Top with remaining cilantro.

Freeze option Omitting remaining cilantro, freeze cooled meatball mixture in freezer containers. To use, partially thaw in the refrigerator overnight. Microwave, covered, on high in a microwave-safe dish until heated through, stirring gently and adding a little water if necessary. To serve, sprinkle with remaining cilantro.

Note Look for garam masala in the spice aisle. To make soft bread crumbs, tear bread into pieces and place in a food processor or blender. Cover and pulse until crumbs form. One slice of bread yields ½ to ¾ cup crumbs.

Per meatball: 40 cal., 2g fat (1g sat. fat), 18mg chol., 87mg sod., 1g carb. (1g sugars, 0 fiber), 3g pro.

ROOT BEER PULLED PORK NACHOS

I count on my slow cooker to do the honors when I have a house full of summer guests. Teenagers especially love DIY nachos. Try cola, ginger ale or lemon-lime soda if you're not into root beer.

—James Schend, Pleasant Prairie, WI

Prep: 20 min. • **Cook:** 8 hours
Makes: 12 servings

- 1 boneless pork shoulder butt roast (3 to 4 lbs.)
- 1 can (12 oz.) root beer or cola
- 12 cups tortilla chips
- 2 cups shredded cheddar cheese
- 2 medium tomatoes, chopped
- Pico de gallo, chopped green onions and sliced jalapeno peppers, optional

1. In a 4- or 5-qt. slow cooker, combine pork roast and root beer. Cook, covered, on low until meat is tender, 8-9 hours.

2. Remove roast; cool slightly. When cool enough to handle, shred meat with two forks. Return to slow cooker; keep warm.

3. To serve, drain pork. Layer tortilla chips with the pork, cheese, tomatoes and, if desired, optional toppings. Serve immediately.

Per serving: 391 cal., 23g fat (8g sat. fat), 86mg chol., 287mg sod., 20g carb. (4g sugars, 1g fiber), 25g pro.

HONEY & ALE PULLED CHICKEN SLIDERS

HONEY & ALE PULLED CHICKEN SLIDERS

Score big with your guests with a little bit of sweet heat! This recipe works well for any party because the extra liquid in the slow cooker keeps it juicy the entire time.

—Julie Peterson, Crofton, MD

Prep: 20 min. • **Cook:** 6 hours
Makes: 12 servings

- ¼ cup honey
- 2 Tbsp. cider vinegar
- 2 Tbsp. Sriracha Asian hot chili sauce
- 1 Tbsp. chili powder
- 1 tsp. smoked paprika
- 1 tsp. garlic powder
- 1 tsp. onion powder
- ½ tsp. salt
- 2 lbs. boneless skinless chicken thighs (about 8 thighs)
- ¾ cup brown ale
- 3 Tbsp. cornstarch
- 3 Tbsp. water
- 12 slider buns
- Sweet pickles and additional Sriracha sauce, optional

1. In a 3- or 4-qt. slow cooker, combine the first eight ingredients. Add chicken and ale; toss to coat. Cook, covered, on low until chicken is tender, 6-8 hours. Remove meat; when cool enough to handle, shred with two forks.

2. Strain cooking juices; skim fat. Transfer juices to a small saucepan; bring to a boil. In a small bowl, mix cornstarch and water until smooth; stir into saucepan. Return to a boil, stirring constantly; cook and stir until thickened, about 5 minutes. Add chicken to the sauce; toss to coat. Serve on buns, with pickles and additional Sriracha sauce if desired.

Per slider: 224 cal., 7g fat (2g sat. fat), 51mg chol., 357mg sod., 22g carb. (8g sugars, 1g fiber), 17g pro.

SLOW-COOKED SMOKIES

SLOW-COOKED SMOKIES

I like to include these little smokies smothered in barbecue sauce on all my appetizer buffets since they're popular with both children and adults.

—Sundra Hauck, Bogalusa, LA

Prep: 5 min. • **Cook:** 5 hours
Makes: 8 servings

- 1 pkg. (14 oz.) miniature smoked sausages
- 1 bottle (28 oz.) barbecue sauce
- 1¼ cups water
- 3 Tbsp. Worcestershire sauce
- 3 Tbsp. steak sauce
- ½ tsp. pepper

In a 3-qt. slow cooker, combine all ingredients. Cover and cook on low for 5-6 hours or until heated through.

Per serving: 331 cal., 14g fat (5g sat. fat), 32mg chol., 1694mg sod., 44g carb. (35g sugars, 1g fiber), 7g pro.

SLOW COOKER SAUSAGE LASAGNA

SLOW COOKER SAUSAGE LASAGNA

My family loves this with mild Italian sausage, especially on cold winter days. I agree about the cold days, but I prefer a spicy sausage, which gives it a bit of a zing.
—Cindi DeClue, Anchorage, AK

Prep: 40 min. **Cook:** 3½ hours + standing
Makes: 8 servings

- 1 lb. ground beef
- 1 lb. ground mild Italian sausage
- 1 medium onion, finely chopped
- 1 garlic clove, minced
- 1 jar (24 oz.) spaghetti sauce
- 1 can (14½ oz.) diced tomatoes in sauce, undrained
- ½ cup water
- 1 tsp. dried basil
- 1 tsp. dried oregano
- 1 carton (15 oz.) whole-milk ricotta cheese
- 2 large eggs, lightly beaten
- ½ cup grated Parmesan cheese
- 9 uncooked lasagna noodles
- 4 cups shredded part-skim mozzarella cheese
- Minced fresh basil, optional

1. Line sides of an oval 6-qt. slow cooker with heavy-duty foil; coat foil with cooking spray. In a Dutch oven, cook beef, sausage, onion and garlic over medium heat for 8-10 minutes or until meat is no longer pink, breaking up beef and sausage into crumbles; drain. Stir in spaghetti sauce, tomatoes, water and herbs; heat through.

2. In a small bowl, mix ricotta cheese, eggs and Parmesan cheese. Spread 1½ cups meat sauce onto bottom of prepared slow cooker. Layer with three noodles (breaking to fit), ¾ cup ricotta mixture, 1 cup mozzarella cheese and 2 cups meat sauce. Repeat layers twice. Sprinkle with the remaining mozzarella cheese.

3. Cook, covered, on low 3½-4 hours or until noodles are tender. Turn off slow cooker; remove insert. Let stand 15 minutes. If desired, sprinkle with fresh basil.

Per serving: 667 cal., 37g fat (17g sat. fat), 164mg chol., 1310mg sod., 41g carb. (14g sugars, 4g fiber), 42g pro.

SLOW COOKER KALUA PORK & CABBAGE

My slow cooker pork has four ingredients and takes less than 10 minutes to prep. The result tastes just like the Kalua pork made in Hawaii that's slow-roasted all day in an underground oven.

—Rholinelle DeTorres, San Jose, CA

Prep: 10 min. • **Cook:** 9 hours
Makes: 12 servings

- 7 bacon strips, divided
- 1 boneless pork shoulder butt roast (3 to 4 lbs.), well trimmed
- 1 Tbsp. coarse sea salt
- 1 medium head cabbage (about 2 lbs.), coarsely chopped

1. Line bottom of a 6-qt. slow cooker with four bacon strips. Sprinkle all sides of roast with salt; place in slow cooker. Arrange remaining bacon over top of roast.

2. Cook, covered, on low 8-10 hours or until pork is tender. Add cabbage, spreading cabbage around roast. Cook, covered, until cabbage is tender, 1-1¼ hours longer.

3. Remove pork to a serving bowl; shred meat with two forks. Using a slotted spoon, add cabbage to pork and toss to combine. If desired, skim fat from cooking juices; stir juices into pork mixture or serve juices on the side.

Per cup: 227 cal., 13g fat (5g sat. fat), 72mg chol., 622mg sod., 4g carb. (2g sugars, 2g fiber), 22g pro.

MADE WITH LOVE

We had Kalua pork and cabbage in Hawaii and loved it, so when I found this recipe I had to try it. I think it was just as delicious as it was there. So easy to make—fantastic flavor!

GUNSLINGER TASTEOFHOME.COM

SLOW COOKER KALUA PORK & CABBAGE

SLOW COOKER
ROAST CHICKEN

SLOW COOKER ROAST CHICKEN

Roast chicken is easy to make in a slow cooker. We shred what's left over and freeze it to use during busy weeks.
—Courtney Stultz, Weir, KS

Prep: 20 min. • **Cook:** 4 hours + standing
Makes: 6 servings

- 2 medium carrots, cut into 1-in. pieces
- 1 medium onion, cut into 1-in. pieces
- 2 garlic cloves, minced
- 2 tsp. olive oil
- 1 tsp. dried parsley flakes
- 1 tsp. pepper
- ¾ tsp. salt
- ½ tsp. dried oregano
- ½ tsp. rubbed sage
- ½ tsp. chili powder
- 1 broiler/fryer chicken (4 to 5 lbs.)

1. Place carrots and onion in a 6-qt. slow cooker. In a small bowl, mix garlic and oil. In another bowl, mix dry seasonings.
2. Tuck wings under chicken; tie drumsticks together. With fingers, carefully loosen skin from chicken breast; rub garlic mixture under the skin. Secure skin to underside of breast with toothpicks.
3. Place chicken in slow cooker over carrots and onions, breast side up; sprinkle with seasoning mixture. Cook, covered, on low 4-5 hours (a thermometer inserted in thigh should read at least 170°).
4. Remove chicken from slow cooker; tent with foil. Discard vegetables. Let chicken stand 15 minutes before carving.

Freeze option Cool chicken pieces and any juices. Freeze in freezer containers. To use, partially thaw in refrigerator overnight. Heat through slowly in a covered skillet until a thermometer inserted in chicken reads 165°, stirring occasionally and adding a little broth or water if necessary.
Per 5 oz. cooked chicken: 408 cal., 24g fat (6g sat. fat), 139mg chol., 422mg sod., 1g carb. (0 sugars, 0 fiber), 44g pro.

PORK CHILI VERDE

Pork slowly stews with jalapenos, onion, green enchilada sauce and spices in this flavor-packed Mexican dish. It's wonderful on its own or stuffed in a warm tortilla with sour cream, grated cheese and olives.
—Kimberly Burke, Chico, CA

Prep: 25 min. • **Cook:** 6½ hours
Makes: 8 servings

- 1 boneless pork sirloin roast (3 lbs.), cut into 1-in. cubes
- 4 medium carrots, sliced
- 1 medium onion, thinly sliced
- 4 garlic cloves, minced
- 3 Tbsp. canola oil
- 1 can (28 oz.) green enchilada sauce
- ¼ cup cold water
- 2 jalapeno peppers, seeded and chopped
- 1 cup minced fresh cilantro
- Hot cooked rice
- Flour tortillas, warmed

In a large skillet, saute the pork, carrots, onion and garlic in oil in batches until the pork is browned. Transfer to a 5-qt. slow cooker. Add the enchilada sauce, water, jalapenos and cilantro. Cover and cook on low for 6 hours or until meat is tender. Serve with rice and tortillas.
Note Wear disposable gloves when cutting hot peppers; the oils can burn skin. Avoid touching your face.
Per cup: 312 cal., 12g fat (4g sat. fat), 102mg chol., 616mg sod., 11g carb. (5g sugars, 1g fiber), 37g pro.

PORK CHILI VERDE

HARVESTTIME CHICKEN WITH COUSCOUS

EDITOR'S CHOICE

HARVESTTIME CHICKEN WITH COUSCOUS

Even on busy days, I can start this chicken in a slow cooker and still get to work on time. When I come home, I add a spinach salad and crescent rolls.

—Heidi Rudolph, Oregon, IL

Prep: 30 min. • **Cook:** 3 hours
Makes: 6 servings

- 2 medium sweet potatoes (about 1¼ lbs.), peeled and cut into ½-in. pieces
- 1 medium sweet red pepper, coarsely chopped
- 1½ lbs. boneless skinless chicken breasts
- 1 can (14½ oz.) stewed tomatoes, undrained
- ½ cup peach or mango salsa
- ¼ cup golden raisins
- ½ tsp. salt
- ¼ tsp. ground cumin
- ¼ tsp. ground cinnamon
- ¼ tsp. pepper

COUSCOUS

- 1 cup water
- ½ tsp. salt
- 1 cup uncooked whole wheat couscous

1. In a 4-qt. slow cooker, layer the sweet potatoes, red pepper and chicken breasts. In a small bowl, mix tomatoes, salsa, raisins and seasonings; pour over chicken. Cook, covered, on low 3-4 hours or until sweet potatoes and chicken are tender.

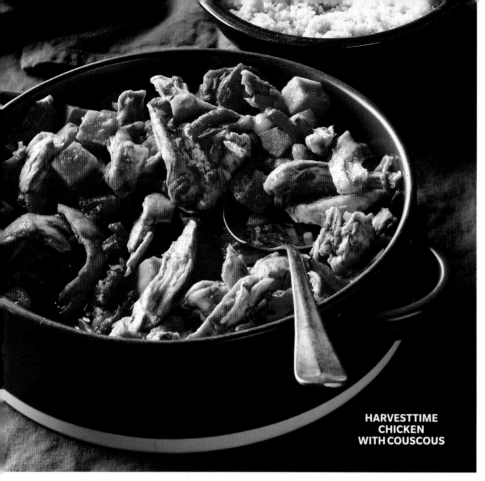

2. About 10 minutes before serving, prepare couscous. In a small saucepan, bring water and salt to a boil. Stir in couscous. Remove from heat; let stand, covered, 5 minutes or until water is absorbed. Fluff with a fork.

3. Remove chicken from slow cooker; coarsely shred with two forks. Return chicken to slow cooker, stirring gently to combine. Serve with couscous.

Freeze option Place cooled chicken mixture in freezer containers. To use, partially thaw in refrigerator overnight. Microwave, covered, on high in a microwave-safe dish until heated through, stirring gently and adding a little broth or water if necessary.

Per 1⅓ cups chicken mixture with ½ cup couscous: 351 cal., 3g fat (1g sat. fat), 63mg chol., 699mg sod., 52g carb. (15g sugars, 7g fiber), 30g pro.

SLOW-COOKED HAM

Entertaining doesn't get much easier than when you serve this tasty five-ingredient ham from the slow cooker. The leftovers are outstanding in casseroles.

—Heather Spring, Sheppard Air Force Base, TX

Prep: 5 min. • **Cook:** 6 hours
Makes: 20 servings

- ½ cup packed brown sugar
- 1 tsp. ground mustard
- 1 tsp. prepared horseradish
- 2 Tbsp. plus ¼ cup cola, divided
- 1 fully cooked boneless ham (5 to 6 lbs.), cut in half

In a small bowl, combine the brown sugar, mustard, horseradish and 2 Tbsp. cola. Rub over ham. Transfer to a 5-qt. slow cooker; add remaining cola to slow cooker. Cover and cook on low for 6-8 hours or until a thermometer reads 140°.

Per serving: 143 cal., 4g fat (1g sat. fat), 58mg chol., 1180mg sod., 6g carb. (6g sugars, 0 fiber), 21g pro.

SLOW COOKER SWEET-AND-SOUR PORK

Chinese food is a big temptation for us, so I lightened up a favorite takeout dish that we could enjoy. As this pork cooks, the aroma is beyond mouthwatering.

—Elyse Ellis, Layton, UT

Prep: 15 min. • **Cook:** 6¼ hours
Makes: 4 servings

- ½ cup sugar
- ½ cup packed brown sugar
- ½ cup chicken broth
- ⅓ cup white vinegar
- 3 Tbsp. lemon juice
- 3 Tbsp. reduced-sodium soy sauce
- 3 Tbsp. tomato paste
- ½ tsp. garlic powder
- ¼ tsp. ground ginger
- ¼ tsp. pepper
- 1½ lbs. boneless pork loin chops, cut into 1-in. cubes
- 1 large onion, cut into 1-in. pieces
- 1 large green pepper, cut into 1-in. pieces
- 1 can (8 oz.) pineapple chunks, drained
- 3 Tbsp. cornstarch
- ⅓ cup chicken broth
- Hot cooked rice

1. In a 3- or 4-qt. slow cooker, mix the first 10 ingredients. Stir in pork, onion, green pepper and pineapple. Cook, covered, on low for 6-8 hours or until pork is tender.

2. In a small bowl, mix the cornstarch and broth until smooth; gradually stir into cooking juices. Cook, covered, on low 15-20 minutes longer or until sauce is thickened. Serve with rice.

Make ahead In a large resealable plastic freezer bag, combine first 10 ingredients. Add pork, onion, green pepper and pineapple; seal bag, turn to coat, then freeze. To use, place filled freezer bag in refrigerator 48 hours or until contents are completely thawed. Cook as directed.

Per 1⅓ cups: 531 cal., 10g fat (4g sat. fat), 83mg chol., 705mg sod., 75g carb. (63g sugars, 2g fiber), 35g pro.

SLOW COOKER SWEET-AND-SOUR PORK

LIME CHICKEN TACOS

Our fun, simple recipe is perfect for taco Tuesdays or a relaxing dinner with friends. If we have any leftover filling, I toss it into a garden-fresh taco salad the next day.
—Tracy Gunter, Boise, ID

Prep: 10 min. • **Cook:** 5½ hours
Makes: 6 servings

- 1½ lbs. boneless skinless chicken breast halves
- 3 Tbsp. lime juice
- 1 Tbsp. chili powder
- 1 cup frozen corn, thawed
- 1 cup chunky salsa
- 12 fat-free flour tortillas (6 in.), warmed
- Sour cream, pickled onions, shredded lettuce, and shredded cheddar or cotija cheese, optional

1. Place chicken in a 3-qt. slow cooker. Combine lime juice and chili powder; pour over chicken. Cook, covered, on low until chicken is tender, 5-6 hours.
2. Remove chicken. When cool enough to handle, shred meat with two forks; return to slow cooker. Stir in corn and salsa. Cook, covered, on low until heated through, about 30 minutes. Place filling on tortillas; if desired, serve with sour cream, pickled onions, lettuce and cheese.

Per 2 tacos: 291 cal., 3g fat (1g sat. fat), 63mg chol., 674mg sod., 37g carb. (2g sugars, 2g fiber), 28g pro. **Diabetic exchanges:** 3 lean meat, 2½ starch.

MEAT LOAF
FROM THE
SLOW COOKER

MEAT LOAF FROM THE SLOW COOKER

This simple, easy-to-make meat loaf is one of my personal favorites. I'm often asked for the recipe.

—Laura Burgess, Mount Vernon, SD

Prep: 25 min. • **Cook:** 3 hours
Makes: 8 servings

- ½ cup tomato sauce
- 2 large eggs, lightly beaten
- ¼ cup ketchup
- 1 tsp. Worcestershire sauce
- 1 small onion, chopped
- ⅓ cup crushed saltines (about 10 crackers)
- ¾ tsp. minced garlic
- ¼ tsp. seasoned salt
- ⅛ tsp. seasoned pepper
- 1½ lbs. lean ground beef (90% lean)
- ½ lb. reduced-fat bulk pork sausage

SAUCE

- ½ cup ketchup
- 3 Tbsp. brown sugar
- ¾ tsp. ground mustard
- ¼ tsp. ground nutmeg

1. Cut three 25x3-in. strips of heavy-duty foil; crisscross so they resemble spokes of a wheel. Place strips on the bottom and up the sides of a 4- or 5-qt. slow cooker. Coat strips with cooking spray.

2. In a large bowl, combine the first nine ingredients. Crumble beef and sausage over mixture and mix well (mixture will be moist). Shape into a loaf. Place meat loaf in the center of the strips.

3. In a small bowl, combine the sauce ingredients. Spoon over meat loaf. Cover and cook on low 3-4 hours or until no pink remains and a thermometer reads 160°. Using foil strips as handles, remove the meat loaf to a platter.

Per slice: 284 cal., 14g fat (5g sat. fat), 119mg chol., 681mg sod., 16g carb. (12g sugars, 1g fiber), 24g pro. **Diabetic exchanges:** 3 lean meat, 1 starch.

TEST KITCHEN TIP

Use a foil-strip crisscross as a tool to remove all sorts of whole foods from the slow cooker. Try it when preparing large cuts of meats or layered dishes such as lasagnas.

PENNSYLVANIA POT ROAST

PENNSYLVANIA POT ROAST

This heartwarming one-dish meal is adapted from a Pennsylvania Dutch recipe. I start the pot roast cooking before I leave for church, add the vegetables when I get home, and then just sit back and relax until it's all done.

—Donna Wilkinson, Monrovia, MD

Prep: 10 min. • **Cook:** 5 hours
Makes: 6 servings

- 1 boneless pork shoulder butt roast (2½ to 3 lbs.), halved
- 1½ cups beef broth
- ½ cup sliced green onions
- 1 tsp. dried basil
- 1 tsp. dried marjoram
- ½ tsp. salt
- ½ tsp. pepper
- 1 bay leaf
- 6 medium red potatoes, cut into 2-in. chunks
- 4 medium carrots, cut into 2-in. chunks
- 7 to 8 fresh mushrooms, quartered
- ¼ cup all-purpose flour
- ½ cup cold water
- Browning sauce, optional

1. Place roast in a 5-qt. slow cooker; add the broth, onions and seasonings. Cook, covered, on high for 4 hours. Add the potatoes, carrots and mushrooms. Cook, covered, on high 1 hour longer or until vegetables are tender. Remove the meat and vegetables; keep warm. Discard the bay leaf.

2. In a saucepan, combine flour and cold water until smooth; stir in 1½ cups cooking juices. Bring to a boil. Cook and stir for 2 minutes or until thickened. If desired, add browning sauce. Serve the gravy with the roast and vegetables.

Per serving: 331 cal., 12g fat (4g sat. fat), 78mg chol., 490mg sod., 28g carb. (5g sugars, 4g fiber), 26g pro.

BEEF IN ONION GRAVY

BEEF IN ONION GRAVY

I double this super recipe to feed our family of four so I'm sure to have leftovers to send with my husband to work for lunch. His co-workers tell him he's lucky to have someone who fixes him such special meals. It's our secret that it's really extras from an easy slow cooker dinner!

—Denise Albers, Freeburg, IL

Prep: 5 min. + standing • **Cook:** 6 hours
Makes: 3 servings

- 1 can (10¾ oz.) condensed cream of mushroom soup, undiluted
- 2 Tbsp. onion soup mix
- 2 Tbsp. beef broth
- 1 Tbsp. quick-cooking tapioca
- 1 lb. beef stew meat, cut into 1-in. cubes
- Hot cooked noodles or mashed potatoes

In a 1½-qt. slow cooker, combine the soup, soup mix, broth and tapioca; let stand for 15 minutes. Stir in the beef. Cover and cook on low for 6-8 hours or until meat is tender. Serve over noodles or mashed potatoes.

Per serving: 326 cal., 15g fat (6g sat. fat), 98mg chol., 1220mg sod., 14g carb. (1g sugars, 1g fiber), 31g pro.

ITALIAN MEATBALL SUBS

This is one of those recipes you always come back to. A flavorful tomato sauce and mildly spiced meatballs make a hearty sandwich filling, or they can be served over pasta. I broil the meatballs first to quickly brown them.

—Jean Glacken, Elkton, MD

Prep: 25 min. • **Cook:** 4 hours
Makes: 7 servings

- 2 large eggs, lightly beaten
- ¼ cup whole milk
- ½ cup dry bread crumbs
- 2 Tbsp. grated Parmesan cheese
- 1 tsp. salt
- ¼ tsp. pepper
- ⅛ tsp. garlic powder
- 1 lb. ground beef
- ½ lb. bulk Italian sausage

SAUCE

- 1 can (15 oz.) tomato sauce
- 1 can (6 oz.) tomato paste
- 1 small onion, chopped
- ½ cup chopped green pepper
- ½ cup dry red wine or beef broth
- ⅓ cup water
- 2 garlic cloves, minced
- 1 tsp. dried oregano
- 1 tsp. salt
- ½ tsp. sugar
- ½ tsp. pepper
- 7 Italian rolls, split
- Shredded Parmesan cheese, optional

1. In a large bowl, combine eggs and milk; add the bread crumbs, cheese, salt, pepper and garlic powder. Add beef and sausage; mix well. Shape into 1-in. balls. Preheat broiler. Place meatballs in a 15x10x1-in. baking pan. Broil 4 in. from the heat for 4 minutes; turn and broil 3 minutes longer.

2. Transfer to a 5-qt. slow cooker. Combine the tomato sauce and paste, onion, green pepper, wine, water and seasonings; pour over meatballs. Cover and cook on low for 4-5 hours. Serve on rolls. Sprinkle with shredded cheese if desired.

Per serving: 482 cal., 21g fat (8g sat. fat), 131mg chol., 1545mg sod., 40g carb. (8g sugars, 4g fiber), 27g pro.

EASY PORK POSOLE

(ALSO PICTURED ON P. 200)

Looking for a meal in a bowl? This Mexican classic—full of pork, sliced sausage, hominy and more—goes into the slow cooker, so you can come home to a table-ready dinner.

—Greg Fontenot, The Woodlands, TX

Prep: 30 min. • **Cook:** 6 hours
Makes: 8 servings (2 qt.)

- 1 Tbsp. canola oil
- ½ lb. boneless pork shoulder butt roast, cubed
- ½ lb. fully cooked andouille sausage links, sliced
- 6 cups reduced-sodium chicken broth
- 2 medium tomatoes, seeded and chopped
- 1 can (16 oz.) hominy, rinsed and drained
- 1 cup minced fresh cilantro
- 1 medium onion, chopped
- 4 green onions, chopped
- 1 jalapeno pepper, seeded and chopped
- 2 garlic cloves, minced
- 1 Tbsp. chili powder
- 1 tsp. ground cumin
- ½ tsp. cayenne pepper
- ½ tsp. coarsely ground pepper
- Corn tortillas, additional chopped onion and minced fresh cilantro, and lime wedges, optional

1. In a large skillet, heat oil over medium-high heat. Brown pork and sausage; drain. Transfer to a 4-qt. slow cooker.

2. Stir in broth, tomatoes, hominy, cilantro, onion, green onions, jalapeno, garlic, chili powder, cumin, cayenne and pepper. Cook, covered, on low for 6-8 hours or until meat is tender. If desired, serve with tortillas, additional onion and cilantro, and lime wedges.

Note Wear disposable gloves when cutting hot peppers; the oils can burn skin. Avoid touching your face.

Per cup: 190 cal., 11g fat (3g sat. fat), 54mg chol., 957mg sod., 12g carb. (2g sugars, 3g fiber), 14g pro.

EASY PORK POSOLE

MARTY'S BEAN BURGER CHILI

EDITOR'S CHOICE

MARTY'S BEAN BURGER CHILI

My husband and I met while working the dinner shift at a homeless shelter that has often served my chili. I've revised the recipe using veggie bean burgers.

—Marty Nickerson, Ellington, CT

Prep: 15 min. • **Cook:** 7 hours
Makes: 6 servings

- 2 cans (14½ oz. each) no-salt-added diced tomatoes, drained
- 1 can (14½ oz.) diced tomatoes, drained
- 1 can (16 oz.) kidney beans, undrained
- 1 can (15 oz.) black beans, undrained
- 1 can (15 oz.) garbanzo beans or chickpeas, rinsed and drained
- 4 frozen spicy black bean veggie burgers, thawed and coarsely chopped
- 1 large onion, finely chopped
- 1 large sweet red or green pepper, chopped
- 2 Tbsp. chili powder
- 1 Tbsp. Worcestershire sauce
- 3 tsp. dried basil
- 3 tsp. dried oregano
- 2 tsp. hot pepper sauce
- 2 garlic cloves, minced

Place all ingredients in a 5- or 6-qt. slow cooker; stir to combine. Cook, covered, on low 7-9 hours to allow flavors to blend.

Per 1½ cups: 348 cal., 6g fat (0 sat. fat), 0 chol., 1151mg sod., 58g carb. (14g sugars, 19g fiber), 21g pro.

BEEF BRISKET IN BEER

One bite of this super tender brisket and your family will be hooked! The rich gravy is perfect for spooning over a side of creamy mashed potatoes.

—Eunice Stoen, Decorah, IA

Prep: 15 min. • **Cook:** 8 hours
Makes: 6 servings

- 1 fresh beef brisket (2½ to 3 lbs.)
- 2 tsp. liquid smoke, optional
- 1 tsp. celery salt
- ½ tsp. pepper
- ¼ tsp. salt
- 1 large onion, sliced
- 1 can (12 oz.) beer or nonalcoholic beer
- 2 tsp. Worcestershire sauce
- 2 Tbsp. cornstarch
- ¼ cup cold water

1. Cut brisket in half; rub with liquid smoke, if desired, and celery salt, pepper and salt. Place in a 3-qt. slow cooker. Top with onion. Combine beer and Worcestershire sauce; pour over meat. Cover and cook on low for 8-9 hours or until tender.

2. Remove brisket from slow cooker and keep warm. Strain cooking juices; transfer to a small saucepan. In a small bowl, combine the cornstarch and water until smooth; stir into juices. Bring to a boil; cook and stir for 2 minutes or until thickened. Serve beef with gravy.

Note This is a fresh beef brisket, not corned beef.

Per 5 oz. cooked meat: 285 cal., 8g fat (3g sat. fat), 80mg chol., 430mg sod., 7g carb. (3g sugars, 0 fiber), 39g pro. **Diabetic exchanges:** 5 lean meat, ½ starch.

TEST KITCHEN TIP

The addition of liquid smoke will give a depth of flavor to this recipe. Be careful not to overdo it; a small amount goes a long way. Look for liquid smoke in the grocery store near the spices and marinades.

EEF BRISKET
IN BEER

CREAMY BRATWURST STEW

CREAMY BRATWURST STEW

I adapted a baked stew recipe from the newspaper to create a simple slow-cooked version. Rich, hearty and creamy, it's the best comfort food for cold winter nights.

—Susan Holmes, Germantown, WI

Prep: 20 min. • **Cook:** $6\frac{1}{2}$ hours
Makes: 8 servings

- $1\frac{3}{4}$ lbs. potatoes (about 4 medium), peeled and cubed
- 2 medium carrots, chopped
- 2 celery ribs, chopped
- 1 medium onion, chopped
- 1 medium green pepper, chopped
- 2 lbs. uncooked bratwurst links
- $\frac{1}{2}$ cup chicken broth
- 1 tsp. salt
- 1 tsp. dried basil
- $\frac{1}{2}$ tsp. pepper
- 2 cups half-and-half cream
- 1 Tbsp. cornstarch
- 3 Tbsp. cold water

1. Place first five ingredients in a 5-qt. slow cooker; toss to combine. Top with the bratwurst. Mix broth and seasonings; pour over top.

2. Cook, covered, on low until sausage is cooked through and vegetables are tender, 6-7 hours. Remove sausages from slow cooker; cut into 1-in. slices. Return sausage to potato mixture; stir in cream.

3. Mix cornstarch and water until smooth; stir into stew. Cook, covered, on high until thickened, about 30 minutes.

Per cup: 544 cal., 39g fat (15g sat. fat), 114mg chol., 1367mg sod., 25g carb. (5g sugars, 2g fiber), 19g pro.

BBQ CHICKEN & SMOKED SAUSAGE

My party-ready barbecue recipe works like a dream for weeknights, too. With just a few minutes of prep time, you still get that low-and-slow flavor everybody craves (thanks, slow cooker!). Throw in minced jalapenos for extra oomph.

—Kimberly Young, Mesquite, TX

Prep: 30 min. • **Cook:** 4 hours
Makes: 8 servings

- **1 medium onion, chopped**
- **1 large sweet red pepper, cut into 1-in. pieces**
- **4 bone-in chicken thighs, skin removed**
- **4 chicken drumsticks, skin removed**
- **1 pkg. (12 oz.) smoked sausage links, cut into 1-in. pieces**
- **1 cup barbecue sauce**
- **Sliced seeded jalapeno pepper, optional**

1. Place first five ingredients in a 4- or 5-qt. slow cooker; top with barbecue sauce. Cook, covered, on low until chicken is tender and a thermometer inserted in chicken reads at least 170°-175°, 4-5 hours.

2. Remove the chicken, sausage and vegetables from slow cooker; keep warm. Transfer cooking juices to a saucepan; bring to a boil. Reduce heat; simmer, uncovered, until thickened, 15-20 minutes, stirring occasionally.

3. Serve chicken, sausage and vegetables with sauce. If desired, top with jalapeno pepper slices.

Per serving: 331 cal., 18g fat (6g sat. fat), 91mg chol., 840mg sod., 17g carb. (13g sugars, 1g fiber), 24g pro.

PORK BURRITOS

PORK BURRITOS

As a working mother, I depend on my slow cooker to help feed my family. We all love the spicy but slightly sweet flavor of these tender burritos.

—Kelly Gengler, Theresa, WI

Prep: 25 min. • **Cook:** 8 hours
Makes: 10 burritos

- **1 boneless pork shoulder butt roast (3 to 4 lbs.)**
- **1 can (14½ oz.) diced tomatoes with mild green chilies, undrained**
- **¼ cup chili powder**
- **3 Tbsp. minced garlic**
- **2 Tbsp. lime juice**
- **2 Tbsp. honey**
- **1 Tbsp. chopped seeded jalapeno pepper**
- **1 tsp. salt**
- **10 flour tortillas (8 in.), warmed**
- **Sliced avocado, sour cream and minced fresh cilantro, optional**

1. Cut roast in half; place in a 5-qt. slow cooker. In a blender, combine the tomatoes, chili powder, garlic, lime juice, honey, jalapeno and salt; cover and process until smooth. Pour over pork. Cover and cook on low for 8-10 hours or until the meat is tender.

2. Remove roast; cool slightly. Shred pork with two forks and return to slow cooker. Using a slotted spoon, place about ½ cup pork mixture down the center of each tortilla; if desired, top with avocado, sour cream and cilantro. Fold sides and ends over filling and roll up.

Freeze option Omit avocado, sour cream and cilantro. Individually wrap cooled burritos in paper towels and foil; freeze in a resealable plastic freezer bag. To use, remove foil; place paper towel-wrapped burrito on a microwave-safe plate. Microwave on high for 3-4 minutes or until heated through, turning once. Let stand 20 seconds. If desired, serve with sliced avocado, sour cream and cilantro.

Note Wear disposable gloves when cutting hot peppers; the oils can burn skin. Avoid touching your face.

Per burrito: 524 cal., 20g fat (6g sat. fat), 155mg chol., 812mg sod., 35g carb. (5g sugars, 2g fiber), 49g pro.

ORANGE SPICE CARROTS

EDITOR'S CHOICE

SLOW COOKER FRENCH ONION SOUP

It's hard to believe something this delightful came from a slow cooker! Topped with French bread and melted provolone cheese, individual servings are sure to be savored by everyone at your dinner table.

—Kris Ritter, Pittsburgh, PA

Prep: 15 min. • **Cook:** 8 hours
Makes: 4 servings

- 2 large sweet onions, thinly sliced (about 4 cups)
- ¼ cup butter, cubed
- 2 cans (14½ oz. each) beef broth
- 2 Tbsp. sherry or additional beef broth
- ½ tsp. pepper
- 4 slices French bread (½ in. thick), toasted
- 4 slices provolone cheese

1. Place onions and butter in a 1½-qt. slow cooker coated with cooking spray. Cover and cook on low for 6 hours or until onions are tender. Stir in the broth, sherry and pepper. Cover and cook 2-3 hours longer or until heated through.
2. Ladle soup into ovenproof bowls. Top each with a slice each of toast and cheese. Broil 4-6 in. from the heat for 2-3 minutes or until cheese is melted. Serve immediately.
Per cup: 267 cal., 20g fat (12g sat. fat), 50mg chol., 1324mg sod., 10g carb. (2g sugars, 1g fiber), 11g pro

MADE WITH LOVE

I love how convenient this recipe is, yet it's so authentic-tasting. I've found that it's the perfect first course for a New Year's Eve dinner. I season it to taste with thyme and salt.

CHRISTINE RUKAVENA
TASTE OF HOME BOOKS

ORANGE SPICE CARROTS

To get my son to eat veggies, I mix and match flavors and spices. Seasoned with orange and cinnamon, these slow-cooked carrots won him over.

—Christina Addison, Blanchester, OH

Prep: 10 min. • **Cook:** 4 hours
Makes: 6 servings

- 2 lbs. medium carrots or baby carrots, cut into 1-in. pieces
- ½ cup packed brown sugar
- ½ cup orange juice
- 2 Tbsp. butter
- ¾ tsp. ground cinnamon
- ½ tsp. salt
- ¼ tsp. ground nutmeg
- 4 tsp. cornstarch
- ¼ cup cold water

1. In a 3-qt. slow cooker, combine the first seven ingredients. Cook, covered, on low 4-5 hours or until carrots are tender.
2. In a small bowl, mix cornstarch and water until smooth; gradually stir into carrot mixture until sauce is thickened, 1-2 minutes.
Per ⅔ cup: 187 cal., 4g fat (3g sat. fat), 10mg chol., 339mg sod., 38g carb. (27g sugars, 4g fiber), 2g pro.

SLOW COOKER BACON MAC & CHEESE

I'm all about easy slow cooker meals. Using more cheese than ever, I've developed an addictive spin on this casserole favorite.

—Kristen Heigl, Staten Island, NY

Prep: 20 min.
Cook: 3 hours + standing
Makes: 18 servings (½ cup each)

- 2 large eggs, lightly beaten
- 4 cups whole milk
- 1 can (12 oz.) evaporated milk
- ¼ cup butter, melted
- 1 Tbsp. all-purpose flour
- 1 tsp. salt
- 1 pkg. (16 oz.) small pasta shells
- 1 cup shredded provolone cheese
- 1 cup shredded Manchego or Monterey Jack cheese
- 1 cup shredded white cheddar cheese
- 8 bacon strips, cooked and crumbled

1. In a large bowl, whisk the first six ingredients until blended. Stir in pasta and the cheeses; transfer to a 4- or 5-qt. slow cooker.

2. Cook, covered, on low 3-3½ hours or until pasta is tender. Turn off slow cooker; remove insert. Let stand, uncovered, for 15 minutes before serving. Top with bacon.

Per ½ cup: 272 cal., 14g fat (8g sat. fat), 59mg chol., 400mg sod., 24g carb. (5g sugars, 1g fiber), 13g pro.

SLOW COOKER BACON MAC & CHEESE

SLOW COOKER RATATOUILLE

SLOW COOKER RATATOUILLE

Not only does this classic recipe make a phenomenal side dish, you can also serve it with sliced French bread for a warm and easy appetizer. Try it in the summer with garden-fresh vegetables.

—Jolene Walters, North Miami, FL

Prep: 20 min. + standing • **Cook:** 3 hours
Makes: 10 servings

- 1 large eggplant, peeled and cut into 1-in. cubes
- 2 tsp. salt, divided
- 3 medium tomatoes, chopped
- 3 medium zucchini, halved lengthwise and sliced
- 2 medium onions, chopped
- 1 large green pepper, chopped
- 1 large sweet yellow pepper, chopped
- 1 can (6 oz.) pitted ripe olives, drained and chopped
- 1 can (6 oz.) tomato paste
- ½ cup minced fresh basil
- 2 garlic cloves, minced
- ½ tsp. pepper
- 2 Tbsp. olive oil

1. Place eggplant in a colander over a plate; sprinkle with 1 tsp. salt and toss. Let stand for 30 minutes. Rinse and drain eggplant well. Transfer to a 5-qt. slow cooker coated with cooking spray.

2. Stir in the tomatoes, zucchini, onions, green and yellow peppers, olives, tomato paste, basil, garlic, pepper and remaining salt. Drizzle with oil. Cover and cook on high for 3-4 hours or until vegetables are tender.

Per ¾ cup: 116 cal., 5g fat (1g sat. fat), 0 chol., 468mg sod., 18g carb. (10g sugars, 6g fiber), 3g pro.

CREAMY HASH BROWN POTATOES

CREAMY HASH BROWN POTATOES

Convenient frozen hash browns are the secret behind the cheesy slow cooker potatoes that I like to cook up for potlucks and other large gatherings.

—Julianne Henson, Streamwood, IL

Prep: 5 min. • **Cook:** 3½ hours
Makes: 14 servings

- 1 pkg. (32 oz.) frozen cubed hash brown potatoes
- 1 can (10¾ oz.) condensed cream of potato soup, undiluted
- 2 cups shredded Colby-Monterey Jack cheese
- 1 cup (8 oz.) sour cream
- ¼ tsp. pepper
- ⅛ tsp. salt
- 1 carton (8 oz.) spreadable chive and onion cream cheese

1. Place potatoes in a lightly greased 4-qt. slow cooker. In a large bowl, combine the soup, cheese, sour cream, pepper and salt. Pour over potatoes and mix well.

2. Cover and cook on low for 3½-4 hours or until the potatoes are tender. Stir in the cream cheese.

Per ¾ cup: 214 cal., 13g fat (9g sat. fat), 42mg chol., 387mg sod., 17g carb. (2g sugars, 2g fiber), 6g pro.

SLOW COOKER CREAMED CORN WITH BACON

Every time we take this super rich corn to a holiday potluck or work party, we leave with an empty slow cooker. It's decadent, homey and so worth the splurge.
—Melissa Pelkey Hass, Waleska, GA

Prep: 10 min.
Cook: 4 hours
Makes: 20 servings (½ cup each)

- 10 cups frozen corn (about 50 oz.), thawed
- 3 pkg. (8 oz. each) cream cheese, cubed
- ½ cup 2% milk
- ½ cup heavy whipping cream
- ½ cup butter, melted
- ¼ cup sugar
- 2 tsp. salt
- ¼ tsp. pepper
- 4 bacon strips, cooked and crumbled
- Chopped green onions

In a 5-qt. slow cooker, combine the first eight ingredients. Cook, covered, on low 4-5 hours or until heated through. Stir just before serving. Sprinkle with crumbled bacon and chopped green onions.

Per ½ cup: 259 cal., 20g fat (11g sat. fat), 60mg chol., 433mg sod., 18g carb. (6g sugars, 1g fiber), 5g pro.

SLOW-COOKED BROCCOLI

This family-favorite side dish is quick to fix and full of flavor. Since it simmers in a slow cooker, it frees up my oven for other things. That's a great help when I'm prepping a big meal at home.

—Connie Slocum, Antioch, TN

Prep: 10 min. • **Cook:** 2¾ hours
Makes: 10 servings

- 6 cups frozen chopped broccoli, partially thawed
- 1 can (10¾ oz.) condensed cream of celery soup, undiluted
- 1½ cups shredded sharp cheddar cheese, divided
- ¼ cup chopped onion
- ½ tsp. Worcestershire sauce
- ¼ tsp. pepper
- 1 cup crushed butter-flavored crackers (about 25)
- 2 Tbsp. butter

1. In a large bowl, combine the broccoli, soup, 1 cup cheese, onion, Worcestershire sauce and pepper. Pour into a greased 3-qt. slow cooker. Sprinkle crackers on top; dot with butter.

2. Cover and cook on high for 2½-3 hours. Sprinkle with remaining cheese. Cook 10 minutes longer or until cheese is melted.

Per ½ cup: 159 cal., 11g fat (6g sat. fat), 25mg chol., 431mg sod., 11g carb. (2g sugars, 1g fiber), 6g pro.

Most frozen vegetables are flash frozen at their peak, so you're getting the ultimate in vitamins and minerals when you work them into your meals.

SLOW-COOKED BROCCOLI

COCONUT-PECAN
SWEET POTATOES

SLOW COOKER DRESSING

Here's an easy dressing that's perfect for holiday get-togethers. Once it's in the slow cooker, you're free to turn your attention to the other dishes.

—Rita Nodland, Bismarck, ND

Prep: 15 min. • **Cook:** 3 hours
Makes: 8 servings

- 2 Tbsp. olive oil
- 1 medium celery rib, chopped
- 1 small onion, chopped
- 8 cups unseasoned stuffing cubes
- 1 tsp. poultry seasoning
- ¼ tsp. salt
- ¼ tsp. pepper
- 2 cups reduced-sodium chicken broth

1. In a large skillet, heat oil over medium-high heat; saute celery and onion until tender. Place stuffing cubes, celery mixture and seasonings in a large bowl; toss to combine. Gradually stir in broth.

2. Transfer to a greased 5-qt. slow cooker. Cook, covered, on low until heated through, 3-4 hours.

Per ½ cup: 226 cal., 5g fat (0 sat. fat), 0 chol., 635mg sod., 40g carb. (3g sugars, 3g fiber), 8g pro.

COCONUT-PECAN SWEET POTATOES

Coconut gives an all-time favorite side dish a new flavor in this version that cooks effortlessly in the slow cooker.

—Raquel Haggard, Edmond, OK

Prep: 15 min.
Cook: 4 hours
Makes: 12 servings (⅔ cup each)

- ½ cup chopped pecans
- ½ cup sweetened shredded coconut
- ⅓ cup sugar
- ⅓ cup packed brown sugar
- ½ tsp. ground cinnamon
- ¼ tsp. salt
- ¼ cup reduced-fat butter, melted
- 4 lbs. sweet potatoes (about 6 medium), peeled and cut into 1-in. pieces
- ½ tsp. coconut extract
- ½ tsp. vanilla extract

1. In a small bowl, combine the first six ingredients; stir in melted butter. Place sweet potatoes in a 5-qt. slow cooker coated with cooking spray. Sprinkle with pecan mixture.

2. Cook, covered, on low 4-4½ hours or until potatoes are tender. Stir in extracts.

Note This recipe was tested with Land O'Lakes light stick butter.

Per ⅔ cup: 211 cal., 7g fat (3g sat. fat), 5mg chol., 103mg sod., 37g carb. (22g sugars, 3g fiber), 2g pro.

SLOW COOKER
DRESSING

CRUNCHY CANDY CLUSTERS

CRUNCHY CANDY CLUSTERS

These cereal and marshmallow clusters are so simple that I always make them for the holidays, as my family looks forward to them each year.

—Faye O'Bryan, Owensboro, KY

Prep: 15 min.
Cook: 1 hour + standing
Makes: about 6½ dozen

- 2 lbs. white candy coating, coarsely chopped
- 1½ cups peanut butter
- ½ tsp. almond extract, optional
- 4 cups Cap'n Crunch cereal
- 4 cups crisp rice cereal
- 4 cups miniature marshmallows

1. Place candy coating in a 5-qt. slow cooker. Cover and cook on high for 1 hour. Add peanut butter. Stir in extract if desired.

2. In a large bowl, combine the cereals and marshmallows. Add the peanut butter mixture and stir until the cereal mixture is well-coated. Drop by tablespoonfuls onto waxed paper. Let stand until set. Store at room temperature.

Per piece: 112 cal., 6g fat (4g sat. fat), 0 chol., 51mg sod., 14g carb. (11g sugars, 0 fiber), 1g pro.

SLOW COOKER LAVA CAKE

I love chocolate—perhaps that's why this decadent cake has long been a family favorite. It can also be served cold.

—Elizabeth Farrell, Hamilton, MT

Prep: 15 min. • **Cook:** 2 hours + standing
Makes: 8 servings

- 1 cup all-purpose flour
- 1 cup packed brown sugar, divided
- 5 Tbsp. baking cocoa, divided
- 2 tsp. baking powder
- ¼ tsp. salt
- ½ cup fat-free milk
- 2 Tbsp. canola oil
- ½ tsp. vanilla extract
- ⅛ tsp. ground cinnamon
- 1¼ cups hot water
- Vanilla ice cream, optional

1. In a large bowl, whisk flour, ½ cup brown sugar, 3 Tbsp. cocoa, baking powder and salt. In another bowl, whisk milk, oil and vanilla until blended. Add to flour mixture; stir just until moistened.

2. Spread into a 3-qt. slow cooker coated with cooking spray. In a small bowl, mix cinnamon and the remaining brown sugar and cocoa; stir in hot water. Pour over batter (do not stir).

3. Cook, covered, on high 2-2½ hours or until a toothpick inserted in cake portion comes out clean. Turn off slow cooker; let stand 15 minutes before serving.

Per serving: 207 cal., 4g fat (0 sat. fat), 0 chol., 191mg sod., 41g carb. (28g sugars, 1g fiber), 3g pro.

SLOW COOKER LAVA CAKE

SLOW-COOKED
BLUEBERRY GRUNT

SLOW-COOKED BLUEBERRY GRUNT

If you love blueberries, then you can't go wrong with this easy dessert. For a special treat, serve it warm with vanilla ice cream.
—Cleo Gonske, Redding, CA

Prep: 20 min. • **Cook:** 2½ hours
Makes: 6 servings

- 4 cups fresh or frozen blueberries
- ¾ cup sugar
- ½ cup water
- 1 tsp. almond extract

DUMPLINGS

- 2 cups all-purpose flour
- 4 tsp. baking powder
- 1 tsp. sugar
- ½ tsp. salt
- 1 Tbsp. cold butter
- 1 Tbsp. shortening
- ¾ cup 2% milk
- Vanilla ice cream, optional

1. Place the blueberries, sugar, water and extract in a 3-qt. slow cooker; stir to combine. Cook, covered, on high 2-3 hours or until bubbly.

2. For dumplings, in a small bowl, whisk flour, baking powder, sugar and salt. Cut in butter and shortening until crumbly. Add milk; stir just until a soft dough forms.

3. Drop dough by tablespoonfuls on top of hot blueberry mixture. Cook, covered, for 30 minutes longer or until a toothpick inserted in center of dumplings comes out clean. Serve warm, with ice cream if desired.

Per cup: 360 cal., 5g fat (2g sat. fat), 7mg chol., 494mg sod., 73g carb. (37g sugars, 3g fiber), 6g pro.

NUTTY APPLE STREUSEL DESSERT

NUTTY APPLE STREUSEL DESSERT

Many people don't think of using a slow cooker to make dessert, but I like having this hot, scrumptious apple treat waiting to be served when we finish up our dinner. I start it in the morning and don't worry about it all day.

—Jacki Every, Rotterdam, NY

Prep: 20 min. • **Cook:** 6 hours
Makes: 8 servings

- 6 cups sliced peeled tart apples
- 1¼ tsp. ground cinnamon
- ¼ tsp. ground allspice
- ¼ tsp. ground nutmeg
- ¾ cup 2% milk
- 2 Tbsp. butter, softened
- ¾ cup sugar
- 2 large eggs
- 1 tsp. vanilla extract
- ½ cup biscuit/baking mix

TOPPING

- 1 cup biscuit/baking mix
- ⅓ cup packed brown sugar
- 3 Tbsp. cold butter
- ½ cup sliced almonds
- Ice cream or whipped cream, optional

1. In a large bowl, toss the apples with cinnamon, allspice and nutmeg. Place in a greased 3-qt. slow cooker. In a small bowl, combine the milk, butter, sugar, eggs, vanilla and biscuit mix. Spoon over apples.

2. For topping, combine biscuit mix and brown sugar in a large bowl; cut in butter until crumbly. Add almonds; sprinkle over the apples.

3. Cover and cook on low for 6-8 hours or until the apples are tender. Serve with ice cream or whipped cream if desired.

Per cup: 378 cal., 16g fat (6g sat. fat), 75mg chol., 387mg sod., 57g carb. (39g sugars, 3g fiber), 5g pro.

FUDGY PEANUT BUTTER CAKE

FUDGY PEANUT BUTTER CAKE

I clipped this recipe from a newspaper years ago. Now, my husband and son like the cake with ice cream and nuts on top. Bonus: The house smells fantastic while it's cooking.
—Bonnie Evans, Norcross, GA

Prep: 10 min. • **Cook:** 1½ hours
Makes: 4 servings

- ⅓ cup whole milk
- ¼ cup peanut butter
- 1 Tbsp. canola oil
- ½ tsp. vanilla extract
- ¾ cup sugar, divided
- ½ cup all-purpose flour
- ¾ tsp. baking powder
- 2 Tbsp. baking cocoa
- 1 cup boiling water
- Chocolate ice cream, optional

1. In a large bowl, beat the milk, peanut butter, oil and vanilla until well blended. In a small bowl, combine ¼ cup sugar, flour and baking powder; gradually beat into milk mixture until blended. Spread into a 1½-qt. slow cooker coated with cooking spray.
2. In a small bowl, combine cocoa and remaining sugar; stir in boiling water. Pour into slow cooker (do not stir).
3. Cover and cook on high for 1½-2 hours or until a toothpick inserted in the center comes out clean. Serve cake warm, with chocolate ice cream if desired.
Note Reduced-fat peanut butter is not recommended for this recipe.
Per piece: 348 cal., 13g fat (3g sat. fat), 3mg chol., 160mg sod., 55g carb. (39g sugars, 2g fiber), 7g pro.

PUMPKIN CRANBERRY BREAD PUDDING

PUMPKIN CRANBERRY BREAD PUDDING

Savor your favorite fall flavors with this scrumptious bread pudding, served warm with a sweet vanilla sauce. Yum!
—Judith Bucciarelli, Newburgh, NY

Prep: 15 min. • **Cook:** 3 hours
Makes: 8 servings (1⅓ cups sauce)

- 8 slices cinnamon bread, cut into 1-in. cubes
- 4 large eggs, beaten
- 2 cups 2% milk
- 1 cup canned pumpkin
- ¼ cup packed brown sugar
- ¼ cup butter, melted
- 1 tsp. vanilla extract
- ½ tsp. ground cinnamon
- ¼ tsp. ground nutmeg
- ½ cup dried cranberries

SAUCE

- 1 cup granulated sugar
- ⅔ cup water
- 1 cup heavy whipping cream
- 2 tsp. vanilla extract
- Vanilla ice cream, optional

1. Place bread cubes in a greased 3- or 4-qt. slow cooker. Combine the next eight ingredients; stir in cranberries. Pour over bread. Cook, covered, on low until a knife inserted in the center comes out clean, 3-4 hours.
2. For sauce, bring granulated sugar and water to a boil in a large saucepan over medium heat. Cook until sugar is dissolved and mixture turns golden amber, about 20 minutes. Gradually stir in cream until smooth. Remove from heat; stir in vanilla. Serve sauce warm with bread pudding. If desired, add a scoop of vanilla ice cream to each serving.
Per serving: 479 cal., 23g fat (13g sat. fat), 147mg chol., 237mg sod., 61g carb. (48g sugars, 4g fiber), 9g pro.

APPLE PIE OATMEAL DESSERT

APPLE PIE OATMEAL DESSERT

This warm and comforting treat brings back memories of time spent with my family around the kitchen table. I serve this dish with sweetened whipped cream or vanilla ice cream as a topper.

—Carol Greer, Earlville, IL

Prep: 15 min. • **Cook:** 4 hours
Makes: 6 servings

- 1 cup quick-cooking oats
- ½ cup all-purpose flour
- ⅓ cup packed brown sugar
- 2 tsp. baking powder
- 1½ tsp. apple pie spice
- ¼ tsp. salt
- 3 large eggs
- 1⅔ cups 2% milk, divided
- 1½ tsp. vanilla extract
- 3 medium apples, peeled and finely chopped
- Vanilla ice cream, optional

1. In a large bowl, whisk oats, flour, brown sugar, baking powder, pie spice and salt. In a small bowl, whisk eggs, 1 cup milk and vanilla until blended. Add to oat mixture, stirring just until moistened. Fold in apples.

2. Transfer to a greased 3-qt. slow cooker. Cook, covered, on low 4-5 hours or until apples are tender and top is set.

3. Stir in remaining milk. Serve warm or cold, with ice cream if desired.

Per ¾ cup: 238 cal., 5g fat (2g sat. fat), 111mg chol., 306mg sod., 41g carb. (22g sugars, 3g fiber), 8g pro.

STRAWBERRY-BANANA PUDDING CAKE

This luscious pink pudding cake is so easy to put together. Top it with fresh fruit, and you have one very happy family.

—Nadine Mesch, Mount Healthy, OH

Prep: 15 min. • **Cook:** 3½ hours + standing
Makes: 10 servings

- 1 pkg. strawberry cake mix (regular size)
- 1 pkg. (3.4 oz.) instant banana cream pudding mix
- 2 cups plain Greek yogurt
- 4 large eggs
- 1 cup water
- ¾ cup canola oil
- 2 Tbsp. minced fresh basil
- 1 cup white baking chips
- Optional toppings: vanilla ice cream, sliced bananas, sliced strawberries and fresh basil

1. In a large bowl, combine the first six ingredients; beat on low speed 30 seconds. Beat on medium 2 minutes; stir in basil. Transfer to a greased 5-qt. slow cooker. Cook, covered, on low until edges of cake are golden brown (center will be moist), 3½-4 hours.

2. Turn off slow cooker; sprinkle cake with baking chips. Remove insert; let stand, uncovered, 10 minutes before serving. Serve warm, with toppings as desired.

Per serving: 373 cal., 29g fat (8g sat. fat), 90mg chol., 239mg sod., 23g carb. (21g sugars, 0 fiber), 5g pro.

STRAWBERRY-BANANA PUDDING CAKE

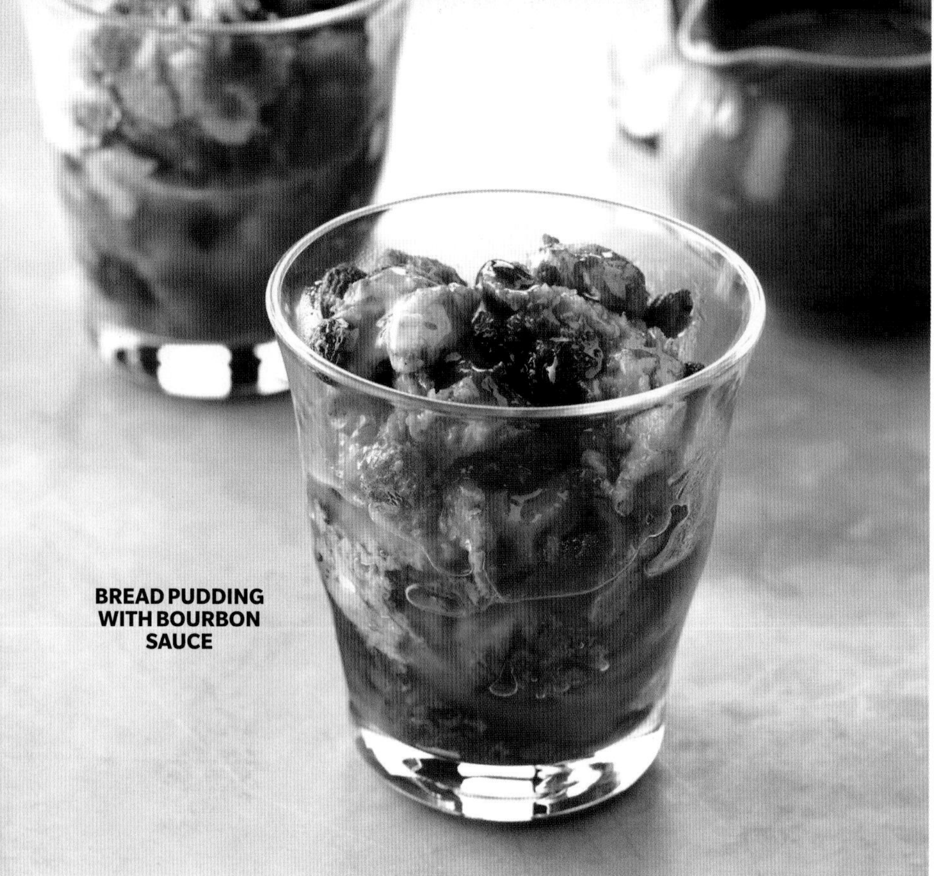

BREAD PUDDING WITH BOURBON SAUCE

MAPLE CREME BRULEE

The slow cooker is the perfect vessel for this classic dessert. The crunchy brown sugar topping in the recipe is wonderful, and the custard is smooth and creamy.
—Taste of Home *Test Kitchen*

Prep: 20 min. • **Cook:** 2 hours + chilling
Makes: 3 servings

- 1⅓ cups heavy whipping cream
- 3 large egg yolks
- ½ cup packed brown sugar
- ¼ tsp. ground cinnamon
- ½ tsp. maple flavoring

TOPPING

- 1½ tsp. sugar
- 1½ tsp. brown sugar

1. In a small saucepan, heat cream until bubbles form around sides of pan. In a small bowl, whisk the egg yolks, brown sugar and cinnamon. Remove cream from the heat; stir a small amount of hot cream into egg mixture. Return all to the pan, stirring constantly. Stir in maple flavoring.
2. Transfer to three 6-oz. ramekins or custard cups. Place in a 6-qt. slow cooker; add 1 in. of boiling water to slow cooker. Cover and cook on high for 2-2½ hours or until centers are just set (mixture will jiggle). Carefully remove ramekins from slow cooker; cool for 10 minutes. Cover and refrigerate for at least 4 hours.
3. For topping, combine sugars and sprinkle over ramekins. Hold a kitchen torch about 2 in. above custard surface; rotate slowly until the sugar is evenly caramelized. Serve immediately.
4. If broiling the custards, preheat broiler and place ramekins on a baking sheet; let stand at room temperature for 15 minutes. Broil 8 in. from heat until sugar is caramelized, 3-5 minutes. Refrigerate until firm, 1-2 hours.
Per serving: 578 cal., 44g fat (26g sat. fat), 350mg chol., 63mg sod., 44g carb. (40g sugars, 0 fiber), 5g pro.

BREAD PUDDING WITH BOURBON SAUCE

There's nothing better than this comforting bread pudding recipe on a cold, wintry day. The bourbon sauce makes the dessert taste special, but it's so easy to prepare—the slow cooker does the most of the work!
—Hope Johnson, Youngwood, PA

Prep: 15 min. • **Cook:** 3 hours.
Makes: 6 servings

- 3 large eggs
- 1¼ cups 2% milk
- ½ cup sugar
- 3 tsp. vanilla extract
- ½ tsp. ground cinnamon
- ¼ tsp. ground nutmeg
- ⅛ tsp. salt
- 4½ cups day-old cubed brioche or egg bread
- 1¼ cups raisins

BOURBON SAUCE

- ¼ cup butter, cubed
- ½ cup sugar
- ¼ cup light corn syrup
- 3 Tbsp. bourbon

1. In a large bowl, whisk together the first seven ingredients; stir in bread and raisins. Transfer to a greased 4-qt. slow cooker. Cook, covered, on low 3 hours. (To avoid scorching, rotate slow cooker insert one-half turn midway through cooking, lifting carefully with oven mitts.)
2. For sauce, place butter, sugar and corn syrup in a small saucepan; bring to a boil, stirring occasionally. Cook and stir until the sugar is dissolved. Remove from heat; stir in bourbon. Serve warm with bread pudding.
Per cup with 2 Tbsp. sauce: 477 cal., 12g fat (6g sat. fat), 130mg chol., 354mg sod., 84g carb. (59g sugars, 2g fiber), 8g pro.

SWEET & TANGY CHICKEN

If you need an easy dish for a casual dinner party, this is just the thing. Spicy barbecue sauce blends with sweet pineapple for a crowd-pleasing entree.

—Mary Zawlocki, Gig Harbor, WA

Prep: 10 min. • **Cook:** 5 hours
Makes: 8 servings

- 8 boneless skinless chicken breast halves (4 oz. each)
- 1 bottle (18 oz.) barbecue sauce
- 1 can (20 oz.) pineapple chunks, undrained
- 1 medium green pepper, chopped
- 1 medium onion, chopped
- 2 garlic cloves, minced
- Hot cooked rice

1. Place four chicken breasts in a 5-qt. slow cooker. Combine the barbecue sauce, pineapple, green pepper, onion and garlic; pour half over the chicken. Top with the remaining chicken and sauce.

2. Cover; cook on low until a thermometer reads 165°, about 5 hours. Thicken sauce if desired. Serve chicken and sauce with rice.

Per serving: 264 cal., 5g fat (1g sat. fat), 63mg chol., 1101mg sod., 28g carb. (24g sugars, 3g fiber), 26g pro.

Chopsticks anyone? How about a fancy orange garnish? Since we first published this recipe and photo in 1999, we try to make entrees look a bit more like they might appear on your own table.

GRILLED GREATS

THERE'S NO BETTER WAY TO FEED THE FAMILY THAN WITH FLAME-KISSED FARE. FROM MEATY MAINSTAYS TO APPS, SIDES AND EVEN DESSERTS, WE'VE GOT THE HOTTEST COOKOUT EATS. TIE ON YOUR APRON, GRAB THE SPATULA AND HEAD TO THE BACKYARD. IT'S GRILLING TIME!

GRILLED SEASONED SHRIMP

A marinade using balsamic vinegar, lemon juice and Italian dressing boosts the flavor of these tender shrimp.

—Diane Harrison, Mechanicsburg, PA

Prep: 10 min. • **Grill:** 5 min. + chilling
Makes: 4 servings

- 1½ lbs. uncooked large shrimp
- 1 small red onion, sliced and separated into rings
- ¼ cup Italian salad dressing
- 2 green onions, chopped
- 2 Tbsp. lemon juice
- 2 Tbsp. balsamic vinegar
- 2 Tbsp. olive oil
- 3 garlic cloves, minced
- Salt and coarsely ground pepper to taste, optional

1. Peel and devein shrimp, leaving tails intact if desired. Coat a grill rack with cooking spray before starting the grill.
2. Grill shrimp, covered, over indirect medium heat for 2-3 minutes on each side or until shrimp turn pink. Cool; cover and refrigerate until chilled.
3. In a large resealable plastic bag, combine the remaining ingredients; add shrimp. Seal bag and turn to coat; refrigerate for at least 2 hours. Serve with a slotted spoon.

Per 3 shrimp: 267 cal., 10g fat (2g sat. fat), 259mg chol., 470mg sod., 7g carb. (0 sugars, 1g fiber), 35g pro. **Diabetic exchanges:** 4 lean meat, 2 fat, ½ fruit.

Shrimp are available fresh or frozen (raw or cooked, peeled or in the shell) or canned. Shrimp in the shell (fresh or frozen) are available in different varieties and sizes—medium, large, extra large and jumbo. Uncooked shrimp will have shells that range in color from gray or brown to pink or red. Fresh shrimp should have a firm texture and a mild odor.

GRILLED GUACAMOLE

Guacamole lovers won't be able to get enough of this smoky grilled version of the classic dip.

—Lindsay Sprunk, Brooklyn, NY

Prep: 10 min.
Grill: 10 min. + cooling
Makes: 12 servings

- 1 medium red onion, cut into ½-in. slices
- 2 plum tomatoes, halved and seeded
- 1 jalapeno pepper, halved and seeded
- 2 Tbsp. canola oil, divided
- 3 medium ripe avocados, halved and pitted
- ¼ cup fresh cilantro leaves, chopped
- 2 Tbsp. lime juice
- 2 tsp. ground cumin
- ¾ tsp. salt
- Tortilla chips

1. In a large bowl, combine the onion, tomatoes, pepper and 1 Tbsp. oil; gently toss to coat. Grill, covered, over medium-high heat or broil 4 in. from heat until tender and charred, turning occasionally, 6-8 minutes. Brush avocados with the remaining oil. Grill or broil avocados, cut side down, 4-6 minutes longer or until charred. Cool vegetables completely.
2. Chop onion, tomatoes and pepper; set aside. Peel avocados; transfer to a large bowl and mash with a fork. Stir in the vegetables, cilantro, lime juice, cumin and salt. Serve immediately with chips.

Note Wear disposable gloves when cutting hot peppers; the oils can burn skin. Avoid touching your face.

Per ¼ cup: 85 cal., 8g fat (1g sat. fat), 0 chol., 152mg sod., 5g carb. (1g sugars, 3g fiber), 1g pro.

COLA HOT WINGS

These delectable wings are so easy to make, and they offer year-round versatility, from summer cookouts to autumn tailgates. My husband likes them so much he'll stand out in the snow to grill them!

—Lisa Linville, Randolph, NE

Prep: 15 min. • **Grill:** 40 min.
Makes: about 2½ dozen

- 3 lbs. chicken wings
- 1 cup Louisiana-style hot sauce
- 1 can (12 oz.) cola
- 1 Tbsp. soy sauce
- ¼ tsp. cayenne pepper
- ¼ tsp. pepper
- Blue cheese salad dressing

1. Cut chicken wings into three sections; discard wing tip sections. In a small bowl, combine hot sauce, cola, soy sauce, cayenne and pepper.

2. Prepare grill for indirect heat, using a drip pan. Grill chicken wings, covered, over indirect medium heat on an oiled rack for 10 minutes. Grill 30-40 minutes longer, turning occasionally and basting frequently with sauce until wings are nicely glazed. Serve with salad dressing.

Note Uncooked chicken wing sections (wingettes) may be substituted for whole chicken wings.

Per chicken wing: 57 cal., 3g fat (1g sat. fat), 15mg chol., 48mg sod., 2g carb. (1g sugars, 0 fiber), 5g pro.

COLORFUL CORN SALSA

COLORFUL CORN SALSA

This salsa is worth the extra time it takes to grill the ears of corn. It's tasty served with chips or as a garnish on grilled meat.

—Nancy Horsburgh, Everett, ON

Prep: 30 min. • **Grill:** 20 min. + cooling
Makes: about 2½ cups

- 2 medium ears sweet corn in husks
- 2 medium tomatoes, chopped
- 1 small onion, chopped
- 2 Tbsp. minced fresh cilantro
- 1 Tbsp. lime juice
- 1 Tbsp. finely chopped green pepper
- 1 Tbsp. finely chopped sweet red pepper
- 1 tsp. minced seeded jalapeno pepper
- ¼ tsp. salt
- Dash pepper
- Tortilla chips

1. Peel back husks of corn but do not remove; remove silk. Replace husks and tie with kitchen string. Place corn in a bowl and cover with water; soak for 20 minutes. Drain. Grill corn, covered, over medium-high heat for 20-35 minutes or until husks are blackened and corn is tender, turning several times. Cool.

2. Remove corn from cobs and place in a bowl. Add tomatoes, onion, cilantro, lime juice, peppers, salt and pepper. Serve salsa with tortilla chips.

Note Wear disposable gloves when cutting hot peppers; the oils can burn skin. Avoid touching your face.

Per ¼ cup: 24 cal., 0 fat (0 sat. fat), 0 chol., 64mg sod., 5g carb. (0 sugars, 1g fiber), 1g pro.

GRILLED NECTARINE & CHEESE CROSTINI

At our house, we love the fresh taste of sweet grilled nectarines and fresh basil over goat cheese. I can usually find all the ingredients at the farmers market.

—Brandy Hollingshead, Grass Valley, CA

Takes: 25 min. • **Makes:** 1 dozen

- ½ cup balsamic vinegar
- 1 Tbsp. olive oil
- 12 slices French bread baguette (¼ in. thick)
- 2 medium nectarines, halved
- ¼ cup fresh goat cheese, softened
- ¼ cup loosely packed basil leaves, thinly sliced

1. In a small saucepan, bring vinegar to a boil; cook 10-15 minutes or until liquid is reduced to 3 Tbsp. Remove from heat.

2. Brush oil over both sides of baguette slices. Grill, uncovered, over medium heat until golden brown on both sides. Grill nectarines 45-60 seconds on each side or until tender and lightly browned. Cool slightly.

3. Spread goat cheese over toasts. Cut nectarines into thick slices; arrange over cheese. Drizzle with balsamic syrup; sprinkle with basil. Serve immediately.

Per appetizer: 48 cal., 2g fat (1g sat. fat), 5mg chol., 55mg sod., 6g carb. (3g sugars, 0 fiber), 1g pro. **Diabetic exchanges:** ½ starch.

GRILLED NECTARINE & CHEESE CROSTINI

MARGARITA CHICKEN QUESADILLAS

MARGARITA CHICKEN QUESADILLAS

My favorite quesadillas are those that are filled with slightly sweet onions and peppers and topped with lime butter and salt—the perfect balance of sweet and savory. These are perfect for an outdoor party or a great way to bring a little bit of summer into the cold winter months.

—Stephanie Bright, Simpsonville, SC

Prep: 35 min. + marinating • **Bake:** 10 min.
Makes: 16 wedges

- 4 boneless skinless chicken breast halves (5 oz. each)
- ¾ cup thawed frozen limeade concentrate
- 1 large onion, sliced
- 1 medium sweet orange pepper, julienned
- 1 medium sweet yellow pepper, julienned
- 1 Tbsp. canola oil
- ¼ tsp. salt
- ¼ tsp. pepper
- 4 flour tortillas (10 in.)
- 1 cup shredded Monterey Jack cheese
- 1 cup shredded cheddar cheese
- 2 Tbsp. butter, melted
- 1 Tbsp. lime juice
- 1 Tbsp. chopped fresh cilantro
- Lime wedges, optional

1. Place chicken in a large bowl. Add limeade concentrate; toss to coat. Cover bowl; refrigerate 6 hours or overnight.

2. In a large nonstick skillet, saute onion and the sweet peppers in oil until tender; season with salt and pepper. Remove and set aside; wipe out skillet. Drain chicken and discard marinade.

3. Grill chicken, covered, on a greased rack over medium heat or broil 4 in. from the heat for 5-8 minutes on each side or until a thermometer reads 170°. Cut chicken into ¼-in. strips; set aside. On one half of each tortilla, layer Monterey Jack cheese, chicken, pepper mixture and cheddar cheese; fold over. Combine butter and lime juice; brush over tortillas.

4. In same skillet used to cook vegetables, cook quesadillas over medium heat until cheese is melted, 2-3 minutes per side. Keep warm in oven while cooking remaining quesadillas. Cut each quesadilla into four wedges. Sprinkle with cilantro; serve with lime wedges if desired.

Per wedge: 204 cal., 9g fat (4g sat. fat), 37mg chol., 288mg sod., 18g carb. (8g sugars, 1g fiber), 12g pro.

GRILLED PINEAPPLE WITH LIME DIP

GRILLED PINEAPPLE WITH LIME DIP

Serve this dish as an appetizer or dessert—the choice is yours! If desired, the pineapple wedges can be rolled in flaked coconut before grilling.

—Taste of Home *Test Kitchen*

Prep: 20 min. + marinating • **Grill:** 10 min.
Makes: 8 servings

- 1 fresh pineapple
- ¼ cup packed brown sugar
- 3 Tbsp. honey
- 2 Tbsp. lime juice

LIME DIP

- 3 oz. cream cheese, softened
- ¼ cup plain yogurt
- 2 Tbsp. honey
- 1 Tbsp. brown sugar
- 1 Tbsp. lime juice
- 1 tsp. grated lime zest

1. Peel and core the pineapple; cut into eight wedges. Cut each wedge into two spears. In a large resealable plastic bag, combine the brown sugar, honey and lime juice; add pineapple. Seal bag and turn to coat; refrigerate for 1 hour.

2. In a small bowl, beat cream cheese until smooth. Beat in the yogurt, honey, brown sugar, lime juice and zest. Cover and refrigerate until serving.

3. Coat grill rack with cooking spray before starting the grill. Drain and discard marinade. Grill pineapple, covered, over medium heat for 3-4 minutes on each side or until golden brown. Serve with lime dip.

Per 2 spears with 2 tablespoons dip: 160 cal., 4g fat (2g sat. fat), 12mg chol., 41mg sod., 32g carb. (28g sugars, 2g fiber), 2g pro.

APPETIZER PIZZAS

To keep a summer kitchen cool, we suggest preparing pizzas on the grill. A mix of ingredients tops flour tortillas for three terrific variations.

—Taste of Home *Test Kitchen*

Prep: 30 min. • **Grill:** 10 min.
Makes: 9 appetizer pizzas (12 servings)

- 9 flour tortillas (6 in.)
- 3 Tbsp. olive oil

TRADITIONAL PIZZA

- ⅓ cup chopped pepperoni
- ¾ cup shredded Colby-Monterey Jack cheese
- 1 jar (14 oz.) pizza sauce

MEDITERRANEAN PIZZA

- ½ cup chopped seeded tomato
- ⅓ cup sliced ripe olives
- ¾ cup crumbled feta cheese
- ¼ cup thinly sliced green onions
- 1 carton (7 oz.) hummus

MARGHERITA PIZZA

- 9 thin slices tomato
- 1 pkg. (8 oz.) small fresh mozzarella cheese balls, sliced
- 1 Tbsp. minced fresh basil
- 1 cup prepared pesto

Brush one side of each tortilla with oil. Place oiled side down on grill rack. Grill, uncovered, over medium heat for 2-3 minutes or until puffed. Brush tortillas with oil; turn and top with pizza toppings.

For traditional pizza: Top three grilled tortillas with pepperoni and cheese. Cover and grill for 2-3 minutes or until cheese is melted. Cut tortillas into wedges; serve with pizza sauce.

For mediterranean pizza: Top three grilled tortillas with tomato, olives, feta cheese and onions. Cover and grill for 2-3 minutes or until cheese is heated through. Cut into wedges; serve with hummus.

For margherita pizza: Top three grilled tortillas with tomato slices, mozzarella cheese and basil. Cover and grill for 2-3 minutes or until cheese is melted. Cut into wedges; serve with pesto.

Per 3 pieces: 238 cal., 16g fat (6g sat. fat), 19mg chol., 551mg sod., 14g carb. (2g sugars, 2g fiber), 8g pro.

BALSAMIC-GLAZED FIG & PORK TENDERLOIN

I have a huge fig tree that produces an abundance of figs. One year I tried drying some and developed this sweet and smoky recipe as a result. Now it's a regular at family gatherings.

—Greg Fontenot, The Woodlands, TX

Prep: 35 min. • **Grill:** 10 min.
Makes: 12 kabobs

- 2 pork tenderloins (about ¾ lb. each), trimmed and silver skin removed
- 1 Tbsp. smoked paprika
- 1 tsp. salt
- 1 tsp. pepper
- 1 tsp. onion powder
- ½ tsp. garlic powder
- ½ tsp. white pepper
- ¼ tsp. cayenne pepper
- ¼ cup balsamic vinegar
- 3 Tbsp. honey
- 1 Tbsp. Dijon mustard
- 2 tsp. olive oil
- 12 dried figs, halved
- 12 cherry tomatoes
- ½ cup crumbled blue cheese
- 4 fresh basil leaves, thinly sliced

1. Cut pork into 1-in. cubes. Combine next seven ingredients; rub over pork. Refrigerate, covered, until ready to grill. Meanwhile, make a glaze by whisking vinegar, honey, mustard and oil. Set aside.
2. On water-soaked wooden skewers, thread pork cubes and fig halves. Grill, covered, on a greased rack over medium-high direct heat, turning occasionally, until a thermometer reads 145°, 8-10 minutes. During last half of grilling, brush cooked surfaces frequently with glaze.
3. Let skewers stand for 5 minutes; add a tomato to each. Transfer to a serving platter and sprinkle lightly with blue cheese and basil.

Per kabob: 139 cal., 4g fat (2g sat. fat), 35mg chol., 306mg sod., 13g carb. (10g sugars, 1g fiber), 13g pro.

BALSAMIC-GLAZED FIG & PORK TENDERLOIN

POLYNESIAN KABOBS

With their explosion of flavors and textures, these kabobs also make a quick, satisfying entree.

—Chris Anderson, Morton, IL

Takes: 30 min. • **Makes:** 14 kabobs

- 1 can (8 oz.) unsweetened pineapple chunks
- 1 pkg. (14 oz.) breakfast turkey sausage links, cut in half
- 1 can (8 oz.) whole water chestnuts, drained
- 1 large sweet red pepper, cut into 1-in. chunks
- 2 Tbsp. honey
- 2 tsp. reduced-sodium soy sauce
- ⅛ tsp. ground nutmeg
- Dash pepper

1. Drain pineapple, reserving 1 Tbsp. juice (discard remaining juice or save for another use). Thread the sausages, water chestnuts, pineapple and red pepper alternately onto 14 metal or soaked wooden skewers.

2. In a small bowl, combine the honey, soy sauce, nutmeg, pepper and reserved pineapple juice.

3. Grill kabobs, uncovered, over medium-hot heat for 6-7 minutes on each side or until the sausages are browned, basting occasionally with marinade.

Per kabob: 95 cal., 6g fat (2g sat. fat), 23mg chol., 199mg sod., 7g carb. (5g sugars, 1g fiber), 5g pro.

HOT DOG SLIDERS WITH MANGO-PINEAPPLE SALSA

For parties, we shrink down lots of foods to slider size, including these quick hot dogs. Pile on the easy but irresistible fruit salsa for a burst of fresh flavor.

—Carole Resnick, Cleveland, OH

Takes: 30 min.
Makes: 2 dozen (2 cups salsa)

- 3 Tbsp. lime juice
- 2 Tbsp. honey
- ¼ tsp. salt
- 1 cup cubed fresh pineapple (½ in.)
- 1 cup cubed peeled mango (½ in.)
- ¼ cup finely chopped red onion
- 2 Tbsp. finely chopped sweet red pepper
- 12 hot dogs
- 12 hot dog buns, split

1. In a small bowl, whisk lime juice, honey and salt until blended. Add pineapple, mango, onion and pepper; toss to coat.

2. Grill hot dogs, covered, over medium heat or broil 4 in. from heat 7-9 minutes or until heated through, turning occasionally.

3. Place hot dogs in buns; cut each crosswise in half. Serve with fruit salsa.

Per slider with 1 tablespoon salsa: 146 cal., 8g fat (3g sat. fat), 13mg chol., 361mg sod., 15g carb. (5g sugars, 1g fiber), 5g pro.

GRILLED ZUCCHINI & PESTO PIZZA

GRILLED ZUCCHINI & PESTO PIZZA

In the great outdoors, we surprise our campmates because they don't think it's possible to have standout pizza in the backwoods. This one with zucchini proves it can be done!

—Jesse Arriaga, Reno, NV

Takes: 20 min. • **Makes:** 6 servings

- 4 naan flatbreads
- ½ cup prepared pesto
- 2 cups shredded part-skim mozzarella cheese
- 1 medium zucchini, thinly sliced
- 1 small red onion, thinly sliced
- ¼ lb. thinly sliced hard salami, chopped
- ½ cup fresh basil leaves, thinly sliced
- ¼ cup grated Romano cheese

1. Over each naan, spread 2 Tbsp. pesto; top with ½ cup mozzarella, ⅓ cup zucchini, ¼ cup onion and one-quarter of the salami.
2. Grill, covered, over medium-low heat until mozzarella has melted and vegetables are tender, 4-6 minutes. Rotate the naan halfway through grilling for an evenly browned crust.
3. Remove from heat. Top each naan with basil and Romano; cut into thirds.

Per 2 pieces: 391 cal., 24g fat (9g sat. fat), 51mg chol., 1276mg sod., 25g carb. (4g sugars, 1g fiber), 20g pro.

SPICY LEMON CHICKEN KABOBS

SPICY LEMON CHICKEN KABOBS

(ALSO PICTURED ON P. 249)

As soon as I see Meyer lemons in the store, I know it must be spring. I use them in this recipe, but regular grilled lemons will also add the same signature smoky tang.

—Terri Crandall, Gardnerville, NV

Prep: 15 min. + marinating • **Grill:** 10 min.
Makes: 6 servings

- ¼ cup lemon juice
- 4 Tbsp. olive oil, divided
- 3 Tbsp. white wine
- 1½ tsp. crushed red pepper flakes
- 1 tsp. minced fresh rosemary or ¼ tsp. dried rosemary, crushed
- 1½ lbs. boneless skinless chicken breasts, cut into 1-in. cubes
- 2 medium lemons, halved
- Minced chives

1. In a large resealable plastic bag, combine lemon juice, 3 Tbsp. oil, wine, pepper flakes and rosemary. Add chicken; seal bag and turn to coat. Refrigerate up to 3 hours.
2. Drain chicken, discarding marinade. Thread chicken onto six metal or soaked wooden skewers. Grill, covered, over medium heat 10-12 minutes or until no longer pink, turning once.
3. Place lemons on grill, cut side down. Grill 8-10 minutes or until lightly browned. Squeeze lemon halves over chicken. Drizzle with remaining oil; sprinkle with chives.

Per kabob: 182 cal., 8g fat (2g sat. fat), 63mg chol., 55mg sod., 2g carb. (1g sugars, 1g fiber), 23g pro. **Diabetic exchanges:** 3 lean meat, 1 fat.

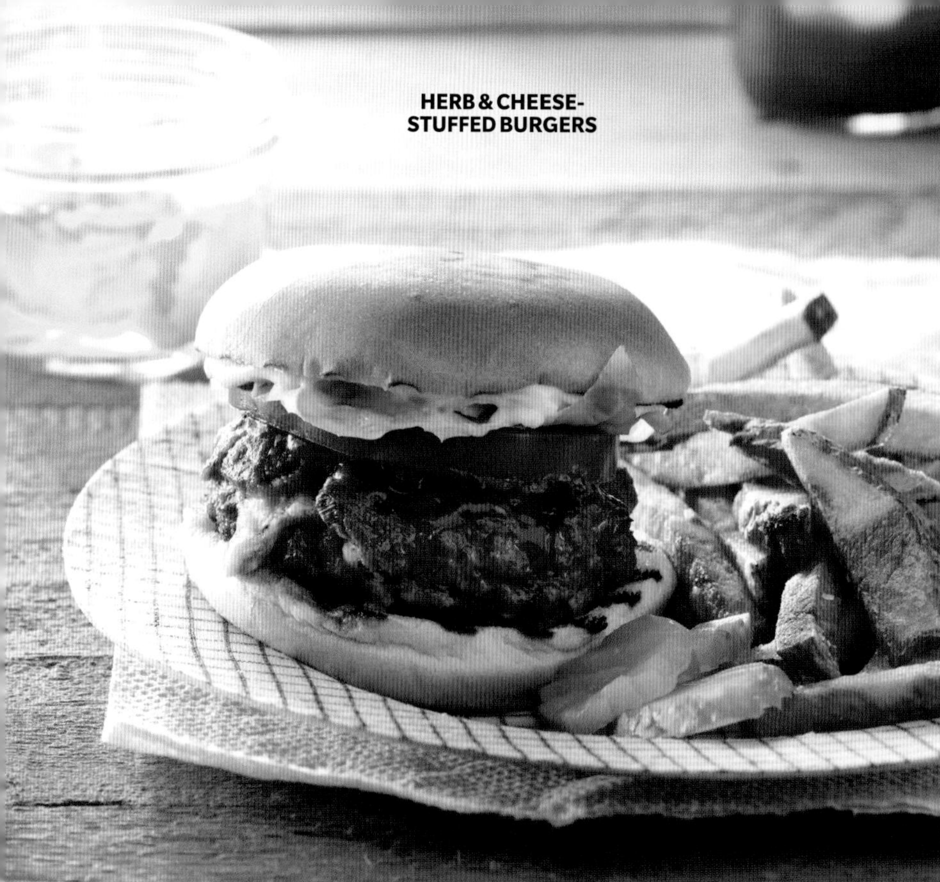

EDITOR'S CHOICE

HERB & CHEESE-STUFFED BURGERS

Tired of the same old ground beef burgers? This quick-fix alternative, with its creamy cheese filling, will wake up your taste buds.
—Sherri Cox, Lucasville, OH

Takes: 30 min. • **Makes:** 4 servings

- ¼ cup shredded cheddar cheese
- 2 Tbsp. cream cheese, softened
- 2 Tbsp. minced fresh parsley
- 3 tsp. Dijon mustard, divided
- 2 green onions, thinly sliced
- 3 Tbsp. dry bread crumbs
- 2 Tbsp. ketchup
- ½ tsp. salt
- ½ tsp. dried rosemary, crushed
- ¼ tsp. dried sage leaves
- 1 lb. lean ground beef (90% lean)
- 4 hamburger buns, split
- Optional toppings: lettuce leaves and tomato slices

1. In a small bowl, mix cheddar cheese, cream cheese, parsley and 1 tsp. mustard. In another bowl, mix green onions, bread crumbs, ketchup, seasonings and the remaining mustard. Add beef; mix lightly but thoroughly.
2. Shape mixture into eight thin patties. Spoon cheese mixture onto the center of four patties; top with remaining patties, pressing edges firmly to seal.
3. Grill burgers, covered, over medium heat or broil 4 in. from heat 4-5 minutes on each side or until a thermometer reads 160°. Serve on buns with toppings as desired.
Per burger: 383 cal., 16g fat (7g sat. fat), 86mg chol., 861mg sod., 29g carb. (5g sugars, 1g fiber), 29g pro.

THE ULTIMATE FISH TACOS

This recipe is my favorite meal to prepare. Adding my own personal touch to the marinade makes my fish tacos pop with flavor. I warm corn tortillas on the grill and add salsa, cilantro, purple cabbage and fresh-squeezed lime.
—Yvonne Molina, Moreno Valley, CA

Prep: 20 min. + marinating • **Grill:** 10 min.
Makes: 6 servings

- ¼ cup olive oil
- 1 tsp. ground cardamom
- 1 tsp. paprika
- 1 tsp. salt
- 1 tsp. pepper
- 6 mahi mahi fillets (6 oz. each)
- 12 corn tortillas (6 in.)
- 2 cups chopped red cabbage
- 1 cup chopped fresh cilantro
- Salsa verde, optional
- 2 medium limes, cut into wedges
- Hot pepper sauce (Tapatio preferred)

1. In a 13x9-in. baking dish, whisk the first five ingredients. Add fillets; turn to coat. Refrigerate, covered, 30 minutes.
2. Drain fish and discard marinade. On an oiled grill rack, grill mahi mahi, covered, over medium-high heat (or broil 4 in. from heat) until it flakes easily with a fork, about 4-5 minutes per side. Remove fish. Place tortillas on grill rack; heat 30-45 seconds. Keep warm.
3. To assemble, divide fish among the tortillas; layer with red cabbage, cilantro and, if desired, salsa verde. Squeeze a little lime juice and hot pepper sauce over fish mixture; fold sides of tortilla over mixture. Serve with lime wedges and additional pepper sauce.
Per 2 tacos: 284 cal., 5g fat (1g sat. fat), 124mg chol., 278mg sod., 26g carb. (2g sugars, 4g fiber), 35g pro. **Diabetic exchanges:** 5 lean meat, 1½ starch, ½ fat.

THE ULTIMATE FISH TACOS

GRILLED HULI HULI CHICKEN

EDITOR'S CHOICE

GRILLED HULI HULI CHICKEN

I received this grilled chicken recipe from a friend while living in Hawaii. (*Huli* means "turn" in Hawaiian.) It sizzles with the flavors of brown sugar, ginger and soy sauce. The sweet and savory glaze is fantastic on pork chops, too.
—Sharon Boling, San Diego, CA

Prep: 15 min. + marinating • **Grill:** 15 min.
Makes: 12 servings

- 1 cup packed brown sugar
- ¾ cup ketchup
- ¾ cup reduced-sodium soy sauce
- ⅓ cup sherry or chicken broth
- 2½ tsp. minced fresh gingerroot
- 1½ tsp. minced garlic
- 24 boneless skinless chicken thighs (about 5 lbs.)

1. In a small bowl, mix the first six ingredients. Reserve 1⅓ cups for basting; cover and refrigerate. Divide remaining marinade between two large resealable plastic bags. Add 12 chicken thighs to each; seal bags and turn to coat. Refrigerate for 8 hours or overnight.
2. Drain and discard marinade from chicken.
3. Grill chicken, covered, on an oiled rack over medium heat for 6-8 minutes on each side or until no longer pink; baste occasionally with reserved marinade during the last 5 minutes.

Per 2 chicken thighs: 391 cal., 16g fat (5g sat. fat), 151mg chol., 651mg sod., 15g carb. (14g sugars, 0 fiber), 43g pro.

MADE WITH LOVE

This is a year-round go-to recipe for me. It tastes just as fab when it's oven-baked!

JEANNE AMBROSE
TASTE OF HOME
ENTHUSIAST TEAM

EDITOR'S CHOICE

GINGER SALMON WITH CUCUMBER LIME SAUCE

Lime and ginger is a favorite flavor combo for me, especially with grilled salmon. You'll be surprised how easy this is.

—Noelle Myers, Grand Forks, ND

Prep: 30 min. • **Grill:** 10 min.
Makes: 10 servings

- 1 Tbsp. grated lime peel
- ¼ cup lime juice
- 2 Tbsp. olive oil
- 2 Tbsp. rice vinegar or white wine vinegar
- 4 tsp. sugar
- ½ tsp. salt
- ½ tsp. ground coriander
- ½ tsp. freshly ground pepper
- ⅓ cup chopped fresh cilantro
- 1 Tbsp. finely chopped onion
- 2 tsp. minced fresh gingerroot
- 2 garlic cloves, minced
- 2 medium cucumbers, peeled, seeded and chopped

SALMON

- ⅓ cup minced fresh gingerroot
- 1 Tbsp. lime juice
- 1 Tbsp. olive oil
- ½ tsp. salt
- ½ tsp. freshly ground pepper
- 10 salmon fillets (6 oz. each)

1. Place the first 13 ingredients in a blender. Cover and process until pureed.
2. In a small bowl, mix ginger, lime juice, oil, salt and pepper. Rub over the flesh side of salmon fillets.
3. Place salmon on an oiled grill rack, skin side down. Grill, covered, over medium-high heat 10-12 minutes or until fish just begins to flake easily with a fork. Serve with sauce.

Per serving: 327 cal., 20g fat (4g sat. fat), 85mg chol., 372mg sod., 7g carb. (4g sugars, 1g fiber), 29g pro. **Diabetic exchanges:** 4 lean meat, 1½ fat, ½ starch.

GINGER SALMON WITH CUCUMBER LIME SAUCE

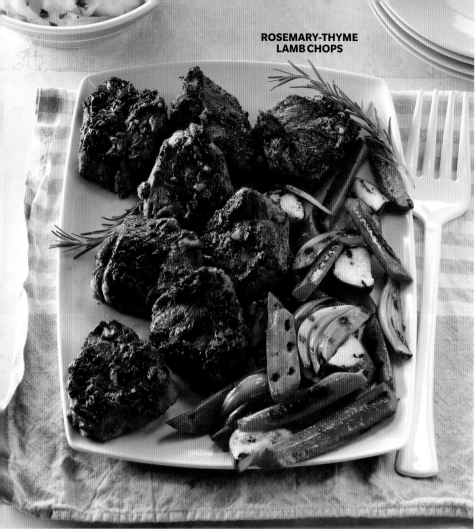

ROSEMARY-THYME
LAMB CHOPS

ROSEMARY-THYME LAMB CHOPS

My father loves lamb, so I make this dish whenever he visits. It's the perfect main course for holidays or get-togethers.
—Kristina Mitchell, Clearwater, FL

Takes: 30 min. • **Makes:** 4 servings

- 8 lamb loin chops (3 oz. each)
- ½ tsp. pepper
- ¼ tsp. salt
- 3 Tbsp. Dijon mustard
- 1 Tbsp. minced fresh rosemary
- 1 Tbsp. minced fresh thyme
- 3 garlic cloves, minced

1. Sprinkle lamb chops with pepper and salt. In a small bowl, mix the mustard, rosemary, thyme and garlic.
2. Grill chops, covered, on an oiled rack over medium heat for 6 minutes. Turn; spread herb mixture over chops. Grill for 6-8 minutes longer or until the meat reaches desired doneness (for medium-rare, a thermometer should read 135°; medium, 140°; medium-well, 145°).
Per 2 lamb chops: 231 cal., 9g fat (4g sat. fat), 97mg chol., 493mg sod., 3g carb. (0 sugars, 0 fiber), 32g pro. **Diabetic exchanges:** 4 lean meat.

EDITOR'S CHOICE

GRILLED PIZZA BURGERS

Pizza burgers are usually a kid's favorite, but by adding spices and cheese to the meat and serving them on English muffins, they've become a favorite for adults as well.
—Mitzi Sentiff, Annapolis, MD

Prep: 20 min. • **Grill:** 15 min.
Makes: 4 servings

- 1 large egg, lightly beaten
- ¾ cup grated Parmesan cheese
- ½ cup chopped onion
- ¼ cup minced fresh parsley
- ¾ tsp. dried basil
- ¾ tsp. dried oregano
- ¾ tsp. dried rosemary, crushed
- ¾ tsp. pepper
- 1 lb. ground beef
- 4 slices provolone cheese
- 4 English muffins, split and toasted
- ½ cup pizza sauce

1. In a large bowl, combine the first eight ingredients. Crumble beef over mixture and mix well. Shape into four patties.
2. Grill burgers, covered, over medium heat for 5-7 minutes on each side or until a thermometer reads 160° and juices run clear. Top burgers with cheese; cover and grill 2-3 minutes longer or until cheese is melted. Serve on muffins with pizza sauce.
Per burger: 572 cal., 29g fat (14g sat. fat), 172mg chol., 902mg sod., 31g carb. (4g sugars, 3g fiber), 45g pro.

MADE WITH LOVE

These remind me of the pizza burgers I loved when I was a kid...only these are from-scratch and way more tasty!

CHRISTINE RUKAVENA
TASTE OF HOME BOOKS

GARLIC GRILLED STEAKS

Skip standard barbecue sauce! Take the flavor of steak to new heights by basting your choice of cuts with this garlicky blend that takes only a few minutes to fix. You're guaranteed a barbecue masterpiece.
—Taste of Home *Test Kitchen*

Takes: 15 min. • **Makes:** 4 servings

- 10 garlic cloves
- 1½ tsp. salt
- ½ tsp. pepper
- 2 Tbsp. olive oil
- 1 Tbsp. lemon juice
- 2 tsp. Worcestershire sauce
- 4 boneless beef strip steaks or ribeye steaks (1 in. thick and 8 oz. each)

1. With a mortar and pestle, crush garlic cloves with salt and pepper. Stir in oil, lemon juice and Worcestershire sauce.
2. Grill steaks, covered, over medium heat 5-7 minutes on each side or until the meat reaches desired doneness (for medium-rare, a thermometer should read 135°; medium, 140°; medium-well, 145°). Brush the steaks generously with garlic mixture during the last four minutes of cooking.
Per serving: 373 cal., 17g fat (5g sat. fat), 100mg chol., 1013mg sod., 3g carb. (0 sugars, 0 fiber), 48g pro.

Trim steaks to avoid flare-ups, leaving a thin layer of fat if desired to help maintain juiciness. Pat dry with paper towels before grilling—a dry steak will brown better than a moist one.

GARLIC GRILLED STEAKS

SWEET HORSERADISH GLAZED RIBS

SWEET HORSERADISH GLAZED RIBS

Go beyond hot dogs for your next camping trip. Roast and wrap these ribs at home before you leave, then finish them with a sweet, savory sauce over the campfire.
—Ralph Jones, San Diego, CA

Prep: 10 min. + chilling • **Cook:** 2¼ hours
Makes: 8 servings

- 3 racks pork baby back ribs (about 8 lbs.)
- 1½ tsp. salt, divided
- 1½ tsp. coarsely ground pepper, divided
- 2 bottles (12 oz. each) beer or 3 cups unsweetened apple juice
- 1 jar (12 oz.) apricot preserves
- ¼ cup prepared horseradish, drained
- 2 Tbsp. honey or maple syrup
- 1 tsp. liquid smoke, optional

1. Preheat oven to 325°. If necessary, remove thin membrane from ribs and discard. Sprinkle 1 tsp. each salt and pepper over ribs. Transfer to a large shallow roasting pan, bone side down; add beer or juice. Bake, covered, until tender, 2-3 hours.
2. Meanwhile, puree the preserves, horseradish, honey, remaining salt and pepper and, if desired, liquid smoke in a blender.
3. Drain ribs. Place 1 rib rack on a large piece of aluminum foil. Brush with apricot-horseradish mixture; wrap tightly. Repeat with remaining ribs. Refrigerate up to 2 days.
4. Prepare campfire or grill for medium heat. Remove ribs from foil; grill until browned, 10-15 minutes, turning occasionally.
Per serving: 690 cal., 42g fat (15g sat. fat), 163mg chol., 674mg sod., 33g carb. (23g sugars, 0 fiber), 45g pro.

GRILLED HAM BURGERS

GRILLED HAM BURGERS

My family loves my ham loaf, so I decided to make the ham loaf mixture into patties and grill them—it was an instant hit. Adding the arugula gives these burgers a peppery bite and honey mustard dressing adds just the right sweet and sour flavor.

—Susan Bickta, Kutztown, PA

Prep: 20 min. + chilling • **Grill:** 10 min.
Makes: 8 servings

- 1½ lbs. fully cooked boneless ham
- ¾ lb. ground pork
- 2 large eggs
- ⅔ cup graham cracker crumbs
- ⅓ cup packed brown sugar
- ⅓ cup unsweetened crushed pineapple plus 3 Tbsp. juice
- 1 Tbsp. spicy brown mustard
- ¼ tsp. ground cloves
- 8 slices Swiss cheese (1 oz. each)
- 8 kaiser rolls, split
- 2 large tomatoes, cut in sixteen ¼-in. slices
- ½ cup honey mustard salad dressing
- 1½ cups fresh baby arugula, packed
- Additional honey mustard salad dressing, optional

1. Pulse ham in food processor until finely ground. Combine with pork, eggs, cracker crumbs, brown sugar, pineapple and juice, brown mustard and cloves. Mix lightly but thoroughly. Shape into eight patties. Using fingertips, make a shallow indentation in center of each patty so it remains flat while grilling. Refrigerate 1 hour.

2. Grill burgers, covered, on a greased rack over medium-high direct heat 5-6 minutes; turn and grill another 3-4 minutes. Add a slice of cheese to each burger; grill, covered, until cheese melts, 1-2 minutes more. Remove burgers from heat when a thermometer reads 160°.

3. Place a burger on bottom half of each roll; add two tomato slices. Drizzle with 1 Tbsp. honey mustard dressing. Divide arugula evenly among rolls; top each burger with a few sprigs. Replace top half of roll. If desired, serve with additional dressing.

Per burger: 632 cal., 28g fat (9g sat. fat), 149mg chol., 1430mg sod., 55g carb. (18g sugars, 2g fiber), 40g pro.

Since you're already firing up the grill, why not make a double batch and freeze the leftovers? Heat for a minute or two in the microwave, and they'll taste like they're hot off the grill.

GRILLED VEGGIES WITH CAPER BUTTER

GRILLED VEGGIES WITH CAPER BUTTER

We like the tart, peppery taste of capers. No one likes a bland veggie, and caper butter helps peppers, squash and zucchini shine.
—Danyelle Crum, Indian Trail, NC

Prep: 25 min. • **Grill:** 10 min.
Makes: 8 servings

- ¼ cup butter, cubed
- 2 garlic cloves, minced
- 1 Tbsp. lemon juice
- 2 tsp. capers, drained and chopped
- 1 Tbsp. minced fresh parsley
- 2 medium zucchini, cut in half lengthwise
- 2 medium crookneck or yellow summer squash, cut in half lengthwise
- 1 medium sweet yellow or orange pepper, quartered
- 1 medium sweet red pepper, quartered
- 2 large portobello mushrooms, stems removed
- 3 green onions, trimmed
- 2 Tbsp. olive oil
- ½ tsp. salt
- ¼ tsp. pepper

1. In a small saucepan, melt butter over medium-low heat. Add the garlic; cook for 2 minutes. Add lemon juice and capers; cook 2 minutes. Stir in parsley.
2. Brush vegetables with oil; sprinkle with salt and pepper.
3. Grill the zucchini, squash and peppers, covered, over medium heat 4-5 minutes on each side or until crisp-tender, basting occasionally with butter mixture. Grill the mushrooms and onions, covered, for 1-2 minutes on each side or until tender, basting occasionally with butter mixture.
4. Cut vegetables as desired; transfer to a serving platter. Drizzle vegetables with remaining butter mixture.

Per serving: 117 cal., 10g fat (4g sat. fat), 15mg chol., 219mg sod., 7g carb. (3g sugars, 2g fiber), 2g pro.

FINGERLING POTATOES WITH FRESH PARSLEY & CHIVES

FINGERLING POTATOES WITH FRESH PARSLEY & CHIVES

We use seasonings like Sazon, adobo, fresh parsley and minced chives to take ordinary potatoes to extraordinary. We sometimes smoke them in our smoker before grilling to amp up the flavor even more.
—Teri Rasey, Cadillac, MI

Prep: 30 min. + marinating • **Grill:** 10 min.
Makes: 6 servings

- 2 lbs. fingerling potatoes
- ¼ cup olive oil
- ½ tsp. Goya Sazon without annatto
- ½ tsp. adobo seasoning
- 2 Tbsp. minced fresh parsley
- 2 Tbsp. minced chives

1. Place potatoes in a 6-qt. stockpot; add water to cover. Bring to a boil. Reduce heat; cook, uncovered, 15-20 minutes or until tender. Drain.
2. In a large bowl, combine olive oil and seasonings; reserve 1 Tbsp. Add potatoes; toss to coat. Let stand 15 minutes.Thread potatoes onto 4 metal or soaked wooden skewers. Grill, covered, over medium heat 8-10 minutes or until browned, turning once. Cool slightly.
3. Remove potatoes from skewers. Transfer potatoes to a large bowl. Add reserved marinade and herbs; toss to coat.

Per serving: 215 cal., 9g fat (1g sat. fat), 0 chol., 172mg sod., 30g carb. (2g sugars, 3g fiber), 4g pro. **Diabetic exchanges:** 2 starch, 2 fat.

GRILLED BRUSSELS SPROUTS

GRILLED BRUSSELS SPROUTS

During a beach vacation, in an effort to cook our entire meal outside on the grill, I turned our not-so-simple veggie choice into an easy grilled side dish. For spicier sprouts, season with red pepper flakes.

—Tiffany Ihle, Bronx, NY

Takes: 25 min. • **Makes:** 4 servings

- **16 fresh Brussels sprouts (about 1½-in. diameter), trimmed**
- **1 medium sweet red pepper**
- **1 medium onion**
- **½ tsp. salt**
- **½ tsp. garlic powder**
- **¼ tsp. coarsely ground pepper**
- **1 Tbsp. olive oil**

1. In a large saucepan, place a steamer basket over 1 in. of water. Bring water to a boil. Place Brussels sprouts in basket. Reduce heat to maintain a simmer; steam, covered, until crisp-tender, 4-6 minutes. Cool slightly; cut each sprout in half.

2. Cut red pepper and onion into 1½-in. pieces. On four metal or soaked wooden skewers, alternately thread Brussels sprouts, red pepper and onion pieces. Mix salt, garlic powder and pepper. Brush vegetables with oil; sprinkle with salt mixture. Grill, covered, over medium heat or broil 4 in. from heat until vegetables are tender, 10-12 minutes, turning occasionally.

Per skewer: 84 cal., 4g fat (1g sat. fat), 0 chol., 316mg sod., 11g carb. (4g sugars, 4g fiber), 3g pro. **Diabetic exchanges:** 1 vegetable, ½ fat.

TEST KITCHEN TIP

To prepare Brussels sprouts, remove any loose or yellowed outer leaves; trim stem end. Rinse sprouts before cooking or steaming.

JALAPENO POPPER MEXICAN STREET CORN

One of the best things about summer is fresh sweet corn, and this recipe is a definite standout. We love its creamy dressing, crunchy panko coating and spicy jalapeno kick. If you're really feeling adventurous, sprinkle with a bit of crumbled bacon.
—Crystal Schlueter, Babbitt, MN

Takes: 30 min. • **Makes:** 4 servings

- 4 ears fresh sweet corn
- 2 jalapeno peppers
- 3 Tbsp. canola oil, divided
- ¾ tsp. salt, divided
- ¼ cup panko (Japanese) bread crumbs
- ½ tsp. smoked paprika
- ½ tsp. dried Mexican oregano
- 4 oz. cream cheese, softened
- ¼ cup media crema table cream or sour cream thinned with 1 tsp. 2% milk
- 2 Tbsp. lime juice
- Ground chipotle pepper or chili powder
- Chopped fresh cilantro, optional

1. Husk corn. Rub the corn and jalapenos with 2 Tbsp. canola oil. Grill vegetables, covered, on a greased grill rack over medium-high direct heat until lightly charred on all sides, 10-12 minutes. Remove from heat. When the jalapenos are cool enough to handle, remove skin, seeds and membranes; chop finely. Set aside.

2. Sprinkle corn with ½ tsp. salt. In a small skillet, heat remaining oil over medium heat. Add panko; cook and stir until starting to brown. Add paprika and oregano; cook until crumbs are toasted and fragrant.

3. Meanwhile, combine the cream cheese, crema, lime juice and remaining salt; spread over corn. Sprinkle with the bread crumbs, jalapenos, chipotle powder and, if desired, chopped fresh cilantro.

Note Wear disposable gloves when cutting hot peppers; the oils can burn skin. Avoid touching your face.

Per ear of corn: 339 cal., 26g fat (9g sat. fat), 39mg chol., 568mg sod., 25g carb. (8g sugars, 3g fiber), 6g pro.

JALAPENO POPPER MEXICAN STREET CORN

GRILLED SWEET POTATOES WITH GORGONZOLA SPREAD

GRILLED SWEET POTATOES WITH GORGONZOLA SPREAD

My husband first tried this recipe with plain baking potatoes. They were so yummy we experimented with sweet potatoes. Dipped in Gorgonzola spread, they're irresistible.
—Kristen Minello, Macomb, MI

Prep: 25 min. • **Grill:** 10 min.
Makes: 8 servings

- 4 large sweet potatoes
- 1 cup (4 oz.) crumbled Gorgonzola cheese
- ½ cup mayonnaise
- 1 to 2 Tbsp. lemon juice
- 3 Tbsp. olive oil
- ½ tsp. salt
- ¼ tsp. pepper
- Minced chives, optional

1. Scrub and pierce sweet potatoes with a fork; place on a microwave-safe plate. Microwave, uncovered, on high just until tender, turning once, 6-8 minutes.
2. Meanwhile, in a small bowl, combine cheese, mayonnaise and lemon juice. Refrigerate until serving.
3. Slice potatoes into ½-in.-thick rounds; brush both sides with oil. Sprinkle with salt and pepper. Grill, covered, over medium heat or broil 4 in. from heat until browned, 4-5 minutes on each side. Serve with spread. If desired, sprinkle with chives.

Per serving with 3 tablespoons spread: 362 cal., 19g fat (5g sat. fat), 14mg chol., 425mg sod., 42g carb. (17g sugars, 6g fiber), 6g pro.

CORN & SQUASH QUESADILLAS

Grilled vegetables give these quesadillas their distinctive flair, while cumin and jalapeno peppers add a little zip.
—Mildred Sherrer, Fort Worth, TX

Prep: 40 min. • **Cook:** 10 min.
Makes: 6 servings

- 2 medium ears sweet corn, husks removed
- 2 medium yellow summer squash, halved lengthwise
- ½ small sweet onion, cut into ¼-in. slices
- 1 to 2 jalapeno peppers
- 1 Tbsp. minced fresh basil
- 1½ tsp. minced fresh oregano
- 1 garlic clove, minced
- ¼ tsp. salt
- ¼ tsp. ground cumin
- 6 flour tortillas (8 in.), warmed
- 1 cup shredded Monterey Jack cheese
- 1 Tbsp. canola oil

1. Grill corn, covered, over medium heat for 10 minutes; turn. Place the squash, onion and jalapenos on grill; cover and cook for 5-6 minutes on each side. When vegetables are cool enough to handle, remove corn from the cobs, chop the squash and onion, and seed and chop the jalapenos. Place in a large bowl.
2. Stir in the basil, oregano, garlic, salt and cumin. Place ½ cup filling on one side of each tortilla; sprinkle with cheese. Fold tortillas over filling. On a griddle or large skillet, cook quesadillas in oil over medium heat for 1-2 minutes on each side or until heated through. Cut into wedges.

Note Wear disposable gloves when cutting hot peppers; the oils can burn skin. Avoid touching your face.

Per quesadilla: 301 cal., 12g fat (5g sat. fat), 17mg chol., 454mg sod., 38g carb. (5g sugars, 3g fiber), 11g pro. **Diabetic exchanges:** 2 starch, 1 medium-fat meat, 1 vegetable, ½ fat.

CORN & SQUASH QUESADILLAS

BACON-WRAPPED ASPARAGUS

BACON-WRAPPED ASPARAGUS

My husband and I grill dinner almost every night, and I love asparagus for a side dish. I serve these bacon-wrapped spears with grilled meat and sliced fresh tomatoes.

—Trisha Kitts, Dickinson, TX

Takes: 30 min. • **Makes:** 2 servings

- 10 fresh asparagus spears, trimmed
- ⅛ tsp. pepper
- 5 bacon strips, halved lengthwise

1. Place asparagus on a sheet of waxed paper; coat with cooking spray. Sprinkle with pepper; turn to coat. Wrap a bacon piece around each asparagus spear; secure ends with toothpicks.

2. Grill, uncovered, over medium heat for 4-6 minutes on each side or until bacon is crisp. Discard toothpicks.

Per 5 pieces: 222 cal., 22g fat (8g sat. fat), 25mg chol., 281mg sod., 2g carb. (1g sugars, 1g fiber), 5g pro.

LEMON GARLIC MUSHROOMS

I baste whole mushrooms with a lemony sauce to prepare this simple side dish. Using skewers or a basket makes it easy to turn them as they grill to perfection.

—Diane Hixon, Niceville, FL

Takes: 15 min. • **Makes:** 4 servings

- ¼ cup lemon juice
- 3 Tbsp. minced fresh parsley
- 2 Tbsp. olive oil
- 3 garlic cloves, minced
- Pepper to taste
- 1 lb. large fresh mushrooms

1. For dressing, whisk together first five ingredients. Toss mushrooms with 2 Tbsp. dressing.

2. Grill mushrooms, covered, over medium-high heat until tender, 5-7 minutes per side. Toss with remaining dressing before serving.

Per serving: 94 cal., 7g fat (1g sat. fat), 0mg chol., 2mg sod., 6g carb. (0g sugars, 0g fiber), 3g pro. **Diabetic exchanges:** 1 vegetable, 1½ fat.

FRESH ARTICHOKES WITH LEMON-YOGURT DIP

Artichokes are at their best when you prepare them simply, without a lot of fuss or seasonings to overdress them. Many people dip the petals in melted butter or mayonnaise, but I think you'll love my tangy lemon-yogurt dip.

—Jill Haapaniemi, Brooklyn, NY

Prep: 10 min. • **Cook:** 45 min.
Makes: 12 servings (1½ cups dip)

- 6 medium artichokes
- 3 Tbsp. olive oil
- Sea salt and coarsely ground pepper to taste
- 1½ cups plain yogurt
- 1 tsp. lemon juice
- ¼ tsp. salt
- ¼ tsp. pepper
- Lemon wedges

1. Using a sharp knife, cut 1 in. from top of each artichoke and trim stem so it will stand upright. Using kitchen scissors, cut off tips of outer leaves. Place artichokes upright in a Dutch oven; cover with water and bring to a boil. Reduce heat; simmer, covered, 35-40 minutes or until a leaf in the center pulls out easily. Invert artichokes to drain. Cool slightly; cut each in half lengthwise. With a spoon, carefully scrape and remove fuzzy center of artichokes.
2. In a grill pan or large skillet, heat oil over medium-high heat. Place artichokes in pan, cut side down. Cook 5-7 minutes or until lightly browned. Sprinkle with salt and pepper. In a small bowl, mix yogurt, lemon juice, salt and pepper. Serve with artichokes and lemon wedges.

Per ½ artichoke with 2 tablespoons dip: 81 cal., 5g fat (1g sat. fat), 4mg chol., 99mg sod., 9g carb. (2g sugars, 3g fiber), 3g pro.

ROOT BEER APPLE BAKED BEANS

ROOT BEER APPLE BAKED BEANS

My family loves roughing it outdoors. My beans with bacon and apples are a must to keep our energy going.

—Nancy Heishman, Las Vegas, NV

Prep: 20 min. • **Cook:** 45 min.
Makes: 12 servings

- 6 thick-sliced bacon strips, chopped
- 4 cans (16 oz. each) baked beans
- 1 can (21 oz.) apple pie filling
- 1 can (12 oz.) root beer
- 1 tsp. ground ancho chili pepper, optional
- 1 cup shredded smoked cheddar cheese, optional

1. Prepare campfire or grill for medium heat, using 32-36 charcoal briquettes or large wood chips.
2. In a 10-in. Dutch oven, cook bacon over campfire until crisp. Remove; discard drippings. Return bacon to pan; stir in baked beans, pie filling, root beer and, if desired, ancho chili pepper
3. Cover Dutch oven. When briquettes or wood chips are covered with ash, place Dutch oven on top of 16-18 briquettes. Place 16-18 briquettes on pan cover.
4. Cook 30-40 minutes to allow flavors to blend. If desired, sprinkle servings with cheese.

Per ¾ cup: 255 cal., 5g fat (2g sat. fat), 16mg chol., 778mg sod., 47g carb. (11g sugars, 9g fiber), 10g pro.

POT OF S'MORES

POT OF S'MORES

Mom's easy Dutch oven version of the popular campout treat is so good and gooey. The hardest part is waiting for this to cool so you can devour it. Yum!
—June Dress, Meridian, ID

Takes: 25 min. • **Makes:** 12 servings

- 1 pkg. (14½ oz.) whole graham crackers, crushed
- ½ cup butter, melted
- 1 can (14 oz.) sweetened condensed milk
- 2 cups (12 oz.) semisweet chocolate chips
- 1 cup butterscotch chips
- 2 cups miniature marshmallows

1. Prepare grill or campfire for low heat, using 16-18 charcoal briquettes or large wood chips.
2. Line a Dutch oven with heavy-duty aluminum foil. Combine cracker crumbs and butter; press onto the bottom of the pan. Pour milk over crust and sprinkle with chocolate and butterscotch chips. Top with marshmallows.
3. Cover Dutch oven. When briquettes or wood chips are covered with white ash, place Dutch oven directly on top of six of them. Using long-handled tongs, place remaining briquettes on pan cover.
4. Cook for 15 minutes or until marshmallows begin to melt. To check for doneness, use the tongs to carefully lift the cover.
Per serving: 584 cal., 28g fat (17g sat. fat), 31mg chol., 326mg sod., 83g carb. (47g sugars, 3g fiber), 8g pro.

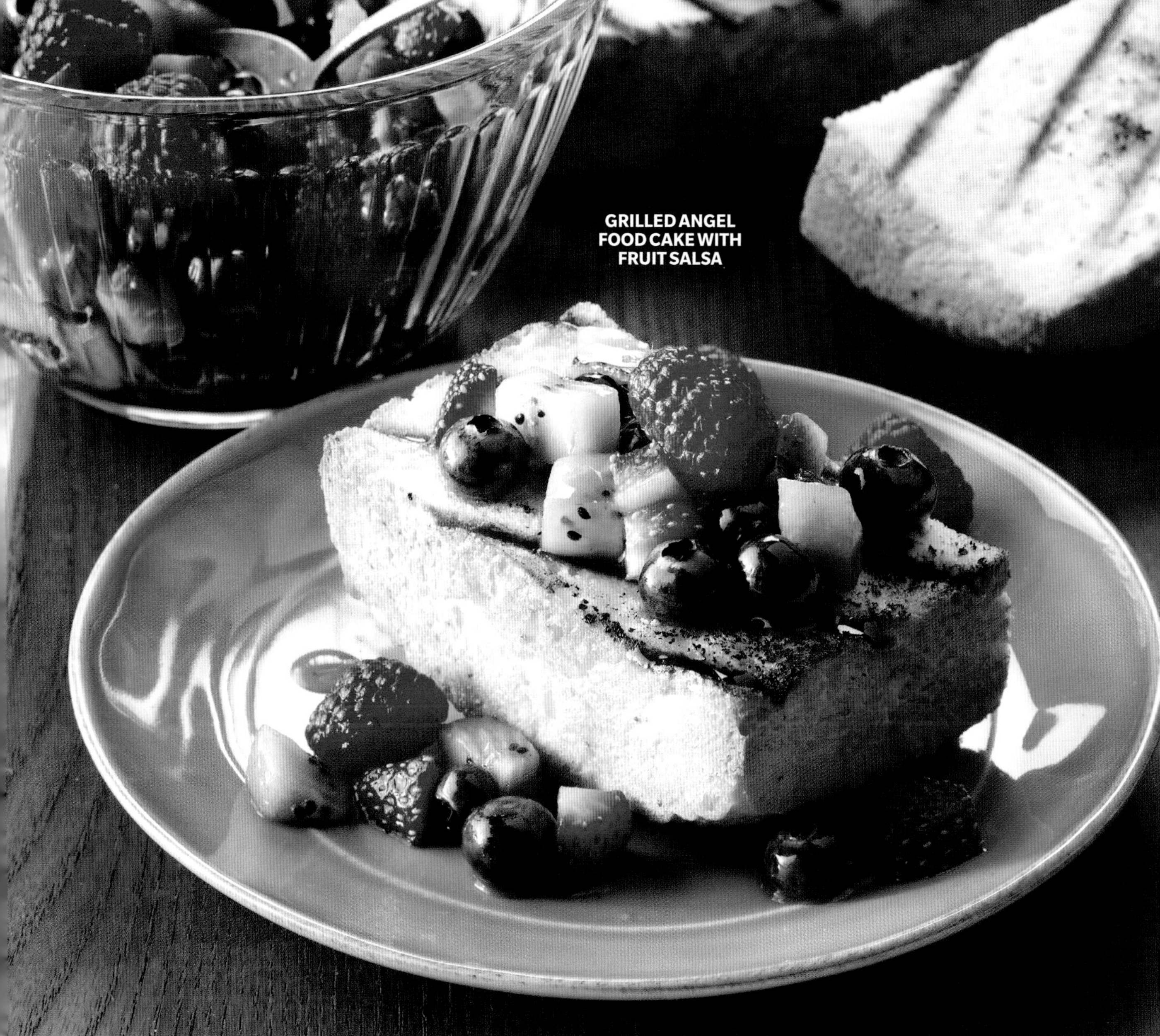

GRILLED ANGEL FOOD CAKE WITH FRUIT SALSA

GRILLED ANGEL FOOD CAKE WITH FRUIT SALSA

When I need quick dessert, I go with a dressed-up angel food cake. Mix the fruit salsa ahead of time, and then pop the cake on the grill. Done and done!

—Glorimar Jimenez, Indianapolis, IN

Takes: 15 min. • Makes: 6 servings

- ½ cup each fresh raspberries, blueberries and chopped strawberries
- 1 kiwifruit, peeled and chopped
- 2 Tbsp. sugar
- 1 Tbsp. lime juice
- 1 loaf-shaped angel food cake (10½ oz.), split horizontally
- Whipped topping, optional

In a small bowl, combine berries, kiwi, sugar and lime juice. Grill cake, cut side down, over medium heat or broil 4 in. from heat until lightly browned, 1-3 minutes. Cut into slices. Serve with the fruit salsa and, if desired, whipped topping.

Per serving: 169 cal., 1g fat (0 sat. fat), 0 chol., 372mg sod., 39g carb. (30g sugars, 2g fiber), 3g pro.

CAKE & BERRY
CAMPFIRE COBBLER

CAKE & BERRY CAMPFIRE COBBLER

This warm cobbler is one of our favorite ways to end a busy day of fishing, hiking, swimming or rafting. It's yummy with ice cream—and so easy to make!
—June Dress, Meridian, ID

Prep: 10 min. • **Grill:** 30 min.
Makes: 12 servings

- 2 cans (21 oz. each) raspberry pie filling
- 1 pkg. yellow cake mix (regular size)
- 1¼ cups water
- ½ cup canola oil
- Vanilla ice cream, optional

1. Prepare grill or campfire for low heat, using 16-20 charcoal briquettes or large wood chips.
2. Line an ovenproof Dutch oven with heavy-duty aluminum foil; add pie filling. In a large bowl, combine the cake mix, water and oil. Spread over pie filling.
3. Cover Dutch oven. When briquettes or wood chips are covered with white ash, place Dutch oven directly on top of 8-10 of them. Using long-handled tongs, place remaining briquettes on pan cover.
4. Cook for 30-40 minutes or until filling is bubbly and a toothpick inserted in the topping comes out clean. To check for doneness, use the tongs to carefully lift the cover. Serve with ice cream if desired.
Note This recipe does not use eggs.
Per serving: 342 cal., 12g fat (2g sat. fat), 0 chol., 322mg sod., 57g carb. (34g sugars, 2g fiber), 1g pro.

ECLAIRS ON THE GRILL

ECLAIRS ON THE GRILL

My best camping treat is an easy eclair cooked on a stick. This is one that makes fellow campers take note of what you're doing and beg to be included in the fun!
—Bonnie Hawkins, Elkhorn, WI

Prep: 5 min. • **Grill:** 5 min./batch
Makes: 6 servings

- Stick or wooden dowel (⅝-in. diameter and 24 in. long)
- 1 tube (8 oz.) refrigerated seamless crescent dough sheet
- 3 snack-size cups (3¼ oz. each) vanilla or chocolate pudding
- ½ cup chocolate frosting
- Whipped cream in a can, optional

1. Prepare campfire or grill for high heat. Wrap one end of a stick or wooden dowel with foil. Unroll crescent dough and cut into six 4-in. squares. Wrap one piece of dough around prepared stick; pinch end and seam to seal.
2. Cook over campfire or grill 5-7 minutes or until golden brown, turning occasionally. When dough is cool enough to handle, remove from stick. Finish cooling. Repeat with remaining dough.
3. Place pudding in a resealable plastic bag; cut a small hole in one corner. Squeeze bag to press mixture into each shell. Spread with frosting. If desired, top with whipped cream.
Per eclair: 293 cal., 12g fat (4g sat. fat), 0 chol., 418mg sod., 43g carb. (27g sugars, 0 fiber), 4g pro.

FRUIT & CAKE KABOBS

A neighbor served these kabobs at a family picnic and brought some over for us to sample. I was pleasantly surprised at the tasty toasted cake and juicy grilled fruit.
—Mary Ann Dell, Phoenixville, PA

Takes: 25 min. • **Makes:** 8 servings

- ½ cup apricot preserves
- 1 Tbsp. water
- 1 Tbsp. butter
- ⅛ tsp. ground cinnamon
- ⅛ tsp. ground nutmeg
- 3 medium nectarines, quartered
- 3 medium peaches, quartered
- 3 medium plums, quartered
- 1 loaf (10¾ oz.) frozen lb. cake, thawed and cut into 1½-in. cubes

1. In a small saucepan, combine first five ingredients; cook and stir over medium heat until blended. Remove from heat.
2. On eight metal or soaked wooden skewers, alternately thread fruit and pound cake. Place on a greased rack over medium heat. Grill, uncovered, until lightly browned and fruit is tender, brushing occasionally with apricot mixture.
Per kabob: 259 cal., 8g fat (4g sat. fat), 58mg chol., 161mg sod., 46g carb. (33g sugars, 3g fiber), 4g pro.

Play with your food! This recipe lends itself to endless experimentation, and any firm fruit will work well. Try substituting apples, pears, pineapple and stone fruits. Stay away from soft fruits like berries, though.

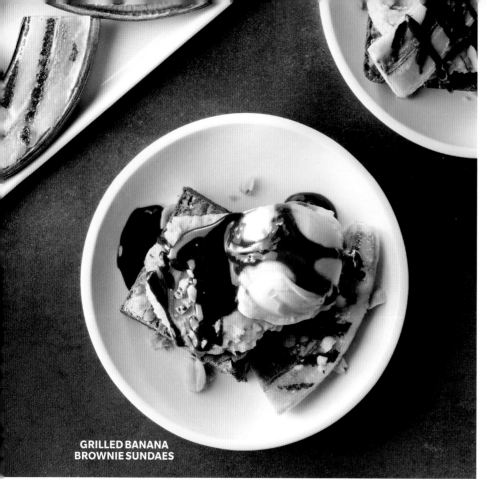

GRILLED BANANA BROWNIE SUNDAES

GRILLED BANANA BROWNIE SUNDAES

My niece Amanda Jean and I have a lot of fun in the kitchen creating different dishes. One of us will start with a recipe idea and it just grows from there—and so does the mess! We always have a blast. That's exactly what happened with these over-the-top brownie sundaes.
—Carol Farnsworth, Greenwood, IN

Prep: 10 min. • **Grill:** 5 min. + cooling
Makes: 8 servings

- 2 medium bananas, unpeeled
- 4 oz. cream cheese, softened
- ¼ cup packed brown sugar
- 3 Tbsp. creamy peanut butter
- 8 prepared brownies (2-in. squares)
- 4 cups vanilla ice cream
- ½ cup hot fudge ice cream topping, warmed
- ½ cup chopped salted peanuts

1. Cut unpeeled bananas crosswise in half, then lengthwise in half. Place quartered bananas on an oiled grill rack, cut side down. Grill, covered, over medium-high heat 2-3 minutes on each side or until lightly browned. Cool slightly.
2. In a small bowl, beat cream cheese, brown sugar and peanut butter until smooth.
3. To serve, remove bananas from their peels; place over brownies. Top with cream cheese mixture, ice cream, fudge topping and peanuts.
Per serving: 505 cal., 28g fat (11g sat. fat), 62mg chol., 277mg sod., 57g carb. (33g sugars, 3g fiber), 10g pro.

FRUIT & CAKE KABOBS

GRILLED FIGGY PIES

GRILLED FIGGY PIES

Delicious figs combined with maple syrup, walnuts and creamy mascarpone make a decadent treat. Try these handheld pies at your next backyard cookout.

—Renee Murby, Johnston, RI

Prep: 50 min. + freezing • **Grill:** 10 min.
Makes: 1 dozen

- 1 sheet refrigerated pie crust
- 12 dried figs
- ¼ cup bourbon
- ½ cup chopped walnuts
- ¼ cup plus 1 Tbsp. maple syrup, divided
- 1 tsp. ground cinnamon
- ½ tsp. ground nutmeg
- ½ tsp. vanilla extract
- ⅔ cup (about 5 oz.) mascarpone cheese
- 1 large egg
- 1 Tbsp. water

1. Warm pie pastry to room temperature following package directions. Meanwhile, in a small saucepan, combine figs and bourbon; add enough water to cover by 1 in. Cook, covered, over low heat until the figs are plump, 15-20 minutes. Remove from heat; drain. Cool 15 minutes; pat dry. Cut each fig into quarters. Set aside.
2. In same saucepan over medium-low heat, combine walnuts with ¼ cup maple syrup, cinnamon and nutmeg. Cook, stirring constantly, until liquid is almost evaporated, 5-7 minutes. Spread nuts on a baking sheet lined with parchment paper; freeze until set, about 10 minutes.
3. Unroll pastry sheets. Using a 4-in. round cutter, cut 12 circles, rolling and cutting scraps as necessary. Stir vanilla and remaining maple syrup into mascarpone cheese. Spread scant 1 Tbsp. mascarpone mixture over half of each circle to within ¼ in. of edge; layer with 2 tsp. maple walnuts and four fig pieces. Make an egg wash by whisking egg and water; use to moisten edge of pastry. Fold dough over filling; press edges with a fork to seal. Repeat with remaining dough and filling. Brush egg wash over pies. Freeze pies on a parchment paper-lined baking sheet for 10 minutes.
4. Remove from baking sheet. Grill pies, covered, on a well-greased grill rack over medium direct heat until golden brown, 5-7 minutes per side.

Per pie: 280 cal., 17g fat (7g sat. fat), 35mg chol., 137mg sod., 28g carb. (10g sugars, 1g fiber), 4g pro.

BANANA BOATS

This recipe, given to me years ago by a good friend, is a favorite with my family when we go camping. It's quick and scrumptious!

—Brenda Loveless, Garland, TX

Takes: 20 min. • **Makes:** 4 servings

- 4 medium unpeeled ripe bananas
- 4 tsp. miniature chocolate chips
- 4 Tbsp. miniature marshmallows

1. Cut banana peel lengthwise about ½ in. deep, leaving ½ in. at both ends. Open peel wider to form a pocket. Fill each with 1 tsp. chocolate chips and 1 Tbsp. marshmallows. Crimp and shape four pieces of heavy-duty foil (about 12 in. square) around bananas, forming boats.
2. Grill, covered, over medium heat until marshmallows melt and are golden brown, 5-10 minutes.

Per serving: 136 cal., 2g fat (1g sat. fat), 0 chol., 3mg sod., 32g carb. (26g sugars, 3g fiber), 1g pro.

STUFFED GRILLED ZUCCHINI

Pair these zucchini boats with charred pork chops, smoked fish and other grilled greats. Not warm enough to cook al fresco? Your oven will do the job, too.

—Nancy Zimmerman, Cape May Court House, NJ

Prep: 25 min. • **Grill:** 10 min.
Makes: 4 servings

- 4 medium zucchini
- 5 tsp. olive oil, divided
- 2 Tbsp. finely chopped red onion
- ¼ tsp. minced garlic
- ½ cup dry bread crumbs
- ½ cup shredded part-skim mozzarella cheese
- 1 Tbsp. minced fresh mint
- ½ tsp. salt
- 3 Tbsp. grated Parmesan cheese

1. Cut zucchini in half lengthwise; scoop out pulp, leaving ¼-in. shells. Brush with 2 tsp. oil; set aside. Chop pulp.

2. In a large skillet, saute pulp and onion in remaining oil. Add garlic; cook 1 minute longer. Add bread crumbs; cook and stir for 2 minutes or until golden brown.

3. Remove pulp mixture from the heat. Stir in the mozzarella cheese, mint and salt. Spoon into zucchini shells. Sprinkle with Parmesan cheese.

4. Grill, covered, over medium heat for 8-10 minutes or until zucchini is tender.

Per 2 zucchini: 186 cal., 10g fat (3g sat. fat), 11mg chol., 553mg sod., 17g carb. (4g sugars, 3g fiber), 9g pro.

"Mr. DeMille, the zucchini is ready for its close-up," said our editor when we originally ran this recipe in the magazine in 2006.

EAT RIGHT, FEEL GREAT

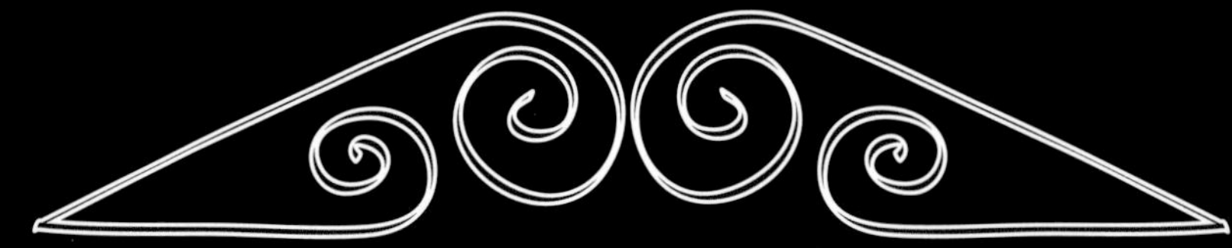

IF YOU LOVE TO SERVE CLASSIC FAMILY FAVORITES BUT WANT TO CUT THE FAT, CALORIES, SODIUM OR CARBS, TURN TO THESE DELICIOUSLY LIGHT, FUSS-FREE RECIPES.

KHMER PICKLED VEGETABLE SALAD

GARDEN CHICKPEA SALAD

Looking for something different on a hot summer's day? This refreshing salad makes a terrific cold side dish or even an entree.
—Sally Sibthorpe, Shelby Township, MI

Takes: 25 min. • **Makes:** 2 servings

- ½ tsp. cumin seeds
- ¼ cup chopped tomato
- ¼ cup lemon juice
- ¼ cup olive oil
- 1 garlic clove, minced
- ¼ tsp. salt
- ¼ tsp. cayenne pepper

SALAD

- ¾ cup canned garbanzo beans or chickpeas, rinsed and drained
- 1 medium carrot, julienned
- 1 small zucchini, julienned
- 2 green onions, thinly sliced
- ½ cup coarsely chopped fresh parsley
- ¼ cup thinly sliced radishes
- ¼ cup crumbled feta cheese
- 3 Tbsp. chopped walnuts
- 3 cups spring mix salad greens

1. For dressing, in a dry small skillet, toast the cumin seeds over medium heat until aromatic, stirring frequently. Transfer to a small bowl. Stir in tomato, lemon juice, oil, garlic, salt and cayenne pepper.
2. In a bowl, combine chickpeas, carrot, zucchini, green onions, parsley, radishes, cheese and walnuts. Stir in ⅓ cup dressing.
3. To serve, divide greens between two plates; top with chickpea mixture. Drizzle with remaining dressing.
Per serving: 492 cal., 38g fat (6g sat. fat), 8mg chol., 619mg sod., 30g carb. (7g sugars, 9g fiber), 12g pro.

KHMER PICKLED VEGETABLE SALAD

I grew up as a missionary kid in Cambodia, and most of my favorite dishes have a Southeast Asian flair. Locals love eating this pickled salad for breakfast, but I like it for lunch or dinner as a side with satay chicken. The best part? It's fat-free!
—Hannah Heavener, Belton, TX

Prep: 25 min. + chilling • **Cook:** 5 min.
Makes: 16 servings

- 2 medium daikon radishes (about 1¼ lbs. each), peeled and thinly sliced
- 4 cups shredded cabbage (about ½ small)
- 1 large cucumber, thinly sliced
- 2 medium carrots, thinly sliced
- 1 cup cut fresh green beans (2 in.)
- ½ medium red onion, thinly sliced
- 1 piece fresh gingerroot (1 in.), thinly sliced
- 2 Thai chili or serrano peppers, halved lengthwise and seeded if desired
- 2 cups rice vinegar
- ¾ cup sugar
- 2 tsp. salt
- 2 Tbsp. chopped fresh cilantro

1. Place first eight ingredients in a large nonreactive bowl. Place vinegar, sugar and salt in a 2-cup or larger glass measure; microwave until warm, 2-3 minutes. Stir until sugar is dissolved. Stir into vegetables. Refrigerate, covered, at least 1 hour before serving.
2. To serve, sprinkle with cilantro. Serve with a slotted spoon.
Per ¾ cup: 99 cal., 0 fat (0 sat. fat), 0 chol., 794mg sod., 25g carb. (22g sugars, 2g fiber), 1g pro.

SPRING PEA & RADISH SALAD

SPRING PEA & RADISH SALAD

Winters are long here in New Hampshire. I look forward to the first veggies of spring so I can finally make light dishes like this fresh pea and radish salad.
—Jolene Martinelli, Fremont, NH

Takes: 20 min. • **Makes:** 6 servings

- ½ lb. fresh wax or green beans
- ½ lb. fresh sugar snap peas
- 2 cups water
- 6 large radishes, halved and thinly sliced
- 2 Tbsp. honey
- 1 tsp. dried tarragon
- ¼ tsp. kosher salt
- ¼ tsp. coarsely ground pepper

1. Snip ends off beans and sugar snap peas; remove strings from snap peas. In a large saucepan, bring water to a boil over high heat. Add beans, reduce heat; simmer, covered, 4-5 minutes. Add sugar snap peas; simmer, covered, until both beans and peas are crisp-tender, another 2-3 minutes. Drain.
2. Toss beans and peas with radishes. Stir together honey, tarragon, salt and pepper. Drizzle over vegetables.
Per ⅔ cup: 50 cal., 0 fat (0 sat. fat), 0 chol., 86mg sod., 11g carb. (8g sugars, 2g fiber), 2g pro. **Diabetic exchanges:** 1 vegetable, ½ starch.

WARM APPLE & PISTACHIO SPINACH SALAD

The inspiration for this salad came from a similar recipe renowned chef and author Barton Seaver published in his book *For Cod and Country*. My tweaks and additions to the original recipe, including ricotta, ginger, and Dijon, result in a fruity salad worthy of bringing to a dinner party or even eating by itself. It's quick and easy to make.
—Justine Kmiecik, Dupont, WA

Takes: 25 min. • **Makes:** 6 servings

- 3 Tbsp. butter
- 2 cups chopped crisp apples, unpeeled (about 2 medium apples)
- 1 tsp. grated fresh gingerroot
- 1 cup shelled roasted pistachios
- 2 tsp. Dijon mustard
- 1 pkg. (5 oz.) fresh baby spinach
- 1 cup whole-milk ricotta cheese
- 2 Tbsp. honey
- Coarsely ground pepper

1. In a large skillet, melt the butter over medium-high heat. Add apples and ginger; cook and stir until apples soften and begin to caramelize, 3-5 minutes. Stir in the pistachios and Dijon mustard. Reduce heat; simmer 5 minutes, stirring occasionally.
2. Pour two-thirds of apple mixture over spinach. Add spoonfuls of ricotta cheese; top with remaining apple mixture. Drizzle with honey. Add fresh pepper to taste.
Per serving: 278 cal., 19g fat (8g sat. fat), 32mg chol., 243mg sod., 20g carb. (14g sugars, 4g fiber), 10g pro.

WARM APPLE & PISTACHIO SPINACH SALAD

GRILLED SOUTHWESTERN POTATO SALAD

This salad is great with a grilled steak for a Tex-Mex meal, and most of it can even be prepared out in the backyard. Poblanos and cayenne make it pop.

—Johnna Johnson, Scottsdale, AZ

Prep: 30 min. • **Grill:** 20 min. + standing
Makes: 6 servings

- 1½ lbs. large red potatoes, quartered lengthwise
- 3 Tbsp. olive oil
- 2 poblano peppers
- 2 medium ears sweet corn, husks removed
- ½ cup buttermilk
- ½ cup sour cream
- 1 Tbsp. lime juice
- 1 jalapeno pepper, seeded and minced
- 1 Tbsp. minced fresh cilantro
- 1½ tsp. garlic salt
- 1 tsp. ground cumin
- ¼ to ½ tsp. cayenne pepper
- Lime wedges

1. Place potatoes in a large saucepan; add water to cover. Bring to a boil. Reduce heat; cook, uncovered, 5 minutes. Drain potatoes and toss with oil.

2. Grill poblanos, covered, over high heat for 8-10 minutes or until the skins are blistered and blackened on all sides, turning occasionally. Immediately place peppers in a small bowl; let stand, covered, 20 minutes. Reduce grill temperature to medium heat.

3. Grill corn and potatoes, covered, over medium heat 12-15 minutes or until tender and lightly browned, turning occasionally. Cool slightly.

4. Peel off and discard charred skin from poblanos; remove stems and seeds. Cut peppers into ½-in. pieces and place in a large bowl. Cut corn from cobs and cut potatoes into ¾-in. pieces; add to peppers.

5. In a small bowl, whisk buttermilk, sour cream and lime juice until blended; stir in jalapeno, cilantro and seasonings. Add to potato mixture, stirring in as much dressing as desired to coat. Serve with lime wedges. Refrigerate leftovers.

Per ¾ cup: 229 cal., 11g fat (4g sat. fat), 14mg chol., 301mg sod., 28g carb. (6g sugars, 3g fiber), 5g pro.

APPLE SAUSAGE SALAD WITH CINNAMON VINAIGRETTE

Making croutons with cinnamon-raisin bread is sweet genius. Toss together the rest of the salad while they toast.

—Kim Van Dunk, Caldwell, NJ

Prep: 25 min. • **Bake:** 10 min.
Makes: 6 servings

- 4 slices cinnamon-raisin bread
- ⅓ cup olive oil
- 3 Tbsp. cider vinegar
- 2 tsp. honey
- ½ tsp. ground cinnamon
- ⅛ tsp. sea salt
- Dash pepper
- 1 pkg. (12 oz.) fully cooked apple chicken sausage links, cut diagonally in ½-in.-thick slices
- 2 pkg. (5 oz. each) spring mix salad greens
- 2 cups sliced fresh Bartlett pears
- ½ cup chopped walnuts, toasted
- ½ cup dried sweet cherries

1. Preheat oven to 375°. Cut each slice of bread into 12 cubes; scatter over a 15x10-in. pan. Bake until toasted, 8-10 minutes, stirring halfway. Cool 5 minutes.

2. Meanwhile, combine next six ingredients in a jar with a tight-fitting lid. Shake until blended. In a large nonstick skillet, cook sausage over medium heat until browned and heated through, 2-3 minutes per side.

3. Divide salad greens among four dinner plates; add sausage to each plate. Top with pear slices, walnuts, cherries and croutons. Shake dressing again; spoon over salad and serve immediately.

Note To toast nuts, bake in a shallow pan in a 350° oven for 5-10 minutes or cook in a skillet over low heat until lightly browned, stirring occasionally.

Per serving: 404 cal., 23g fat (4g sat. fat), 40mg chol., 441mg sod., 39g carb. (23g sugars, 5g fiber), 14g pro.

APPLE SAUSAGE SALAD WITH CINNAMON VINAIGRETTE

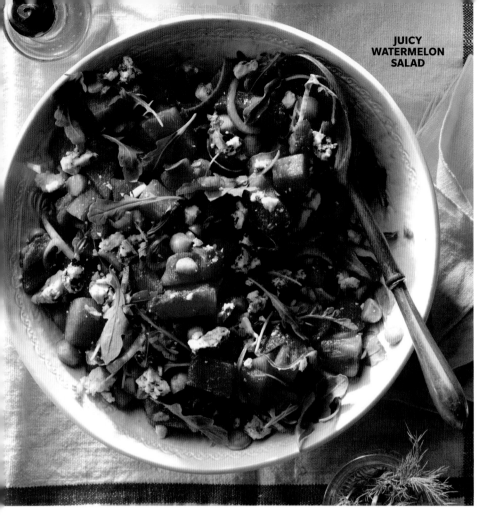

JUICY WATERMELON SALAD

JUICY WATERMELON SALAD

(PICTURED ON P. 286)

This fresh fruit salad has a surprising yet fabulous mix of flavors. Combine seedless watermelon varieties in yellow, red and pink for a colorful twist.

—Heidi Haight, Macomb, MI

Prep: 20 min. + chilling • **Makes:** 10 servings

- 8 cups cubed seedless watermelon (about 1 medium)
- 1 small red onion, cut into rings
- 1 cup coarsely chopped macadamia nuts or slivered almonds, toasted
- 1 cup fresh arugula or baby spinach
- ⅓ cup balsamic vinaigrette
- 3 Tbsp. canola oil
- Watermelon slices, optional
- 1 cup (4 oz.) crumbled blue cheese

In a large bowl, combine watermelon and onion; cover and refrigerate until cold, about 30 minutes. Just before serving, add the macadamia nuts and arugula to watermelon mixture. In a small bowl, whisk vinaigrette and oil; drizzle over salad and toss to coat. Serve over sliced watermelon, if desired. Sprinkle with cheese.

Note To toast nuts, bake in a shallow pan in a 350° oven for 5-10 minutes or cook in a skillet over low heat until lightly browned, stirring occasionally.

Per cup: 232 cal., 20g fat (5g sat. fat), 10mg chol., 295mg sod., 15g carb. (12g sugars, 2g fiber), 4g pro.

ITALIAN ORZO SALAD

A light pasta salad is ideal in summer when you need a dish to pass. It also makes a delicious accompaniment to your favorite weeknight dinner.

—Cindy Grischo, Denver, CO

Takes: 30 min. • **Makes:** 12 servings

- 6 cups chicken broth
- 1 pkg. (16 oz.) orzo pasta
- ⅓ cup olive oil
- ¼ cup red wine vinegar
- 2 Tbsp. lemon juice
- 1 Tbsp. honey
- ½ tsp. salt
- ½ tsp. pepper
- 2 cups chopped plum tomatoes
- 1 cup chopped seeded peeled cucumber
- 1 cup fresh basil leaves, thinly sliced
- 4 green onions, chopped
- ½ cup fresh baby spinach, chopped
- 1¾ cups (7 oz.) crumbled feta cheese
- ½ cup pine nuts, toasted

1. In a large saucepan, bring the broth to a boil; add pasta. Return to a boil. Cook, uncovered, for 10-12 minutes or until pasta is tender. Meanwhile, in a small bowl, whisk the oil, vinegar, lemon juice, honey, salt and pepper.

2. In a large bowl, combine the tomatoes, cucumber, basil, onions and spinach. Drain pasta; add to tomato mixture. Drizzle with dressing; toss to coat. Chill until serving.

3. Just before serving, stir in cheese and pine nuts.

Per ⅔ cup: 288 cal., 12g fat (3g sat. fat), 11mg chol., 630mg sod., 34g carb. (4g sugars, 2g fiber), 10g pro.

TEST KITCHEN TIP

Because of orzo's shape and mild flavor, it can be substituted for rice in many recipes.

POTATO-BEAN SALAD WITH HERB DRESSING

My veggie garden inspired this creamy combo of beans, potatoes and fresh herbs. I toss them with a ranch-style dressing sparked with Creole mustard.

—Christopher Cummer, Rincon, GA

Prep: 15 min. • **Cook:** 20 min. + chilling
Makes: 6 servings

- 1 lb. potatoes (about 2 medium), peeled and cubed
- ½ lb. fresh green beans, trimmed and cut into 2-in. pieces

DRESSING

- ⅓ cup buttermilk
- 2 Tbsp. mayonnaise
- 2 Tbsp. sour cream
- 1 Tbsp. Creole mustard
- 1 Tbsp. minced chives
- 1 Tbsp. minced fresh parsley or 1 tsp. dried parsley flakes
- 1½ tsp. snipped fresh dill or ½ tsp. dill weed
- 1½ tsp. cider vinegar
- 1 garlic clove, minced
- ½ tsp. salt
- ⅛ tsp. celery seed
- ⅛ tsp. pepper

1. Place potatoes in a large saucepan; add water to cover. Bring to a boil. Reduce heat; cook, uncovered, 10-15 minutes or until tender, adding green beans during the last 4 minutes of cooking. Drain; cool potatoes completely.

2. In a small bowl, mix dressing ingredients. Pour over potato mixture; toss to coat. Refrigerate, covered, until cold.

Per ⅔ cup: 109 cal., 5g fat (1g sat. fat), 6mg chol., 305mg sod., 14g carb. (3g sugars, 2g fiber), 2g pro. **Diabetic exchanges:** 1 starch, 1 fat.

POTATO-BEAN SALAD WITH HERB DRESSING

EMILY'S HONEY
LIME COLESLAW

EMILY'S HONEY LIME COLESLAW

Here's a refreshing take on slaw made with a honey-lime vinaigrette instead of traditional mayo. It's a great take-along for summer picnics and potlucks.

—Emily Tyra, Milwaukee, WI

Prep: 20 min. + chilling
Makes: 8 servings

- 1½ tsp. grated lime peel
- ¼ cup lime juice
- 2 Tbsp. honey
- 1 garlic clove, minced
- ½ tsp. salt
- ¼ tsp. pepper
- ¼ tsp. crushed red pepper flakes
- 3 Tbsp. canola oil
- 1 small head red cabbage (about ¾ lb.), shredded
- 1 cup shredded carrots (about 2 medium carrots)
- 2 green onions, thinly sliced
- ½ cup fresh cilantro leaves

Whisk together the first seven ingredients until smooth. Gradually whisk in oil until blended. Combine cabbage, carrots and green onions; toss with lime mixture to lightly coat. Refrigerate, covered, 2 hours. Sprinkle with cilantro.

Per ½ cup: 86 cal., 5g fat (0 sat. fat), 0 chol., 170mg sod., 10g carb. (7g sugars, 2g fiber), 1g pro. **Diabetic exchanges:** 1 vegetable, 1 fat.

MADE WITH LOVE

My brother and I bond over cooking. I wasn't about to make an attempt at improving his classic creamy slaw recipe so instead I created one of my own. We decided to let the best sibling—and slaw—reign at a get-together. I'm still not sure who won, but this colorful dish is now a staple at family barbecues!

EMILY TYRA
TASTE OF HOME MAGAZINE

CHICKEN & BRUSSELS SPROUTS SALAD

My mom made the best salads, and that's where my love for them started. I turned one of her recipes into this delish meal filled with chicken, veggies, nuts and cranberries.
—Lindsay Tanner, Cathedral City, CA

Takes: 30 min. • **Makes:** 6 servings

- 3 Tbsp. olive oil
- 20 fresh Brussels sprouts, trimmed and halved
- 2 shallots, sliced
- ½ tsp. salt
- ½ cup balsamic vinegar
- 1 skinned rotisserie chicken, shredded
- 3 cups torn romaine
- ⅔ cup chopped roasted sweet red peppers
- ½ cup chopped sun-dried tomatoes (not oil-packed)
- ½ cup balsamic vinaigrette
- ¾ cup pistachios, toasted
- ¾ cup dried cranberries
- Fresh goat cheese, optional

1. In a large skillet, heat oil over medium heat. Add Brussels sprouts and shallots; cook and stir until browned and tender, 10-12 minutes. Sprinkle with salt; drizzle with balsamic vinegar. Cook 2-3 minutes, reducing liquid and stirring to loosen browned bits from pan.

2. Combine chicken, romaine, red pepper and sun-dried tomatoes. Toss with Brussels sprouts mixture and balsamic vinaigrette. Top with pistachios and dried cranberries; serve with goat cheese if desired.

Note To toast nuts, bake in a shallow pan in a 350° oven for 5-10 minutes or cook in a skillet over low heat until lightly browned, stirring occasionally.

Per 1⅓ cups: 500 cal., 25g fat (4g sat. fat), 73mg chol., 657mg sod., 39g carb. (24g sugars, 7g fiber), 30g pro.

GRILLED PEACH, RICE & ARUGULA SALAD

GRILLED PEACH, RICE & ARUGULA SALAD

This hearty salad was created on a day when I needed to clear out some leftovers from the fridge—and it became an instant hit! The grilled peaches are the ultimate "tastes like summer" salad booster.

—Lauren Wyler, Dripping Springs, TX

Takes: 30 min. • **Makes:** 6 servings

- 3 Tbsp. cider vinegar
- 2 Tbsp. Dijon mustard
- 2 Tbsp. canola oil
- 2 Tbsp. maple syrup
- 1 Tbsp. finely chopped shallot
- ¼ tsp. cayenne pepper

SALAD

- 1 pkg. (8.8 oz.) ready-to-serve long grain and wild rice
- 2 medium peaches, quartered
- 6 cups fresh arugula (about 4 oz.)
- 6 bacon strips, cooked and crumbled
- ½ cup crumbled goat cheese

1. For dressing, whisk together first six ingredients.

2. Prepare rice according to the package directions; cool slightly. Place peaches on an oiled grill rack over medium heat. Grill, covered, until lightly browned, 6-8 minutes, turning occasionally.

3. To serve, add bacon and ¼ cup dressing to rice. Line a platter with arugula; top with rice mixture and peaches. Drizzle with remaining dressing; top with cheese.

Per serving: 218 cal., 11g fat (3g sat. fat), 20mg chol., 530mg sod., 23g carb. (9g sugars, 2g fiber), 7g pro. **Diabetic exchanges:** 1 starch, 1 vegetable, 2 fat.

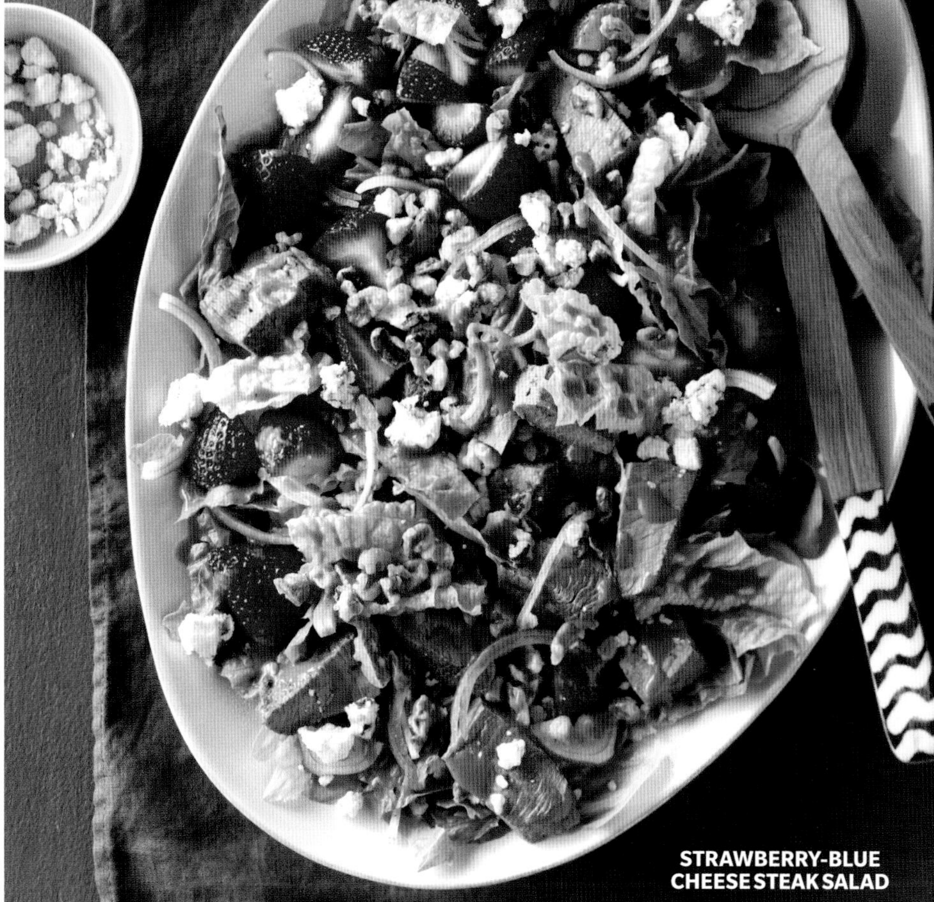

STRAWBERRY-BLUE CHEESE STEAK SALAD

STRAWBERRY-BLUE CHEESE STEAK SALAD

At lunch one day, a friend told me about a steak salad she'd had at a party. It sounded so good, I had to try it for myself. My family and I would eat it every day if we could. We love the sweet, tangy flavors.

—Alma Winberry, Great Falls, MT

Takes: 30 min. • **Makes:** 4 servings

- 1 beef top sirloin steak (¾ in. thick and 1 lb.)
- ½ tsp. salt
- ¼ tsp. pepper
- 2 tsp. olive oil
- 2 Tbsp. lime juice

SALAD

- 1 bunch romaine, torn (about 10 cups)
- 2 cups fresh strawberries, halved
- ¼ cup thinly sliced red onion
- ¼ cup crumbled blue cheese
- ¼ cup chopped walnuts, toasted
- Reduced-fat balsamic vinaigrette

1. Season steak with salt and pepper. In a large skillet, heat oil over medium heat. Add steak; cook 5-7 minutes on each side until meat reaches desired doneness (for medium-rare, a thermometer should read 135°; medium, 140°; medium-well, 145°). Remove from the pan; let stand 5 minutes. Cut the steak into bite-size strips; toss with lime juice.

2. On a platter, combine the romaine, strawberries and onion; top with steak. Sprinkle with blue cheese and walnuts. Serve with vinaigrette.

Per serving: 289 cal., 15g fat (4g sat. fat), 52mg chol., 452mg sod., 12g carb. (5g sugars, 4g fiber), 29g pro. **Diabetic exchanges:** 4 lean meat, 2 vegetable, 2 fat, ½ fruit.

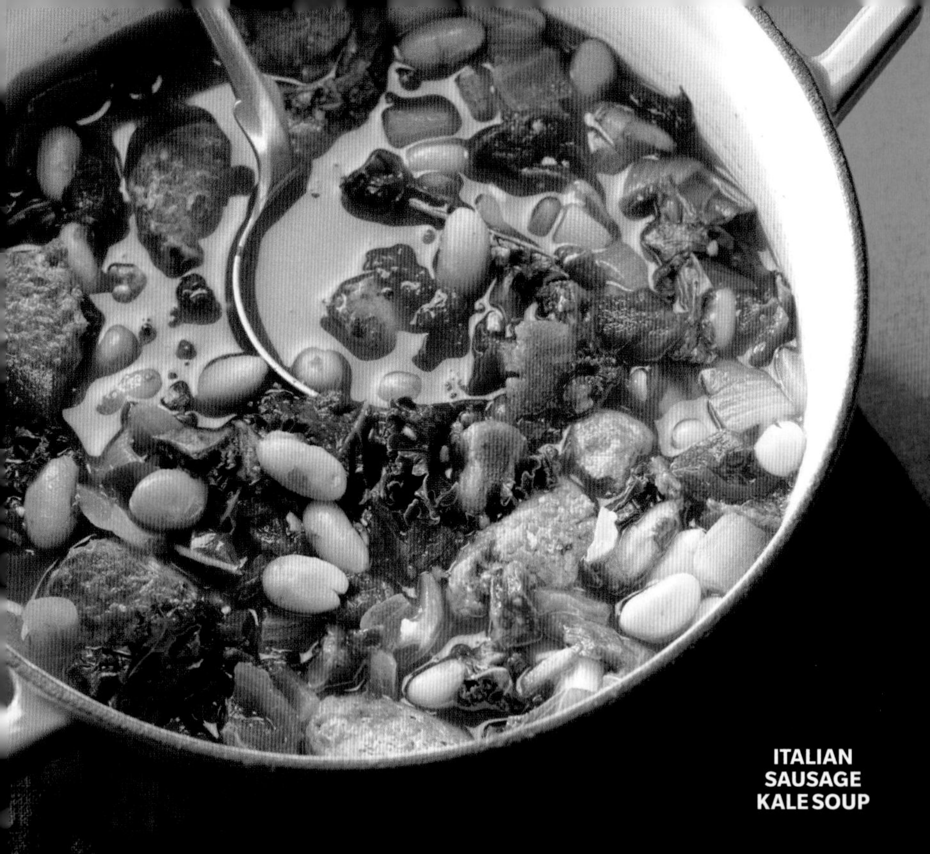

HERBED TURKEY BREAST

Like many home cooks, I always serve turkey for our family's Thanksgiving meal. But instead of roasting a whole bird, I opt for a turkey breast since most of us prefer white meat. The herb butter basting sauce keeps it so moist, and it's easy to carve.
—Ruby Williams, Bogalusa, LA

Prep: 10 min. • **Bake:** 1½ hours + standing
Makes: 12 servings

- ½ cup butter, cubed
- ¼ cup lemon juice
- 2 Tbsp. reduced-sodium soy sauce
- 2 Tbsp. finely chopped green onions
- 1 Tbsp. rubbed sage
- 1 tsp. dried thyme
- 1 tsp. dried marjoram
- ¼ tsp. pepper
- 1 bone-in turkey breast (5½ to 6 lbs.)

1. In a small saucepan, combine the first eight ingredients; bring to a boil. Remove from the heat. Place turkey in a shallow roasting pan; drizzle with butter mixture.
2. Bake, uncovered, at 325° for 1½-2 hours or until a thermometer reads 165°, basting every 30 minutes. Let stand for 10 minutes before carving.
Per 5 ounces cooked turkey: 291 cal., 11g fat (3g sat. fat), 112mg chol., 192mg sod., 1g carb. (0 sugars, 0 fiber), 44g pro.

 **MADE WITH LOVE**

This is the only way to cook a turkey breast. I've been cooking turkey for over 40 years and this is the most flavorful and moist recipe ever! Did a trial run in early November (yum!) and then served it on Thanksgiving.

NANCHEBERT TASTEOFHOME.COM

EDITOR'S CHOICE

ITALIAN SAUSAGE KALE SOUP

My mother dehydrates the last pick of tomatoes from her garden each fall. They are perfect for quick soups like this. When I have time, I like to prepare dried beans for it, but canned beans are just as good.
—Lori Terry, Chicago, IL

Prep: 15 min. • **Cook:** 20 min.
Makes: 8 servings (2 qt.)

- 1 pkg. (19½ oz.) Italian turkey sausage links, casings removed
- 1 medium onion, chopped
- 8 cups chopped fresh kale
- 2 garlic cloves, minced
- ¼ tsp. crushed red pepper flakes, optional
- ½ cup white wine or chicken stock
- 3¼ cups chicken stock (26 oz.)
- 1 can (15 oz.) white kidney or cannellini beans, rinsed and drained
- 1 can (14½ oz.) no-salt-added diced tomatoes, undrained
- ½ cup sun-dried tomatoes (not packed in oil), chopped
- ¼ tsp. pepper

1. In a 6-qt. stockpot, cook sausage and onion over medium heat 6-8 minutes or until no longer pink, breaking meat into crumbles. Remove with a slotted spoon.
2. Add kale to pot; cook and stir 2 minutes. Add garlic and, if desired, pepper flakes; cook 1 minute. Add wine; cook 2 minutes.
3. Stir in sausage mixture and remaining ingredients. Bring to a boil. Reduce heat; simmer, covered, 15-20 minutes or until kale is tender.
Per cup: 217 cal., 8g fat (2g sat. fat), 51mg chol., 868mg sod., 15g carb. (5g sugars, 4g fiber), 18g pro.

HERBED TURKEY BREAST

CHICKEN PROVOLONE

My easy-to-make baked chicken topped with prosciutto and provolone is also one of my husband's favorite dishes. I often serve it on a dark plate and add a garnish of fresh parsley or basil for a fancy touch.

—Dawn Bryant, Thedford, NE

Takes: 25 min.
Makes: 4 servings

- 4 boneless skinless chicken breast halves (4 oz. each)
- ¼ tsp. pepper
- Butter-flavored cooking spray
- 8 fresh basil leaves
- 4 thin slices prosciutto or deli ham
- 4 slices provolone cheese

1. Sprinkle chicken with pepper. In a large nonstick skillet coated with butter-flavored cooking spray, cook chicken over medium heat for 4-5 minutes on each side or until a thermometer reads 170°.

2. Transfer to an ungreased baking sheet; top with the basil, prosciutto and cheese. Broil 6-8 in. from the heat for 1-2 minutes or until cheese is melted.

Per serving: 236 cal., 11g fat (6g sat. fat), 89mg chol., 435mg sod., 1g carb. (0 sugars, 0 fiber), 33g pro. **Diabetic exchanges:** 4 lean meat.

TACO SALAD TACOS

I was making tacos one night and noticed I was out of spicy taco sauce. Using a combination of spices and fat-free Catalina salad dressing saved our family taco night.
—Cheryl Plainte, Prudenville, MI

Takes: 30 min. • **Makes:** 4 servings

- 1 lb. extra-lean ground beef (95% lean)
- 1 medium onion, chopped
- 1 Tbsp. chili powder
- 1 tsp. garlic powder
- 1 tsp. reduced-sodium beef bouillon granules
- 1 tsp. ground cumin
- ¼ tsp. salt

SALAD

- 3 cups torn romaine
- 1 large tomato, seeded and chopped
- 1 medium sweet orange pepper, chopped
- 3 green onions, chopped
- 8 taco shells, warmed
- ½ cup fat-free Catalina salad dressing
- Shredded reduced-fat Colby-Monterey Jack cheese and reduced-fat sour cream, optional

1. In a large skillet, cook beef and onion over medium heat until the meat is no longer pink. Stir in the chili powder, garlic powder, bouillon, cumin and salt; remove from the heat.

2. In a large bowl, combine the romaine, tomato, orange pepper and green onions. Spoon beef mixture into taco shells; top with salad mixture. Drizzle with dressing. Serve with cheese and sour cream if desired.

Per 2 tacos: 334 cal., 11g fat (4g sat. fat), 65mg chol., 722mg sod., 33g carb. (13g sugars, 6g fiber), 26g pro. **Diabetic exchanges:** 3 lean meat, 2 vegetable, 1½ starch.

TACO SALAD TACOS

CREAMY TUNA-NOODLE CASSEROLE

EDITOR'S CHOICE

CREAMY TUNA-NOODLE CASSEROLE

When you need to get supper on the table fast, this tuna casserole with peas, peppers and onions makes a super one-dish meal. Cooked chicken breast works well in place of the tuna.

—Edie DeSpain, Logan, UT

Prep: 20 min.
Bake: 25 min.
Makes: 6 servings

- 5 cups uncooked egg noodles
- 1 cup frozen peas
- 1 can (10¾ oz.) reduced-fat reduced-sodium condensed cream of mushroom soup, undiluted
- 1 cup fat-free sour cream
- ⅔ cup grated Parmesan cheese
- ⅓ cup 2% milk
- ¼ tsp. salt
- 2 cans (5 oz. each) light tuna in water, drained and flaked
- ¼ cup finely chopped onion
- ¼ cup finely chopped green pepper

TOPPING

- ½ cup soft bread crumbs
- 1 Tbsp. butter, melted

1. Preheat oven to 350°. Cook noodles according to package directions for al dente, adding peas during the last minute of cooking; drain.

2. Meanwhile, in a large bowl, combine soup, sour cream, cheese, milk and salt; stir in tuna, onion and pepper. Add noodles and peas; toss to combine.

3. Transfer to an 11x7-in. baking dish coated with cooking spray. In a small bowl, toss bread crumbs with melted butter; sprinkle over top. Bake, uncovered, 25-30 minutes or until bubbly.

Per 1⅓ cups: 340 cal., 8g fat (4g sat. fat), 63mg chol., 699mg sod., 41g carb. (7g sugars, 3g fiber), 25g pro. **Diabetic exchanges:** 3 starch, 2 lean meat, ½ fat.

EDITOR'S CHOICE

LEMON THYME CHICKEN

Buttered onions are a great addition to the lemon sauce of this easy supper. Best of all, it takes only a few minutes to brown the lightly breaded chicken on the stovetop.

—Kay Shimonek, Corsicana, TX

Prep: 10 min. • **Cook:** 25 min.
Makes: 4 servings

- 3 Tbsp. all-purpose flour
- ½ tsp. salt
- ¼ tsp. pepper
- 4 boneless skinless chicken breast halves (4 oz. each)
- 2 tsp. olive oil
- 1 medium onion, chopped
- 1 Tbsp. butter
- ½ tsp. dried thyme
- 1 cup chicken broth
- 3 Tbsp. lemon juice
- 2 Tbsp. minced fresh parsley

1. In a small bowl, combine the flour, salt and pepper. Set aside 4½ tsp. for sauce. Sprinkle the remaining flour mixture over both sides of chicken.

2. In a large nonstick skillet coated with cooking spray, cook chicken in oil over medium heat for 7-9 minutes on each side or until the juices run clear. Remove and keep warm.

3. In the same pan, saute onion in butter until tender. Add thyme and the reserved flour mixture; stir until blended. Gradually stir in the broth and lemon juice, scraping up any browned bits from bottom of pan. Bring to a boil; cook and stir for 2 minutes or until thickened. Serve the onions over chicken. Sprinkle with parsley.

Per serving: 213 cal., 8g fat (3g sat. fat), 70mg chol., 614mg sod., 10g carb. (3g sugars, 1g fiber), 25g pro. **Diabetic exchanges:** 3 lean meat, 1 fat, ½ starch.

BLACK BEAN & PUMPKIN CHILI

BLACK BEAN & PUMPKIN CHILI

My family is crazy about this slow cooker chili because it calls for pumpkin and other ingredients not usually found in chili. Cook up a big batch and freeze some for later—it tastes even better reheated.

—Deborah Vliet, Holland, MI

Prep: 20 min. • **Cook:** 4 hours
Makes: 10 servings (2½ qt.)

- 2 Tbsp. olive oil
- 1 medium onion, chopped
- 1 medium sweet yellow pepper, chopped
- 3 garlic cloves, minced
- 2 cans (15 oz. each) black beans, rinsed and drained
- 1 can (15 oz.) solid-pack pumpkin
- 1 can (14½ oz.) diced tomatoes, undrained
- 3 cups chicken broth
- 2½ cups cubed cooked turkey
- 2 tsp. dried parsley flakes
- 2 tsp. chili powder
- 1½ tsp. ground cumin
- 1½ tsp. dried oregano
- ½ tsp. salt
- Cubed avocado and thinly sliced green onions, optional

1. In a large skillet, heat oil over medium-high heat. Add onion and pepper; cook and stir until onions are tender. Add garlic; cook 1 minute longer.

2. Transfer to a 5-qt. slow cooker; stir in the next 10 ingredients. Cook, covered, on low 4-5 hours. If desired, top with avocado and green onions.

Per cup: 192 cal., 5g fat (1g sat. fat), 28mg chol., 658mg sod., 21g carb. (5g sugars, 7g fiber), 16g pro. **Diabetic exchanges:** 2 lean meat, 1½ starch, ½ fat.

SPICY BEEF VEGETABLE STEW

SPICY BEEF VEGETABLE STEW

This zesty beef and veggie soup is flavorful and fast to fix. It makes a complete meal when served with warm cornbread or French bread.

—Lynnette Davis, Tullahoma, TN

Prep: 10 min. • **Cook:** 8 hours
Makes: 8 servings (3 qt.)

- 1 lb. lean ground beef (90% lean)
- 1 cup chopped onion
- 1 jar (24 oz.) meatless pasta sauce
- 3½ cups water
- 1 pkg. (16 oz.) frozen mixed vegetables
- 1 can (10 oz.) diced tomatoes and green chilies
- 1 cup sliced celery
- 1 tsp. beef bouillon granules
- 1 tsp. pepper

1. In a large skillet, cook beef and onion over medium heat until meat is no longer pink; drain.

2. Transfer to a 5-qt. slow cooker. Stir in the remaining ingredients. Cover and cook on low for 8 hours or until the vegetables are tender.

Per 1½ cups: 177 cal., 5g fat (2g sat. fat), 35mg chol., 675mg sod., 19g carb. (8g sugars, 5g fiber), 15g pro. **Diabetic exchanges:** 2 meat, 1 starch.

TEST KITCHEN TIP

Got leftover stew? Pour it into a pie dish the next night and reheat it in the oven with a pastry crust on top for a tasty beef potpie.

SHRIMP & BROCCOLI BROWN RICE PAELLA

EDITOR'S CHOICE

SHRIMP & BROCCOLI BROWN RICE PAELLA

Years ago, my husband and I came across an open market in France where a Spanish gentleman was making paella. We've been hooked ever since. I whip this up for large groups, but if the gathering is small, I know I can freeze leftovers for another time.
—Joni Hilton, Rocklin, CA

Prep: 45 min. • **Cook:** 50 min.
Makes: 8 servings

- 1 Tbsp. olive oil
- 1 medium onion, chopped
- 1 medium sweet red pepper, chopped
- 1 cup sliced fresh mushrooms
- 2 cups uncooked long grain brown rice
- 2 garlic cloves, minced
- 2 tsp. paprika
- ½ tsp. salt
- ½ tsp. cayenne pepper
- ¼ tsp. saffron threads
- 6 cups chicken stock
- 2 lbs. uncooked large shrimp, peeled and deveined
- 1½ cups fresh broccoli florets
- 1 cup frozen peas

1. In a Dutch oven, heat oil over medium-high heat. Add the onion, red pepper and mushrooms; cook and stir the vegetable mixture 6-8 minutes or until tender. Stir in the rice, garlic and seasonings; cook for 1-2 minutes longer.

2. Stir in stock; bring to a boil. Reduce heat; simmer, covered, 40-45 minutes or until liquid is absorbed and rice is tender. Add shrimp and broccoli; cook 8-10 minutes longer or until shrimp turn pink. Stir in peas; heat through.

Freeze option Place cooled paella in freezer containers. To use, partially thaw in refrigerator overnight. Microwave, covered, on high in a microwave-safe dish until heated through, stirring gently and adding a little stock or water if necessary.

Per 1½ cups: 331 cal., 5g fat (1g sat. fat), 138mg chol., 693mg sod., 44g carb. (4g sugars, 4g fiber), 27g pro. **Diabetic exchanges:** 3 lean meat, 2½ starch.

ORANGE-GLAZED
PORK LOIN

ORANGE-GLAZED PORK LOIN

When it comes to pork recipes, this one is definitely my favorite. My family looks forward to this roast for dinner, and guests always want the recipe. The flavorful rub and a glaze sparked with orange juice are also outstanding on pork chops.
—Lynnette Miete, Alna, ME

Prep: 10 min.
Bake: 1 hour 20 min. + standing
Makes: 16 servings

- 1 tsp. salt
- 1 garlic clove, minced
- 2 to 3 fresh thyme sprigs or ¼ tsp. dried thyme
- ¼ tsp. ground ginger
- ¼ tsp. pepper
- 1 boneless pork loin roast (5 lbs.)

GLAZE

- 1 cup orange juice
- ¼ cup packed brown sugar
- 1 Tbsp. Dijon mustard
- ⅓ cup cold water
- 1 Tbsp. cornstarch

1. Preheat oven to 350°. Combine the first five ingredients; rub over roast. Place fat side up on a rack in a shallow roasting pan. Bake, uncovered, for 1 hour.
2. Meanwhile, in a saucepan over medium heat, combine orange juice, brown sugar and mustard. In a small bowl, mix water and cornstarch until smooth. Add to orange juice mixture. Bring to a boil; cook and stir 2 minutes. Reserve 1 cup glaze for serving; brush half of remaining glaze over roast.
3. Bake until a thermometer reads 145°, about 20-40 minutes longer, brushing occasionally with remaining glaze. Let stand 10 minutes before slicing. Reheat reserved glaze; serve with roast.

Per 4 ounces cooked pork with 1 Tbsp. glaze: 199 cal., 7g fat (2g sat. fat), 71mg chol., 212mg sod., 6g carb. (5g sugars, 0 fiber), 28g pro. **Diabetic exchanges:** 4 lean meat, ½ starch.

LEMON-PARSLEY BAKED COD

LEMON-PARSLEY BAKED COD

After trying a few cod recipes, this was the first fish recipe that got two thumbs up from my picky meat-only eaters. The tangy lemon gives the cod some oomph.
—Trisha Kruse, Eagle, ID

Takes: 30 min. • **Makes:** 4 servings

- 3 Tbsp. lemon juice
- 3 Tbsp. butter, melted
- ¼ cup all-purpose flour
- ½ tsp. salt
- ¼ tsp. paprika
- ¼ tsp. lemon-pepper seasoning
- 4 cod fillets (6 oz. each)
- 2 Tbsp. minced fresh parsley
- 2 tsp. grated lemon peel

1. Preheat oven to 400°. In a shallow bowl, mix lemon juice and butter. In a separate bowl, mix flour and seasonings. Dip fillets in lemon juice mixture, then in flour mixture to coat both sides; shake off excess.
2. Place in a 13x9-in. baking dish coated with cooking spray. Drizzle with remaining lemon juice mixture. Bake 12-15 minutes or until fish just begins to flake easily with a fork. Mix parsley and lemon peel; sprinkle over fish.

Per fillet: 232 cal., 10g fat (6g sat. fat), 87mg chol., 477mg sod., 7g carb. (0 sugars, 0 fiber), 28g pro. **Diabetic exchanges:** 4 lean meat, 2 fat, ½ starch.

EASY CRAB CAKES

STEAK FAJITAS

Zesty salsa and tender strips of steak make these traditional fajitas extra-special.

—Rebecca Baird, Salt Lake City, UT

Takes: 30 min. • **Makes:** 6 servings

- 2 large tomatoes, seeded and chopped
- ½ cup diced red onion
- ¼ cup lime juice
- 1 jalapeno pepper, seeded and minced
- 3 Tbsp. minced fresh cilantro
- 2 tsp. ground cumin, divided
- ¾ tsp. salt, divided
- 1 beef flank steak (about 1½ lbs.)
- 1 Tbsp. canola oil
- 1 large onion, halved and sliced
- 6 whole wheat tortillas (8 in.), warmed
- Sliced avocado and lime wedges, optional

1. For salsa, place first five ingredients in a small bowl; stir in 1 tsp. cumin and ¼ tsp. salt. Let stand until serving.

2. Sprinkle steak with the remaining cumin and salt. Grill, covered, over medium heat or broil 4 in. from the heat until meat reaches desired doneness (for medium-rare, a thermometer should read 135°), 6-8 minutes. Let stand 5 minutes.

3. Meanwhile, in a skillet, heat oil over medium-high heat; saute onion until crisp-tender. Slice steak thinly across the grain; serve in tortillas with onion and salsa. If desired, serve fajitas with sliced avocado and lime wedges.

Per fajita: 329 cal., 12g fat (4g sat. fat), 54mg chol., 498mg sod., 29g carb. (3g sugars, 5g fiber), 27g pro. **Diabetic exchanges:** 3 lean meat, 2 starch, ½ fat.

EASY CRAB CAKES

Ready-to-go crabmeat makes these patties easier to prep than other crab cakes. You can also form the crab mixture into four thick patties instead of eight cakes.

—Charlene Spelock, Apollo, PA

Takes: 25 min. • **Makes:** 4 servings

- 1 cup seasoned bread crumbs, divided
- 2 green onions, finely chopped
- ¼ cup finely chopped sweet red pepper
- 1 large egg, lightly beaten
- ¼ cup reduced-fat mayonnaise
- 1 Tbsp. lemon juice
- ½ tsp. garlic powder
- ⅛ tsp. cayenne pepper
- 2 cans (6 oz. each) crabmeat, drained, flaked and cartilage removed
- 1 Tbsp. butter

1. In a large bowl, combine ⅓ cup bread crumbs, green onions, red pepper, egg, mayonnaise, lemon juice, garlic powder and cayenne; fold in crab.

2. Place remaining crumbs in a shallow bowl. Divide mixture into eight portions; shape into 2-in. balls. Gently coat in bread crumbs and shape into ½-in.-thick patties.

3. In a large nonstick skillet, heat butter over medium-high heat. Add crab cakes; cook until golden brown, 3-4 minutes per side.

Per 2 crab cakes: 239 cal., 11g fat (3g sat. fat), 141mg chol., 657mg sod., 13g carb. (2g sugars, 1g fiber), 21g pro.

STEAK FAJITAS

MASHED PEPPERY TURNIPS

MASHED PEPPERY TURNIPS

I created this recipe to use up a great turnip harvest from our garden as well as to lighten up one of our favorite side dishes—mashed potatoes. By using turnips in place of spuds, we can enjoy a delicious side without all the carbohydrates.

—Courtney Stultz, Weir, KS

Takes: 30 min. • Makes: 4 servings

- 4 medium turnips (about 1 lb.), peeled and cut into 1¼-in. pieces
- 1 large potato (about ¾ lb.), peeled and cut into 1¼-in. pieces
- 2 Tbsp. reduced-fat cream cheese
- 1 Tbsp. butter
- 1 Tbsp. minced fresh parsley
- 1 tsp. sea salt
- ½ tsp. garlic powder
- ¼ tsp. pepper
- ⅛ tsp. chili powder
- ⅛ tsp. ground chipotle pepper

1. Place turnips, potato and enough water to cover in a large saucepan; bring to a boil. Reduce heat; cook, uncovered, until tender, 15-20 minutes. Drain; return to pan.

2. Mash vegetables to desired consistency. Stir in remaining ingredients.

Per ¾ cup: 140 cal., 5g fat (3g sat. fat), 13mg chol., 608mg sod., 23g carb. (5g sugars, 3g fiber), 3g pro. **Diabetic exchanges:** 1½ starch, 1 fat.

TEST KITCHEN TIP

When shopping for turnips or other root vegetables, select those that are smooth-skinned, unblemished, heavy and firm. Look for turnips no larger than 2 inches in diameter. Keep unwashed turnips in a plastic bag in your refrigerator's crisper drawer for up to one week. Just before using, wash, trim ends and peel.

BAKED PARMESAN BROCCOLI

I began making this creamy side dish years ago as a way to get my kids to eat broccoli. They're grown now, but still request this satisfying casserole when they come to visit. It's truly a family favorite.

—Barbara Uhl, Wesley Chapel, FL

Prep: 30 min. • **Bake:** 15 min.
Makes: 12 servings

- 4 bunches broccoli, cut into florets
- 6 Tbsp. butter, divided
- 1 small onion, finely chopped
- 1 garlic clove, minced
- ¼ cup all-purpose flour
- 2 cups 2% milk
- 1 large egg yolk, beaten
- 1 cup grated Parmesan cheese
- ½ tsp. salt
- ⅛ tsp. pepper
- ½ cup seasoned bread crumbs

1. Preheat oven to 400°. Place half of broccoli in a steamer basket; place in a large saucepan over 1 in. of water. Bring to a boil; cover and steam 3-4 minutes or until crisp-tender. Place in a greased 13x9-in. baking dish; repeat with the remaining broccoli.

2. Meanwhile, in a small saucepan over medium heat, melt 4 Tbsp. butter. Add onion; cook and stir until tender. Add garlic; cook 1 minute longer.

3. Stir in flour until blended; gradually add milk. Bring to a boil; cook and stir 2 minutes or until thickened. Stir a small amount of hot mixture into egg yolk; return all to the pan, stirring constantly. Cook and stir 1 minute longer. Remove from the heat; stir in the cheese, salt and pepper. Pour over broccoli.

4. In a small skillet, cook bread crumbs in remaining butter until golden brown; sprinkle over the top.

5. Bake, uncovered, 15-18 minutes or until heated through.

Per ¾ cup: 191 cal., 10g fat (5g sat. fat), 41mg chol., 388mg sod., 19g carb. (7g sugars, 6g fiber), 11g pro.

BAKED PARMESAN BROCCOLI

SKILLET ZUCCHINI & SAUSAGE

I lived on the Oregon coast for 20 years, and during that time I had plenty of guests. I often turned to this tasty dish when folks dropped by because it's quick and easy. And judging by the requests I received for the recipe, everyone seemed to love it! This dish goes well with skillet cornbread or garlic bread.

—LaBelle Doster, Vancouver, WA

Takes: 30 min. • **Makes:** 10 servings

- 2 Tbsp. vegetable oil
- ½ lb. fully cooked smoked Polish sausage, cut into ½-in. diagonal slices
- 1 cup chopped onion
- 1 cup sliced celery
- ½ cup chopped green pepper
- 1 garlic clove, minced
- ½ tsp. dried oregano
- ½ tsp. pepper
- 4 to 5 medium zucchini, sliced
- 4 to 5 medium tomatoes, coarsely chopped
- Herb seasoning blend to taste

Heat oil in a large skillet, lightly brown sausage. Add onion, celery, green pepper, garlic, oregano and pepper. Cook and stir until vegetables are almost tender. Add zucchini and tomatoes; cook and stir until zucchini is just tender. Sprinkle with herb seasoning blend.

Per cup: 130 cal., 9g fat (3g sat. fat), 16mg chol., 211mg sod., 8g carb. (4g sugars, 2g fiber), 5g pro.

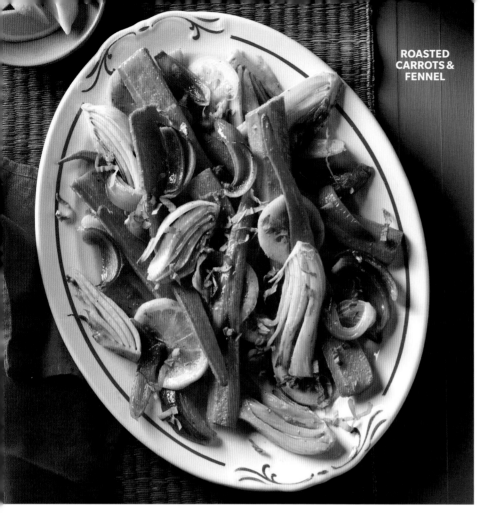

ROASTED CARROTS & FENNEL

This addictive vegetable combo is a fresh take on one of my mother's standard wintertime dishes. I usually add more carrots—as many as the pans will hold.

—Lily Julow, Lawrenceville, GA

Prep: 15 min. • **Bake:** 40 min.
Makes: 8 servings

- 2½ lbs. medium carrots, peeled and cut in half lengthwise
- 1 large fennel bulb, cut into ½-in. wedges
- 1 large red onion, cut into ½-in. wedges
- 1 medium lemon, thinly sliced
- ¼ cup olive oil
- 2 tsp. ground coriander
- 1 tsp. ground cumin
- ½ tsp. salt
- ¼ tsp. pepper
- Thinly sliced fresh basil leaves

1. Preheat oven to 375°. In a bowl, combine carrots, fennel, onion and lemon. Mix oil, coriander, cumin, salt and pepper; drizzle over vegetables and toss to coat. Transfer to two foil-lined 15x10x1-in. baking pans.

2. Roast 40-50 minutes or until vegetables are tender, stirring occasionally. Sprinkle with basil.

Per serving: 139 cal., 7g fat (1g sat. fat), 0 chol., 262mg sod., 18g carb. (9g sugars, 6g fiber), 2g pro. **Diabetic exchanges:** 2 vegetable, 1½ fat.

SKILLET ZUCCHINI & SAUSAGE

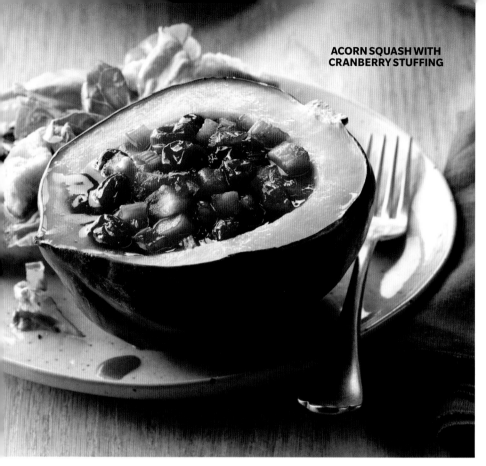

ACORN SQUASH WITH CRANBERRY STUFFING

BEST-EVER STUFFED MUSHROOMS

I make these every Christmas Eve. If you don't have mushrooms on hand, spread the filling on baguette slices or crackers. It's a good veggie dip, too.

—Debby Beard, Eagle, CO

Prep: 20 min. • **Bake:** 15 min.
Makes: 2½ dozen

- 1 lb. bulk pork sausage
- ¼ cup finely chopped onion
- 1 garlic clove, minced
- 1 pkg. (8 oz.) reduced-fat cream cheese
- ¼ cup shredded Parmesan cheese
- ⅓ cup seasoned bread crumbs
- 3 tsp. dried basil
- 1½ tsp. dried parsley flakes
- 30 large fresh mushrooms (about 1½ lbs.), stems removed
- 3 Tbsp. butter, melted

1. Preheat oven to 400°. In a large skillet, cook the sausage, onion and garlic over medium heat 6-8 minutes or until sausage is no longer pink and onion is tender, breaking up sausage into crumbles; drain. Add cream cheese and Parmesan cheese; cook and stir until melted. Stir in bread crumbs, basil and parsley.

2. Meanwhile, place the mushroom caps in a greased 15x10x1-in. baking pan, stem side up. Brush with butter. Spoon sausage mixture into caps. Bake, uncovered, 12-15 minutes or until the mushrooms are tender.

Per appetizer: 79 cal., 6g fat (3g sat. fat), 17mg chol., 167mg sod., 2g carb. (1g sugars, 0 fiber), 3g pro.

ACORN SQUASH WITH CRANBERRY STUFFING

Have squash or cranberry lovers at your table? They're sure to love this colorful dish and its delicious blend of flavors.

—Dorothy Pritchett, Wills Point, TX

Prep: 10 min. • **Bake:** 55 min.
Makes: 4 servings

- 2 medium acorn squash
- ¼ cup chopped celery
- 2 Tbsp. chopped onion
- 2 Tbsp. butter
- 1 medium tart apple, peeled and diced
- ½ tsp. salt
- ½ tsp. lemon juice
- ⅛ tsp. pepper
- 1 cup fresh or frozen cranberries
- ½ cup sugar
- 2 Tbsp. water

1. Cut squash in half; discard seeds. Cut a thin slice from the bottom of squash halves so they sit flat. Place squash hollow side down in an ungreased 13x9-in. baking dish. Add ½ in. of water. Cover and bake at 375° for 45 minutes.

2. Meanwhile, in a small skillet, saute celery and onion in butter until tender. Add the apple, salt, lemon juice and pepper. Cook, uncovered, over medium-low heat until apple is tender, stirring occasionally. Stir in the cranberries, sugar and water. Cook and stir until berries pop and liquid is syrupy.

3. Turn squash halves over; fill with cranberry mixture. Cover and bake 10-15 minutes longer or until squash is tender.

Per serving: 270 cal., 6g fat (4g sat. fat), 15mg chol., 367mg sod., 57g carb. (36g sugars, 5g fiber), 2g pro.

ROASTED CARROTS WITH CILANTRO-WALNUT PESTO

ROASTED CARROTS WITH CILANTRO-WALNUT PESTO

Lightly baked and lightly flavored, this carrot dish uses cilantro, walnuts, extra virgin olive oil, garlic, parsley, Parmesan and basil.

—Aysha Schurman, Ammon, ID

Prep: 15 min.
Bake: 20 min.
Makes: 4 servings

- 2 Tbsp. chopped walnuts
- 2 Tbsp. fresh cilantro leaves
- 1 Tbsp. grated Parmesan cheese
- 1 garlic clove, chopped
- 1 tsp. fresh parsley leaves
- 1 tsp. chopped fresh basil
- ¼ cup olive oil
- 1 lb. medium carrots, halved lengthwise

Preheat oven to 400°. Pulse the first six ingredients in a small food processor until finely chopped. Continue processing while gradually adding oil in a steady stream. Drizzle carrots with herb mixture; toss to coat. Transfer to a greased 15x10x1-in. baking pan. Roast, stirring occasionally, until tender, 20-25 minutes.

Per serving: 196 cal., 17g fat (2g sat. fat), 1mg chol., 102mg sod., 12g carb. (5g sugars, 3g fiber), 2g pro.

ROASTED VEGGIE ORZO

ROASTED VEGGIE ORZO

My sister inspired this recipe. I added a few more spices, but the concept is hers. It's easy to vary, and a simple way to add veggies to your diet.

—Jackie Termont, Ruther Glen, VA

Prep: 25 min. • **Bake:** 20 min.
Makes: 8 servings

- 1½ cups fresh mushrooms, halved
- 1 medium zucchini, chopped
- 1 medium sweet yellow pepper, chopped
- 1 medium sweet red pepper, chopped
- 1 small red onion, cut into wedges
- 1 cup cut fresh asparagus (1-in. pieces)
- 1 Tbsp. olive oil
- 1 tsp. each dried oregano, thyme and rosemary, crushed
- ½ tsp. salt
- 1¼ cups uncooked orzo pasta
- ¼ cup crumbled feta cheese

1. Place vegetables in a 15x10x1-in. baking pan coated with cooking spray. Drizzle with oil and sprinkle with seasonings; toss to coat. Bake at 400° for 20-25 minutes or until tender, stirring occasionally.

2. Meanwhile, cook orzo according to package directions. Drain; transfer to a serving bowl. Stir in roasted vegetables. Sprinkle with cheese.

Per ¾ cup: 164 cal., 3g fat (1g sat. fat), 2mg chol., 188mg sod., 28g carb. (3g sugars, 3g fiber), 6g pro. **Diabetic exchanges:** 1½ starch, 1 vegetable, ½ fat.

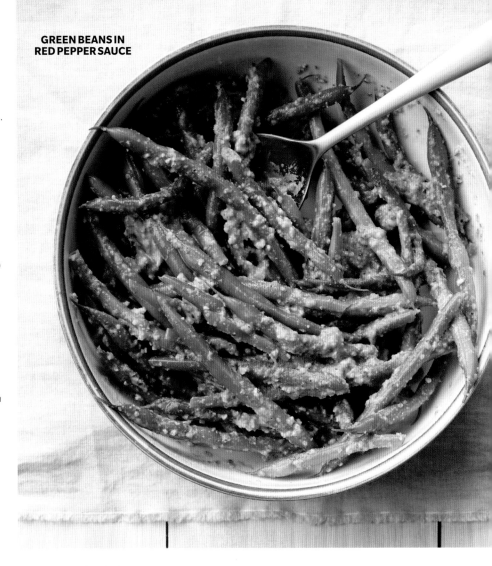

GREEN BEANS IN RED PEPPER SAUCE

GREEN BEANS IN RED PEPPER SAUCE

For easy veggies, I make a simple sauce of sweet red peppers, almonds and parsley. We also like this sauce with zucchini or roasted cauliflower.

—Elisabeth Larsen, Pleasant Grove, UT

Takes: 30 min. • **Makes:** 6 servings

- 1 lb. fresh green beans, trimmed
- ½ cup roasted sweet red peppers
- ¼ cup sliced almonds
- 2 Tbsp. olive oil
- 2 Tbsp. minced fresh parsley
- 2 Tbsp. lemon juice
- 2 garlic cloves, halved
- ½ tsp. salt

Place beans in a large saucepan; add water to cover. Bring to a boil. Cook, covered, until crisp-tender, 2-4 minutes. Drain. Pulse remaining ingredients in a food processor until smooth. Toss with beans.

Per ¾ cup: 95 cal., 7g fat (1g sat. fat), 0 chol., 276mg sod., 8g carb. (3g sugars, 3g fiber), 2g pro. **Diabetic exchanges:** 1 vegetable, 1 fat.

MOIST LEMON CHIFFON CAKE

Looking for a low-fat dessert? You'll love my airy chiffon cake drizzled with a sweet-tart lemon glaze.
—Rebecca Baird, Salt Lake City, UT

Prep: 15 min. • **Bake:** 45 min. + cooling
Makes: 16 servings

- ½ cup fat-free evaporated milk
- ½ cup reduced-fat sour cream
- ¼ cup lemon juice
- 2 Tbsp. canola oil
- 2 tsp. vanilla extract
- 1 tsp. grated lemon peel
- 1 tsp. lemon extract
- 2 cups cake flour
- 1½ cups sugar
- 1 Tbsp. baking powder
- ½ tsp. salt
- 1 cup large egg whites (about 7)
- ½ tsp. cream of tartar

LEMON GLAZE

- 1¾ cups confectioners' sugar
- 3 Tbsp. lemon juice

1. In a large bowl, combine the first seven ingredients. Sift together the flour, sugar, baking powder and salt; gradually beat into lemon mixture until smooth. In a small bowl, beat egg whites until foamy. Add cream of tartar; beat until stiff peaks form. Gently fold into the lemon mixture.
2. Pour into an ungreased 10-in. tube pan. Bake at 325° for 45-55 minutes or until the cake springs back when lightly touched. Immediately invert pan; cool completely. Remove cake to a serving platter. Combine glaze ingredients; drizzle over cake.
Per slice: 230 cal., 3g fat (1g sat. fat), 3mg chol., 189mg sod., 47g carb. (33g sugars, 0 fiber), 4g pro.

MAKEOVER FRUIT PIZZA

The calories and fat have been trimmed from a traditional fruit pizza to create this gorgeous, refreshing treat.
—Taste of Home *Test Kitchen*

Prep: 25 min. + chilling
Bake: 10 min. + cooling
Makes: 16 servings

- 1 cup all-purpose flour
- ¼ cup confectioners' sugar
- ½ cup cold butter, cubed

GLAZE

- 5 tsp. cornstarch
- 1¼ cups unsweetened pineapple juice
- 1 tsp. lemon juice

TOPPINGS

- 1 pkg. (8 oz.) reduced-fat cream cheese
- ⅓ cup sugar
- 1 tsp. vanilla extract
- 2 cups halved fresh strawberries
- 1 cup fresh blueberries
- 1 can (11 oz.) mandarin oranges, drained

1. Preheat oven to 350°. In a large bowl, mix flour and confectioners' sugar; cut in butter until crumbly. Press onto an ungreased 12-in. pizza pan. Bake until very lightly browned, 10-12 minutes. Cool completely on a wire rack.
2. In a saucepan, mix the glaze ingredients until smooth; bring to a boil. Cook and stir until thickened, 2 minutes. Cool slightly.
3. In a bowl, beat cream cheese, sugar and vanilla until smooth. Spread over crust. Top with berries and mandarin oranges. Drizzle with glaze. Refrigerate until cold.
Per slice: 170 cal., 9g fat (6g sat. fat), 25mg chol., 120mg sod., 20g carb. (13g sugars, 1g fiber), 3g pro. **Diabetic exchanges:** 1½ fat, 1 starch, ½ fruit.

MOIST LEMON CHIFFON CAKE

GRAPEFRUIT, LIME & MINT YOGURT PARFAIT

Tart grapefruit and lime are balanced with a bit of honey in this cool and easy parfait.
—Lois Enger, Colorado Springs, CO

Takes: 15 min. • **Makes:** 6 servings

- 4 large red grapefruit
- 4 cups (32 oz.) reduced-fat plain yogurt
- 2 tsp. grated lime peel
- 2 Tbsp. lime juice
- 3 Tbsp. honey
- Torn fresh mint leaves

1. Cut a thin slice from the top and bottom of each grapefruit; stand fruit upright on a cutting board. With a knife, cut off peel and outer membrane from grapefruit. Cut along the membrane of each segment to remove fruit.

2. In a large bowl, mix yogurt, lime peel and juice. Layer half of the grapefruit and half of the yogurt mixture into six parfait glasses. Repeat layers. Drizzle parfaits with honey; top with mint.

Per parfait: 207 cal., 3g fat (2g sat. fat), 10mg chol., 115mg sod., 39g carb. (36g sugars, 3g fiber), 10g pro.

SPICED BUTTERNUT SQUASH PIE

My mom always made this dessert with her homegrown squash. It was my dad's favorite after-dinner treat. I continue to make it to this day.

—Johnna Poulson, Celebration, FL

Prep: 20 min.
Bake: 40 min. + cooling
Makes: 8 servings

- 1 refrigerated pie crust
- 3 large eggs
- 1½ cups mashed cooked butternut squash
- 1 cup fat-free milk
- ⅔ cup fat-free evaporated milk
- ¾ cup sugar
- ½ tsp. salt
- 1 tsp. ground cinnamon
- ½ tsp. ground ginger
- ¼ tsp. ground nutmeg
- ¼ tsp. ground cloves
- Sweetened whipped cream, optional

1. Preheat oven to 450°. Unroll pie crust into a 9-in. pie plate; flute edge. Place eggs, squash, milks, sugar, salt and spices in a food processor; process until smooth. Pour into crust. Bake on a lower oven rack for 10 minutes.

2. Reduce oven setting to 350°. Bake until a knife inserted in the center comes out clean, 30-40 minutes longer. Cool on a wire rack; serve or refrigerate within 2 hours. If desired, serve with whipped cream.

Per piece: 266 cal., 9g fat (4g sat. fat), 76mg chol., 313mg sod., 41g carb. (24g sugars, 2g fiber), 7g pro.

CHOCOLATE CHIFFON CAKE

CHOCOLATE CHIFFON CAKE

This dessert stands out from the rest. Beautiful high layers of rich sponge cake are drizzled with a succulent chocolate glaze.
—Erma Fox, Memphis, MO

Prep: 25 min. + cooling
Bake: 1 hour + cooling • **Makes:** 20 servings

- 7 large eggs, separated
- ½ cup baking cocoa
- ¾ cup boiling water
- 1¾ cups cake flour
- 1¾ cups sugar
- 1½ tsp. baking soda
- 1 tsp. salt
- ½ cup canola oil
- 2 tsp. vanilla extract
- ¼ tsp. cream of tartar

ICING

- ⅓ cup butter
- 2 cups confectioners' sugar
- 2 oz. unsweetened chocolate, melted and cooled
- 1½ tsp. vanilla extract
- 3 to 4 Tbsp. hot water
- Chopped nuts, optional

1. Let eggs stand at room temperature for 30 minutes. In a bowl, combine cocoa and water until smooth; cool for 20 minutes. In a large bowl, combine flour, sugar, baking soda and salt. In another bowl, whisk the egg yolks, oil and vanilla; add to the dry ingredients along with the cocoa mixture. Beat until well blended. In another large bowl and with clean beaters, beat the egg whites and cream of tartar on high speed until stiff peaks form. Gradually fold into the egg yolk mixture.

2. Gently spoon batter into an ungreased 10-in. tube pan. Cut through the batter with a knife to remove air pockets. Bake on the lowest rack at 325° for 60-65 minutes or until top springs back when lightly touched. Immediately invert pan; cool completely. Run a knife around sides and center tube of pan. Invert cake onto a serving plate.

3. For icing, melt butter in a saucepan. Remove from heat; stir in the confectioners' sugar, chocolate, vanilla and water. Drizzle over cake. Sprinkle with nuts if desired.

Per slice: 268 cal., 11g fat (3g sat. fat), 73mg chol., 262mg sod., 40g carb. (30g sugars, 1g fiber), 4g pro.

PRETTY PEACH TART

When ripe peaches finally arrive at fruit stands, this is the first recipe I reach for. It's just plain perfection—and a delightful way to celebrate their arrival! You can make the tart with other varieties of fruit, too.

—Lorraine Caland, Shuniah, ON

Prep: 30 min. • **Bake:** 40 min. + cooling
Makes: 8 servings

- ¼ cup butter, softened
- 3 Tbsp. sugar
- ¼ tsp. ground nutmeg
- 1 cup all-purpose flour

FILLING

- 2 lbs. peaches (about 7 medium), peeled and sliced
- ⅓ cup sugar
- 2 Tbsp. all-purpose flour
- ¼ tsp. ground cinnamon
- ⅛ tsp. almond extract
- ¼ cup sliced almonds
- Whipped cream, optional

1. Preheat oven to 375°. Cream butter, sugar and nutmeg until light and fluffy. Beat in flour until blended (mixture will be dry). Press firmly onto bottom and up sides of an ungreased 9-in. fluted tart pan with removable bottom.

2. Place on a baking sheet. Bake on a middle oven rack until lightly browned, 10-12 minutes. Cool on a wire rack.

3. In a large bowl, toss peaches with sugar, flour, cinnamon and extract; add to crust. Sprinkle with almonds.

4. Bake tart on a lower oven rack until crust is golden brown and peaches are tender, 40-45 minutes. Cool on a wire rack. If desired, serve with whipped cream.

Per piece: 222 cal., 8g fat (4g sat. fat), 15mg chol., 46mg sod., 36g carb. (21g sugars, 3g fiber), 4g pro.

PRETTY PEACH TART

BERRY-CREAM COOKIE SNAPS

BERRY-CREAM COOKIE SNAPS

My mom and I came up with this cookie by combining two different recipes. These beauties are crispy on the outside and light and fluffy inside. It's also fun to bake the cookies flat and serve the filling as a dip.

—Crystal Briddick, Colfax, IL

Prep: 40 min. + chilling
Bake: 5 min/batch + cooling
Makes: about 2 dozen

- 4 oz. cream cheese, softened
- ¼ cup sugar
- 2 Tbsp. seedless strawberry jam
- ¼ cup heavy whipping cream, whipped
- 1 to 3 drops red food coloring, optional

BATTER

- ½ cup sugar
- ⅓ cup all-purpose flour
- ⅛ tsp. salt
- 2 large egg whites
- ¼ tsp. vanilla extract
- ¼ cup butter, melted and cooled

1. Preheat oven to 400°. Beat the cream cheese, sugar and jam until blended. Fold in whipped cream and, if desired, food coloring. Refrigerate.

2. For cookie batter, whisk sugar, flour and salt; stir in the egg whites and vanilla until smooth. Whisk in the butter until blended. Line baking sheets with parchment paper. Preparing four cookies at a time, drop the batter by 1½ teaspoonfuls 4 in. apart onto the prepared baking pans. Bake until the edges of the cookies are lightly browned, about 5-8 minutes.

3. Loosen each cookie and curl around a wooden spoon handle. Press lightly to seal; hold until set, 20 seconds. Place on waxed paper to cool. Repeat steps with remaining cookies. If cookies become too cool to shape, return to oven for 1 minute to soften.

4. Just before serving, spoon filling into cookie shells. Or pipe it by cutting a small hole in the tip of a pastry bag or in a corner of a food-safe plastic bag and inserting a star tip, then transferring filling to bag. Refrigerate any leftovers.

Per cookie: 72 cal., 4g fat (3g sat. fat), 12mg chol., 44mg sod., 8g carb. (7g sugars, 0 fiber), 1g pro.

CARROT COOKIE BITES

This recipe is a longtime family favorite. The cookies are soft and delicious, and the aroma while baking...absolutely irresistible!
—Jeanie Petrik, Greensburg, KY

Prep: 15 min. • **Bake:** 10 min./batch
Makes: 7 dozen

- ⅔ cup shortening
- 1 cup packed brown sugar
- 2 large eggs
- ½ cup buttermilk
- 1 tsp. vanilla extract
- 2 cups all-purpose flour
- 1 tsp. ground cinnamon
- ½ tsp. salt
- ¼ tsp. baking powder
- ¼ tsp. baking soda
- ¼ tsp. ground nutmeg
- ¼ tsp. ground cloves
- 2 cups quick-cooking oats
- 1 cup shredded carrots
- ½ cup chopped pecans

1. In a large bowl, cream shortening and brown sugar until light and fluffy. Beat in the eggs, buttermilk and vanilla. Combine the flour, cinnamon, salt, baking powder, baking soda, nutmeg and cloves; gradually add to creamed mixture. Stir in the oats, carrots, and pecans.

2. To freeze cookie dough, see freeze option. To bake immediately, drop dough by rounded teaspoonfuls 2 in. apart onto ungreased baking sheets. Bake at 375° until lightly browned, 6-8 minutes. Remove to wire racks to cool.

Freeze option Drop dough by rounded teaspoonfuls onto baking sheets. Freeze until firm. Transfer cookie dough balls to a resealable plastic freezer bag. Dough may be frozen up to 3 months. To bake, place 2 in. apart on ungreased baking sheets. Bake at 375° for 10-15 minutes or until lightly browned. Remove to wire racks to cool.

Per cookie: 50 cal., 2g fat (0 sat. fat), 5mg chol., 24mg sod., 6g carb. (3g sugars, 0 fiber), 1g pro. **Diabetic exchanges:** ½ starch, ½ fat.

LEMON BLUEBERRY DROP SCONES

EDITOR'S CHOICE

LEMON BLUEBERRY DROP SCONES

I serve these fruity scones for baby and bridal showers. They're a bit lower in fat than other scones, so you can indulge with little guilt.
—Jacqueline Hendershot, Orange, CA

Takes: 30 min. • **Makes:** 14 scones

- 2 cups all-purpose flour
- ⅓ cup sugar
- 2 tsp. baking powder
- 1 tsp. grated lemon peel
- ½ tsp. baking soda
- ¼ tsp. salt
- 1 cup (8 oz.) lemon yogurt
- 1 large egg
- ¼ cup butter, melted
- 1 cup fresh or frozen blueberries

GLAZE

- ½ cup confectioners' sugar
- 1 Tbsp. lemon juice
- ½ tsp. grated lemon peel

1. In a large bowl, combine the first six ingredients. In another bowl, combine the yogurt, egg and butter. Stir into the dry ingredients just until moistened. Fold in blueberries.

2. Drop by heaping tablespoonfuls 2 in. apart onto a greased baking sheet. Bake at 400° for 15-18 minutes or until lightly browned. Combine glaze ingredients; drizzle over warm scones.

Note If using frozen blueberries, use without thawing to avoid discoloring the batter.

Per scone: 158 cal., 4g fat (2g sat. fat), 25mg chol., 192mg sod., 28g carb. (13g sugars, 1g fiber), 3g pro.

GANACHE-TOPPED CHOCOLATE CAKE

GANACHE-TOPPED CHOCOLATE CAKE

To say this cake is elegant would be an understatement. It's worthy of special occasions, but so easy to whip together you can enjoy it any day of the week.
—Taste of Home *Test Kitchen*

Prep: 20 min. • **Bake:** 20 min. + cooling
Makes: 12 servings

- ¾ cup boiling water
- 2 oz. 53% cacao dark baking chocolate, coarsely chopped
- 2 Tbsp. butter
- ¾ cup sugar
- ¼ cup buttermilk
- 1 large egg
- 1 tsp. vanilla extract
- ½ tsp. orange extract
- 1 cup all-purpose flour
- 1 tsp. baking soda
- ½ tsp. salt

GANACHE
- ¼ cup half-and-half cream
- 3 oz. 53% cacao dark baking chocolate, coarsely chopped
- Fresh raspberries, optional

1. Preheat oven to 350°. Pour boiling water over the chocolate and butter; stir until smooth. Cool slightly. Whisk in sugar, buttermilk, egg and extracts. Combine flour, baking soda and salt; whisk into chocolate mixture just until blended.
2. Transfer to a 9-in. round baking pan coated with cooking spray. Bake until a toothpick inserted in center comes out clean, 18-22 minutes. Cool 10 minutes before removing from pan to a wire rack to cool completely. Place rack on a waxed paper-lined baking sheet.
3. For ganache, bring cream just to a boil in a small saucepan. Pour over chocolate; whisk until smooth. Cool until slightly thickened, about 10 minutes. Slowly pour over cake, allowing some ganache to drape over sides.
4. Refrigerate cake until serving. If desired, sprinkle with raspberries. Cut into wedges.
Per slice: 179 cal., 7g fat (4g sat. fat), 26mg chol., 236mg sod., 28g carb. (18g sugars, 1g fiber), 3g pro. **Diabetic exchanges:** 2 starch, 1 fat.

OLD-FASHIONED RICE PUDDING

This dessert is a comforting way to end any meal. When I was a little girl, I could hardly wait for the first heavenly bite. For extra indulgence, enjoy it the way my husband does—with a scoop of ice cream on top.
—Sandra Melnychenko, Grandview, MB

Prep: 10 min. • **Bake:** 1 hour
Makes: 6 servings

- 3½ cups 2% milk
- ½ cup uncooked long grain rice
- ⅓ cup sugar
- ½ tsp. salt
- ½ cup raisins
- 1 tsp. vanilla extract
- Ground cinnamon, optional

1. Preheat oven to 325°. Place first four ingredients in a large saucepan; bring to a boil over medium heat, stirring constantly. Transfer to a greased 1½-qt. baking dish.
2. Bake, covered, 45 minutes, stirring every 15 minutes. Stir in raisins and vanilla; bake, covered, until rice is tender, about 15 minutes. If desired, sprinkle with cinnamon. Serve warm or refrigerate and serve cold.
Per ¾ cup: 214 cal., 3g fat (2g sat. fat), 11mg chol., 266mg sod., 41g carb. (25g sugars, 1g fiber), 6g pro.

PLUM UPSIDE-DOWN CAKE

The delicate flavor of plums is a pleasing change of pace in this upside-down cake.
—Bobbie Talbott, Veneta, OR

Prep: 15 min. • **Bake:** 40 min.
Makes: 10 servings

- ⅓ cup butter
- ½ cup packed brown sugar
- 1¾ to 2 lbs. medium plums, pitted and halved
- 2 large eggs
- ⅔ cup sugar
- 1 cup all-purpose flour
- 1 tsp. baking powder
- ¼ tsp. salt
- ⅓ cup hot water
- ½ tsp. lemon extract

1. Melt butter in a 10-in. cast-iron or ovenproof skillet. Sprinkle brown sugar over butter. Arrange plum halves, cut side down, in a single layer over sugar; set aside.
2. In a large bowl, beat eggs until thick and lemon-colored; gradually beat in sugar. Combine the flour, baking powder and salt; add to egg mixture and mix well. Blend water and lemon extract; beat into batter. Pour over plums.
3. Bake at 350° for 40-45 minutes or until a toothpick inserted in the center comes out clean. Immediately invert onto a serving plate. Serve warm.
Per serving: 245 cal., 7g fat (4g sat. fat), 53mg chol., 173mg sod., 43g carb. (32g sugars, 1g fiber), 3g pro.

We've played down propping and played up lighing in photos since this recipe was first published in 1996.

UNFORGETTABLE
DESSERTS

FOR 25 YEARS, READERS HAVE SHARED THEIR FAVORITE SWEETS, TREATS AND DESSERTS. THAT'S WHY WE COULD'T WAIT TO ASSEMBLE THIS BEST-OF-THE-BEST COLLECTION OF BAKED GOODS AND DINNER FINALES. LIFE IS SHORT! EAT DESSERT FIRST!

CARDAMOM SPRITZ

EDITOR'S CHOICE

FIVE-CHIP COOKIES

With peanut butter, oats and five kinds of chips, these cookies make a hearty snack that appeals to kids of all ages. I sometimes double the recipe to share with my friends and neighbors.

—Sharon Hedstrom, Minnetonka, MN

Takes: 25 min. • **Makes:** 4½ dozen

- 1 cup butter, softened
- 1 cup peanut butter
- 1 cup sugar
- ⅔ cup packed brown sugar
- 2 large eggs
- 1 tsp. vanilla extract
- 2 cups all-purpose flour
- 1 cup old-fashioned oats
- 2 tsp. baking soda
- ½ tsp. salt
- ⅔ cup each milk chocolate chips, semisweet chocolate chips, peanut butter chips, white baking chips and butterscotch chips

1. Preheat oven to 350°. In a large bowl, cream butter, peanut butter and sugars until light and fluffy. Add eggs, one at a time, beating well after each addition. Beat in vanilla. Combine flour, oats, baking soda and salt; gradually add to creamed mixture and mix well. Stir in chips.

2. Drop by rounded tablespoonfuls 2 in. apart onto ungreased baking sheets. Bake 10-12 minutes or until lightly browned. Cool 1 minute before removing to wire racks.

Note Reduced-fat peanut butter is not recommended for this recipe.

Per 2 cookies: 332 cal., 19g fat (10g sat. fat), 36mg chol., 280mg sod., 37g carb. (23g sugars, 2g fiber), 6g pro.

CARDAMOM SPRITZ

I have loved cardamom for as long as I can remember. My grandmother often added the spice to her baked goods. I usually make these cookies in a camel design with a camel spritz press I found at a thrift shop—it reminds me of a time when I rode a camel in the desert while deployed with the Navy. Of course, any design will do!

—Crystal Schlueter, Babbitt, MN

Prep: 20 min. • **Bake:** 10 min./batch + cooling • **Makes:** about 6 dozen

- 1 cup butter, softened
- 1 cup plus 2 Tbsp. sugar, divided
- 1 large egg
- 1½ tsp. vanilla extract
- 1 tsp. lemon extract
- 2½ cups all-purpose flour
- 2 tsp. ground cardamom, divided
- ¼ tsp. salt

1. Preheat oven to 350°. Cream butter and 1 cup sugar until light and fluffy. Beat in egg and extracts. In another bowl, whisk flour, ½ tsp. cardamom and salt; gradually beat into creamed mixture.

2. Using a cookie press fitted with a disk of your choice, press dough 1 in. apart onto ungreased baking sheets. Mix remaining sugar and remaining cardamom; sprinkle over cookies. Bake until set, 8-10 minutes (do not brown). Remove from pans to wire racks to cool.

Per cookie: 52 cal., 3g fat (2g sat. fat), 9mg chol., 30mg sod., 7g carb. (3g sugars, 0 fiber), 1g pro.

LAYERED CHOCOLATE MARSHMALLOW PEANUT BUTTER BROWNIES

A friend gave me a recipe for layered brownies, but I added my own touches.

—Judy Sims, Weatherford, TX

Prep: 30 min. • **Bake:** 20 min. + chilling
Makes: 4 dozen

- 1½ cups butter, divided
- ¾ cup baking cocoa, divided
- 4 large eggs
- 2 cups sugar
- 1 tsp. vanilla extract
- 1½ cups all-purpose flour
- ½ tsp. salt
- 1 jar (16.3 oz.) chunky peanut butter
- ⅓ cup 2% milk
- 10 large marshmallows
- 2 cups confectioners' sugar

1. Preheat oven to 350°. In a saucepan, melt 1 cup butter; stir in ½ cup cocoa until smooth. Remove from heat. In a large bowl, beat eggs, sugar and vanilla until blended. Combine flour and salt; gradually add to egg mixture. Beat in cocoa mixture.

2. Transfer to a greased 15x10x1-in. baking pan. Bake until a toothpick inserted in the center comes out clean, 18-22 minutes. Cool on a wire rack for 3-4 minutes.

3. Meanwhile, in a microwave, heat peanut butter, uncovered, on high until softened, about 30 seconds. Stir and spread over warm brownies. Refrigerate until peanut butter is set, about 45 minutes.

4. In a heavy saucepan, combine milk, marshmallows, remaining cocoa and the remaining butter. Cook and stir over medium-low heat until the butter and marshmallows are melted and mixture is smooth. Remove from heat. Gradually stir in confectioners' sugar until smooth. Spread over peanut butter layer. Refrigerate for at least 30 minutes. Cut into squares.

Per brownie: 189 cal., 11g fat (5g sat. fat), 31mg chol., 125mg sod., 21g carb. (15g sugars, 1g fiber), 4g pro.

EDITOR'S CHOICE

RHUBARB CUSTARD BARS

Once I tried these rich, gooey bars, I just had to have the recipe so I could make them for my family and friends. The shortbread-like crust and creamy layers inspire people to fix a batch for themselves.

—Shari Roach, South Milwaukee, WI

Prep: 25 min. • **Bake:** 50 min. + chilling
Makes: 3 dozen

- 2 cups all-purpose flour
- ¼ cup sugar
- 1 cup cold butter

FILLING

- 2 cups sugar
- 7 Tbsp. all-purpose flour
- 1 cup heavy whipping cream
- 3 large eggs, beaten
- 5 cups finely chopped fresh or frozen rhubarb, thawed and drained

TOPPING

- 6 oz. cream cheese, softened
- ½ cup sugar
- ½ tsp. vanilla extract
- 1 cup heavy whipping cream, whipped

1. In a bowl, combine the flour and sugar; cut in butter until the mixture resembles coarse crumbs. Press into a greased 13x9-in. baking pan. Bake at 350° for 10 minutes.

2. Meanwhile, for filling, combine sugar and flour in a bowl. Whisk in cream and the eggs. Stir in rhubarb. Pour over the crust. Bake at 350° until the custard is set, 40-45 minutes. Cool.

3. For topping, beat cream cheese, sugar and vanilla until smooth; fold in whipped cream. Spread over top. Cover and chill. Cut into bars. Store in the refrigerator.

Per bar: 198 cal., 11g fat (7g sat. fat), 52mg chol., 70mg sod., 23g carb. (16g sugars, 1g fiber), 2g pro.

LAYERED CHOCOLATE MARSHMALLOW PEANUT BUTTER BROWNIES

CHEWY PEANUT BUTTER PAN SQUARES

CHEWY PEANUT BUTTER PAN SQUARES

With seven of us in our family, including two teenage boys, these sweet cookie bars never last long! It's hard to believe how simple the peanut butter squares are to prepare. Just 10 minutes of prep!
—Deb DeChant, Milan, OH

Prep: 10 min. • **Bake:** 30 min.
Makes: 2 dozen

- ½ cup butter, cubed
- ½ cup creamy peanut butter
- 1½ cups sugar
- 1 cup all-purpose flour
- 2 large eggs, lightly beaten
- 1 tsp. vanilla extract

1. In a microwave-safe bowl, melt butter and peanut butter; stir until smooth. Combine sugar and flour; gradually add to butter mixture and mix well. Beat in eggs and vanilla.

2. Spread into a greased 13x9-in. baking pan. Bake at 350° for 28-32 minutes or until lightly browned and edges start to pull away from sides of pan. Cool on a wire rack.

Note Reduced-fat peanut butter is not recommended for this recipe.

Per square: 139 cal., 7g fat (3g sat. fat), 28mg chol., 69mg sod., 18g carb. (13g sugars, 0 fiber), 2g pro.

For a bit of chocolate flair, stir a handful of mini chocolate chips into the mixture just before spreading it into the baking pan.

CHOCOLATE CHIP & COOKIE BUTTER THUMBPRINTS

I wanted to make a more festive version of chocolate chip cookies for the holidays. Since my mom's thumbprints are what I look forward to the most, I decided to combine the two classics into one.
—Crystal Schlueter, Babbitt, MN

Prep: 35 min. • **Bake:** 10 min./batch
Makes: about 2½ dozen

- ½ cup butter, softened
- ½ cup packed brown sugar
- ¼ tsp. salt
- 1 large egg, separated
- 2 Tbsp. 2% milk
- 1 tsp. vanilla extract
- 1½ cups all-purpose flour
- ½ cup miniature semisweet chocolate chips
- 1 cup chopped pecans
- ⅔ cup Biscoff creamy cookie spread or Nutella
- Additional miniature semisweet chocolate chips, optional

1. Preheat oven to 350°. In a large bowl, cream butter, brown sugar and salt until light and fluffy. Beat in egg yolk, milk and vanilla. Gradually beat flour into creamed mixture. Stir in chocolate chips. Cover and refrigerate 1 hour or until dough is firm enough to shape.
2. Shape tablespoons of dough into balls. Dip balls into egg white; roll in pecans. Place 2 in. apart on lightly greased baking sheets. Press a deep indentation in center of each with your thumb. Bake until light golden brown, 12-14 minutes.
3. Remove from pans to wire racks to cool completely. Fill each with 1 tsp. cookie spread. If desired, sprinkle with additional chocolate chips.
Per cookie: 138 cal., 9g fat (3g sat. fat), 14mg chol., 48mg sod., 14g carb. (7g sugars, 1g fiber), 2g pro.

CHOCOLATE CHIP & COOKIE BUTTER THUMBPRINTS

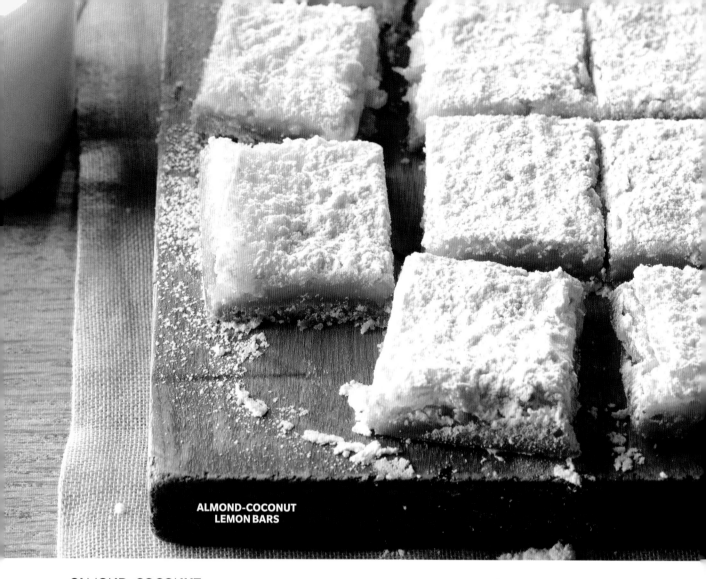

ALMOND-COCONUT
LEMON BARS

ALMOND-COCONUT LEMON BARS

Give traditional lemon bars a tasty twist with the addition of almonds and coconut.
—Taste of Home *Test Kitchen*

Prep: 10 min. • **Bake:** 40 min. + cooling
Makes: 2 dozen

- 1½ cups all-purpose flour
- ½ cup confectioners' sugar
- ⅓ cup blanched almonds, toasted
- 1 tsp. grated lemon zest
- ¾ cup cold butter, cubed

FILLING

- 3 large eggs
- 1½ cups sugar
- ½ cup sweetened shredded coconut
- ¼ cup lemon juice
- 3 Tbsp. all-purpose flour
- 1 tsp. grated lemon zest
- ½ tsp. baking powder
- Confectioners' sugar

1. In a food processor, combine the flour, confectioners' sugar, almonds and lemon zest; cover and process until nuts are finely chopped. Add butter; pulse just until mixture is crumbly. Press into a greased 13x9-in. baking dish. Bake at 350° for 20 minutes.

2. Meanwhile, in a large bowl, whisk eggs, sugar, coconut, lemon juice, flour, lemon zest and baking powder; pour over the hot crust. Bake until light golden brown, 20-25 minutes. Cool on a wire rack. Dust with confectioners' sugar. Cut into squares.

Per bar: 173 cal., 8g fat (5g sat. fat), 39mg chol., 70mg sod., 23g carb. (16g sugars, 1g fiber), 2g pro.

CHOCOLATE CHIP BROWNIES

People love these very rich brownies so much that I never take them anywhere without bringing along several copies of the recipe to hand out. The treats are a no-brainer to take on a picnic because you don't have to worry about frosting melting.
—Brenda Kelly, Ashburn, VA

Prep: 10 min. • **Bake:** 30 min. + cooling
Makes: 4 dozen

- 1 cup butter, softened
- 3 cups sugar
- 6 large eggs
- 1 Tbsp. vanilla extract
- 2¼ cups all-purpose flour
- ½ cup baking cocoa
- 1 tsp. baking powder
- ½ tsp. salt
- 1 cup (6 oz.) semisweet chocolate chips
- 1 cup vanilla or white chips
- 1 cup chopped walnuts

1. In a large bowl, cream butter and sugar until light and fluffy. Add eggs and vanilla; mix well. Combine the flour, cocoa, baking powder and salt; gradually add to creamed mixture just until blended (do not overmix).
2. Pour into two greased 9-in. square baking pans. Sprinkle with chips and nuts. Bake at 350° for 30-35 minutes or until toothpick inserted in the center comes out clean. Cool.

Per brownie: 167 cal., 8g fat (4g sat. fat), 38mg chol., 83mg sod., 22g carb. (14g sugars, 1g fiber), 3g pro.

CHOCOLATE CHIP BROWNIES

COOKIES & CREAM BROWNIES

COOKIES & CREAM BROWNIES

You won't want to frost these brownies, since the marbled top is too pretty to cover up. Besides, the cream cheese layer makes them taste as if they're already frosted. The crushed cookies add extra chocolate flavor and a fun crunch.

—Darlene Brenden, Salem, OR

Prep: 15 min. • **Bake:** 25 min. + cooling
Makes: 2 dozen

- 1 pkg. (8 oz.) cream cheese, softened
- ¼ cup sugar
- 1 large egg
- ½ tsp. vanilla extract

BROWNIE LAYER

- ½ cup butter, melted
- ½ cup sugar
- ½ cup packed brown sugar
- ½ cup baking cocoa
- 2 large eggs
- 1 tsp. vanilla extract
- ½ cup all-purpose flour
- 1 tsp. baking powder
- 12 Oreo cookies, crushed
- 8 Oreo cookies, coarsely chopped

1. In a small bowl, beat the cream cheese, sugar, egg and vanilla until smooth; set aside. For brownie layer, combine the butter, sugars and cocoa in a large bowl. Beat in eggs. Combine flour and baking powder; gradually add to cocoa mixture. Stir in crushed cookie crumbs.

2. Pour into a greased 11x7-in. baking pan. Spoon cream cheese mixture over batter. Sprinkle with coarsely chopped cookies. Bake at 350° for 25-30 minutes or until a toothpick inserted in the center comes out with moist crumbs. Cool completely on a wire rack. Cut into 24 bars. Store in the refrigerator.

Per brownie: 159 cal., 9g fat (5g sat. fat), 47mg chol., 130mg sod., 18g carb. (13g sugars, 1g fiber), 2g pro.

FIRST PLACE COCONUT MACAROONS

FIRST PLACE COCONUT MACAROONS

These cookies earned me a first-place ribbon at the county fair. They remain my husband's favorites—whenever I make them to give away, he always asks me where his batch is! I especially like the fact that the recipe makes just enough for the two of us to nibble on.

—Penny Ann Habeck, Shawano, WI

Prep: 10 min.
Bake: 20 min. + cooling
Makes: about 1½ dozen

- 1⅓ cups sweetened shredded coconut
- ⅓ cup sugar
- 2 Tbsp. all-purpose flour
- ⅛ tsp. salt
- 2 large egg whites
- ½ tsp. vanilla extract

1. In a small bowl, combine the coconut, sugar, flour and salt. Add egg whites and vanilla; mix well.

2. Drop by rounded teaspoonfuls onto greased baking sheets. Bake at 325° for 18-20 minutes or until golden brown. Cool on a wire rack.

Per cookie: 54 cal., 2g fat (2g sat. fat), 0 chol., 41mg sod., 8g carb. (7g sugars, 0 fiber), 1g pro. **Diabetic exchanges:** ½ starch, ½ fat.

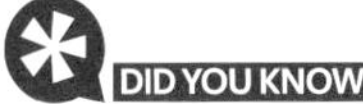

While many no-calorie sweeteners are fine in beverages, they do not maintain sweetness at high temperatures and can take on a bitter taste in baked goods.

HUNGARIAN WALNUT COOKIES

HUNGARIAN WALNUT COOKIES

As a child, I always looked forward to these goodies at Christmastime. Now I make them for my own family.
—Sharon Kurtz, Emmaus, PA

Prep: 50 min. + chilling
Bake: 10 min./batch + cooling
Makes: 4 dozen

- 1 cup butter, softened
- 1 pkg. (8 oz.) cream cheese, softened
- 2½ cups all-purpose flour

FILLING

- 3 large egg whites
- ¾ tsp. vanilla extract
- ⅓ cup sugar
- 3½ cups ground walnuts
- Confectioners' sugar

1. In a large bowl, cream butter and cream cheese until blended. Gradually beat flour into creamed mixture. Divide dough into three portions. Shape each into a disk; wrap in plastic. Refrigerate 1 hour or until firm enough to roll.
2. Preheat oven to 375°. For filling, in a small bowl, beat egg whites and vanilla on medium speed until foamy. Gradually add sugar, 1 Tbsp. at a time, beating on medium after each addition until well blended. Stir in walnuts.
3. Generously coat a work surface with confectioners' sugar. Roll one portion of dough into a 12-in. square about ⅛ in. thick, sprinkling with additional confectioners' sugar as necessary to coat well. Cut into sixteen 3-in. squares.
4. Shape 2 tsp. filling into a small log about 2 in. long. Place diagonally onto a square. Overlap opposite corners of dough over filling; pinch tightly to seal. Place 2 in. apart on greased baking sheets. Repeat with remaining dough and filling.
5. Bake until bottoms are golden brown, 9-11 minutes. Remove from pans to wire racks to cool completely. Dust with confectioners' sugar.

Make ahead Dough can be made 2 days in advance. Wrap in plastic and place in a resealable bag. Store in the refrigerator.
Freeze option Freeze cookies in freezer containers. To use, thaw before serving. If desired, dust with confectioners' sugar.
Per cookie: 129 cal., 9g fat (4g sat. fat), 15mg chol., 49mg sod., 10g carb. (4g sugars, 1g fiber), 2g pro.

M&M & PRETZEL COOKIES

M&M & PRETZEL COOKIES

Kids and grown-ups alike adore these sweet and crunchy no-bake cookies. Add more candy for M&M's lovers, or toss in a few additional pretzels for an extra-salty bite.
—Madison Allen, Destrehan, LA

Prep: 20 min. + chilling • **Makes:** 6 dozen

- ½ cup butter, cubed
- 2 cups sugar
- ½ cup 2% milk
- 2 Tbsp. baking cocoa
- 1 cup creamy peanut butter
- 2 tsp. vanilla extract
- 3 cups quick-cooking oats
- 1 cup coarsely crushed pretzels
- 1 cup milk chocolate M&M's

1. In a large saucepan, combine the butter, sugar, milk and cocoa. Bring to a boil over medium heat, stirring constantly. Cook and stir 1 minute.
2. Remove from heat; stir in peanut butter and vanilla until blended. Stir in the oats; let stand 5 minutes to cool. Fold in pretzels and M&M's. Drop mixture by tablespoonfuls onto waxed paper-lined baking sheets. Refrigerate until set.
Per cookie: 87 cal., 4g fat (2g sat. fat), 4mg chol., 46mg sod., 12g carb. (8g sugars, 1g fiber), 2g pro.

GRANDMA'S PECAN BARS

My grandmother handed down the recipe for these gooey bars, which we all love. The candied cherries are a must.

—Deborah Pennington, Decatur, AL

Prep: 20 min. • **Bake:** 1 hour + cooling
Makes: about 2 dozen

- 4 large eggs
- 4 cups chopped pecans, divided
- 1 cup butter, softened
- 2¼ cups packed brown sugar
- 2 Tbsp. vanilla extract
- 1 cup all-purpose flour
- 2¼ cups red candied cherries
- 1½ cups chopped candied pineapple
- ½ cup chopped candied citron
- ⅓ cup rum

1. Let eggs stand at room temperature 30 minutes. Sprinkle 3 cups pecans over a greased 15x10x1-in. baking pan.
2. Preheat oven to 350°. Cream butter and brown sugar until light and fluffy. Add the eggs, one at a time, beating well after each addition. Beat in vanilla. Gradually add flour to creamed mixture, beating well.
3. Spread batter into the prepared pan. Combine candied fruit and remaining pecans. Spread fruit and pecans evenly over creamed mixture; press gently to help mixtures adhere. Bake until a toothpick inserted in center comes out clean, about 1 hour. Sprinkle rum over the bars; cool completely in pan on a wire rack. Cut into bars. Store in an airtight container.
Per bar: 401 cal., 22g fat (6g sat. fat), 51mg chol., 123mg sod., 49g carb. (40g sugars, 2g fiber), 4g pro.

FROSTED BUTTER RUM BRICKLE BITES

The rum, real butter and toffee bits made these cookies my husband's new favorite. If you'd like them less sweet, forget the frosting and sprinkle them with a bit of confectioners' sugar while still warm.

—Cindy Nerat, Menominee, MI

Prep: 35 min.
Bake: 10 min./batch + cooling
Makes: about 4 dozen

- 1 cup butter, softened
- ¾ cup confectioners' sugar
- 2 tsp. rum extract
- ½ tsp. salt
- 2 cups all-purpose flour
- 1 pkg. (8 oz.) brickle toffee bits

ICING

- ⅓ cup butter, cubed
- 2 cups confectioners' sugar
- ½ tsp. rum extract
- 2 to 3 Tbsp. 2% milk

1. Preheat oven to 375°. Beat the first four ingredients until blended. Beat in flour. Stir in toffee bits. Shape dough into 1-in. balls; place 2 in. apart on parchment paper-lined baking sheets.
2. Bake until edges are light brown and toffee bits begin to melt, 8-10 minutes. Cool on pans 5 minutes. Remove to wire racks to cool completely.
3. In a small heavy saucepan, melt butter over medium heat. Heat until golden brown, about 5 minutes, stirring constantly. Remove from heat; stir in confectioners' sugar, rum extract and enough milk to reach desired consistency. Spread icing over cookies.
Per cookie: 81 cal., 4g fat (2g sat. fat), 9mg chol., 59mg sod., 10g carb. (7g sugars, 0 fiber), 1g pro.

FROSTED BUTTER RUM BRICKLE BITES

HOMEMADE CHERRY CRISP

HOMEMADE CHERRY CRISP

Only 15 minutes for dessert? It's true! This treat relies on canned pie filling and takes mere minutes to heat in the microwave. We all love it.

—Laurie Todd, Columbus, MS

Takes: 15 min. • Makes: 4 servings

- 1 can (21 oz.) cherry pie filling
- 1 tsp. lemon juice
- 1 cup all-purpose flour
- ¼ cup packed brown sugar
- ¾ tsp. ground cinnamon
- ¼ tsp. ground allspice
- ⅓ cup cold butter, cubed
- ½ cup chopped walnuts
- Vanilla ice cream

1. Combine the pie filling and lemon juice in an ungreased 1½-qt. microwave-safe dish; set aside.

2. In a small bowl, combine flour, brown sugar, cinnamon and allspice; cut in butter until mixture resembles coarse crumbs. Add walnuts. Sprinkle over filling.

3. Microwave, uncovered, on high until bubbly, 3-4 minutes. Serve warm with ice cream.

Per cup: 567 cal., 24g fat (10g sat. fat), 41mg chol., 187mg sod., 81g carb. (50g sugars, 3g fiber), 8g pro.

PLUM GOOD CRISP

This delightful crisp hits the spot any time of day—from breakfast treats to late-night snack attacks. Bubbly and warm from the oven, it just can't be beat!

—Peter Halferty, Corpus Christi, TX

Prep: 20 min. • **Bake:** 30 min. + standing
Makes: 8 servings

- 4 cups sliced fresh plums (about 1½ lbs.)
- 3 medium nectarines, sliced
- 1½ cups fresh blueberries
- 3 Tbsp. brown sugar
- 2 Tbsp. cornstarch
- ¼ tsp. ground ginger
- ⅛ tsp. ground nutmeg
- ¼ cup maple syrup
- 2 Tbsp. lemon juice

TOPPING

- ½ cup old-fashioned oats
- ½ cup all-purpose flour
- ¼ cup packed brown sugar
- ¼ tsp. salt
- 4 tsp. unsweetened apple juice
- 4 tsp. canola oil
- 1½ tsp. butter, melted

1. Preheat oven to 400°. Place fruit in a large bowl. Mix brown sugar, cornstarch, spices, syrup and lemon juice; toss with fruit. Transfer to an 11x7-in. baking dish coated with cooking spray.

2. For topping, mix oats, flour, brown sugar and salt; stir in remaining ingredients until crumbly. Sprinkle over fruit.

3. Bake, uncovered, until filling is bubbly and topping is golden brown, about 30 minutes. Let stand 15 minutes before serving.

Per ¾ cup: 233 cal., 4g fat (1g sat. fat), 2mg chol., 85mg sod., 49g carb. (33g sugars, 3g fiber), 3g pro.

PLUM GOOD CRISP

ENGLISH RHUBARB CRUMBLE

ENGLISH RHUBARB CRUMBLE

When I met my English husband and served him this crumble, he said it was fantastic but really needed a custard sauce. We found a terrific sauce recipe from England that pairs just perfectly with the dessert. Now, I wouldn't serve it any other way.
—Amy Freeman, Cave Creek, AZ

Prep: 45 min. • **Bake:** 30 min.
Makes: 12 servings (2½ cups sauce)

- 8 cups chopped fresh or frozen rhubarb
- 1¼ cups sugar, divided
- 2½ cups all-purpose flour
- ¼ cup packed brown sugar
- ¼ cup quick-cooking oats
- 1 cup cold butter

CUSTARD SAUCE

- 6 large egg yolks
- ½ cup sugar
- 2 cups heavy whipping cream
- 1¼ tsp. vanilla extract

1. In a saucepan, combine rhubarb and ¾ cup sugar. Cover and cook over medium heat, stirring occasionally, until the rhubarb is tender, about 10 minutes.

2. Pour into a greased 13x9-in. baking dish. In a bowl, combine flour, brown sugar, oats and remaining sugar. Cut in butter until crumbly; sprinkle over rhubarb. Bake at 400° for 30 minutes.

3. Meanwhile, in a saucepan, whisk the egg yolks and sugar; stir in cream. Cook and stir over low heat until a thermometer reads 160° and mixture thickens, 15-20 minutes. Remove from the heat; stir in vanilla. Serve warm over rhubarb crumble.

Note If using frozen rhubarb, measure rhubarb while still frozen, then thaw completely. Drain in a colander, but do not press liquid out.

Per serving: 550 cal., 33g fat (19g sat. fat), 202mg chol., 179mg sod., 60g carb. (37g sugars, 2g fiber), 6g pro.

CHOCOLATE COBBLER

Talk about comfort food! This ultra moist dessert makes a decadent end to any meal. Best of all, it comes together in no time with just a few ingredients.

—Margaret McNeil, Germantown, TN

Prep: 10 min. • **Bake:** 40 min.
Makes: 8 servings

- 1 cup self-rising flour
- ½ cup sugar
- 2 Tbsp. plus ¼ cup baking cocoa, divided
- ½ cup whole milk
- 3 Tbsp. vegetable oil
- 1 cup packed brown sugar
- 1¾ cups hot water
- Vanilla ice cream, optional

In a bowl, combine the flour, sugar and 2 Tbsp. cocoa. Stir in milk and oil until smooth. Pour into a greased 8-in. square baking pan. Combine the brown sugar and remaining cocoa; sprinkle over batter. Pour hot water over top (do not stir). Bake at 350° for 40-45 minutes or until top of cake springs back when lightly touched. Serve warm, with ice cream if desired.

Note As a substitute for 1 cup self-rising flour, place 1½ tsp. baking powder and ½ tsp. salt in a measuring cup. Add all-purpose flour to measure 1 cup.

Per serving: 267 cal., 6g fat (1g sat. fat), 2mg chol., 198mg sod., 53g carb. (40g sugars, 1g fiber), 3g pro.

CHOCOLATE COBBLER

CRAN-APPLE PECAN CRISP

Even folks who claim not to like cranberries rave about this crisp. I cherish the recipe from my mother, who truly inspired my love of cooking and baking.

—Debbie Daly, Florence, KY

Prep: 20 min. • **Bake:** 40 min.
Makes: 12 servings

- 1 cup sugar
- 1 Tbsp. cornstarch
- 3 cups chopped tart apples
- 2 cups fresh or frozen cranberries
- 1 cup old-fashioned oats
- ½ cup packed brown sugar
- ½ cup chopped pecans
- ⅓ cup all-purpose flour
- ⅓ cup cold butter

In a large bowl, combine the sugar and cornstarch; stir in apples and cranberries. Transfer to a greased 2-qt. baking dish. In another bowl, combine the oats, brown sugar, pecans and flour; cut in butter until mixture is crumbly. Sprinkle over apple mixture. Bake, uncovered, at 375° until golden brown, 40-45 minutes. Serve warm.

Per ½ cup: 244 cal., 9g fat (4g sat. fat), 14mg chol., 56mg sod., 41g carb. (30g sugars, 3g fiber), 2g pro.

SKILLET BLUEBERRY SLUMP

We've been eating slump for nearly six decades! My mother-in-law started the tradition with a recipe calling for wild blueberries. She served hers warm with a pitcher of farm-fresh cream.
—Eleanore Ebeling, Brewster, MN

Prep: 25 min. • **Bake:** 20 min.
Makes: 6 servings

- 4 cups fresh or frozen blueberries
- ½ cup sugar
- ½ cup water
- 1 tsp. grated lemon zest
- 1 Tbsp. lemon juice
- 1 cup all-purpose flour
- 2 Tbsp. sugar
- 2 tsp. baking powder
- ½ tsp. salt
- 1 Tbsp. butter
- ½ cup 2% milk
- Vanilla ice cream

1. Preheat oven to 400°. In a 10-in. ovenproof skillet, combine the first five ingredients; bring to a boil. Reduce heat; simmer, uncovered, 9-11 minutes or until slightly thickened, stirring occasionally.

2. Meanwhile, in a small bowl, whisk flour, sugar, baking powder and salt. Cut in butter until mixture resembles coarse crumbs. Add milk; stir just until moistened.

3. Drop batter in six portions on top of the simmering blueberry mixture. Transfer to oven. Bake, uncovered, 17-20 minutes or until dumplings are golden brown. Serve warm with ice cream.

Per serving: 239 cal., 3g fat (2g sat. fat), 7mg chol., 355mg sod., 52g carb. (32g sugars, 3g fiber), 4g pro.

SKILLET CARAMEL APRICOT GRUNT

SKILLET CARAMEL APRICOT GRUNT

Here's an old-fashioned pantry dessert made with items you can easily keep on hand. Mix up a second batch of the dry ingredients for the dumplings to save a few minutes the next time you prepare it.
—Shannon Roum, Cudahy, WI

Prep: 20 min. + standing • **Bake:** 20 min.
Makes: 8 servings

- 2 cans (15¼ oz. each) apricot halves, undrained
- 2 tsp. quick-cooking tapioca
- ⅓ cup packed brown sugar
- 1 Tbsp. butter
- 1 Tbsp. lemon juice

DUMPLINGS

- 1½ cups all-purpose flour
- ½ cup sugar
- 2 tsp. baking powder
- 2 Tbsp. cold butter
- ½ cup milk

TOPPING

- ¼ cup packed brown sugar
- 1 Tbsp. water
- Half-and-half cream, optional

1. In a large saucepan, combine apricots and tapioca; let stand for 15 minutes. Add the brown sugar, butter and lemon juice. Cook and stir until mixture comes to a full boil. Reduce heat to low; keep warm.

2. For dumplings, in a large bowl, combine the flour, sugar and baking powder; cut in butter until crumbly. Add milk; mix just until combined. Pour warm fruit mixture into an ungreased 9- or 10-in. cast-iron skillet. Drop the batter into six mounds onto the fruit mixture.

3. Bake, uncovered, at 425° for 15 minutes or until a toothpick inserted into a dumpling comes out clean. Stir together brown sugar and water; microwave 30 seconds or until sugar is dissolved, stirring frequently. Spoon over dumplings; bake 5 minutes longer. Serve with cream if desired.

Per serving: 336 cal., 5g fat (3g sat. fat), 13mg chol., 170mg sod., 71g carb. (51g sugars, 2g fiber), 4g pro.

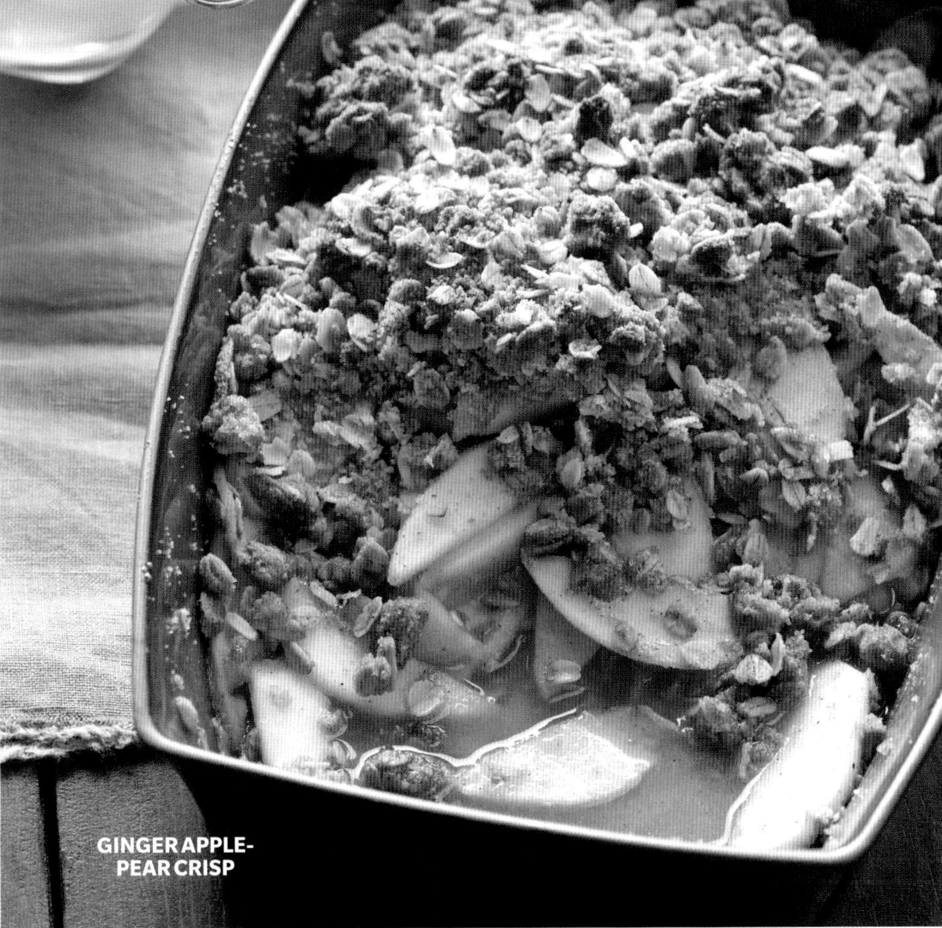

GINGER APPLE-PEAR CRISP

GINGER APPLE-PEAR CRISP

Taste autumn aromas—apples, cinnamon and spices—in this delicious recipe. Pumpkin-flavored ice cream is a logical accompaniment, but whipped cream is always a tasty option.
—Holly Battiste, Barrington, NJ

Prep: 20 min.
Bake: 40 min.
Makes: 8 servings

- 4 medium tart apples, peeled and sliced
- 4 medium pears, peeled and sliced
- ¼ cup sugar
- 1 Tbsp. lemon juice
- 1 Tbsp. grated fresh gingerroot
- ½ tsp. salt
- ½ tsp. vanilla extract

TOPPING

- 1 cup old-fashioned oats
- ½ cup all-purpose flour
- ½ cup packed brown sugar
- 1 tsp. ground cinnamon
- ¼ tsp. ground nutmeg
- ⅛ tsp. salt
- ⅓ cup cold butter, cubed

1. Preheat oven to 375°. In a large bowl, toss first seven ingredients. Transfer to a greased 2½-qt. baking dish.

2. In another bowl, mix the first six topping ingredients; cut in butter until crumbly. Sprinkle over fruit.

3. Bake until golden brown and fruit is tender, 40-45 minutes. Serve warm.

Per serving: 295 cal., 9g fat (5g sat. fat), 20mg chol., 250mg sod., 55g carb. (35g sugars, 5g fiber), 3g pro.

BUTTERMILK LEMON MERINGUE PIE

EDITOR'S CHOICE

BUTTERMILK LEMON MERINGUE PIE

This tasty take on a classic dessert brings meringue pies to a new level. Compliments roll in whenever I serve it.

—Ellen Riley, Murfreesboro, TN

Prep: 30 min. • **Bake:** 15 min. + chilling
Makes: 8 servings

- 1½ cups graham cracker crumbs
- ¼ cup sugar
- ⅓ cup butter, melted

FILLING

- ¾ cup sugar
- 3 Tbsp. cornstarch
- 1½ cups buttermilk
- 3 large egg yolks
- 2 Tbsp. butter
- 2 Tbsp. lemon juice
- 2 tsp. grated lemon zest

MERINGUE

- 3 large egg whites
- ½ tsp. vanilla extract
- ¼ tsp. cream of tartar
- 6 Tbsp. sugar

1. Combine the cracker crumbs, sugar and butter; press onto the bottom and up the sides of an ungreased 9-in. pie plate. Bake at 350° for 10-12 minutes or until crust is lightly browned. Cool on a wire rack.

2. For filling, in a large saucepan, combine sugar and cornstarch. Stir in buttermilk until smooth. Cook and stir over medium-high heat until thickened and bubbly. Reduce heat to low; cook and stir for 2 minutes longer. Remove from the heat. Stir 1 cup of hot mixture into egg yolks; return all to pan, stirring constantly. Bring to a gentle boil; cook and stir for 2 minutes longer. Remove from the heat. Stir in butter. Gently stir in lemon juice and zest. Pour hot filling into pastry shell.

3. For meringue, in a small mixing bowl, beat the egg whites, vanilla and cream of tartar on medium speed until soft peaks form. Gradually beat in sugar, 1 Tbsp. at a time, on high until stiff peaks form. Spread over hot filling, sealing edges to crust.

4. Bake for 15-20 minutes or until golden brown. Cool on a wire rack for 1 hour; refrigerate for 1-2 hours before serving. Refrigerate leftovers.

Per piece: 350 cal., 14g fat (8g sat. fat), 106mg chol., 242mg sod., 52g carb. (42g sugars, 1g fiber), 5g pro.

GRAHAM STREUSEL COFFEE CAKE

I use this sweet coffee cake recipe often because it's quick and easy to make.

—Blanche Whytsell, Arnoldsburg, WV

Prep: 20 min. • **Bake:** 40 min. + cooling
Makes: 16 servings

- 1½ cups graham cracker crumbs
- ¾ cup packed brown sugar
- ¾ cup chopped pecans
- 1½ tsp. ground cinnamon
- ⅔ cup butter, melted
- 1 pkg. yellow cake mix (regular size)
- ½ cup confectioners' sugar
- 1 Tbsp. milk

1. In a small bowl, combine the cracker crumbs, brown sugar, pecans and cinnamon. Stir in butter; set aside. Prepare cake mix according to package directions.

2. Pour half of the batter into a greased 13x9-in. baking pan. Sprinkle with half the graham cracker mixture. Spoon remaining batter on top. Sprinkle with the remaining graham cracker mixture.

3. Bake at 350° until a toothpick inserted in center comes out clean, 40-45 minutes. Cool on a rack. Combine confectioners' sugar and milk; drizzle over coffee cake.

Per piece: 329 cal., 15g fat (6g sat. fat), 21mg chol., 332mg sod., 46g carb. (30g sugars, 2g fiber), 3g pro.

GRAHAM STREUSEL COFFEE CAKE

UPSIDE-DOWN APPLE PIE

UPSIDE-DOWN APPLE PIE

This pie has won eight ribbons at area fairs. People say it looks and tastes like a giant apple-cinnamon bun. The recipe has become everyone's favorite.

—Susan Frisch, Germansville, PA

Prep: 30 min. + chilling
Bake: 50 min. + cooling
Makes: 8 servings

- 2 cups all-purpose flour
- ½ tsp. salt
- 6 Tbsp. shortening
- 2 Tbsp. cold butter
- 5 to 7 Tbsp. orange juice

FILLING

- 6 Tbsp. butter, melted, divided
- ½ cup packed brown sugar
- ½ cup chopped pecans
- 8 cups thinly sliced peeled tart apples (about ⅛ in. thick)
- 1 cup sugar
- ⅓ cup all-purpose flour
- ¾ tsp. ground cinnamon
- ¼ tsp. ground nutmeg

GLAZE

- ½ cup confectioners' sugar
- 2 to 3 tsp. orange juice

1. In a large bowl, combine flour and salt; cut in shortening and butter until crumbly. Gradually add orange juice, tossing with a fork until dough forms a ball. Divide dough into two balls. Wrap in plastic; refrigerate for at least 30 minutes.

2. Line a 9-in. deep-dish pie plate with heavy-duty foil, leaving 1½ in. beyond edge; coat the foil with cooking spray. Combine 4 Tbsp. butter, brown sugar and pecans; spoon into prepared pie plate.

3. In a large bowl, combine the apples, sugar, flour, cinnamon, nutmeg and remaining butter; toss gently.

4. On waxed paper, roll out one ball of pastry to fit pie plate. Place pastry over nut mixture, pressing firmly against mixture and sides of plate; trim to 1 in. beyond plate edge. Fill with apple mixture.

5. Roll out remaining pastry to fit top of pie; place over filling. Trim to ¼ in. beyond plate edge. Fold bottom pastry over top pastry; seal and flute edges. Cut four 1-in. slits in top pastry.

6. Bake at 375° for 50-55 minutes or until apples are tender and crust is golden brown (cover edges with foil during the last 20 minutes to prevent overbrowning if necessary).

7. Cool for 15 minutes on a wire rack. Invert pie onto a serving platter; carefully remove the foil. Combine the glaze ingredients; drizzle over pie.

Per slice: 613 cal., 26g fat (10g sat. fat), 31mg chol., 270mg sod., 92g carb. (60g sugars, 4g fiber), 5g pro.

PEAR CAKE WITH SOUR CREAM TOPPING

Terrific with morning coffee, this treat combines cake with sweet pears and an inviting topping.

—Norma Bluma, Emporia, KS

Prep: 20 min. • **Bake:** 30 min.
Makes: 16 servings

- ½ cup butter, softened
- ½ cup granulated sugar
- 3 large eggs, lightly beaten
- 1 tsp. grated lemon zest
- 1¾ cups all-purpose flour
- 2 tsp. baking powder
- 1 tsp. salt
- ½ cup whole milk
- 1 can (29 oz.) pear halves, drained

TOPPING

- 1 cup (8 oz.) sour cream
- 2 Tbsp. brown sugar
- 1 Tbsp. grated lemon zest

1. Preheat oven to 350°. Cream butter and sugar until fluffy. Add eggs and lemon zest; mix well. In another bowl, combine flour, baking powder and salt; add to creamed mixture alternately with milk, beating well after each addition.

2. Spread batter into a greased 13x9-in. or 3-qt. baking dish. Slice pear halves; arrange slices in rows on top of batter. Mix topping ingredients until smooth; spread over pears. Bake until a toothpick inserted in center comes out clean, 30-35 minutes.

Per piece: 218 cal., 10g fat (6g sat. fat), 66mg chol., 282mg sod., 29g carb. (17g sugars, 1g fiber), 4g pro.

PEAR CAKE WITH SOUR CREAM TOPPING

PUMPKIN SPICE CUPCAKES

I make these from-scratch cupcakes for an annual Halloween party, but they are also wonderful year-round. I sometimes bake them in decorative liners and top them with sprinkles instead of nuts.
—Amber Butzer, Gladstone, OR

Prep: 30 min. • **Bake:** 30 min. + cooling
Makes: 2 dozen

- 2 cups granulated sugar
- 1 can (15 oz.) solid-pack pumpkin
- 4 large eggs
- 1 cup canola oil
- 2 cups all-purpose flour
- 2 tsp. baking powder
- 2 tsp. ground cinnamon
- 1 tsp. baking soda
- ½ tsp. salt
- ½ tsp. ground ginger
- ¼ tsp. ground cloves
- 1 cup raisins

CREAM CHEESE FROSTING

- ⅓ cup butter, softened
- 3 oz. cream cheese, softened
- 1 tsp. vanilla extract
- 2 cups confectioners' sugar
- ½ cup chopped walnuts, toasted

1. Preheat oven to 350°. Beat granulated sugar, pumpkin, eggs and oil until well blended. In another bowl, whisk next seven ingredients; gradually beat into pumpkin mixture. Stir in raisins.

2. Fill each of 24 paper-lined muffin cups with ¼ cup plus 1 tsp. batter. Bake until a toothpick inserted in center comes out clean, 28-32 minutes. Cool 10 minutes before removing from pans to wire racks to cool completely.

3. For frosting, beat butter and cream cheese until smooth. Beat in vanilla. Gradually add the confectioners' sugar. Frost cupcakes; sprinkle with chopped walnuts. Refrigerate.

Note To toast nuts, bake in a shallow pan in a 350° oven for 5-10 minutes or cook in a skillet over low heat until lightly browned, stirring occasionally.

Per cupcake: 313 cal., 16g fat (3g sat. fat), 41mg chol., 187mg sod., 42g carb. (31g sugars, 1g fiber), 3g pro.

EDITOR'S CHOICE

MAMAW EMILY'S STRAWBERRY CAKE

My husband loved his Mamaw's strawberry cake. He thought no one could duplicate it. I made it, and I'm happy to report that it's just as scrumptious as he remembers.
—Jennifer Bruce, Manitou, KY

Prep: 15 min. • **Bake:** 25 min. + cooling
Makes: 12 servings

- 1 pkg. white cake mix (regular size)
- 1 pkg. (3 oz.) strawberry gelatin
- 3 Tbsp. sugar
- 3 Tbsp. all-purpose flour
- 1 cup water
- ½ cup canola oil
- 2 large eggs
- 1 cup finely chopped strawberries

FROSTING

- ½ cup butter, softened
- ½ cup crushed strawberries
- 4½ to 5 cups confectioners' sugar

1. Preheat oven to 350°. Line the bottoms of two greased 8-in. round baking pans with parchment paper; grease paper.
2. In a large bowl, combine cake mix, gelatin, sugar and flour. Add water, oil and eggs; beat on low speed 30 seconds. Beat on medium 2 minutes. Fold in chopped strawberries. Transfer to prepared pans.
3. Bake 25-30 minutes or until a toothpick inserted in center comes out clean. Cool in pans 10 minutes before removing to wire racks; remove paper. Cool completely.
4. For frosting, in a small bowl, beat butter until creamy. Beat in crushed strawberries. Gradually beat in enough confectioners' sugar to reach desired consistency. Spread frosting between layers and over top and sides of cake.
Per slice: 532 cal., 21g fat (7g sat. fat), 51mg chol., 340mg sod., 85g carb. (69g sugars, 1g fiber), 4g pro.

MAMAW EMILY'S STRAWBERRY CAKE

CAPE COD BLUEBERRY PIE

CAPE COD BLUEBERRY PIE

Talk about an all-time classic dessert! Northeasterners have been baking this pie since the 18th century. I'm quite sure it'll stand the test of time in your home, too.
—Nancy O'Connell, Biddeford, ME

Prep: 45 min. + chilling
Cook: 10 min. + chilling
Makes: 8 servings

- Pastry for single-crust pie (9 in.)
- 3 Tbsp. all-purpose flour
- ¼ tsp. salt
- 1 cup water, divided
- ¾ cup sugar
- 6 cups fresh blueberries, divided
- ½ tsp. white vinegar
- Sweetened whipped cream or vanilla ice cream

1. On a lightly floured surface, roll crust to a ⅛-in.-thick circle; transfer to a 9-in. pie plate. Trim crust to ½ in. beyond rim of plate; flute edge. Refrigerate 30 minutes. Preheat oven to 425°.
2. Line crust with a double thickness of foil. Fill with pie weights, dried beans or uncooked rice. Bake on a lower oven rack 20-25 minutes or until edges are golden brown. Remove foil and weights; bake 3-6 minutes longer or until bottom is golden brown. Cool completely on a wire rack.
3. In a small bowl, mix flour, salt and ⅓ cup water until smooth. In a large saucepan, combine sugar, 1 cup blueberries and remaining water; bring to a boil. Stir in flour mixture. Return to a boil, stirring constantly; cook and stir 4-6 minutes or until thickened. Stir in vinegar and remaining blueberries; pour into crust.
4. Refrigerate 4 hours or until filling is set. Serve with whipped cream.
Per slice: 307 cal., 12g fat (7g sat. fat), 30mg chol., 230mg sod., 49g carb. (28g sugars, 3g fiber), 3g pro.

CREAMY LIME PIE WITH FRESH BERRIES

CREAMY LIME PIE WITH FRESH BERRIES

I combined the tangy taste of lime and cilantro with cream cheese for this unusual berry pie that showcases seasonal fruit. The ginger cookies add zip to the crust.
—Anneliese Barz, Fort Mill, SC

Prep: 30 min. + chilling
Bake: 10 min. + cooling • **Makes:** 8 servings

- 1¾ cups finely crushed gingersnap cookies (about 30 cookies)
- ¼ cup sugar
- 2 Tbsp. all-purpose flour
- ⅓ cup butter, melted

FILLING

- 1 pkg. (8 oz.) cream cheese, softened
- 4 tsp. grated lime zest
- 2 Tbsp. lime juice
- 1 cup confectioners' sugar
- 1 tsp. vanilla extract
- ½ cup coarsely chopped fresh cilantro

TOPPING

- 2 cups fresh strawberries, sliced
- 2 cups fresh blueberries
- 2 Tbsp. apricot preserves

1. Preheat oven to 375°. In a small bowl, mix the crushed cookies, sugar and flour; stir in butter. Press onto bottom and up sides of a greased 9-in. pie plate. Bake until set, 8-10 minutes. Cool completely on a wire rack.

2. In a small bowl, beat cream cheese, lime zest and lime juice until blended. Beat in confectioners' sugar and vanilla. Stir in cilantro. Transfer to crust. Refrigerate, covered, at least 4 hours or until the filling is firm.

3. Just before serving, arrange berries over the pie. In a microwave, warm preserves just until melted. Brush over berries.

Per slice: 441 cal., 21g fat (12g sat. fat), 51mg chol., 370mg sod., 61g carb. (35g sugars, 3g fiber), 5g pro.

SALTED CARAMEL WALNUT TART

SALTED CARAMEL WALNUT TART

It took me a while to figure out a way to convert one of my favorite ice cream flavors into a pie—one of my favorite desserts. The result was so worth it.

—Ruth Ealy, Plain City, OH

Prep: 20 min. + chilling
Bake: 20 min. + cooling
Makes: 12 servings

- 2 large eggs, lightly beaten
- ¼ cup plus 2 Tbsp. heavy whipping cream
- ¾ cup packed light brown sugar
- ¼ cup plus 2 Tbsp. golden syrup or light corn syrup
- 3 Tbsp. unsalted butter, cubed
- 1½ tsp. vanilla extract
- ¾ tsp. sea salt
- 1 sheet refrigerated pie crust
- 1 cup chopped walnuts, toasted

1. Let eggs stand at room temperature 30 minutes. In a microwave, heat cream on high for 20 seconds. Keep warm. Meanwhile, in a large, heavy saucepan over medium heat, combine sugar and syrup, stirring frequently. Bring to a boil; cook, stirring constantly, for 1 minute. Remove from heat. Slowly pour cream into pan; continue stirring constantly (cream may spatter) until well blended. Gradually add butter, stirring until melted. Add vanilla and sea salt; stir until smooth. Cool.

2. Unroll crust into a 9-in. tart pan; trim edges. Refrigerate 30 minutes. Preheat oven to 400°. Line unpricked crust with a double thickness of foil. Fill with pie weights, dried beans or uncooked rice. Bake on a lower oven rack until edges are golden brown, 10-12 minutes. Remove foil and weights; bake until bottom is golden brown, 3-5 minutes longer. Cool on a wire rack.

3. Reduce oven setting to 350°. Whisk eggs into caramel mixture; stir in walnuts. Add filling to crust. Bake until center is just set (mixture will jiggle), 20-25 minutes. Cool completely. Refrigerate leftovers.

GRANDMA'S APPLE CAKE

Per slice: 293 cal., 17g fat (6g sat. fat), 50mg chol., 238mg sod., 32g carb. (23g sugars, 1g fiber), 3g pro.

GRANDMA'S APPLE CAKE

My husband's German family calls this *Oma's apfelkuchen*, "Grandma's apple cake." They've been sharing the recipe for more than 150 years. I use Granny Smith apples, but any variety works.

—Amy Kirchen, Loveland, OH

Prep: 20 min. • **Bake:** 45 min. + cooling
Makes: 10 servings

- 5 large egg yolks
- 2 medium tart apples, peeled, cored and halved
- 1 cup plus 2 Tbsp. unsalted butter, softened
- 1¼ cups sugar
- 2 cups all-purpose flour
- 2 Tbsp. cornstarch
- 2 tsp. cream of tartar
- 1 tsp. baking powder
- ½ tsp. salt
- ¼ cup 2% milk
- Confectioners' sugar

1. Preheat oven to 350°. Let the egg yolks stand at room temperature for 30 minutes. Starting ½ in. from one end, cut apple halves lengthwise into ¼-in. slices, leaving them attached at the top so they fan out slightly. Set aside.

2. Cream butter and sugar until light and fluffy. Add egg yolks, one at a time, beating well after each addition. In another bowl, sift flour, cornstarch, cream of tartar, baking powder and salt twice. Gradually beat into creamed mixture. Add milk; mix well (batter will be thick).

3. Spread the batter into a greased 9-in. springform pan wrapped in a sheet of heavy-duty foil. Gently press apples, round side up, into batter. Bake until a toothpick inserted in the center comes out with moist crumbs, 45-55 minutes. Cool on a wire rack 10 minutes. Loosen sides from the pan with a knife; remove the foil. Cool 1 hour longer. Remove rim from pan. Dust the cake with confectioners' sugar.

Per slice: 422 cal., 23g fat (14g sat. fat), 50mg chol., 177mg sod., 50g carb. (28g sugars, 1g fiber), 4g pro.

COFFEE-CHOCOLATE CAKE

This dark, moist cake is perfect for parties and special occasions. The buttery frosting has an unmatchable homemade flavor.
—Taste of Home *Test Kitchen*

Prep: 25 min. • Bake: 25 min. + cooling
Makes: 12 servings

- 2 cups sugar
- 1 cup canola oil
- 1 cup whole milk
- 1 cup brewed coffee, room temperature
- 2 large eggs
- 1 tsp. vanilla extract
- 2 cups all-purpose flour
- ¾ cup baking cocoa
- 2 tsp. baking soda
- 1 tsp. baking powder
- 1 tsp. salt

BUTTERCREAM FROSTING

- 1 cup butter, softened
- 8 cups confectioners' sugar
- 2 tsp. vanilla extract
- ½ to ¾ cup whole milk

1. In a large bowl, beat the sugar, oil, milk, coffee, eggs and vanilla until well blended. Combine the flour, cocoa, baking soda, baking powder and salt; gradually beat into sugar mixture until blended.
2. Pour into two greased and floured 9-in. round baking pans. Bake at 325° for 25-30 minutes or until a toothpick inserted in the center comes out clean. Cool in the pans for 10 minutes before removing to wire racks to cool completely.
3. For frosting, in a large bowl, beat butter until fluffy. Beat in confectioners' sugar and vanilla. Add milk until frosting reaches desired consistency. Spread the frosting between layers and over top and sides of the cake.

Per slice: 859 cal., 36g fat (13g sat. fat), 80mg chol., 621mg sod., 133g carb. (109g sugars, 2g fiber), 5g pro.

RUSTIC CARAMEL APPLE TART

Like an apple pie without the pan, this scrumptious tart has a crispy crust that cuts nicely and a yummy caramel topping.
—Betty Fulks, Onia, AR

Prep: 20 min. + chilling • **Bake:** 25 min.
Makes: 4 servings

- ⅔ cup all-purpose flour
- 1 Tbsp. sugar
- ⅛ tsp. salt
- ¼ cup cold butter, cubed
- 6½ tsp. cold water
- ⅛ tsp. vanilla extract

FILLING

- 1½ cups chopped peeled tart apples
- 3 Tbsp. sugar
- 1 Tbsp. all-purpose flour

TOPPING

- 1 tsp. sugar
- ¼ tsp. ground cinnamon
- 1 large egg
- 1 Tbsp. water
- 2 Tbsp. caramel ice cream topping, warmed

1. In a large bowl, combine flour, sugar and salt; cut in butter until crumbly. Gradually add water and vanilla, tossing with a fork until dough forms a ball. Cover the dough and refrigerate for 30 minutes or until easy to handle.
2. Preheat oven to 400°. On a lightly floured surface, roll dough into a 10-in. circle. Transfer to a parchment paper-lined baking sheet. Combine the filling ingredients; spoon over crust to within 2 in. of edges. Fold up edges of crust over filling, leaving center uncovered. Combine sugar and cinnamon; sprinkle over filling. Whisk egg and water; brush over crust.
3. Bake tart 25-30 minutes or until the crust is golden and the filling is bubbly. Using parchment paper, slide tart onto a wire rack. Drizzle with caramel topping. Serve tart warm.
Per slice: 298 cal., 13g fat (8g sat. fat), 77mg chol., 218mg sod., 42g carb. (24g sugars, 1g fiber), 4g pro.

RUSTIC CARAMEL APPLE TART

CREAMY PINEAPPLE PIE

Here's one of our favorite ways to end a hearty meal, especially during the warm summer months.

—Sharon Bickett, Chester, SC

Takes: 10 min. • **Makes:** 8 servings

- 1 can (14 oz.) sweetened condensed milk
- 1 can (8 oz.) crushed pineapple, undrained
- ¼ cup lemon juice
- 1 carton (8 oz.) frozen whipped topping, thawed
- 1 prepared graham cracker crust (9 in.) Chopped toasted macadamia nuts and additional crushed pineapple, optional

Combine the milk, pineapple and lemon juice; fold in whipped topping. Pour into prepared crust. Refrigerate until serving. If desired, serve with toasted macadamia nuts and additional crushed pineapple.

Note To toast nuts, bake in a shallow pan in a 350° oven for 5-10 minutes or cook in a skillet over low heat until lightly browned, stirring occasionally.

Per slice: 367 cal., 14g fat (9g sat. fat), 17mg chol., 185mg sod., 54g carb. (46g sugars, 1g fiber), 5g pro.

AUNT RUTH'S FAMOUS BUTTERSCOTCH CHEESECAKE

Aunt Ruth was our nanny when I was little, and she made this cheesecake often. Since it had to chill overnight ,it was torture when my sister and I had to wait until the next day to have a piece.

—Trisha Kruse, Eagle, ID

Prep: 30 min. • **Bake:** 65 min. + chilling
Makes: 12 servings

- 1½ cups graham cracker crumbs
- ⅓ cup packed brown sugar
- ⅓ cup butter, melted
- 1 can (14 oz.) sweetened condensed milk
- ¾ cup cold 2% milk
- 1 pkg. (3.4 oz.) instant butterscotch pudding mix
- 3 pkg. (8 oz. each) cream cheese, softened
- 1 tsp. vanilla extract
- 3 large eggs, lightly beaten Whipped cream and crushed butterscotch candies, optional

1. Place a greased 9-in. springform pan on a double thickness of heavy-duty foil (about 18 in. square). Securely wrap foil around pan. In a small bowl, combine the cracker crumbs and sugar; stir in butter. Press onto bottom of the prepared pan. Place pan on a baking sheet. Bake at 325° for 10 minutes. Cool on a wire rack.

2. In a small bowl, whisk the milks and pudding mix for 2 minutes. Let stand for 2 minutes or until soft-set.

3. Meanwhile, in a large bowl, beat cream cheese until smooth. Beat in pudding and vanilla. Add eggs; beat on low speed just until combined. Pour over crust. Place springform pan in a large baking pan; add 1 in. of hot water to larger pan.

4. Bake at 325° for 65-75 minutes or until center is almost set and top appears dull. Remove springform pan from water bath. Cool on a wire rack for 10 minutes.

5. Carefully run a knife around edge of pan to loosen; cool 1 hour longer. Refrigerate overnight. Garnish with whipped cream and butterscotch candies if desired.

Per piece: 473 cal., 30g fat (18g sat. fat), 141mg chol., 460mg sod., 42g carb. (34g sugars, 0 fiber), 10g pro.

When I visited my old neighborhood, I stopped by Aunt Ruth's, where she offered me a piece of her cheesecake. She was kind enough to make sure I left with a copy of the recipe. I think of her every time I make this.

TRISHA KRUSE EAGLE, ID

MOCHA TRUFFLE CHEESECAKE

I went through a phase when I couldn't get enough cheesecake or coffee, so I created this rich dessert. Its brownielike crust and creamy mocha layer really hit the spot. It's ideal for get-togethers because it can be made in advance.

—Shannon Dormady, Great Falls, MT

Prep: 20 min.
Bake: 50 min. + chilling
Makes: 16 servings

- 1 pkg. devil's food cake mix (regular size)
- 6 Tbsp. butter, melted
- 1 large egg
- 1 to 3 Tbsp. instant coffee granules

FILLING/TOPPING

- 2 pkg. (8 oz. each) cream cheese, softened
- 1 can (14 oz.) sweetened condensed milk
- 2 cups (12 oz.) semisweet chocolate chips, melted and cooled
- 3 to 6 Tbsp. instant coffee granules
- ¼ cup hot water
- 3 large eggs, lightly beaten
- 1 cup heavy whipping cream
- ¼ cup confectioners' sugar
- ½ tsp. almond extract
- 1 Tbsp. baking cocoa, optional

1. In a large bowl, combine the cake mix, butter, egg and coffee granules until well blended. Press mixture onto the bottom and 2 in. up the sides of a greased 10-in. springform pan.

2. In another large bowl, beat cream cheese until smooth. Beat in milk and melted chips. Dissolve coffee granules in water. Add the coffee to cream cheese mixture. Add eggs; beat on low speed just until combined. Pour into crust. Carefully place pan on a baking sheet.

3. Bake at 325° for 50-55 minutes or until center is almost set. Cool on a wire rack for 10 minutes. Carefully run a knife around edge of pan to loosen; cool 1 hour longer. Chill overnight.

4. Just before serving, in a large bowl, beat cream until soft peaks form. Beat in sugar and extract until stiff peaks form. Spread over top of cheesecake. Sprinkle with cocoa powder if desired. Refrigerate leftovers.

Per slice: 484 cal., 28g fat (16g sat. fat), 109mg chol., 389mg sod., 55g carb. (41g sugars, 2g fiber), 7g pro.

MOCHA TRUFFLE CHEESECAKE

RASPBERRY CHOCOLATE PUFFS

These flaky, chocolate-filled puffs are one of my favorite show-off desserts because they make a spectacular presentation, especially with the gorgeous berry sauce. The best part? They're easy to make.

—Anneliese Deising, Plymouth, MI

Prep: 25 min. • **Bake:** 20 min. + cooling
Makes: 8 servings

- 1 cup milk chocolate chips
- 1 cup white baking chips
- 1 cup chopped pecans
- 1 pkg. (17.3 oz.) frozen puff pastry, thawed
- 1 pkg. (12 oz.) frozen unsweetened raspberries, thawed
- 1 cup confectioners' sugar
- Additional confectioners' sugar
- Optional ingredients: fresh raspberries and additional chocolate and white baking chips

1. Preheat oven to 425°. Toss together chocolate chips, baking chips and pecans. On a lightly floured surface, roll each pastry sheet into a 12-in. square; cut each sheet into quarters, making four 6-in. squares.
2. Place squares on ungreased baking sheets; top each square with about ⅓ cup chocolate mixture. Lightly brush edges of pastry with water; bring together all the corners, pinching seams to seal.
3. Bake until golden brown, 18-20 minutes. Remove to a wire rack to cool slightly. Puree frozen raspberries with 1 cup confectioners' sugar in a food processor. Strain to remove the seeds.
4. Before serving, dust the pastries with confectioners' sugar. Serve with raspberry sauce and, if desired, fresh berries and additional chips.

Per pastry: 699 cal., 39g fat (13g sat. fat), 9mg chol., 238mg sod., 81g carb. (40g sugars, 7g fiber), 9g pro.

BLACK WALNUT LAYER CAKE

My sister gave me the recipe for this cake years ago, and everyone loves it. The thin layer of frosting spread on the outside gives it a beautiful modern look.

—Lynn Glaze, Warren, OH

Prep: 25 min.
Bake: 20 min. + cooling
Makes: 16 servings

- ½ cup butter, softened
- ½ cup shortening
- 2 cups sugar
- 2 tsp. vanilla extract
- 4 large eggs
- 3¾ cups all-purpose flour
- 2 tsp. baking soda
- ½ tsp. salt
- 1½ cups buttermilk
- 1¼ cups finely chopped black or English walnuts

FROSTING

- ½ cup butter, softened
- 1 pkg. (8 oz.) cream cheese, softened
- 1 tsp. vanilla extract
- 4½ cups confectioners' sugar
- 1 to 3 Tbsp. buttermilk
- Additional black walnuts
- Thin orange slices, optional

1. Preheat oven to 350°. Line bottoms of three greased 9-in. round baking pans with parchment paper; grease paper.
2. Cream butter, shortening and sugar until light and fluffy. Add vanilla and eggs, one at a time, beating well after each addition. In another bowl, whisk together flour, baking soda and salt; add to creamed mixture alternately with buttermilk, beating after each addition. Fold in walnuts.
3. Transfer to prepared pans. Bake until a toothpick inserted in center comes out clean, 20-25 minutes. Cool in pans for 10 minutes before removing to wire racks; remove paper. Cool completely.
4. For frosting, beat butter and cream cheese until smooth. Beat in the vanilla. Gradually beat in confectioners' sugar and enough buttermilk to reach spreading consistency.
5. Spread 1 cup frosting between each cake layer. Spread top of cake with an additional 1 cup frosting. Spread remaining frosting in a thin layer over side of cake. Top cake with additional walnuts and, if desired, orange slices.

Per slice: 630 cal., 30g fat (13g sat. fat), 92mg chol., 432mg sod., 84g carb. (60g sugars, 1g fiber), 9g pro.

BLACK WALNUT LAYER CAKE

GINGER PLUM TART

GINGER PLUM TART

Sweet cravings, begone! This free-form plum tart is sure to satisfy, and it's done in only 35 minutes. Plus, it's extra-awesome served warm.

—Taste of Home *Test Kitchen*

Prep: 15 min. • **Bake:** 20 min. + cooling
Makes: 8 servings

- 1 sheet refrigerated pie crust
- 3½ cups sliced fresh plums (about 10 medium)
- 3 Tbsp. plus 1 tsp. coarse sugar, divided
- 1 Tbsp. cornstarch
- 2 tsp. finely chopped crystallized ginger
- 1 large egg white
- 1 Tbsp. water

1. Preheat oven to 400°. On a work surface, unroll crust. Roll to a 12-in. circle. Carefully transfer to a parchment paper-lined baking sheet.

2. In a large bowl, toss plums with 3 Tbsp. sugar and cornstarch. Arrange plums on crust to within 2 in. of edges; sprinkle with ginger. Fold crust edge over plums, pleating as you go.

3. In a small bowl, whisk egg white and water; brush over folded crust. Sprinkle with remaining sugar.

4. Bake 20-25 minutes or until crust is golden brown. Cool on pan on a wire rack. Serve warm or at room temperature.

Per piece: 190 cal., 7g fat (3g sat. fat), 5mg chol., 108mg sod., 30g carb. (14g sugars, 1g fiber), 2g pro. **Diabetic exchanges:** 1½ starch, 1 fat, ½ fruit.

Think you're too busy to make dessert? Convenient store-bought individual tart shells make it as easy as pie to end dinner on a sweet note. Simply fill a tart shell with your favorite berries and dollop with whipped topping

EDITOR'S CHOICE

LOVELY LEMON CHEESECAKE

Wait for the oohs and aahs when you present this luxurious lemon cheesecake.
—Margaret Allen, Abingdon, VA

Prep: 25 min. • **Bake:** 70 min. + chilling
Makes: 14 servings

- ¾ cup graham cracker crumbs
- 2 Tbsp. sugar
- 3 tsp. ground cinnamon
- 2 Tbsp. butter, melted

FILLING

- 5 pkg. (8 oz. each) cream cheese, softened
- 1⅔ cups sugar
- ⅛ tsp. salt
- ¼ cup lemon juice
- 1½ tsp. vanilla extract
- 5 large eggs, lightly beaten
- Thin lemon slices, optional

1. Preheat oven to 325°. Place a greased 10-in. springform pan on a double thickness of heavy-duty foil (about 18 in. square). Wrap foil securely around pan.
2. In a small bowl, mix cracker crumbs, sugar and cinnamon; stir in butter. Press onto bottom of prepared pan; refrigerate while preparing filling.
3. In a large bowl, beat cream cheese, sugar and salt until smooth. Beat in lemon juice and vanilla. Add eggs; beat on low speed just until blended. Pour over crust. Place springform pan in a larger baking pan; add 1 in. of hot water to larger pan.
4. Bake 70-80 minutes or until center is just set and top appears dull. Remove springform pan from water bath. Cool cheesecake on a wire rack 10 minutes. Loosen sides from pan with a knife; remove the foil. Cool 1 hour longer. Refrigerate overnight, covering when completely cool.
5. Remove rim from pan. If desired, top cheesecake with lemon slices.
Per slice: 444 cal., 32g fat (19g sat. fat), 169mg chol., 325mg sod., 32g carb. (27g sugars, 0 fiber), 9g pro.

SWEDISH CREME

SWEDISH CREME

This thick and creamy dessert is my interpretation of my mother's recipe for Swedish *krem*. It has just a hint of almond flavor and looks spectacular with bright red berries on top. Serve it in glasses to match the occasion.
—Linda Nilsen, Anoka, MN

Prep: 20 min. + chilling • **Makes:** 8 servings

- 2 cups heavy whipping cream
- 1 cup plus 2 tsp. sugar, divided
- 1 envelope unflavored gelatin
- 1 tsp. vanilla extract
- 1 tsp. almond extract
- 2 cups (16 oz.) sour cream
- 1 cup fresh or frozen raspberries

1. In a large saucepan, combine cream and 1 cup sugar; cook and stir over low heat until a thermometer reads 160° (do not allow to boil). Stir in the gelatin until completely dissolved.
2. Remove from the heat; stir in extracts. Cool for 10 minutes. Whisk in sour cream. Pour into eight dessert dishes. Refrigerate at least 1 hour.
3. Just before serving, lightly crush the raspberries; gently stir in remaining sugar. Spoon over tops.
Per serving: 440 cal., 32g fat (21g sat. fat), 122mg chol., 55mg sod., 32g carb. (30g sugars, 1g fiber), 4g pro.

BERRY-PATCH
BROWNIE PIZZA

BERRY-PATCH BROWNIE PIZZA

I just love the combination of fruit, almonds and chocolate that makes this brownie so unique. The fruit lightens the chocolate a bit and makes it feel as though you are eating something sinfully healthy.

—Sue Kauffman, Columbia City, IN

Prep: 20 min. + chilling
Bake: 15 min. + cooling
Makes: 12 servings

- 1 pkg. fudge brownie mix (13x9-in. pan size)
- ⅓ cup chopped unblanched almonds
- 1 tsp. almond extract

TOPPING

- 1 pkg. (8 oz.) cream cheese, softened
- 1 Tbsp. sugar
- 1 tsp. vanilla extract
- ½ tsp. grated lemon peel
- 2 cups whipped topping
- Assorted fresh berries
- Fresh mint leaves and coarse sugar, optional

1. Preheat oven to 375°. Prepare brownie batter according to package directions for fudgelike brownies, adding almonds and almond extract. Spread into a greased 14-in. pizza pan.

2. Bake until a toothpick inserted in center comes out clean, 15-18 minutes. Cool completely on a wire rack.

3. Beat the first four topping ingredients until smooth; fold in whipped topping. Spread over crust to within ½ in. of edges; refrigerate, loosely covered, 2 hours.

4. To serve, cut into slices; top with berries of choice. If desired, top with mint and sprinkle with coarse sugar.

Per slice: 404 cal., 26g fat (8g sat. fat), 51mg chol., 240mg sod., 39g carb. (26g sugars, 2g fiber), 5g pro.

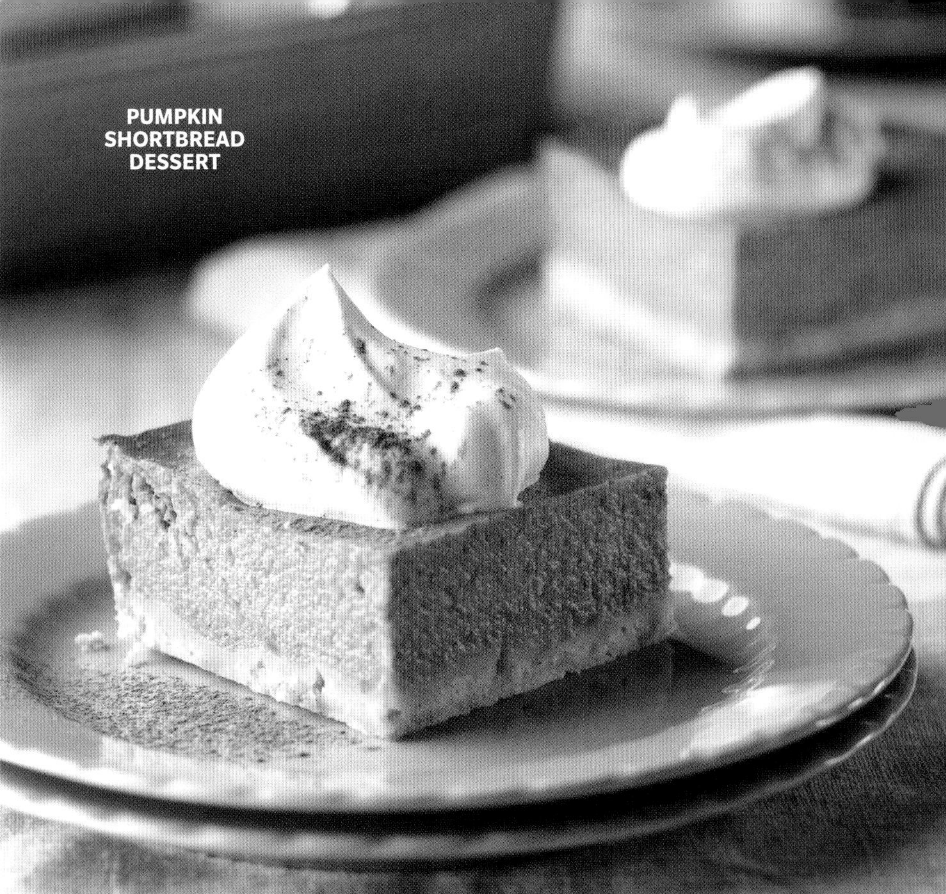

PUMPKIN SHORTBREAD DESSERT

PUMPKIN SHORTBREAD DESSERT

My family prefers this to traditional pumpkin pie, which is just fine with me. It feeds a crowd, so I need to make only one dessert instead of several pies.

—Edie DeSpain, Logan, UT

Prep: 15 min. • **Bake:** 65 min. + chilling
Makes: 15 servings

- 1¾ cups sugar, divided
- 1½ cups all-purpose flour
- ½ cup cold butter
- 4 large eggs, lightly beaten
- 1 can (29 oz.) solid-pack pumpkin
- 1 tsp. salt
- 1 tsp. ground cinnamon
- 1 tsp. ground ginger
- ½ tsp. ground cloves
- 2 cans (12 oz. each) evaporated milk
- Whipped cream and additional ground cinnamon, optional

1. In a bowl, combine ¼ cup sugar and the flour; cut in butter until the mixture resembles coarse crumbs. Press into an ungreased 13x9-in. baking pan.

2. In a bowl, combine the eggs, pumpkin, salt, spices and remaining sugar. Stir in the milk. Pour over crust.

3. Bake at 425° for 15 minutes. Reduce heat to 350°; bake 50-55 minutes longer or until filling is set. Cool on a wire rack. Cover and refrigerate overnight.

4. Cut into 15 squares. If desired, top squares with whipped cream and sprinkle with cinnamon.

Per piece: 258 cal., 9g fat (5g sat. fat), 80mg chol., 260mg sod., 40g carb. (27g sugars, 3g fiber), 5g pro.

GRANDMA'S STRAWBERRY SHORTCAKE

When my grandma served this shortcake, she usually topped it with homemade vanilla ice cream.

—Angela Lively, Conroe, TX

Prep: 30 min. + standing • **Bake:** 20 min.
Makes: 8 servings

- 6 cups sliced fresh strawberries
- ½ cup sugar
- 1 tsp. vanilla extract

SHORTCAKE

- 3 cups all-purpose flour
- 5 Tbsp. sugar, divided
- 3 tsp. baking powder
- 1 tsp. baking soda
- ½ tsp. salt
- ¾ cup cold butter, cubed
- 1 cup buttermilk
- 2 Tbsp. heavy whipping cream

TOPPING

- 1½ cups heavy whipping cream
- 2 Tbsp. sugar
- ½ tsp. vanilla extract

1. Combine strawberries with sugar and vanilla; mash slightly. Let stand at least 30 minutes, tossing occasionally.

2. Preheat oven to 400°. For shortcake, whisk together flour, 4 Tbsp. sugar, baking powder, baking soda and salt. Cut in butter until crumbly. Add buttermilk; stir just until combined (do not overmix). Drop batter by ⅓ cupfuls 2 in. apart onto an ungreased baking sheet. Brush with 2 Tbsp. heavy cream; sprinkle with the remaining 1 Tbsp. sugar. Bake 18-20 minutes. Remove to wire racks to cool.

3. For topping, beat heavy whipping cream until it begins to thicken. Add sugar and vanilla; beat until soft peaks form. To serve, cut biscuits in half; top with strawberries and whipped cream.

Per 1 shortcake with ½ cup strawberries and ⅓ cup whipped cream: 635 cal., 36g fat (22g sat. fat), 102mg chol., 696mg sod., 72g carb. (33g sugars, 4g fiber), 8g pro.

SALTED CARAMEL CAPPUCCINO CHEESECAKE

After spending years living in Seattle, I've become a coffee junkie! I had to relocate across the country for a time, so I created this cheesecake with the flavors of salted caramel, coffee and espresso. It lifted me up on days when I felt blue about leaving one of the world's great coffee destinations.
—Julie Merriman, Seattle, WA

Prep: 30 min.
Bake: 55 min. + chilling
Makes: 12 servings

- 1 pkg. (9 oz.) chocolate wafers
- 1 cup (6 oz.) semisweet chocolate chips
- ½ cup packed brown sugar
- 2 Tbsp. instant espresso powder
- ⅛ tsp. ground nutmeg
- ½ cup butter, melted

FILLING

- 3 pkg. (8 oz. each) cream cheese, softened
- 1 cup packed brown sugar
- ½ cup sour cream
- ¼ cup Kahlua (coffee liqueur)
- 2 Tbsp. all-purpose flour
- 2 Tbsp. instant espresso powder
- 4 large eggs, lightly beaten

TOPPING

- ½ cup hot caramel ice cream topping
- ½ tsp. coarse sea salt

1. Preheat oven to 350°. Place a greased 9-in. springform pan on a double thickness of heavy-duty foil (about 18 in. square). Securely wrap foil around pan.
2. Place the first five ingredients in a food processor; cover and pulse into fine crumbs. Gradually add melted butter, pulsing until combined. Press mixture onto the bottom and 2 in. up sides of prepared pan.
3. In a large bowl, beat cream cheese and brown sugar until smooth. Beat in sour cream, Kahlua, flour and espresso powder. Add eggs; beat on low speed just until blended. Pour into crust. Place springform pan in a larger baking pan; add 1 in. of hot water to larger pan.
4. Bake 55-65 minutes or until center is just set and top appears dull. Remove the springform pan from water bath; remove the foil. Cool cheesecake on a wire rack 10 minutes; loosen sides from pan with a knife. Cool 1 hour longer. Refrigerate overnight, covering cheesecake when completely cooled.
5. Pour caramel topping over cheesecake. Refrigerate at least 15 minutes. Remove rim from pan. Sprinkle with the sea salt just before serving.
Per slice: 618 cal., 38g fat (22g sat. fat), 160mg chol., 530mg sod., 64g carb. (42g sugars, 2g fiber), 9g pro.

BLACK FOREST CHOCOLATE TORTE

BLACK FOREST CHOCOLATE TORTE

If you want to pull out all the stops for dessert, look no further. This cherry-crowned beauty stacked with layers of chocolate cake and cream filling will have everyone talking.

—Doris Grotz, York, NE

Prep: 1 hour • **Bake:** 15 min. + cooling
Makes: 16 servings

- ⅔ cup butter, softened
- 1¾ cups sugar
- 4 large eggs
- 1¼ cups water
- 4 oz. unsweetened chocolate, chopped
- 1 tsp. vanilla extract
- 1¾ cups all-purpose flour
- 1 tsp. baking powder
- ¼ tsp. baking soda

CHOCOLATE FILLING

- 6 oz. German sweet chocolate, chopped
- ¾ cup butter, cubed
- ½ cup sliced almonds, toasted

WHIPPED CREAM

- 2 cups heavy whipping cream
- 1 Tbsp. sugar
- 1½ tsp. vanilla extract

TOPPING

- 1 cup cherry pie filling
- 1½ cups sliced almonds, toasted

1. Preheat oven to 350°. Line bottoms of four greased 9-in. round baking pans with parchment paper; grease paper.

2. Cream butter and sugar until light and fluffy. Add eggs, one at a time, beating well after each addition. Beat in the water just until blended.

3. In a microwave, melt unsweetened chocolate; stir until smooth. Stir in vanilla. In a small bowl, whisk together flour, baking powder and baking soda; add to creamed mixture alternately with chocolate mixture, beating after each addition. Divide batter among prepared pans.

4. Bake until a toothpick inserted in center comes out clean, 15-20 minutes. Cool for 10 minutes before removing from pans to wire racks; remove paper. Cool completely.

5. For chocolate filling, melt chocolate in a microwave; stir until smooth. Stir in butter until blended. Stir in almonds.

6. For whipped cream, in a small bowl, beat cream until it begins to thicken. Add sugar and vanilla; beat until soft peaks form.

7. To assemble, place one cake layer on a serving plate; spread with ⅓ cup chocolate filling and 1 cup whipped cream. Repeat layers twice. Top with the remaining cake and chocolate filling.

8. Spread remaining whipped cream over sides of cake. Press almonds onto sides. Spoon cherry pie filling over top of cake. Refrigerate until serving.

Note To toast nuts, bake in a shallow pan in a 350° oven for 5-10 minutes or cook in a skillet over low heat until lightly browned, stirring occasionally.

Per slice: 535 cal., 37g fat (21g sat. fat), 128mg chol., 295mg sod., 48g carb. (39g sugars, 2g fiber), 8g pro.

WHITE CHOCOLATE MOUSSE

Simply elegant is a fitting description for this smooth treat. Whipped cream teams up with white chocolate to make this four-item recipe extra special.

—Laurinda Johnston, Belchertown, MA

Prep: 20 min. + chilling • **Makes:** 8 servings

- 12 oz. white baking chocolate, coarsely chopped
- 2 cups heavy whipping cream, divided
- 1 Tbsp. confectioners' sugar
- 1 tsp. vanilla extract

1. In a small heavy saucepan, combine white chocolate and ⅔ cup cream; cook and stir over medium-low heat until smooth. Transfer to a large bowl; cool to room temperature.

2. In a small bowl, beat the remaining cream until it begins to thicken. Add the confectioners' sugar and vanilla; beat until soft peaks form. Fold ¼ cup of the whipped cream into chocolate mixture, then fold in remaining whipped cream.

3. Spoon into dessert dishes. Refrigerate, covered, at least 2 hours.

Per ½ cup: 230 cal., 23g fat (14g sat. fat), 82mg chol., 26mg sod., 5g carb. (5g sugars, 0 fiber), 1g pro.

Overbeating cream may cause it to break down, resulting in curdling and separating. Avoid this by simply stopping the beating process as soon as soft peaks begin to form.

WHITE CHOCOLATE MOUSSE

CHOCOLATE MINT APPLE FONDUE

CHOCOLATE MINT APPLE FONDUE

Fondue is simple to make, and this version has a hint of peppermint. You can dip just about any fruit, bread or cookie that pairs well with the chocolate.

—Deb Danner, Dayton, OH

Takes: 10 min. • **Makes:** 2½ cups

- 1 can (14 oz.) sweetened condensed milk
- 1 cup (6 oz.) semisweet chocolate chips
- 10 chocolate-covered peppermint patties, chopped
- Sliced apples

In a small saucepan, combine the milk, chocolate chips and peppermint patties. Cook and stir over medium-low heat until smooth. Serve warm with apples.

Per ¼ cup: 273 cal., 10g fat (6g sat. fat), 14mg chol., 57mg sod., 46g carb. (42g sugars, 1g fiber), 4g pro.

EDITOR'S CHOICE

LAYERED MOCHA CHEESECAKE

A while back, I was on the hunt for the perfect coffee-flavored cheesecake. I ended up combining a few of my best to create this mouthwatering version. Now, it's a favorite with family and friends.

—Sue Gronholz, Beaver Dam, WI

Prep: 30 min.
Bake: 1 hour + chilling
Makes: 16 servings

- 1½ cups Oreo cookie crumbs
- ¼ cup butter, melted

FILLING

- 2 Tbsp. plus 1½ tsp. instant coffee granules
- 1 Tbsp. hot water
- ¼ tsp. ground cinnamon
- 4 pkg. (8 oz. each) cream cheese, softened
- 1½ cups sugar
- ¼ cup all-purpose flour
- 2 tsp. vanilla extract
- 4 large eggs, lightly beaten
- 2 cups (12 oz.) semisweet chocolate chips, melted and cooled

GLAZE

- ½ cup semisweet chocolate chips
- 3 Tbsp. butter
- Chocolate-covered coffee beans, optional

1. Place a greased 9-in. springform pan on a double thickness of heavy-duty foil (about 18 in. square). Securely wrap the foil around the pan.

2. In a bowl, mix cookie crumbs and butter; press onto the bottom of prepared pan. In another bowl, mix the coffee granules, hot water and cinnamon; set aside.

3. In a large bowl, beat cream cheese, sugar, flour and vanilla until smooth. Add the eggs; beat on low speed just until combined.

4. Divide batter in half. Stir melted chocolate into one portion; pour over crust. Stir coffee mixture into the remaining batter; spoon over chocolate layer. Place springform pan in a large baking pan; add 1 in. of hot water to larger pan.

5. Bake at 325° for 60-65 minutes or until center is just set and top appears dull. Remove springform pan from water bath; remove foil. Cool cheesecake on a wire rack for 10 minutes; loosen sides from pan with a knife. Cool for 1 hour longer. Refrigerate cheesecake overnight.

6. Remove rim from pan. For glaze, in a microwave, melt chocolate chips and butter; stir until smooth. Spread over cheesecake. If desired, top with coffee beans.

Per slice: 535 cal., 37g fat (21g sat. fat), 128mg chol., 295mg sod., 48g carb. (39g sugars, 2g fiber), 8g pro.

MACAROON-TOPPED RHUBARB COBBLER

Crumbled macaroons are a surprising addition to this cobbler's topping. We love that you can make the sweet treat in a baking dish or a cast-iron skillet.
—Taste of Home *Test Kitchen*

Takes: 30 min. • **Makes:** 4 servings

- 4 cups sliced fresh or frozen rhubarb (1-in. pieces)
- 1 large apple, peeled and sliced
- ½ cup packed brown sugar
- ½ tsp. ground cinnamon, divided
- 1 Tbsp. cornstarch
- 2 Tbsp. cold water
- 8 macaroons, crumbled
- 1 Tbsp. butter, melted
- 2 Tbsp. sugar
- Vanilla ice cream, optional

1. In a large skillet, combine the rhubarb, apple, brown sugar and ¼ tsp. cinnamon; bring to a boil. Reduce heat; cover and simmer for 10-13 minutes or until rhubarb is very tender. Combine cornstarch and water until smooth; gradually add to the fruit mixture. Bring to a boil; cook and stir for 2 minutes or until thickened. Transfer to an ungreased 1-qt. baking dish.
2. In a small bowl, combine the crumbled cookies, butter, sugar and remaining cinnamon. Sprinkle over fruit mixture.
3. Broil 4 in. from the heat until lightly browned, 3-5 minutes. Serve warm, with ice cream if desired.
Note If using frozen rhubarb, measure rhubarb while still frozen, then thaw completely. Drain in a colander, but do not press liquid out.
Per serving: 368 cal., 12g fat (7g sat. fat), 8mg chol., 45mg sod., 62g carb. (55g sugars, 5g fiber), 3g pro.

As you can see, we've given the photo of this recipe a downhome spin since it was published in 2004.

RETRO DINNER
REVIVALS

SPECIAL DINNERS SHOULDN'T BE CONFINED TO HOLIDAYS AND NOTABLE OCCASIONS. EVERY DAY IS WORTHY OF A CELEBRATORY MEAL THAT BRINGS TOGETHER LOVED ONES, CHERISHED TRADITIONS AND GOOD FOOD. LET THESE TRIED-AND-TRUE RECIPES INSPIRE YOUR OWN UNIQUE MENUS.

MEXICAN FIESTA

Take your party south of the border with the fresh ingredients and bold flavors in this zesty lineup of festive favorites. Cue up the mariachi music—it's fiesta time!

CHICKEN TAMALES

I love making tamales. They take a little time to make but are so worth the effort. I usually make them for Christmas, but my family wants them more often, so I freeze a big batch to enjoy throughout the year.
—Cindy Pruitt, Grove, OK

Prep: 2½ hours + soaking • **Cook:** 50 min.
Makes: 20 tamales

- 24 dried corn husks
- 1 broiler/fryer chicken (3 to 4 lbs.), cut up
- 1 medium onion, quartered
- 2 tsp. salt
- 1 garlic clove, crushed
- 3 qt. water

DOUGH

- 1 cup shortening
- 3 cups masa harina

FILLING

- 6 Tbsp. canola oil
- 6 Tbsp. all-purpose flour
- ¾ cup chili powder
- ½ tsp. salt
- ¼ tsp. garlic powder
- ¼ tsp. pepper
- 2 cans (2¼ oz. each) sliced ripe olives, drained
- Hot water

CHICKEN TAMALES

1. Cover corn husks with cold water; soak until softened, at least 2 hours.

2. Place chicken, onion, salt and garlic in a 6-qt. stockpot. Pour in water; bring to a boil. Reduce heat; simmer, covered, until chicken is tender, 45-60 minutes. Remove chicken from broth. When cool enough to handle, remove bones and skin; discard. Shred chicken. Strain cooking juices; skim fat. Reserve 6 cups stock.

3. For dough, beat shortening until light and fluffy, about 1 minute. Beat in small amounts of masa harina alternately with small amounts of reserved stock, using no more than 2 cups stock. Drop a small amount of dough into a cup of cold water; dough should float. If not, continue beating, rechecking every 1-2 minutes

4. For filling, heat oil in a Dutch oven; stir in flour until blended. Cook and stir over medium heat until lightly browned, about 7-9 minutes. Stir in seasonings, chicken and remaining chicken stock; bring to a boil. Reduce the heat; simmer, uncovered, stirring occasionally, until thickened, about 45 minutes.

5. Drain corn husks and pat dry; tear four husks to make 20 strips for tying tamales. (To prevent husks from drying out, cover with plastic wrap and a damp towel until ready to use.) On the wide end of each remaining husk, spread 3 Tbsp. dough to within ½ in. of side edges; top each with 2 Tbsp. chicken filling and 2 tsp. olives. Fold long sides of husk over filling, overlapping slightly. Fold over narrow end of husk; tie with a strip of husk to secure.

6. Place a large steamer basket in the stockpot over water; place tamales upright in steamer. Bring to a boil; steam, covered, adding hot water as needed, until dough peels away from husk, about 45 minutes.

Per 2 tamales: 564 cal., 35g fat (7g sat. fat), 44mg chol., 835mg sod., 43g carb. (2g sugars, 7g fiber), 20g pro.

SOUTHWESTERN RICE

I created this colorful rice dish after eating something similar at a restaurant. It makes a great complement to Tex-Mex fare. Add cubed grilled chicken breast to make it a meal in itself.

—Michelle Dennis, Clarks Hill, IN

Takes: 30 min. • **Makes:** 8 servings

- 1 Tbsp. olive oil
- 1 medium green pepper, diced
- 1 medium onion, chopped
- 2 garlic cloves, minced
- 1 cup uncooked long grain rice
- ½ tsp. ground cumin
- ⅛ tsp. ground turmeric
- 1 can (14½ oz.) reduced-sodium chicken broth
- 2 cups frozen corn (about 10 oz.), thawed
- 1 can (15 oz.) black beans, rinsed and drained
- 1 can (10 oz.) diced tomatoes and green chilies, undrained

1. In a large nonstick skillet, heat oil over medium-high heat; saute pepper and onion 3 minutes. Add garlic; cook and stir for 1 minute.

2. Stir in rice, spices and broth; bring to a boil. Reduce heat; simmer, covered, until rice is tender, about 15 minutes. Stir in remaining ingredients; cook, covered, until heated through.

Per ¾ cup: 198 cal., 3g fat (1g sat. fat), 1mg chol., 339mg sod., 37g carb. (0 sugars, 5g fiber), 7g pro.

TOPSY-TURVY SANGRIA

SOUTHWESTERN RICE

TOPSY-TURVY SANGRIA

I got this recipe from a friend a few years ago. It's perfect for relaxed get-togethers. It's even better if you make it the night before and let the flavors steep. But watch out—it goes down easy!

—Tracy Field, Bremerton, WA

Takes: 10 min.
Makes: 10 servings

- 1 bottle (750 milliliters) merlot
- 1 cup sugar
- 1 cup orange liqueur
- ½ to 1 cup brandy
- 3 cups cold lemon-lime soda
- 1 cup sliced fresh strawberries
- 1 medium orange, sliced
- 1 medium lemon, sliced
- 1 medium peach, sliced
- Ice cubes

In a pitcher, stir first four ingredients until sugar is dissolved. Stir in soda and fruit. Serve over ice.

Per ¾ cup: 292 cal., 0 fat (0 sat. fat), 0 chol., 11mg sod., 42g carb. (39g sugars, 0 fiber), 0 pro.

HOMEMADE GUACAMOLE

Nothing is better than fresh guacamole when you're eating something spicy. It's easy to whip together in a matter of minutes, and it quickly tames anything that's too hot.
—Joan Hallford, North Richland Hills, TX

Takes: 10 min. • **Makes:** 2 cups

- 3 medium ripe avocados, peeled and cubed
- 1 garlic clove, minced
- ¼ to ½ tsp. salt
- 2 medium tomatoes, seeded and chopped, optional
- 1 small onion, finely chopped
- ¼ cup mayonnaise, optional
- 1 to 2 Tbsp. lime juice
- 1 Tbsp. minced fresh cilantro

Mash avocados with garlic and salt. Stir in remaining ingredients.

Per ¼ cup: 90 cal., 8g fat (1g sat. fat), 0 chol., 78mg sod., 6g carb. (1g sugars, 4g fiber), 1g pro. **Diabetic exchanges:** 1½ fat.

MEXICAN CINNAMON COOKIES

HOMEMADE GUACAMOLE

MEXICAN CINNAMON COOKIES

My extended family shares a meal every Sunday. The aunts and uncles take turns bringing everything from main dishes to desserts like this traditional Mexican cinnamon cookie called *reganadas*.
—Adan Franco, Milwaukee, WI

Prep: 25 min. + standing
Bake: 10 min./batch
Makes: 12 dozen

- 1 large egg, separated
- 2 cups lard
- 4 cups all-purpose flour
- 3 tsp. baking powder
- 1½ tsp. ground cinnamon
- Dash salt
- ¾ cup sugar

COATING

- ⅔ cup sugar
- 4 tsp. ground cinnamon
- Confectioners' sugar, optional

1. Place egg white in a small bowl; let stand at room temperature 30 minutes.

2. Preheat oven to 375°. In a large bowl, beat lard until creamy. In another bowl, whisk flour, baking powder, cinnamon and salt; gradually beat into lard.

3. Beat egg white on high speed until stiff peaks form. Gently whisk in sugar and egg yolk. Gradually beat into lard mixture. Turn onto a lightly floured surface; knead gently 8-10 times.

4. Divide dough into six portions. On a lightly floured surface, roll each portion into a 24-in.-long rope; cut diagonally into 1-in. pieces. Place 1 in. apart on ungreased baking sheets. Bake 8-10 minutes or until edges are light brown. Cool on pans for 2 minutes.

5. In a small bowl, mix sugar and cinnamon. Roll warm cookies in cinnamon sugar mixture or confectioners' sugar. Cool on wire racks.

Per cookie: 47 cal., 3g fat (1g sat. fat), 4mg chol., 10mg sod., 5g carb. (2g sugars, 0 fiber), 0 pro.

Sundays are meant to be savored. It's a breeze to plan a memorable brunch with these stress-free stunners. Each one makes the weekend worth celebrating.

CHICKEN & SWISS CASSEROLE

It's nice to have an alternative to omelets and egg bakes at brunch. Folks can't get enough of this comforting casserole. Using rotisserie chicken from the deli keeps prep simple and quick.

—Christina Petri, Alexandria, MN

Prep: 30 min. • **Bake:** 10 min.
Makes: 8 servings

- 5 1/2 cups uncooked egg noodles (about 1/2 lb.)
- 3 Tbsp. olive oil
- 3 shallots, chopped
- 3 small garlic cloves, minced
- 1/3 cup all-purpose flour
- 2 cups chicken broth
- 3/4 cup 2% milk
- 1 1/2 tsp. dried thyme
- 3/4 tsp. grated lemon peel
- 1/2 tsp. salt
- 1/4 tsp. ground nutmeg
- 1/4 tsp. pepper
- 5 cups cubed rotisserie chicken
- 1 1/2 cups frozen peas
- 2 cups shredded Swiss cheese
- 3/4 cup dry bread crumbs
- 2 Tbsp. butter, melted

1. Preheat oven to 350°. Cook noodles according to package directions; drain. In a large skillet, heat oil over medium heat. Add the shallots and garlic; cook and stir 45 seconds. Stir in the flour; cook and stir 1 minute. Add broth, milk, thyme, lemon peel, salt, nutmeg and pepper. Stir in the chicken and peas; heat through. Stir in the noodles and cheese.

2. Transfer to a greased 13x9-in. baking dish. In a small bowl, mix bread crumbs and butter; sprinkle over top. Bake 8-10 minutes or until top is browned.

Per 1 1/4 cups: 551 cal., 25g fat (10g sat. fat), 136mg chol., 661mg sod., 38g carb. (4g sugars, 3g fiber), 41g pro.

CHICKEN & SWISS CASSEROLE

GARLIC-DILL DEVILED EGGS

In my family, brunch isn't complete without deviled eggs. Fresh dill and garlic perk up the flavor of these irresistible appetizers you'll want to have for every occasion.
—Kami Horch, Calais, ME

Prep: 20 min. + chilling • **Makes:** 2 dozen

- 12 hard-boiled large eggs
- ⅔ cup mayonnaise
- 4 tsp. dill pickle relish
- 2 tsp. snipped fresh dill
- 2 tsp. Dijon mustard
- 1 tsp. coarsely ground pepper
- ¼ tsp. garlic powder
- ⅛ tsp. paprika or cayenne pepper

1. Cut eggs lengthwise in half. Remove yolks, reserving whites. In a bowl, mash yolks. Stir in all remaining ingredients except paprika. Spoon or pipe filling into egg whites.
2. Refrigerate, covered, at least 30 minutes before serving. Sprinkle with paprika.
Per stuffed egg half: 81 cal., 7g fat (1g sat. fat), 94mg chol., 81mg sod., 1g carb. (0 sugars, 0 fiber), 3g pro.

TEST KITCHEN TIP

Try this fuss-free way to fill deviled eggs. Put the cooked yolks and other ingredients in a large resealable food-safe plastic bag, seal the bag and knead everything together by hand. Then snip a corner off the bag and use it like a pastry bag to squeeze the mixture into the egg white halves. It's easier than spooning the filling into the eggs, and cleanup is a breeze—just toss out the bag!

GARLIC-DILL DEVILED EGGS

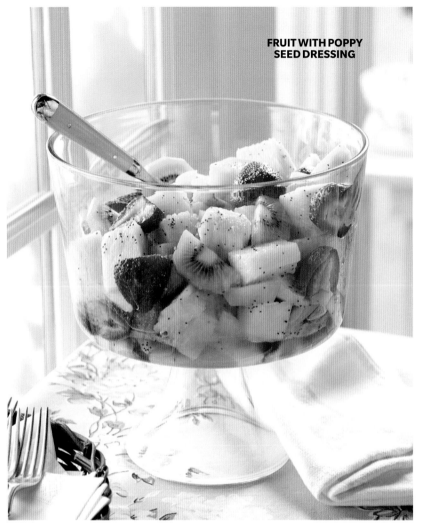

FRUIT WITH POPPY SEED DRESSING

STRAWBERRY MIMOSAS

Here's a tasty twist on the classic mimosa. To make this refreshing drink friendly for kids or mamas-to-be, substitute lemon-lime soda or ginger ale for the champagne.

—Kelly Maxwell, Plainfield, IL

Takes: 15 min.
Makes: 12 servings

- **7 cups sliced fresh strawberries (about 2 qt.)**
- **3 cups orange juice**
- **4 cups champagne, chilled**

GARNISHES

- **Fresh strawberries and orange slices, optional**

1. Place half of the strawberries and orange juice in a blender; cover and process until smooth. Press through a fine mesh strainer. Repeat with remaining strawberries and orange juice.

2. Pour a scant ⅔ cup strawberry mixture into each champagne flute or wine glass. Top with about ⅓ cup champagne. If desired, serve with a strawberry and an orange slice.

Per cup: 112 cal., 0 fat (0 sat. fat), 0 chol., 1mg sod., 15g carb. (10g sugars, 2g fiber), 1g pro.

STRAWBERRY MIMOSAS

FRUIT WITH POPPY SEED DRESSING

Easy to prepare, cool and colorful, this refreshing, good-for-you fruit medley pairs well with breakfast and lunch fare alike.

—Peggy Mills, Texarkana, AR

Prep: 20 min. + standing
Makes: 12 servings

- **3 Tbsp. honey**
- **1 Tbsp. white vinegar**
- **1 tsp. ground mustard**
- **¼ tsp. salt**
- **¼ tsp. onion powder**
- **⅓ cup canola oil**
- **1 tsp. poppy seeds**
- **1 fresh pineapple, cut into 1½-in. cubes**
- **3 medium kiwifruit, halved and sliced**
- **2 cups fresh strawberries, halved**

1. In a small bowl, whisk the first five ingredients. Gradually whisk in oil until blended. Stir in poppy seeds; let mixture stand 1 hour.

2. In a large bowl, combine fruits. Drizzle with dressing; toss gently to coat.

Per cup: 129 cal., 7g fat (0 sat. fat), 0 chol., 51mg sod., 19g carb. (14g sugars, 2g fiber), 1g pro.

CHOCOLATE-COCONUT LAYER BARS

I'm a huge fan of Nanaimo bars, the no-bake layered dessert named for the city in British Columbia. For fun, I reinvented this treat with coconut lovers in mind.

—Shannon Dobos, Calgary, AB

Prep: 20 min. + chilling • **Makes:** 3 dozen

- ¾ cup butter, cubed
- 3 cups Oreo cookie crumbs
- 2 cups sweetened shredded coconut
- ½ cup cream of coconut

FILLING

- ⅓ cup butter, softened
- 3 Tbsp. cream of coconut
- ¼ tsp. coconut extract
- 3 cups confectioners' sugar
- 1 to 2 Tbsp. 2% milk

TOPPING

- 1½ cups semisweet chocolate chips
- 4 tsp. canola oil
- 3 Mounds candy bars (1¾ oz. each), coarsely chopped, optional

1. Microwave butter on high until melted; stir until smooth. Stir in cookie crumbs, coconut and cream of coconut until blended (mixture will be wet). Spread onto bottom of an ungreased 13x9-in. baking pan. Refrigerate until set, about 30 minutes.

2. For filling, beat butter, cream of coconut and extract until smooth. Gradually beat in confectioners' sugar and enough milk to reach a spreading consistency. Spread over the crust.

3. For topping, microwave chocolate chips and oil until melted; stir until smooth. Cool slightly; spread over filling. If desired, sprinkle with chopped candy bars. Refrigerate.

Per bar: 229 cal., 13g fat (8g sat. fat), 15mg chol., 124mg sod., 28g carb. (23g sugars, 1g fiber), 1g pro.

CHOCOLATE-COCONUT LAYER BARS

SOUP & BREAD

Steamy homemade soup plus warm bread equals the coziest comfort food ever. Grab the bowls, spoons and crackers. Winter's chill doesn't stand a chance!

CARAWAY CHEESE BREAD

Cheddar cheese blends beautifully with just the right amount of caraway in this savory bread.

—Homer Wooten, Ridgetown, ON

Prep: 10 min. • **Bake:** 30 min. + cooling
Makes: 1 loaf (16 servings)

- 2½ cups all-purpose flour
- 2 cups shredded cheddar cheese
- 1½ to 2 tsp. caraway seeds
- ¾ tsp. salt
- ½ tsp. baking powder
- ½ tsp. baking soda
- 2 large eggs
- 1 cup plain yogurt
- ½ cup butter, melted
- 1 Tbsp. Dijon mustard

Preheat oven to 375°. Combine the first six ingredients. In another bowl, combine the remaining ingredients. Stir into the dry ingredients just until moistened. Pour into a greased 9x5-in. loaf pan. Bake until a toothpick comes out clean, 30-35 minutes. Cool 10 minutes before removing from pan to a wire rack. Serve warm. Refrigerate leftovers.

Per slice: 199 cal., 12g fat (7g sat. fat), 55mg chol., 338mg sod., 16g carb. (1g sugars, 1g fiber), 7g pro.

THYME-SEA SALT CRACKERS

These homemade crackers are decidedly light and crispy. They're an addictive snack on their own, but they also pair well with a sharp white cheddar.

—Jessica Wirth, Charlotte, NC

Prep: 25 min. • **Bake:** 10 min./batch
Makes: about 7 dozen

- 2½ cups all-purpose flour
- ½ cup white whole wheat flour
- 1 tsp. salt
- ¾ cup water
- ¼ cup plus 1 Tbsp. olive oil, divided
- 1 to 2 Tbsp. minced fresh thyme
- ¾ tsp. sea or kosher salt

1. Preheat oven to 375°. In a large bowl, whisk flours and salt. Gradually add water and ¼ cup oil, tossing with a fork until dough holds together when pressed. Divide dough into three portions. On a lightly floured surface, roll each portion of dough to ⅛-in. thickness. Cut with a floured 1½-in. round cookie cutter. Place 1 in. apart on ungreased baking sheets. Prick each cracker with a fork; brush lightly with remaining oil. Mix thyme and sea salt; sprinkle over crackers.

2. Bake 9-11 minutes or until bottoms are lightly browned.

Per cracker: 23 cal., 1g fat (0 sat. fat), 0 chol., 45mg sod., 3g carb. (0 sugars, 0 fiber), 0 pro.

BROCCOLI BEER CHEESE SOUP

This recipe combines two classic cheese soups into one. I always make extra and pop individual servings in the freezer to enjoy later.

—Lori Lee, Brooksville, FL

Prep: 20 min. • **Cook:** 30 min.
Makes: 10 servings (2½ qt.)

- 3 Tbsp. butter
- 5 celery ribs, finely chopped
- 3 medium carrots, finely chopped
- 1 small onion, finely chopped
- 4 cups fresh broccoli florets, chopped
- ¼ cup chopped sweet red pepper
- 4 cans (14½ oz. each) chicken broth
- ½ tsp. pepper
- ½ cup all-purpose flour
- ½ cup water
- 3 cups shredded cheddar cheese
- 1 pkg. (8 oz.) cream cheese, cubed
- 1 bottle (12 oz.) beer or nonalcoholic beer
- Additional shredded cheddar cheese, optional
- Bacon strips, cooked and crumbled, optional
- Chopped green onions, optional
- Sour cream, optional
- Salad croutons, optional

1. In a Dutch oven, melt the butter over medium-high heat. Add celery, carrots and onion; saute until crisp-tender. Add the broccoli and red pepper; stir in broth and pepper. Combine the flour and water until smooth; gradually stir into pan. Bring to a boil. Reduce heat; simmer, uncovered, until thickened and the vegetables are tender, 25-30 minutes.

2. Stir in cheeses and beer until cheeses are melted (do not boil). If desired, top with additional shredded cheese, bacon, green onions, sour cream and croutons.

Freeze option Before adding toppings, cool soup; transfer to freezer containers. Freeze up to 3 months. To use, partially thaw in refrigerator overnight; heat through in a large saucepan over medium-low heat, stirring occasionally (do not boil). Add toppings if desired.

Per cup: 316 cal., 23g fat (13g sat. fat), 69mg chol., 1068mg sod., 13g carb. (5g sugars, 2g fiber), 12g pro.

To cool soup quickly before freezing, place the kettle in a sink filled with ice water. When cool, transfer to airtight freezer-safe containers, leaving about ¼-in. headspace for expansion. Don't freeze soups for longer than 3 months as they don't retain their fantastic flavor much beyond that.

CARAWAY
CHEESE BREAD
BROCCOLI BEER
CHEESE SOUP

WENDY'S APPLE POMEGRANATE SALAD

WENDY'S APPLE POMEGRANATE SALAD

My grandparents grew pomegranates, pecans and walnuts. Some of my best memories are the days I spent with my grandmother learning how to cook. Now whenever I make this salad, it's like having lunch with her again.

—Wendy Ball, Battle Creek, MI

Takes: 20 min. • **Makes:** 8 servings

- 1 bunch romaine, torn (about 8 cups)
- ½ cup pomegranate seeds
- ½ cup chopped pecans or walnuts, toasted
- ½ cup shredded Parmesan cheese
- 1 large Granny Smith apple, chopped
- 1 Tbsp. lemon juice
- ¼ cup olive oil
- ¼ cup white wine vinegar
- 2 Tbsp. sugar
- ¼ tsp. salt

1. In a large bowl, combine the romaine, pomegranate seeds, pecans and cheese. Toss chopped apple with lemon juice and add to salad.

2. In a small bowl, whisk the remaining ingredients until well blended. Drizzle vinaigrette over salad; toss to coat. Serve salad immediately.

Note To toast nuts, bake in a shallow pan in a 350° oven for 5-10 minutes or cook in a skillet over low heat until lightly browned, stirring occasionally.

Per cup: 165 cal., 13g fat (2g sat. fat), 4mg chol., 163mg sod., 10g carb. (8g sugars, 2g fiber), 3g pro. **Diabetic exchanges:** 2½ fat, 1 vegetable.

The seeds and surrounding juice sacs (also called arils) are the only parts of the pomegranate that are edible. One medium pomegranate (about 8 oz.) yields roughly ¾ cup arils.

COKECOLA CAKE

We live in Coca-Cola country, where everyone loves a chocolaty, moist sheet cake made with the iconic soft drink. Our rich version does the tradition proud.
—Heidi Jobe, Carrollton, GA

Prep: 25 min. • **Bake:** 25 min.
Makes: 15 servings

- 2 cups all-purpose flour
- 2 cups sugar
- 1 tsp. baking soda
- ½ tsp. salt
- ½ tsp. ground cinnamon
- 1 can (12 oz.) cola
- 1 cup butter, cubed
- ¼ cup baking cocoa
- 2 large eggs
- ½ cup buttermilk
- 1 tsp. vanilla extract

GLAZE

- 1 can (12 oz.) cola
- ½ cup butter, cubed
- ¼ cup baking cocoa
- 4 cups confectioners' sugar, sifted

1. Preheat oven to 350°. Grease a 13x9-in. baking pan.
2. In a large bowl, whisk the first five ingredients. In a small saucepan, combine cola, butter and cocoa; bring just to a boil, stirring occasionally. Add to flour mixture, stirring just until moistened.
3. In a small bowl, whisk eggs, buttermilk and vanilla until blended; add to flour mixture, whisking constantly.
4. Transfer to prepared pan. Bake until a toothpick inserted in center comes out clean, 25-30 minutes.
5. About 15 minutes before cake is done, prepare glaze. In a small saucepan, bring cola to a boil; cook 12-15 minutes or until liquid is reduced to ½ cup. Stir in butter and cocoa until butter is melted; remove from heat. Add confectioners' sugar; stir until smooth. Pour immediately over hot cake.
Per piece: 491 cal., 20g fat (12g sat. fat), 74mg chol., 346mg sod., 78g carb. (63g sugars, 1g fiber), 4g pro.

FRIED CHICKEN DINNER

Nothing's more comforting than chicken when it's seasoned, battered and fried to golden perfection. Pair it with mashed potatoes and biscuits for a meal that's down-home delicious.

BEST-EVER FRIED CHICKEN

(PICTURED ON P. 380)

Family reunions and neighborly gatherings will never be the same when you serve this crispy, juicy and perfectly seasoned fried chicken. I grew up on a farm and every year when it was time to bale hay, my dad would hire farm hands to help. The crew looked forward to coming because they knew they would be treated to my mom's delicious fried chicken.

—Lola Clifton, Vinton, VA

Prep: 15 min. • **Cook:** 20 min.
Makes: 4 servings

- 1¾ cups all-purpose flour
- 1 Tbsp. dried thyme
- 1 Tbsp. paprika
- 2 tsp. salt
- 2 tsp. garlic powder
- 1 tsp. pepper
- 1 large egg
- ⅓ cup whole milk
- 2 Tbsp. lemon juice
- 1 broiler/fryer chicken (3 to 4 lbs.), cut up
- Oil for deep-fat frying

1. In a shallow bowl, mix the first six ingredients. In a separate shallow bowl, whisk egg, milk and lemon juice until blended. Dip chicken in flour mixture to coat all sides; shake off excess. Dip in egg mixture, then again in flour mixture.

2. In an electric skillet or deep fryer, heat oil to 375°. Fry chicken, a few pieces at a time, for 6-10 minutes on each side or until golden brown and chicken juices run clear. Drain on paper towels.

Per serving: 811 cal., 57g fat (9g sat. fat), 176mg chol., 725mg sod., 26g carb. (2g sugars, 2g fiber), 47g pro.

BEST-EVER FRIED CHICKEN

MASHED POTATOES

Mashed potatoes are sensational alongside fried chicken, so keep this recipe handy.
—Taste of Home *Test Kitchen*

Takes: 30 min.
Makes: 6 servings (about 4½ cups)

- 6 medium russet potatoes, (about 2 lbs.), peeled and cubed
- ½ cup warm whole milk or heavy whipping cream
- ¼ cup butter, cubed
- ¾ tsp. salt
- Dash pepper

Place potatoes in a large saucepan; add water to cover. Bring to a boil. Reduce heat to medium; cook, uncovered, until very tender, 20-25 minutes. Drain. Add the remaining ingredients; mash until light and fluffy.
Per ¾ cup: 168 cal., 8g fat (5g sat. fat), 22mg chol., 367mg sod., 22g carb. (3g sugars, 1g fiber), 3g pro.

HERBED GRAVY

This traditional gravy recipe works for any roasted meat or poultry.
—Taste of Home *Test Kitchen*

Takes: 20 min. • **Makes:** 2 cups

- Turkey drippings
- 1 to 1½ cups chicken broth
- ¼ cup all-purpose flour
- ¼ tsp. dried thyme
- ¼ tsp. rubbed sage
- ¼ tsp. pepper

1. Pour drippings and loosened browned bits into a 2-cup measuring cup. Skim fat, reserving ¼ cup. Add enough broth to the drippings to measure 2 cups.
2. In a small saucepan, combine flour and reserved fat until smooth. Gradually stir in the drippings mixture. Stir in the thyme, sage and pepper. Bring to a boil; cook and stir gravy for 2 minutes or until thickened.
Per 2 Tbsp.: 102 cal., 10g fat (5g sat. fat), 11mg chol., 115mg sod., 2g carb. (0 sugars, 0 fiber), 0 pro.

MASHED POTATOES

CREAMY SUCCOTASH

Succotash is famous in the South, and my sister Jenny came up with this colorful and delicious take on it.

—Shannon Koene, Blacksburg, VA

Prep: 10 min. • **Cook:** 20 min. + cooling
Makes: 10 servings

- 4 cups frozen lima beans
- 1 cup water
- 4 cups frozen corn
- ⅔ cup reduced-fat mayonnaise
- 2 tsp. Dijon mustard
- ½ tsp. onion powder
- ½ tsp. garlic powder
- ¼ tsp. salt
- ¼ tsp. pepper
- 2 medium tomatoes, finely chopped
- 1 small onion, finely chopped

1. In a large saucepan, bring lima beans and water to a boil. Reduce heat; cover and simmer for 10 minutes. Add the corn; return to a boil. Reduce heat; cover and simmer 5-6 minutes longer or until vegetables are tender. Drain; cool for 10-15 minutes.
2. Meanwhile, in a large bowl, combine the mayonnaise, mustard, onion powder, garlic powder, salt and pepper. Stir in the bean mixture, tomatoes and onion. Serve immediately or refrigerate.
Per ¾ cup: 198 cal., 6g fat (1g sat. fat), 6mg chol., 238mg sod., 31g carb. (5g sugars, 6g fiber), 7g pro.

DILL & CHIVE PEAS

Growing my own vegetables and herbs makes it easy for me to prepare fresh meals. This recipe is a breeze.

—Tanna Richard, Cedar Rapids, IA

Takes: 10 min. • **Makes:** 4 servings

- 1 pkg. (16 oz.) frozen peas
- ¼ cup snipped fresh dill
- 2 Tbsp. minced fresh chives
- 1 Tbsp. butter
- 1 tsp. lemon-pepper seasoning
- ¼ tsp. kosher salt

Cook the peas according to the package directions. Stir in the remaining ingredients; serve immediately.
Per ¾ cup: 113 cal., 3g fat (2g sat. fat), 8mg chol., 346mg sod., 16g carb. (6g sugars, 5g fiber), 6g pro.

SOUTHERN BUTTERMILK BISCUITS

(PICTURED ON P. 381)

What's fried chicken without traditional buttermilk biscuits? The recipe for these four-ingredient biscuits has been handed down for many generations in my family.

—Fran Thompson, Tarboro, NC

Takes: 30 min. • **Makes:** 8 biscuits

- ½ cup cold butter, cubed
- 2 cups self-rising flour
- ¾ cup buttermilk
- Melted butter

1. In a large bowl, cut butter into flour until mixture resembles coarse crumbs. Stir in buttermilk just until moistened. Turn onto a lightly floured surface; knead 3-4 times. Pat or lightly roll to ¾-in. thickness. Cut with a floured 2½-in. biscuit cutter.
2. Place on a greased baking sheet. Bake at 425° until golden brown, 11-13 minutes. Brush tops with butter. Serve warm.
Per biscuit: 197 cal., 11 g fat (7 g sat. fat), 28 mg chol., 451 mg sod., 22 g carb., 1 g fiber, 4 g pro.

DILL & CHIVE PEAS

EASY FRESH STRAWBERRY PIE

EDITOR'S CHOICE

EASY FRESH STRAWBERRY PIE

We combined my mother's 70th birthday and Mother's Day into one celebration. I decided to make two of these strawberry pies instead of a cake. Since it was mid-May in Texas, the berries were perfect. It was a memorable occasion for the whole family.
—Josh Carter, Birmingham, AL

Prep: 20 min. + cooling
Bake: 15 min. + chilling
Makes: 8 servings

- 1 sheet refrigerated pie crust (9 in.)
- ¾ cup sugar
- 2 Tbsp. cornstarch
- 1 cup water
- 1 pkg. (3 oz.) strawberry gelatin
- 4 cups sliced fresh strawberries
- Fresh mint, optional

1. Line unpricked pie crust with a double thickness of heavy-duty foil. Bake at 450° for 8 minutes. Remove foil; bake 5 minutes longer. Cool on a wire rack.

2. In a small saucepan, combine the sugar, cornstarch and water until smooth. Bring to a boil; cook and stir for 2 minutes or until thickened. Remove from the heat; stir in gelatin until dissolved. Refrigerate for 15-20 minutes or until slightly cooled.

3. Meanwhile, arrange strawberries in the crust. Pour gelatin mixture over berries. Refrigerate until set. Garnish with mint if desired.

Per slice: 264 cal., 7g fat (3g sat. fat), 5mg chol., 125mg sod., 49g carb. (32g sugars, 2g fiber), 2g pro.

CHILI NIGHT

Craving something hot and hearty? Chili to the rescue! Whether it's for a game-day block party or an easy weeknight dinner, this one-pot classic and its accompaniments will hit the spot.

FIREHOUSE CHILI

FIREHOUSE CHILI

As one of the cooks at the firehouse, I used to prepare meals for 10 fighfighters. This chili was among their favorites.

—Richard Clements, San Dimas, CA

Prep: 20 min. • **Cook:** 1½ hours
Makes: 12 servings (about 3 qt.)

- 2 Tbsp. canola oil
- 4 lbs. lean ground beef (90% lean)
- 2 medium onions, chopped
- 1 medium green pepper, chopped
- 4 cans (16 oz. each) kidney beans, rinsed and drained
- 3 cans (14½ oz. each) stewed tomatoes, cut up
- 1 can (14½ oz.) beef broth
- 3 Tbsp. chili powder
- 2 Tbsp. ground coriander
- 2 Tbsp. ground cumin
- 4 garlic cloves, minced
- 1 tsp. dried oregano

In a Dutch oven, heat canola oil over medium heat. Brown beef in batches, crumbling meat, until no longer pink; drain. Add onions and green pepper; cook until tender. Return meat to Dutch oven. Stir in remaining ingredients. Bring to a boil. Reduce heat; simmer, covered, until flavors are blended, about 1½ hours.

Per cup: 444 cal., 16g fat (5g sat. fat), 94mg chol., 703mg sod., 36g carb. (9g sugars, 10g fiber), 41g pro. **Diabetic exchanges:** 5 lean meat, 2½ starch, ½ fat.

TEST KITCHEN TIP

Got leftover chili? Spoon it over baked potatoes, bake into a meat pie, use it to fill burritos or stir it into a prepared box of macaroni and cheese.

OVEN-FRIED CORN BREAD

OVEN-FRIED CORNBREAD

Nothing complements a pot of chili like a crisp cornbread baked in a cast-iron skillet.

—Emory Doty, Jasper, GA

Prep: 20 min. • **Bake:** 15 min.
Makes: 8 servings

- 4 Tbsp. canola oil, divided
- 1½ cups finely ground white cornmeal
- ¼ cup sugar
- 2 tsp. baking powder
- 1 tsp. baking soda
- 1 tsp. salt
- 2 large eggs
- 2 cups buttermilk

1. Place 2 Tbsp. oil in a 10-in. cast-iron skillet; place in oven. Preheat oven to 450°. Whisk together cornmeal, sugar, baking powder, baking soda and salt. In another bowl, whisk together eggs, buttermilk and remaining oil. Add to cornmeal mixture; stir just until moistened.

2. Carefully remove hot skillet from oven. Add batter; bake until golden brown and a toothpick inserted in center comes out clean, 15-20 minutes. Cut into slices; serve warm.

Per serving: 238 cal., 9g fat (1g sat. fat), 49mg chol., 709mg sod., 33g carb. (10g sugars, 1g fiber), 6g pro.

COOL & CREAMY SPINACH DIP

I always keep this easy dip on hand—it encourages me to eat more fresh veggies. The light cottage cheese adds protein and calcium without a lot of added fat.

—Melissa Hansen, Milwaukee, WI

Prep: 10 min. + chilling • **Makes:** 2½ cups

- 1 cup 2% cottage cheese
- 1 pkg. (10 oz.) frozen chopped spinach, thawed and squeezed dry
- 1 cup fat-free sour cream
- 2 Tbsp. fat-free milk
- 1 Tbsp. grated Parmesan-Romano or Parmesan cheese
- 1 Tbsp. reduced-fat ranch salad dressing
- ¼ tsp. dill weed
- ⅛ tsp. garlic powder
- Assorted fresh vegetables

In a food processor, cover and process cottage cheese until smooth. Transfer to a bowl; stir in the spinach, sour cream, milk, Parmesan-Romano cheese, ranch dressing, dill and garlic powder. Cover and refrigerate for 3-4 hours. Serve with vegetables.

Per ¼ cup: 56 cal., 1g fat (0 sat. fat), 8mg chol., 145mg sod., 7g carb. (3g sugars, 1g fiber), 5g pro. **Diabetic exchanges:** ½ starch.

EDITOR'S CHOICE

SOFT BEER PRETZELS

What goes together better than beer and pretzels? Not much that I can think of. That's why I put them together into one delicious recipe. I'm always looking for new ways to unite fun flavors, and these fun bites are proof just how good this combo can be.

—Alyssa Wilhite, Whitehouse, TX

Prep: 1 hour + rising • **Bake:** 10 min.
Makes: 8 pretzels

- 1 bottle (12 oz.) amber beer or nonalcoholic beer
- 1 pkg. (¼ oz.) active dry yeast
- 2 Tbsp. unsalted butter, melted
- 2 Tbsp. sugar
- 1½ tsp. salt
- 4 to 4½ cups all-purpose flour
- 10 cups water
- ⅔ cup baking soda

TOPPING

- 1 large egg yolk
- 1 Tbsp. water
- Coarse salt, optional

1. In a small saucepan, heat the beer to 110°-115°; remove from heat. Stir in yeast until dissolved. In a large bowl, combine butter, sugar, 1½ tsp. salt, yeast mixture and 3 cups flour; beat on medium speed until smooth. Stir in enough remaining flour to form a soft dough (dough will be sticky).

2. Turn dough onto a floured surface; knead until smooth and elastic, 6-8 minutes. Place in a greased bowl, turning once to grease the top. Cover with plastic wrap and let rise in a warm place until doubled, about 1 hour.

3. Preheat oven to 425°. Punch dough down. Turn onto a lightly floured surface; divide and shape into eight balls. Roll each ball into a 24-in. rope. Curve ends of each rope to form a circle; twist ends once and lay over opposite side of circle, pinching ends to seal.

4. In a Dutch oven, bring water and baking soda to a boil. Drop pretzels, two at a time, into boiling water. Cook for 30 seconds. Remove with a slotted spoon; drain well on paper towels.

5. Place 2 in. apart on greased baking sheets. In a small bowl, whisk egg yolk and water; brush over pretzels. Sprinkle with coarse salt, if desired. Bake 10-12 minutes or until golden brown. Remove from pans to a wire rack to cool.

Freeze option Freeze cooled pretzels in resealable plastic freezer bags. To use, thaw at room temperature or, if desired, microwave each pretzel on high until heated through, 20-30 seconds.

Per pretzel: 288 cal., 4g fat (2g sat. fat), 16mg chol., 604mg sod., 53g carb. (6g sugars, 2g fiber), 7g pro.

SOFT BEER PRETZELS

PEANUT BUTTER CHOCOLATE DESSERT

I love the classic combo of chocolate and peanut butter. So when I came up with this no-bake treat, I was in heaven.

—Debbie Price, La Rue, OH

Prep: 20 min. + chilling • **Makes:** 16 servings

- 20 chocolate cream-filled chocolate sandwich cookies, divided
- 2 Tbsp. butter, softened
- 1 pkg. (8 oz.) cream cheese, softened
- ½ cup peanut butter
- 1½ cups confectioners' sugar, divided
- 1 carton (16 oz.) frozen whipped topping, thawed, divided
- 15 miniature peanut butter cups, chopped
- 1 cup whole cold milk
- 1 pkg. (3.9 oz.) instant chocolate fudge pudding mix

1. Crush 16 cookies; toss with the butter. Press into an ungreased 9-in. square dish; set aside.

2. In a large bowl, beat the cream cheese, peanut butter and 1 cup confectioners' sugar until smooth. Fold in half of the whipped topping. Spread over crust. Sprinkle with peanut butter cups.

3. In another large bowl, beat the milk, pudding mix and remaining confectioners' sugar on low speed for 2 minutes. Let stand for 2 minutes or until soft-set. Fold in the remaining whipped topping.

4. Spread over peanut butter cups. Crush remaining cookies; sprinkle over the top. Cover and chill for at least 3 hours.

Per piece: 366 cal., 21g fat (11g sat. fat), 22mg chol., 307mg sod., 40g carb. (28g sugars, 1g fiber), 5g pro.

REFRESHING RASPBERRY ICED TEA

This recipe makes 2 gallons, so it's a great choice for a party when you have a medium-size crowd. It freezes well, so feel free to make it ahead of time.

—Arlana Hendricks, Manchester, TN

Takes: 20 min.
Makes: 16 servings

- 6 cups water
- 1¾ cups sugar
- 8 individual tea bags
- ¾ cup frozen apple-raspberry juice concentrate
- 8 cups cold water
- Ice cubes
- Fresh raspberries, optional

In a large saucepan, bring 6 cups water and sugar to a boil; remove from heat. Add tea bags; steep, covered, 3-5 minutes according to taste. Discard tea bags. Add the juice concentrate; stir in cold water. Serve over ice, with raspberries if desired.

Per cup: 108 cal., 0 fat (0 sat. fat), 0 chol., 7mg sod., 28g carb. (27g sugars, 0 fiber), 0 pro.

BEST OF
TASTE OF HOME
HOLIDAYS

FROM EASTER MORNING BRUNCHES AND FESTIVE CHRISTMAS DINNERS TO HAUNTING HALLOWEEN PARTIES, THERE'S ALWAYS A REASON TO GATHER WITH FAMILY AND FRIENDS FOR FUN AND, OF COURSE, FOOD! WITH THESE DELISH RECIPES, IT'S NEVER BEEN EASIER TO MAKE THE MOST OF EVERY OCCASION—ALL YEAR LONG!

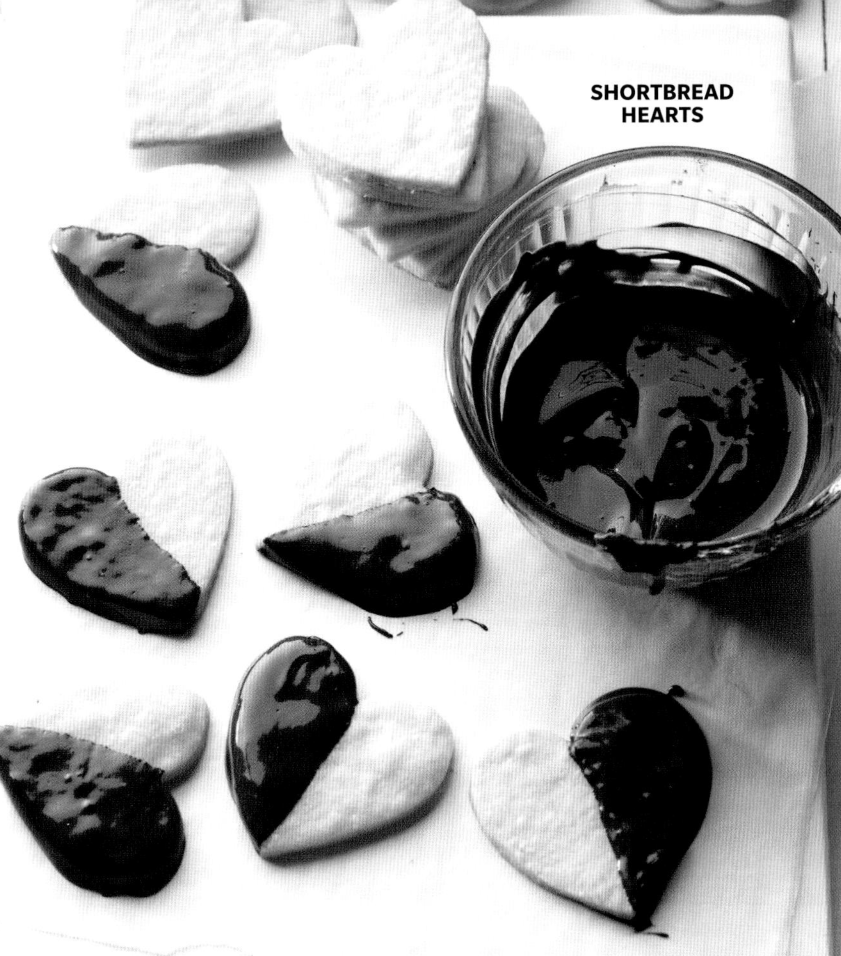

SHORTBREAD HEARTS

These flaky cookies melt in your mouth. Dipped in chocolate, they look festive. If you have time, write names or initials on the hearts with red icing for Valentine's Day.
—Barbara Birk, St. George, UT

Prep: 20 min. + chilling
Bake: 15 min. + cooling
Makes: about 2 dozen

- 2 cups all-purpose flour
- ½ cup sugar
- Dash salt
- 1 cup cold butter, cubed
- 1 Tbsp. cold water
- 1 tsp. almond extract
- ½ lb. dark chocolate candy coating, melted

1. In a large bowl, combine the flour, sugar and salt; cut in the butter until the mixture resembles coarse crumbs. Stir in water and extract until mixture forms a ball.
2. On a lightly floured surface, roll out dough to ¼-in. thickness. Cut with a lightly floured 2½-in. cookie cutter. Place 1 in. apart on ungreased baking sheets. Cover and refrigerate for 30 minutes.
3. Bake at 325° for 13-16 minutes or until edges are lightly browned. Cool cookies for 2 minutes before removing to wire racks to cool completely. Dip one side of cookies in candy coating; allow excess to drip off. Place on waxed paper; let stand until set.

Per cookie: 171 cal., 10g fat (7g sat. fat), 20mg chol., 83mg sod., 19g carb. (10g sugars, 0 fiber), 1g pro.

EDITOR'S CHOICE

CONTEST-WINNING ORANGE-GLAZED CORNISH HENS

This is an elegant, impressive entree to serve at a cozy Valentine's Day dinner.
—Laurie Bartley, Lake Hiawatha, NJ

Prep: 10 min. • **Bake:** 1¼ hours
Makes: 4 servings

- 4 Cornish game hens (20 to 24 oz. each)
- ¼ cup butter, melted
- 1 tsp. salt
- ½ tsp. pepper
- ¾ cup orange juice
- ½ cup packed brown sugar
- ½ cup Madeira wine, sherry or chicken broth
- 2 Tbsp. lemon juice
- 1 tsp. ground mustard
- ¼ tsp. ground allspice

1. Tie legs of each hen together; turn wing tips under backs. Place on a greased rack in a roasting pan. Brush with butter; sprinkle with salt and pepper. Bake, uncovered, at 350° for 1 hour.
2. In a saucepan, combine the remaining ingredients; bring to a boil. Reduce heat; simmer, uncovered, for 15 minutes. Spoon over hens. Bake 15 minutes longer or until a thermometer reads 180°.

Per serving: 682 cal., 40g fat (15g sat. fat), 235mg chol., 819mg sod., 36g carb. (35g sugars, 0 fiber), 35g pro.

MADE WITH LOVE

These Cornish hens were the winners of the first contest I judged for *Taste of Home* back in 2001. They were so delicious, they instantly became a staple on my holiday menus.

MARK HAGEN
TASTE OF HOME BOOKS

SHRIMP GUMBO

What's Mardi Gras without a traditional shrimp gumbo? A crisp green salad and crusty French bread complete this for me. Don't be afraid to add extra hot sauce.
—Jo Ann Graham, Ovilla, TX

Prep: 30 min. • **Cook:** 1 hour
Makes: 11 servings

- ¼ cup all-purpose flour
- ¼ cup canola oil
- 3 celery ribs, chopped
- 1 medium green pepper, chopped
- 1 medium onion, chopped
- 1 carton (32 oz.) chicken broth
- 3 garlic cloves, minced
- 1 tsp. salt
- 1 tsp. pepper
- ½ tsp. cayenne pepper
- 2 lbs. uncooked large shrimp, peeled and deveined
- 1 pkg. (16 oz.) frozen sliced okra
- 4 green onions, sliced
- 1 medium tomato, chopped
- 1½ tsp. gumbo file powder
- Hot cooked rice

1. In a Dutch oven over medium heat, cook and stir flour and oil until caramel-colored, about 12 minutes (do not burn). Add the celery, green pepper and onion; cook and stir for 5-6 minutes or until tender. Stir in the broth, garlic, salt, pepper and cayenne; bring to a boil. Reduce heat; cover and simmer for 30 minutes.
2. Stir in the shrimp, okra, green onions and tomato. Return to a boil. Reduce the heat; cover and simmer for 10 minutes or until shrimp turn pink. Stir in file powder. Serve with rice.
Note Gumbo file powder, used to thicken and flavor Creole recipes, is available in spice shops. If you can't find file powder, combine 2 Tbsp. each cornstarch and water until smooth. Gradually stir into gumbo. Bring to a boil; cook and stir for 2 minutes or until thickened.
Per cup: 159 cal., 7g fat (1g sat. fat), 102mg chol., 681mg sod., 9g carb. (3g sugars, 2g fiber), 15g pro. **Diabetic exchanges:** 2 lean meat, 1 vegetable, 1 fat.

SWEET CORN BEIGNETS WITH BACON-SUGAR DUST

Opposites attract deliciously in these irresistible beignets—crispy outside and soft and fluffy inside. Salty bacon sugar contrasts nicely with the sweet corn in the pastries.
—Cheryl Perry, Hertford, NC

Prep: 25 min. + rising • **Cook:** 5 min/batch
Makes: 4 dozen

- 1 pkg. (¼ oz.) active dry yeast
- 1 cup warm 2% milk (110° to 115°)
- 1¼ cups fresh or frozen corn, thawed
- ¼ cup sugar
- 2 large eggs
- ¼ cup butter, melted
- 1 tsp. salt
- 1 tsp. vanilla extract
- 4½ to 5 cups all-purpose flour
- 2 cups confectioners' sugar
- 6 cooked bacon strips
- Oil for deep-fat frying

1. In a large bowl, dissolve yeast in warm milk. Add the corn, sugar, eggs, butter, salt, vanilla and 4½ cups flour. Beat until smooth. Stir in enough remaining flour to form a soft dough (dough will be sticky).
2. Turn onto a floured surface; knead until smooth and elastic, about 6-8 minutes. Place in a greased bowl, turning once to grease the top. Cover and let rise in a warm place until doubled, about 1 hour.
3. Meanwhile, in a food processor, combine confectioners' sugar and bacon. Process until combined; set aside.
4. Punch dough down. Turn onto a lightly floured surface; roll dough into a 16x12-in. rectangle. Cut into 2-in. squares.
5. In an electric skillet or deep-fat fryer, heat oil to 375°. Fry squares, a few at a time, until golden brown, about 1½ minutes on each side. Drain on paper towels. Dust with bacon-sugar mixture. Serve warm.
Note These beignets are best served the day they're made.
Per beignet: 117 cal., 5g fat (1g sat. fat), 13mg chol., 84mg sod., 17g carb. (7g sugars, 0 fiber), 2g pro.

TRADITIONAL NEW ORLEANS KING CAKE

TRADITIONAL NEW ORLEANS KING CAKE

Get in on the fun of the king cake. Hide a little toy baby in the cake. Whoever finds it has one year of good luck!

—Rebecca Baird, Salt Lake City, UT

Prep: 40 min. + rising
Bake: 25 min. + cooling
Makes: 1 cake (12 slices)

- 2 pkg. (¼ oz. each) active dry yeast
- ½ cup warm water (110° to 115°)
- ¾ cup sugar, divided
- ½ cup butter, softened
- ½ cup warm 2% milk (110° to 115°)
- 2 large egg yolks
- 1¼ tsp. salt
- 1 tsp. grated lemon peel
- ¼ tsp. ground nutmeg
- 3¼ to 3¾ cups all-purpose flour
- 1 tsp. ground cinnamon
- 1 large egg, beaten

GLAZE

- 1½ cups confectioners' sugar
- 2 tsp. lemon juice
- 2 to 3 Tbsp. water
- Green, purple and yellow sugars

1. In a large bowl, dissolve yeast in warm water. Add ½ cup sugar, butter, milk, egg yolks, salt, lemon peel, nutmeg and 2 cups flour. Beat until smooth. Stir in enough remaining flour to form a soft dough (dough will be sticky).

2. Turn onto a floured surface; knead until smooth and elastic, about 6-8 minutes. Place in a greased bowl, turning once to grease the top. Cover and let rise in a warm place until doubled, about 1 hour.

3. Punch dough down. Turn onto a lightly floured surface. Roll into a 16 x10-in. rectangle. Combine cinnamon and remaining sugar; sprinkle over dough to within ½ in. of edges. Roll up jelly-roll style, starting with a long side; pinch seam to seal. Place seam side down on a greased baking sheet; pinch ends together to form a ring. Cover and let rise until doubled, about 1 hour. Brush with egg.

4. Bake at 375° for 25-30 minutes or until golden brown. Cool completely on a wire rack. For glaze, combine the confectioners' sugar, lemon juice and enough water to achieve desired consistency. Spread over cake. Sprinkle with colored sugars.

Per slice: 168 cal., 8g fat (5g sat. fat), 22mg chol., 367mg sod., 22g carb. (3g sugars, 1g fiber), 3g pro.

HOMEMADE IRISH CREAM

Add some creamy goodness to your cup of joe with a splash of this alcohol-free version of the Irish favorite.

—Marcia Severson, Hallock, MN

Takes: 10 min. • **Makes:** 3⅓ cups

- 1 can (12 oz.) evaporated milk
- 1 cup heavy whipping cream
- ½ cup 2% milk
- ¼ cup sugar
- 2 Tbsp. chocolate syrup
- 1 Tbsp. instant coffee granules
- 2 tsp. vanilla extract
- ¼ tsp. almond extract

EACH SERVING

- ½ cup brewed coffee

In a blender, combine the first eight ingredients; cover and process until smooth. Store in the refrigerator. For each serving, place coffee in a mug. Stir in ⅓ cup Irish cream. Heat mixture in a microwave if desired.

Per serving: 165 cal., 11g fat (7g sat. fat), 44mg chol., 53mg sod., 12g carb. (11g sugars, 0 fiber), 3g pro.

MADE WITH LOVE

Very good! I made a practice round before St. Patrick's Day and served it alone over some ice. Everyone loved it...perfect amount of chocolate and coffee and cream flavor.

MIKIBUNNY31 TASTEOFHOME.COM

HOMEMADE IRISH CREAM

NANNY'S PARMESAN MASHED POTATOES

My grandsons rave over these creamy potatoes loaded with Parmesan. That's all the endorsement I need. Sometimes I use golden or red potatoes, with skins on.
—Kallee Krong-McCreery, Escondido, CA

Prep: 20 min. • **Cook:** 20 min.
Makes: 12 servings

- 5 lbs. potatoes, peeled and cut into 1-in. pieces
- ¾ cup butter, softened
- ¾ cup sour cream
- ½ cup grated Parmesan cheese
- 1¼ tsp. garlic salt
- 1 tsp. salt
- ½ tsp. pepper
- ¾ to 1 cup 2% milk, warmed
- 2 Tbsp. minced fresh parsley

1. Place potatoes in a 6-qt. stockpot; add water to cover. Bring to a boil. Reduce heat; cook, uncovered, 10-15 minutes or until tender. Drain potatoes; return to pot and stir over low heat 1 minute to dry.
2. Coarsely mash potatoes, gradually adding butter, sour cream, cheese, seasonings and enough milk to reach desired consistency. Stir in parsley.
Per ¾ cup: 264 cal., 15g fat (10g sat. fat), 45mg chol., 456mg sod., 27g carb. (3g sugars, 2g fiber), 5g pro.

TOASTED REUBENS

TOASTED REUBENS

New Yorkers say my Reubens taste like those served in the famous delis there. Omit the horseradish for a milder flavor.
—Patricia Kile, Elizabethtown, PA

Takes: 20 min. • **Makes:** 4 servings

- 4 tsp. prepared mustard
- 8 slices rye bread
- 4 slices Swiss cheese
- 1 lb. thinly sliced deli corned beef
- 1 can (8 oz.) sauerkraut, rinsed and well drained
- ½ cup mayonnaise
- 3 Tbsp. ketchup
- 2 Tbsp. sweet pickle relish
- 1 Tbsp. prepared horseradish
- 2 Tbsp. butter

1. Spread mustard over four slices of bread. Layer with the cheese, corned beef and sauerkraut. In a bowl, mix mayonnaise, ketchup, relish and horseradish; spread over remaining the bread. Place over the sauerkraut. Spread outsides of sandwiches with butter.
2. In a large skillet, toast sandwiches over medium heat 3-4 minutes on each side or until golden brown and cheese is melted.
Per sandwich: 705 cal., 45g fat (15g sat. fat), 124mg chol., 2830mg sod., 41g carb. (9g sugars, 6g fiber), 34g pro.

CREME DE MENTHE CUPCAKES

CREME DE MENTHE CUPCAKES

We use creme de menthe, a liqueur that means mint cream in French, to add a cool touch to these impressive mascarpone-frosted cupcakes.

—Keri Whitney, Castro Valley, CA

Prep: 30 min. • Bake: 15 min. + cooling
Makes: about 1 dozen

- ¾ cup butter, softened
- 1 cup granulated sugar
- 2 large eggs, room temperature
- ½ tsp. mint extract
- 1½ cups cake flour
- 1½ tsp. baking powder
- ¼ tsp. salt
- ⅔ cup 2% milk
- 2 Tbsp. white (clear) creme de menthe
- Green paste food coloring

FROSTING

- 1 carton (8 oz.) mascarpone cheese
- ⅓ cup heavy whipping cream
- ¼ cup confectioners' sugar
- 4 tsp. white (clear) creme de menthe
- Green paste food coloring

1. Preheat oven to 350°. Cream butter and granulated sugar until light and fluffy. Add the eggs, one at a time, beating well after each addition. Add mint extract. In another bowl, whisk flour, baking powder and salt; add to creamed mixture alternately with milk and creme de menthe, beating well after each addition. Transfer two cups batter to a separate bowl. Mix food coloring paste into remaining batter.

2. Cut a small hole in the tip of a pastry bag or in a corner of a food-safe plastic bag; insert a #12 round tip. Spoon the batters alternately into bag. Pipe batter into 12 paper-lined muffin cups until three-fourths full. Bake until a toothpick comes out clean, 15-20 minutes. Cool 10 minutes; remove from pan to a wire rack to cool completely.

3. For frosting, stir the mascarpone and whipping cream together until smooth. Add the confectioners' sugar and creme de menthe; stir until blended. Transfer half the frosting to a separate bowl and mix food coloring paste into remaining frosting. Stir each portion vigorously until stiff peaks form (do not overmix).

4. Cut a small hole in the tip of a pastry bag or corner of a food-safe plastic bag; insert a #12 round tip. Add frostings alternately into bag. Pipe onto cupcakes. Refrigerate leftovers.

Per cupcake: 372 cal., 24g fat (14g sat. fat), 95mg chol., 222mg sod., 35g carb. (21g sugars, 0 fiber), 5g pro.

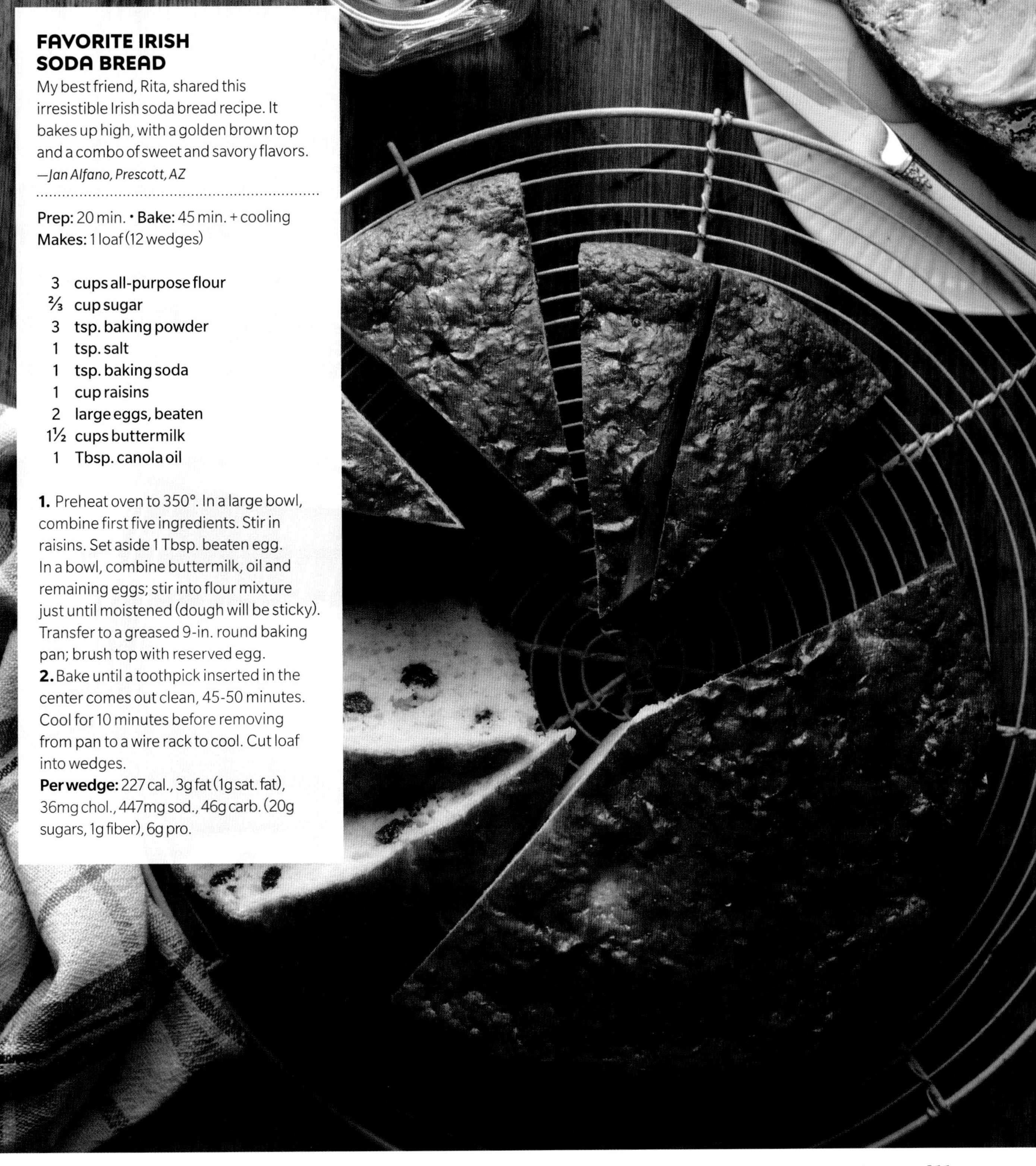

FAVORITE IRISH SODA BREAD

My best friend, Rita, shared this irresistible Irish soda bread recipe. It bakes up high, with a golden brown top and a combo of sweet and savory flavors.
—Jan Alfano, Prescott, AZ

Prep: 20 min. • **Bake:** 45 min. + cooling
Makes: 1 loaf (12 wedges)

- 3 cups all-purpose flour
- ⅔ cup sugar
- 3 tsp. baking powder
- 1 tsp. salt
- 1 tsp. baking soda
- 1 cup raisins
- 2 large eggs, beaten
- 1½ cups buttermilk
- 1 Tbsp. canola oil

1. Preheat oven to 350°. In a large bowl, combine first five ingredients. Stir in raisins. Set aside 1 Tbsp. beaten egg. In a bowl, combine buttermilk, oil and remaining eggs; stir into flour mixture just until moistened (dough will be sticky). Transfer to a greased 9-in. round baking pan; brush top with reserved egg.
2. Bake until a toothpick inserted in the center comes out clean, 45-50 minutes. Cool for 10 minutes before removing from pan to a wire rack to cool. Cut loaf into wedges.

Per wedge: 227 cal., 3g fat (1g sat. fat), 36mg chol., 447mg sod., 46g carb. (20g sugars, 1g fiber), 6g pro.

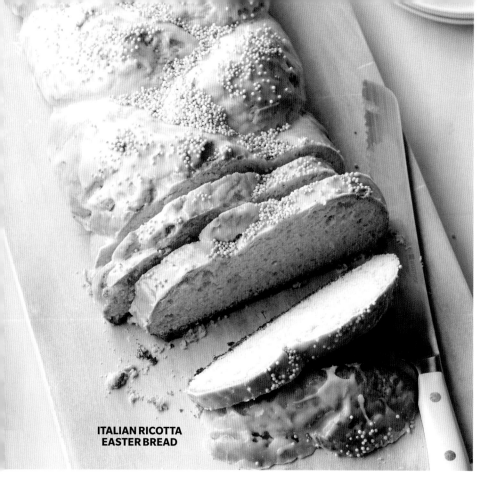

ITALIAN RICOTTA EASTER BREAD

ITALIAN RICOTTA EASTER BREAD

I tweaked our family's traditional Easter bread by adding ricotta cheese. The almond extract yields a delicately sweet taste but you can add any flavor you choose.
—Tina Mirilovich, Johnstown, PA

Prep: 30 min. • **Bake:** 45 min.
Makes: 18 servings

- ¾ cup plain or butter-flavored shortening, room temperature
- 1½ cups granulated sugar
- 3 large eggs, room temperature
- 3 large egg yolks, room temperature
- 1 cup whole-milk ricotta cheese
- 1 tsp. almond extract (or flavor of choice)
- 6 cups all-purpose flour
- 1 Tbsp. baking powder
- 1 tsp. salt
- ½ cup 2% milk

GLAZE

- 1½ cups confectioners' sugar
- 3 Tbsp. 2% milk
- ½ tsp. almond extract (or flavor of choice)
- Sliced toasted almonds or assorted sprinkles

1. Preheat oven to 350°. Cream shortening and sugar until light and fluffy. Add eggs and egg yolks, one at a time, beating well after each addition. Beat in ricotta and extract. In another bowl, whisk flour, baking powder and salt; add to creamed mixture alternately with milk, beating well after each addition, stirring in final 1 cup flour by hand.

2. Turn onto a lightly floured surface; divide into thirds. Roll each into an 18-in. rope. Place ropes on a parchment paper-lined baking sheet and braid. Pinch ends to seal; tuck under braid. Bake until a toothpick inserted in the center comes out clean, 45-55 minutes (do not overbake). Remove to wire racks to cool.

3. Meanwhile, beat confectioners' sugar, milk and extract until smooth. Brush on bread while still warm; top with sliced almonds or sprinkles.

Note To toast nuts, bake in a shallow pan in a 350° oven for 5-10 minutes or cook in a skillet over low heat until lightly browned, stirring occasionally.

Per piece: 376 cal., 11g fat (4g sat. fat), 68mg chol., 247mg sod., 60g carb. (28g sugars, 1g fiber), 8g pro.

TANGY POPPY SEED FRUIT SALAD

For a fruit salad that's delightful, we combine berries and citrus with a honey lime dressing flecked with poppy seeds.
—Carrie Howell, Lehi, UT

Takes: 20 min. • **Makes:** 10 servings

- 1 can (20 oz.) unsweetened pineapple chunks, drained
- 1 lb. fresh strawberries, quartered
- 2 cups fresh blueberries
- 2 cups fresh raspberries
- 2 medium navel oranges, peeled and sectioned
- 2 medium kiwifruit, peeled, halved and sliced

DRESSING

- 2 to 4 Tbsp. honey
- ½ tsp. grated lime peel
- 2 Tbsp. lime juice
- 2 tsp. poppy seeds

Place all fruit in a large bowl. In a small bowl, whisk dressing ingredients. Drizzle over fruit; toss gently to combine.

Per ⅔ cup: 117 cal., 1g fat (0 sat. fat), 0 chol., 3mg sod., 29g carb. (21g sugars, 5g fiber), 2g pro. **Diabetic exchanges:** 2 fruit.

BIRD NESTS

BIRD NESTS

I love Peeps, the perennial springtime favorite. They make perfect mother birds for these pretzel nests with candy eggs.
—Jessica Boivin, Nekoosa, WI

Prep: 40 min. • **Makes:** 2 dozen

- 2 pkg. (10 to 12 oz. each) white baking chips
- 1 pkg. (10 oz.) pretzel sticks
- 24 yellow chicks Peeps candy
- 1 pkg. (12 oz.) M&M's eggs or other egg-shaped candy

1. In a large metal bowl over simmering water, melt white baking chips; stir until smooth. Reserve ½ cup melted chips for decorations; keep warm.
2. Add pretzel sticks to remaining chips; stir to coat evenly. Drop mixture into 24 mounds on waxed paper; shape into bird nests using two forks.
3. Dip bottoms of Peeps in reserved chips; place in nests. Attach eggs with remaining chips. Let stand until set.
Per nest: 276 cal., 11g fat (7g sat. fat), 7mg chol., 215mg sod., 41g carb. (30g sugars, 1g fiber), 4g pro.

APRICOT & MANGO-GLAZED HAM

Mango chutney adds pleasant sweetness to the glaze on this elegant ham, which bakes up moist and juicy. It's perfect for festive spring occasions like Easter.
—Chinarose, TasteOfHome.com

Prep: 20 min. • **Bake:** 2 hours + standing
Makes: 18 servings

- 1 boneless fully cooked ham (6 lbs.)
- 2 tsp. whole cloves
- 2 cups apple cider or juice
- ¼ cup apricot preserves
- 3 Tbsp. mango chutney
- 3 Tbsp. Dijon mustard
- 1 cup packed brown sugar

1. Place ham on a rack in a shallow roasting pan. Score the surface of the ham, making diamond shapes ½ in. deep; insert a clove in each diamond. Pour cider into pan.
2. In a small saucepan, combine the preserves, chutney and mustard. Cook and stir over medium heat until preserves are melted; brush over ham. Press brown sugar onto ham.
3. Bake, uncovered, at 325° for 2-2½ hours or until a thermometer reads 140°, basting occasionally with pan drippings. Cover loosely with foil if ham browns too quickly. Let stand for 10 minutes before slicing.
Per 5 oz.: 243 cal., 5g fat (2g sat. fat), 77mg chol., 1666mg sod., 21g carb. (18g sugars, 0 fiber), 28g pro.

MEXICAN STREET CORN BAKE

MEXICAN STREET CORN BAKE

We discovered Mexican street corn at a festival. This easy one-pan version saves on prep and cleanup. Every August, I freeze a lot of our own fresh sweet corn, and I use that in this recipe, but store-bought corn works just as well.

—Erin Wright, Wallace, KS

Prep: 10 min. • **Bake:** 35 min.
Makes: 6 servings

- 6 cups frozen corn (about 30 oz.), thawed and drained
- 1 cup mayonnaise
- 1 tsp. ground chipotle pepper
- ¼ tsp. salt
- ¼ tsp. pepper
- 6 Tbsp. chopped green onions, divided
- ½ cup grated Parmesan cheese
- Lime wedges, optional

1. Preheat oven to 350°. Mix first five ingredients and 4 Tbsp. green onions; transfer to a greased 1½-qt. baking dish. Sprinkle with cheese.

2. Bake, covered, 20 minutes. Uncover; bake until bubbly and lightly browned, 15-20 minutes. Sprinkle with remaining green onions. If desired, serve with lime wedges.

Per ⅔ cup: 391 cal., 30g fat (5g sat. fat), 8mg chol., 423mg sod., 30g carb. (4g sugars, 3g fiber), 6g pro.

Add a jar of drained pimientos or chopped red or orange bell pepper to this corn casserole for a little extra pop of color.

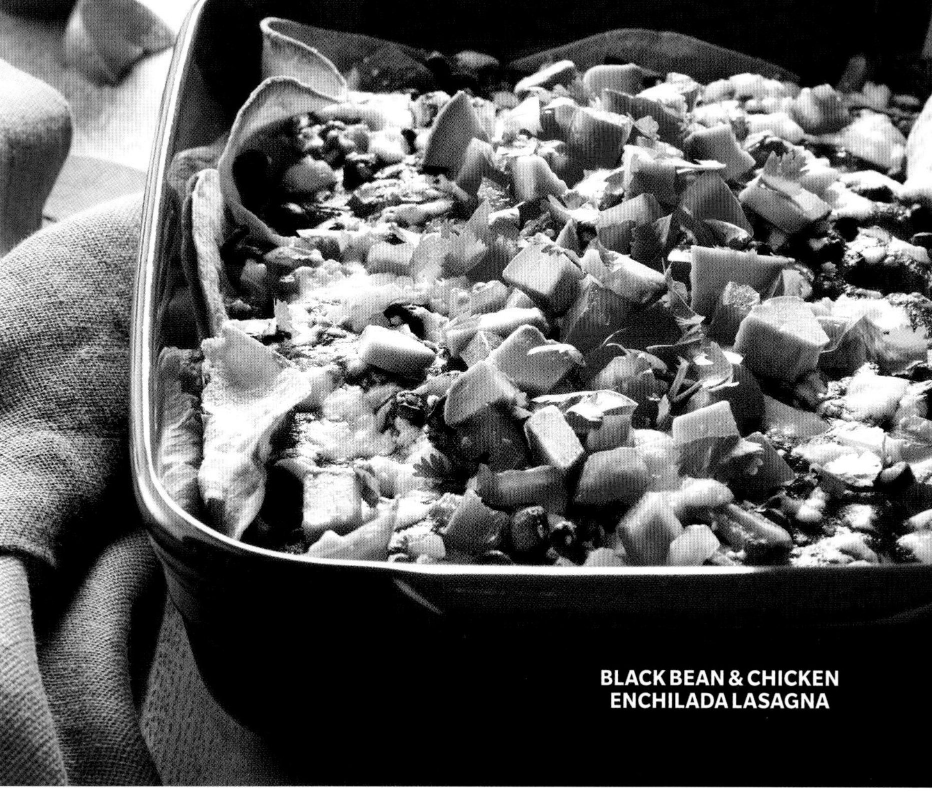

BLACK BEAN & CHICKEN ENCHILADA LASAGNA

BLACK BEAN & CHICKEN ENCHILADA LASAGNA

Twice a month I make chicken enchiladas, lasagna-style. It's a regular with us because assembly is easy and my whole family gives it a thumbs-up.

—Cheryl Snavely, Hagerstown, MD

Prep: 30 min.
Bake: 25 min. + standing
Makes: 8 servings

- 2 cans (10 oz. each) enchilada sauce
- 12 corn tortillas (6 in.)
- 2 cups coarsely shredded rotisserie chicken
- 1 small onion, chopped
- 1 can (15 oz.) black beans, rinsed and drained
- 3 cans (4 oz. each) whole green chilies, drained and coarsely chopped
- 3 cups crumbled queso fresco or shredded Mexican cheese blend
- 2 medium ripe avocados
- 2 Tbsp. sour cream
- 2 Tbsp. lime juice
- ½ tsp. salt
- Chopped fresh tomatoes and cilantro

1. Preheat oven to 350°. Spread ½ cup enchilada sauce into a greased 13x9-in. baking dish; top with four tortillas, 1 cup chicken, ¼ cup onion, ¼ cup beans, ⅓ cup green chilies and 1 cup cheese. Repeat layers. Drizzle with ½ cup enchilada sauce; top with the remaining tortillas, onion, beans, chilies, sauce and cheese.

2. Bake, uncovered, 25-30 minutes or until bubbly and cheese is melted. Let stand for 10 minutes before serving.

3. Meanwhile, quarter, peel and pit one avocado; place avocado in a food processor. Add sour cream, lime juice and salt; process until smooth. Peel, pit and cut remaining avocado into small cubes.

4. Top lasagna with tomatoes, cilantro and cubed avocado. Serve with avocado sauce.

Per piece with 1 Tbsp. sauce: 407 cal., 18g fat (7g sat. fat), 64mg chol., 857mg sod., 39g carb. (4g sugars, 8g fiber), 28g pro.

SHAVED BRUSSELS SPROUT SALAD

FRUITY CHICKEN SALAD MINI SANDWICHES

Chicken salad ranks among the classics, and this version is great for parties of all kinds. Feel free to substitute green grapes for the red, or toss in extra strawberries when they're in season. The filling can also be served on a bed of salad greens.
—Marcy Kamery, Blasdell, NY

Takes: 25 min. • **Makes:** 12 servings

- 6 cups chopped cooked chicken
- ¾ cup sliced fresh strawberries
- ½ cup halved seedless red grapes
- 2 celery ribs, finely chopped
- ⅓ cup chopped pecans, toasted
- ¾ cup sour cream
- ¾ cup mayonnaise
- ⅓ cup chopped fresh basil
- 2 tsp. lemon juice
- ¾ tsp. salt
- ¼ tsp. garlic powder
- ¼ tsp. pepper
- 24 potato dinner rolls or Hawaiian sweet rolls, split

1. Place first five ingredients in a large bowl. In a small bowl, mix sour cream, mayonnaise, basil, lemon juice and seasonings; stir into chicken mixture. Refrigerate, covered, until serving.
2. To serve, fill each sandwich with ⅓ cup chicken mixture.
Note To toast nuts, bake in a shallow pan in a 350° oven for 5-10 minutes or cook in a skillet over low heat until lightly browned, stirring occasionally.
Per 2 sandwiches: 524 cal., 23g fat (5g sat. fat), 67mg chol., 669mg sod., 49g carb. (8g sugars, 3g fiber), 29g pro.

SHAVED BRUSSELS SPROUTS SALAD

The first time my friends tasted this tasty side dish they said it was phenomenal. The sprouts will become more tender the longer the salad chills in the fridge.
—Nick Iverson, Denver, CO

Prep: 20 min. + chilling • **Makes:** 6 servings

- 1 Tbsp. cider vinegar
- 1 Tbsp. Dijon mustard
- 2 tsp. honey
- 1 small garlic clove, minced
- 2 Tbsp. olive oil
- 1 lb. Brussels sprouts, halved and thinly sliced
- 1 small red onion, halved and thinly sliced
- ⅓ cup dried cherries, chopped
- ⅓ cup chopped pecans, toasted

1. Whisk together first four ingredients; gradually whisk in oil until blended.
2. Place the Brussels sprouts, onion and cherries in a large bowl; toss with dressing. Refrigerate, covered, at least 1 hour. Stir in pecans just before serving.
Per ¾ cup: 156 cal., 9g fat (1g sat. fat), 0 chol., 79mg sod., 18g carb. (10g sugars, 4g fiber), 3g pro. **Diabetic exchanges:** 2 fat, 1 vegetable, ½ starch.

FRUITY CHICKEN SALAD MINI SANDWICHES

HAZELNUT ASPARAGUS SOUP

My heart is happy when bundles of tender local asparagus start to appear at my grocery store in spring. No one would ever guess this restaurant-quality vegetarian soup can be prepared in less than 30 minutes.

—Cindy Beberman, Orland Park, IL

Prep: 20 min. • **Cook:** 15 min.
Makes: 4 servings (3 cups)

- 1 Tbsp. olive oil
- ½ cup chopped sweet onion
- 3 garlic cloves, sliced
- Dash crushed red pepper flakes
- 2½ cups cut fresh asparagus (about 1½ lbs.), trimmed
- 2 cups vegetable broth
- ⅓ cup whole hazelnuts, toasted
- 2 Tbsp. chopped fresh basil
- 2 Tbsp. lemon juice
- ½ cup unsweetened almond milk
- 2 tsp. gluten-free reduced-sodium tamari soy sauce
- ¼ tsp. salt
- Shaved asparagus, optional

1. In a large saucepan, heat oil over medium heat. Add onion, garlic and pepper flakes; cook and stir until onion is softened, 4-5 minutes. Add asparagus and broth; bring to a boil. Reduce heat; simmer, covered, until asparagus is tender, 6-8 minutes. Remove from heat; cool slightly.

2. Place nuts, basil and lemon juice in a blender. Add asparagus mixture. Process until smooth and creamy. Return to saucepan. Stir in almond milk, tamari sauce and salt. Heat through, taking care not to boil soup. If desired, top with shaved asparagus.

Note To toast nuts, bake in a shallow pan in a 350° oven for 5-10 minutes or cook in a skillet over low heat until lightly browned, stirring occasionally.

Per ¾ cup: 164 cal., 13g fat (1g sat. fat), 0 chol., 623mg sod., 11g carb. (4g sugars, 4g fiber), 5g pro. **Diabetic exchanges:** 2½ fat, ½ starch.

APRICOT-ROSEMARY SCONES

Make these easy sweet-savory scones a family project. Baking them is a delightful way to show your love on Mother's Day.
—Charlene Chambers, Ormond Beach, FL

Prep: 25 min. • **Bake:** 15 min.
Makes: 16 scones

- 4 cups all-purpose flour
- 2 Tbsp. sugar
- 2 Tbsp. baking powder
- ¾ tsp. salt
- 1½ cups cold butter, cubed
- 1 cup chopped dried apricots
- 1 Tbsp. minced fresh rosemary
- 4 large eggs, lightly beaten
- 1 cup cold heavy whipping cream

TOPPING

- 1 large egg, lightly beaten
- 2 Tbsp. 2% milk
- 2 tsp. sugar

1. Preheat oven to 400°. Whisk together flour, sugar, baking powder and salt. Cut in cold butter until the size of peas. Stir in apricots and rosemary.
2. In a separate bowl, whisk eggs and whipping cream until blended. Stir into flour-butter mixture just until moistened.
3. Turn onto a well-floured surface. Roll dough into a 10-in. square. Cut into four squares; cut each square into four triangles. Place on baking sheets lined with parchment paper.
4. For topping, combine egg and milk. Brush tops of scones with egg mixture; sprinkle with sugar. Bake until golden brown, 12-15 minutes.

Freeze option Freeze cooled scones in resealable plastic freezer bags. To use, reheat in a preheated 350° oven for 20-25 minutes, adding time as necessary to heat through.

Per scone: 372 cal., 25g fat (15g sat. fat), 121mg chol., 461mg sod., 32g carb. (7g sugars, 1g fiber), 6g pro.

APRICOT-ROSEMARY SCONES

STAR-SPANGLED LEMON ICEBOX PIE

STAR-SPANGLED LEMON ICEBOX PIE

With a little chill time, my no-bake lemon pie turns into a potluck superstar. My kids like to arrange the berries in a star pattern.

—Lauren Katz, Ashburn, VA

Prep: 35 min. + chilling • **Makes:** 8 servings

- 15 pecan shortbread cookies (about 8 oz.)
- 1 Tbsp. sugar
- 3 Tbsp. butter, melted

FILLING

- 8 oz. cream cheese, softened
- ½ cup mascarpone cheese
- 1 Tbsp. grated lemon zest
- ½ cup lemon juice
- 1 can (14 oz.) sweetened condensed milk
- 1 cup sliced fresh strawberries
- 1 cup fresh blueberries

1. Preheat oven to 350°. Place cookies and sugar in a food processor; process until cookies are ground. Add melted butter; pulse just until combined. Press mixture onto bottom and up sides of an ungreased 9-in. pie plate. Bake for 15-20 minutes or until lightly browned. Cool completely on a wire rack.

2. In a large bowl, beat cream cheese, mascarpone cheese, lemon zest and lemon juice until smooth; gradually beat in milk.

3. Spread into prepared crust. Refrigerate, covered, at least 4 hours or until filling is set. Top with berries before serving.

Per serving: 591 cal., 41g fat (20g sat. fat), 104mg chol., 310mg sod., 52g carb. (38g sugars, 1g fiber), 10g pro.

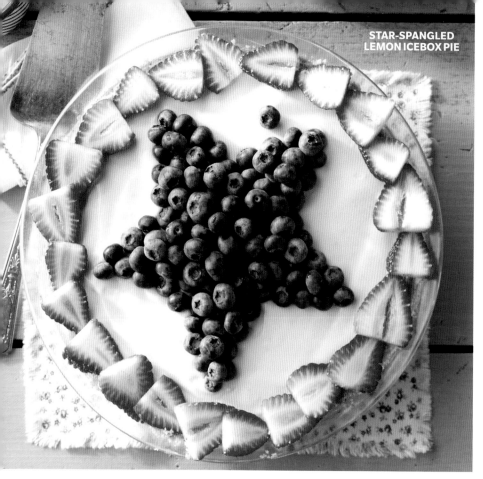

COLORFUL CORNBREAD SALAD

When my garden comes in, I harvest the veggies for potluck dishes. I live in the South, and we think bacon and cornbread make everything better, even salad!

—Rebecca Clark, Warrior, AL

Prep: 45 min. + chilling
Makes: 14 servings

- 1 pkg. (8½ oz.) cornbread/muffin mix
- 1 cup mayonnaise
- ½ cup sour cream
- 1 envelope ranch salad dressing mix
- 1 to 2 Tbsp. adobo sauce from canned chipotle peppers
- 4 to 6 cups torn romaine
- 4 medium tomatoes, chopped
- 1 medium green pepper, chopped
- 1 medium onion, chopped
- 1 lb. bacon strips, cooked and crumbled
- 4 cups shredded cheddar cheese
- Additional tomato and crumbled bacon, optional

1. Preheat oven to 400°. Prepare cornbread batter according to package directions. Pour into a greased 8-in. square baking pan. Bake 15-20 minutes or until a toothpick inserted in center comes out clean. Cool completely in pan on a wire rack.

2. Coarsely crumble the cornbread into a large bowl. In a small bowl, mix the mayonnaise, sour cream, salad dressing mix and adobo sauce.

3. In a 3-qt. trifle bowl or glass bowl, layer a third of the cornbread and half of each of the following: romaine, tomatoes, pepper, onion, bacon, cheese and mayonnaise mixture. Repeat layers. Top with remaining cornbread and, if desired, additional chopped tomato and bacon. Refrigerate, covered, 2-4 hours before serving.

Per ¾ cup: 407 cal., 31g fat (11g sat. fat), 61mg chol., 821mg sod., 18g carb. (6g sugars, 2g fiber), 14g pro.

FOURTH OF JULY BAKED BEANS

We always choose this family recipe for July Fourth or for any picnic because it's a meaty twist on everyday baked beans and it has a nice sweetness.

—Wendy Hodorowski, Bellaire, OH

Prep: 10 min. • **Bake:** 55 min.
Makes: 8 servings

- ½ lb. ground beef
- 1 large onion, finely chopped
- ½ cup sugar
- ½ cup packed brown sugar
- ½ cup ketchup
- ½ cup barbecue sauce
- 2 Tbsp. yellow mustard
- 2 Tbsp. molasses
- ½ tsp. chili powder
- 2 cans (13.7 oz. each) beans with tomato sauce
- ½ lb. bacon strips, cooked and crumbled

1. Preheat oven to 350°. In a large skillet, cook beef and onion over medium heat 6-8 minutes or until beef is no longer pink, breaking up beef into crumbles; drain. Stir in sugars, ketchup, barbecue sauce, mustard, molasses and chili powder. Add beans and bacon.

2. Transfer to a greased 13x9-in. baking dish. Bake, covered, 45 minutes. Bake, uncovered, 10-15 minutes longer or until heated through.

Per ¾ cup: 323 cal., 8g fat (3g sat. fat), 28mg chol., 970mg sod., 51g carb. (41g sugars, 4g fiber), 14g pro.

FOURTH OF JULY BAKED BEANS

GRILLED GARDEN PIZZA

EDITOR'S CHOICE

GRILLED GARDEN PIZZA

Dazzle your family and friends with pizzas fresh off the grill. We top them with Asiago, Parmesan, veggies and fresh basil. Pile on the toppings you love.

—Teri Rasey, Cadillac, MI

Takes: 30 min. • **Makes:** 6 servings

- 2 plum tomatoes, thinly sliced
- ½ tsp. sea salt or kosher salt
- 1 loaf (1 lb.) frozen pizza dough, thawed
- 2 Tbsp. olive oil, divided
- ½ cup shredded Parmesan or Asiago cheese
- ½ cup fresh or frozen corn, thawed
- ¼ cup thinly sliced red onion
- 8 oz. fresh mozzarella cheese, sliced
- ½ cup thinly sliced fresh spinach
- 3 Tbsp. chopped fresh basil

1. Sprinkle tomatoes with salt; set aside. On a lightly floured surface, divide dough in half. Roll or press each to ¼-in. thickness; place each on a greased sheet of foil (about 10 in. square). Brush tops with 1 Tbsp. oil.

2. Carefully invert crusts onto a grill rack, removing foil. Brush tops with remaining oil. Grill, covered, over medium heat for 2-3 minutes or until the bottom is golden brown. Remove from grill; reduce grill temperature to low.

3. Top grilled sides of crusts with Parmesan or Asiago cheese, tomatoes, corn, onion and mozzarella cheese. Grill, covered, over low heat 4-6 minutes or until cheese is melted. Sprinkle with spinach and basil.

Per piece: 375 cal., 16g fat (7g sat. fat), 35mg chol., 680mg sod., 40g carb. (4g sugars, 1g fiber), 15g pro.

PAPA BURGER

PAPA BURGER

When whipping up something for Father's Day or the Fourth of July, I go big and tall with this fully loaded, juicy yumburger.
—Chase Bailey, Costa Mesa, CA

Takes: 30 min. • **Makes:** 4 servings

- 1 lb. ground beef
- ⅓ cup finely chopped onion
- 1 slice whole wheat or white bread, broken into small pieces
- 2 Tbsp. red wine vinegar
- 1 Tbsp. liquid smoke
- 2 tsp. Worcestershire sauce
- 1 tsp. hamburger or steak seasoning
- ¼ to ½ tsp. garlic salt
- ¼ to ½ tsp. pepper
- ¼ cup all-purpose flour
- 4 onion hamburger buns, split
- 4 Bibb or Boston lettuce leaves
- ⅓ cup prepared Thousand Island salad dressing
- 4 slices red onion
- 1 large heirloom tomato, sliced

1. Combine the first nine ingredients; mix lightly. Shape into four ¾-in.-thick patties. Press patties into flour to lightly coat both sides.

2. In a large nonstick skillet, cook burgers over medium heat until a thermometer reads 160°, about 4-5 minutes per side. Layer bun bottoms with lettuce, burgers, salad dressing and onion and tomato slices. Replace bun tops.

Per burger: 464 cal., 22g fat (6g sat. fat), 77mg chol., 713mg sod., 37g carb. (8g sugars, 3g fiber), 26g pro.

CATCH-A-WAVE SUGAR COOKIES

CATCH-A-WAVE SUGAR COOKIES

These soft, tender cookies are always a hit, so I often stir up a big batch. You can tint the frosting and decorate the tops to match any season or occasion.

—Coleen Walter, Bancroft, MI

Prep: 30 min.
Bake: 10 min./batch + cooling
Makes: about 2½ dozen

- 1 cup butter, softened
- ¾ cup sugar
- 1 tsp. vanilla extract
- ½ tsp. almond extract
- 2 large eggs
- 2¼ cups all-purpose flour
- 1 tsp. cream of tartar
- ½ tsp. baking soda
- ¼ tsp. salt
- ¼ tsp. ground nutmeg

FROSTING

- ¼ cup butter, softened
- 3 cups confectioners' sugar
- 1 tsp. almond extract
- 2 to 4 Tbsp. hot water
- Food coloring, optional

1. Preheat oven to 350°. Cream butter and sugar until light and fluffy; beat in extracts and eggs, one at a time. In another bowl, whisk together flour, cream of tartar, baking soda, salt and nutmeg; gradually beat into creamed mixture.

2. Drop dough by rounded tablespoonfuls 3 in. apart onto parchment paper-lined baking sheets; flatten slightly with bottom of a glass dipped in sugar. Bake until edges begin to brown, 8-10 minutes. Remove from pan to wire racks; cool completely.

3. For frosting, beat butter, confectioners' sugar, extract and enough water to reach desired consistency. If desired, tint with food coloring. Spread over cookies.

Per cookie: 174 cal., 8g fat (5g sat. fat), 33mg chol., 107mg sod., 24g carb. (17g sugars, 0 fiber), 1g pro.

RHUBARB MINT TEA

RHUBARB MINT TEA

A bumper crop of rhubarb and mint from my garden inspired me to create this thirst-quenching pick-me-up. Raspberries deepen the tea's vibrant red color, making the drinks a pretty addition to your table.

—Laurie Bock, Lynden, WA

Prep: 15 min. • **Cook:** 45 min. + chilling
Makes: 12 servings

- 4 cups chopped fresh or frozen rhubarb
- 2 cups fresh or frozen raspberries
- 2 pkg. (¾ oz. each) fresh mint leaves
- 3 qt. water
- 4 black tea bags
- 2 cups sugar
- 12 mint sprigs

In a 6-qt. stockpot, combine the rhubarb, raspberries, mint and water; bring to a boil. Reduce heat; simmer, uncovered, for 30 minutes. Remove from heat. Add tea bags; steep, covered, 3-5 minutes according to taste. Using a fine mesh strainer, strain tea, discarding tea bags and pulp. Stir in sugar until dissolved; cool slightly. Transfer to a pitcher; refrigerate until cooled completely. Serve over ice with mint sprigs.

Per cup: 151 cal., 0 fat (0 sat. fat), 0 chol., 3mg sod., 38g carb. (35g sugars, 2g fiber), 1g pro.

BLUEBERRY-CINNAMON CAMPFIRE BREAD

GARDEN PESTO PASTA SALAD

My family and I live on a homestead in the Missouri Ozarks and produce much of our own food. In the summer, when the garden is bursting with fresh vegetables and it's too hot to cook, I use our seasonal veggies for pasta salads and other cool meals.
—Sarah Mathews, Ava, MO

Prep: 15 min. + chilling • **Makes:** 10 servings

- 3 cups uncooked spiral pasta (about 9 oz.)
- ½ cup prepared pesto
- 3 Tbsp. white wine vinegar
- 1 Tbsp. lemon juice
- ½ tsp. salt
- ¼ tsp. pepper
- ¼ cup olive oil
- 1 medium zucchini, halved and sliced
- 1 medium sweet red pepper, chopped
- 1 medium tomato, seeded and chopped
- 1 small red onion, halved and thinly sliced
- ½ cup grated Parmesan cheese

1. Cook pasta according to package directions; drain. Rinse with cold water and drain well.
2. Meanwhile, whisk together pesto, vinegar, lemon juice and seasonings. Gradually whisk in oil until blended.
3. Combine vegetables and the pasta. Drizzle with pesto dressing; toss to coat. Refrigerate, covered, until cold, about 1 hour. Serve with Parmesan cheese.

Per serving: 217 cal., 11g fat (2g sat. fat), 3mg chol., 339mg sod., 23g carb. (3g sugars, 2g fiber), 6g pro. **Diabetic exchanges:** 2 fat, 1½ starch.

TEST KITCHEN TIP

To cook pasta more evenly, prevent it from sticking together and avoid boilovers, always cook it in a large kettle or Dutch oven. Unless you have a very large kettle, don't cook more than 2 pounds of pasta at a time.

BLUEBERRY-CINNAMON CAMPFIRE BREAD

A neighboring camper made a bread so tempting, I had to ask for the details. Here's my version, best enjoyed with a steaming cup of coffee by the campfire.
—Joan Hallford, North Richland Hills, TX

Prep: 10 min.
Cook: 30 min. + standing
Makes: 8 servings

- 1 loaf (1 lb.) cinnamon-raisin bread
- 6 large eggs
- 1 cup 2% milk or half-and-half cream
- 2 Tbsp. maple syrup
- 1 tsp. vanilla extract
- ½ cup chopped pecans, toasted
- 2 cups fresh blueberries, divided

1. Prepare campfire or grill for low heat. Arrange bread slices on a greased double thickness of heavy-duty foil (about 24x18 in.). Bring foil up the sides, leaving the top open. Whisk eggs, milk, syrup and vanilla. Pour over bread; sprinkle with nuts and 1 cup blueberries. Fold edges over top, crimping to seal.
2. Place on a grill grate over campfire or grill until eggs are cooked through, 30-40 minutes. Remove from heat; let stand 10 minutes. Sprinkle with remaining blueberries; serve with additional maple syrup if desired.

Per 2 slices: 266 cal., 10g fat (2g sat. fat), 142mg chol., 185mg sod., 36g carb. (14g sugars, 5g fiber), 12g pro. **Diabetic exchanges:** 2 starch, 1 medium-fat meat, ½ fruit, ½ fat.

GARDEN PESTO PASTA SALAD

BROWNIE SPIDERS

BROWNIE SPIDERS

Spiders petrify me, but I can make an exception for these cute ones made from chocolate. They make perfectly adorable Halloween treats.

—Ali Ebright, Kansas City, MO

Prep: 20 min. • **Bake:** 30 min. + cooling
Makes: 9 brownie spiders

- 1 pkg. (15.8 oz.) brownie mix
- ½ cup semisweet chocolate chips
- 2 cups crispy chow mein noodles
- 18 candy eyeballs

1. Prepare and bake brownies according to package directions using an 8-in. square baking pan lined with parchment paper. Cool completely in pan on a wire rack.

2. In a microwave, melt chocolate chips; stir until smooth. Remove 1 Tbsp. melted chocolate to a bowl; reserve for attaching eyes. Add noodles to remaining chocolate; stir gently to coat. Spread onto a waxed paper-lined baking sheet, separating noodles slightly. Freeze until set.

3. Cut nine brownies with a 2¼-in. round cutter for spider bodies. Attach eyeballs using reserved melted chocolate. With a bamboo skewer or toothpick, poke eight holes in top of each spider for inserting legs. Insert a coated noodle into each hole. Store in an airtight container.

Per brownie: 367 cal., 16g fat (4g sat. fat), 16mg chol., 346mg sod., 54g carb. (31g sugars, 2g fiber), 5g pro.

MUMMY POPPERS

I wrapped these spicy jalapeno poppers in puff pastry like a mummy. You can tame the heat by adjusting the amount of chipotle.

—Nick Iverson, Denver, CO

Prep: 30 min. • **Bake:** 30 min.
Makes: 32 appetizers

- 1 pkg. (8 oz.) cream cheese, softened
- 2 cups shredded cheddar cheese
- 2 green onions, finely chopped
- 1 to 2 chipotle peppers in adobo sauce, finely chopped
- 2 Tbsp. lime juice
- 1 Tbsp. honey
- ½ tsp. salt
- ½ tsp. ground cumin
- ¼ tsp. pepper
- 16 jalapeno peppers, halved lengthwise and seeded
- 1 pkg. (17.3 oz.) frozen puff pastry, thawed and cut lengthwise into 32 strips

1. Preheat oven to 400°. Beat the first nine ingredients until blended. Spoon or pipe cheese mixture into pepper halves.

2. Wrap puff pastry strips around pepper halves. Transfer wrapped peppers to parchment paper-lined baking sheets. Bake until golden brown and cheese is melted, 30-40 minutes.

Per popper: 133 cal., 9g fat (4g sat. fat), 14mg chol., 159mg sod., 10g carb. (1g sugars, 1g fiber), 3g pro.

TEST KITCHEN TIP

Vary the sizes and shape of the peppers to create visual interest. A measuring teaspoon is a handy tool for removing seeds. Use a food-safe plastic bag to pipe filling. Snip off a corner, transfer cheese mixture and pipe away.

MUMMY POPPERS

CITRUS HERB TURKEY

turkey in prepared pan, breast side up.

3. Bring edges of foil over turkey to cover. Roast, covered, 1 hour. Carefully open foil and fold it down. Reduce oven setting to 325°. Roast, uncovered, 1½-2 hours longer or until a thermometer inserted in thickest part of thigh reads 170°-175°. Cover loosely with foil if turkey browns too quickly.

4. Remove turkey from oven; tent with foil. Let stand 20 minutes before carving. Discard fruit mixture from cavity. If desired, skim fat and thicken pan drippings for gravy. Serve with turkey.

Per 8 oz. cooked turkey: 651 cal., 36g fat (14g sat. fat), 276mg chol., 430mg sod., 4g carb. (2g sugars, 1g fiber), 73g pro.

CHIPOTLE-ORANGE CRANBERRY SAUCE

(PICTURED ON P. 402)

With brown sugar, cinnamon and chipotle powder for a little kick, this cranberry sauce will earn a permanent spot in the holiday lineup.

—Chris Michalowski, Dallas, TX

Prep: 15 min. + chilling • **Makes:** 1¾ cups

- 1 medium orange
- 1 pkg. (12 oz.) fresh or frozen cranberries
- ½ cup packed brown sugar
- 1 cinnamon stick (3 in.)
- ¼ to ¾ tsp. ground chipotle pepper
- ¼ tsp. pepper

1. Finely grate zest from the orange. Cut orange crosswise in half; squeeze juice from orange. Place zest and orange juice in a large saucepan. Add the remaining ingredients.

2. Bring to a boil, stirring to dissolve sugar. Reduce heat to a simmer; cook, uncovered, 5-7 minutes or until berries pop, stirring occasionally. Remove from heat.

3. Transfer to a small bowl; cool slightly. Refrigerate, covered, until cold.

Per ¼ cup: 103 cal., 0 fat (0 sat. fat), 0 chol., 10mg sod., 26g carb. (21g sugars, 2g fiber), 0 pro.

CITRUS HERB TURKEY

(PICTURED ON P. 403)

When it came to a roasting turkey, my grandmother had the magic touch: She would wrap a turkey in foil and cook it on low heat for 8 hours so it would bake up juicy and tender. This version doesn't take that long, but it's just as good.

—Portia Gorman, Los Angeles, CA

Prep: 40 min. • **Bake:** 2½ hours + standing
Makes: 12 servings

- 1 pkg. (1 oz.) fresh rosemary, divided
- 1 pkg. (1 oz.) fresh thyme, divided
- ¾ cup softened unsalted butter, divided
- 1 turkey (12 to 14 lbs.)
- 2 tsp. seasoned salt
- ½ tsp. garlic powder
- ½ tsp. pepper
- 1 medium apple, chopped
- 1 medium orange, chopped
- 1 small red onion, chopped
- 1 small sweet orange pepper, chopped

1. Preheat oven to 400°. Line a roasting pan with three pieces of heavy-duty foil (pieces should be long enough to cover turkey). Mince half the rosemary and thyme from each package (about ¼ cup total). In a small bowl, beat ½ cup butter and minced herbs until blended. With fingers, carefully loosen skin from turkey breast; rub butter mixture under the skin. Secure skin to underside of breast with toothpicks. Mix seasoned salt, garlic powder and pepper; sprinkle over turkey and inside the turkey cavity.

2. Cube remaining butter. In a large bowl, combine butter, apple, orange, onion, orange pepper and remaining herb sprigs; spoon inside cavity. Tuck wings under turkey; tie drumsticks together. Place

EASY PUMPKIN PIE

Pumpkin pie does not have to be difficult to make. This recipe has a wonderful taste and will be a hit at your holiday meal.

—Marty Rummel, Trout Lake, WA

Prep: 10 min. • **Bake:** 50 min. + cooling
Makes: 8 servings

- 3 large eggs
- 1 cup canned pumpkin
- 1 cup evaporated milk
- ½ cup sugar
- ¼ cup maple syrup
- 1 tsp. ground cinnamon
- ½ tsp. salt
- ½ tsp. ground nutmeg
- ½ tsp. maple flavoring
- ½ tsp. vanilla extract
- 1 frozen deep-dish pie dough (9 in.)
- Additional pie pastry, optional
- Whipped cream, optional

1. In a bowl, beat the first 10 ingredients until smooth; pour into crust. Cover edge loosely with foil.

2. Bake at 400° for 10 minutes. Reduce heat to 350°; bake 40-45 minutes longer or until a knife inserted in the center comes out clean. Remove foil. Cool on a wire rack.

3. If leaf cutouts are desired, roll additional pastry to ⅛-in. thickness; cut out with 1-in. to 1½-in. leaf-shaped cookie cutters. With a sharp knife, score leaf veins on cutouts.

4. Place on an ungreased baking sheet. Bake cutouts at 400° for 6-8 minutes or until golden brown. Remove to a wire rack to cool. Arrange around edge of pie. Garnish with whipped cream if desired.

Per piece: 275 cal., 11g fat (5g sat. fat), 94mg chol., 306mg sod., 38g carb. (24g sugars, 1g fiber), 6g pro.

EASY PUMPKIN PIE

BRAISED HANUKKAH BRISKET

My mother, Enid, always used the most marbled cut of brisket she could find to make this recipe so she'd get top flavor. When she added carrots to the pan, she threw in some potatoes, too. The best thing about this dish is that it's even tastier the next day.

—Ellen Ruzinsky, Yorktown Heights, NY

Prep: 25 min. • Cook: 2¾ hours
Makes: 12 servings (4 cups vegetables)

- 2 Tbsp. canola oil
- 1 fresh beef brisket (4 to 5 lbs.)
- 3 celery ribs, cut into 1-in. pieces
- 3 large carrots, cut into ¼-in. slices
- 2 large onions, sliced
- 1 lb. medium fresh mushrooms
- ¾ cup cold water
- ¾ cup tomato sauce
- 3 Tbsp. Worcestershire sauce
- 1 Tbsp. prepared horseradish

1. In a Dutch oven, heat oil over medium heat. Brown brisket on both sides. Remove from pan.

2. Add celery, carrots and onions to same pan; cook and stir 4-6 minutes or until crisp-tender. Stir in remaining ingredients.

3. Return brisket to pan, fat side up. Bring mixture to a boil. Reduce heat; simmer, covered, 2½-3 hours or until the meat is tender. Remove beef and vegetables; keep warm. Skim fat from pan juices. If desired, thicken juices.

4. Cut brisket diagonally across the grain into thin slices. Serve with vegetables and pan juices.

Note This is a fresh beef brisket, not corned beef.

4 oz. cooked meat with ⅓ cup vegetables and ½ cup juices: 247 cal., 9g fat (3g sat. fat), 64mg chol., 189mg sod., 8g carb. (3g sugars, 2g fiber), 33g pro. **Diabetic exchanges:** 4 lean meat, 1 vegetable, ½ fat.

TZIMMES

I found this recipe a long time ago. It has become our traditional side dish for every Hanukkah and Passover feast and is a favorite of young and old alike. It also complements chicken and turkey well.
—Cheri Bragg, Viola, DE

Prep: 20 min. • **Bake:** 1¾ hours
Makes: 12 servings

- 3 lbs. sweet potatoes (about 4 large), peeled and cut into chunks
- 2 lbs. medium carrots, cut into ½-in. chunks
- 1 pkg. (12 oz.) pitted dried plums, halved
- 1 cup orange juice
- 1 cup water
- ¼ cup honey
- ¼ cup packed brown sugar
- 2 tsp. ground cinnamon
- ¼ cup butter, cubed

1. In a greased 13x9-in. baking dish, combine the sweet potatoes, carrots and plums. Combine the orange juice, water, honey, brown sugar and cinnamon; pour over vegetables.
2. Cover; bake at 350° for 1 hour. Uncover; dot with butter. Bake for 45-60 minutes longer, carefully stirring every 15 minutes, until vegetables are tender and sauce is thickened.
Per ¾ cup: 262 cal., 4g fat (1g sat. fat), 0 chol., 109mg sod., 55g carb. (32g sugars, 6g fiber), 3g pro.

PARSNIP LATKES WITH LOX & HORSERADISH CREME

A horseradish-flavored creme fraiche brings zip to these crispy homemade latkes, which get a touch of sweetness from the parsnips. Add fresh dill sprigs for a garnish.
—Todd Schmeling, Gurnee, IL

Prep: 30 min. • **Cook:** 5 min./batch
Makes: about 3 dozen

- 1 lb. potatoes, peeled
- 1 lb. parsnips, peeled
- ⅔ cup chopped green onions
- 2 large eggs, lightly beaten
- 1 tsp. salt
- ½ tsp. pepper
- Oil for deep-fat frying
- 1 pkg. (3 oz.) smoked salmon or lox, cut into ½-in.-wide strips
- 1 cup creme fraiche or sour cream
- 1 Tbsp. snipped fresh dill
- 1 Tbsp. prepared horseradish
- ¼ tsp. salt
- ⅛ tsp. white pepper
- Fresh dill sprigs

1. Coarsely grate potatoes and parsnips. Place the grated vegetables on a double thickness of cheesecloth; bring up corners and squeeze out any liquid. Transfer to a large bowl; stir in the onions, eggs, salt and pepper.
2. In an electric skillet, heat ⅛ in. of oil to 375°. Drop potato mixture by heaping tablespoonfuls into hot oil. Flatten to form patties. Fry until golden brown; turn and cook the other side. Drain on paper towels.
3. Roll salmon to form rose shapes; set aside. Combine the creme fraiche, dill, horseradish, salt and pepper. Top latkes with a dollop of creme fraiche mixture and a salmon rose. Garnish with dill.
Per appetizer: 71 cal., 5g fat (2g sat. fat), 17mg chol., 110mg sod., 4g carb. (1g sugars, 1g fiber), 1g pro.

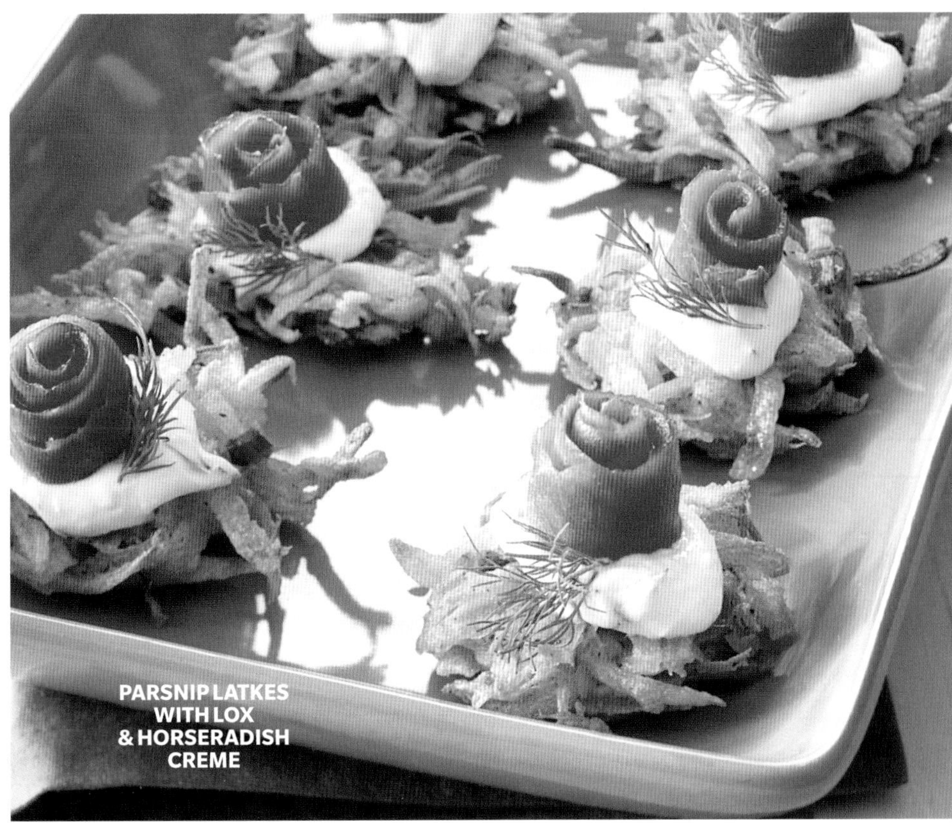

PARSNIP LATKES WITH LOX & HORSERADISH CREME

HOLIDAY DANISH PUFFS

It's worth the extra effort to make this candy cane-shaped dessert. The recipe makes two pastries, so it's perfect for gift-giving.

—Susan Garoutte, Georgetown, TX

Prep: 45 min.
Bake: 1 hour + cooling
Makes: 2 pastries (8 servings each)

- 1 cup all-purpose flour
- ½ cup cold butter, cubed
- 2 to 3 Tbsp. cold water

TOPPING

- 1 cup water
- ½ cup butter, cubed
- ¼ tsp. salt
- 1 cup all-purpose flour
- 3 large eggs
- ½ tsp. almond extract

FROSTING

- 1½ cups confectioners' sugar
- 2 Tbsp. butter, softened
- 2 Tbsp. water
- 1½ tsp. vanilla extract
- ½ cup sliced almonds, toasted

1. Place flour in a small bowl; cut in butter until crumbly. Gradually add water, tossing with a fork until dough holds together when pressed. Divide dough in half. On a lightly floured surface, roll each into a 14x2½-in. rectangle. Transfer to an ungreased baking sheet; curve one end of each pastry to form tops of canes. Refrigerate while preparing the topping.

2. Preheat the oven to 350°. In a large saucepan, combine water, butter and salt; bring to a rolling boil. Add flour all at once and beat until blended. Cook over medium heat, stirring vigorously until mixture pulls away from sides of pan and forms a ball. Remove from heat; let stand 5 minutes.

3. Add eggs, one at a time, beating well after each addition until smooth. Add the extract; continue beating until the mixture is smooth and shiny. Spread over pastry dough.

4. Bake for 60-70 minutes or until puffed and golden brown. Cool on pans for 10 minutes before removing to a wire rack; cool completely.

5. In a small bowl, beat confectioners' sugar, butter, water and extract until smooth. Spread over pastries; sprinkle with almonds. Refrigerate leftovers.

Note To toast nuts, bake in a shallow pan in a 350° oven for 5-10 minutes or cook in a skillet over low heat until lightly browned, stirring occasionally.

Per piece: 247 cal., 15g fat (9g sat. fat), 69mg chol., 154mg sod., 24g carb. (11g sugars, 1g fiber), 4g pro.

HOLIDAY DANISH PUFFS

EDITOR'S CHOICE

COQUITO

An all-time family favorite, this creamy frozen adult beverage features cream of coconut blended with cloves, cinnamon, vanilla and rum.

—Evelyn Robles, Oak Creek, WI

Prep: 15 min. + chilling • **Makes:** 8 servings

- 1 can (15 oz.) cream of coconut
- 1 can (14 oz.) sweetened condensed milk
- 1 can (12 oz.) evaporated milk
- ½ cup water
- 1 tsp. vanilla extract
- ½ tsp. ground cinnamon
- ¼ tsp. ground cloves
- 1 cup rum

Place the first seven ingredients in a blender; cover and process until blended. Refrigerate until chilled. Stir in rum before serving.

Per ¾ cup: 488 cal., 17g fat (12g sat. fat), 30mg chol., 132mg sod., 63g carb. (63g sugars, 0 fiber), 7g pro.

HERB-CRUSTED PRIME RIB

HERB-CRUSTED PRIME RIB

Prime rib always makes an impression on a holiday dinner table. This roast is flavored with a bounty of fresh herbs.

—Jennifer Dennis, Alhambra, CA

Prep: 20 min. • **Bake:** 1¾ hours + standing
Makes: 8 servings

- 1 large shallot, coarsely chopped
- 6 garlic cloves, quartered
- 3 Tbsp. minced fresh rosemary or 1 Tbsp. dried rosemary
- 2 Tbsp. minced fresh oregano or 2 tsp. dried oregano
- 2 Tbsp. minced fresh thyme or 2 tsp. dried thyme
- 2 Tbsp. minced fresh sage or 2 tsp. rubbed sage
- 2 Tbsp. olive oil
- 3 tsp. pepper
- 1 tsp. salt
- 1 bone-in beef rib roast (4 lbs.)

SAUCE

- 1½ cups reduced-sodium beef broth
- 1 cup dry red wine or additional reduced-sodium beef broth
- 1 tsp. butter
- ½ tsp. salt

1. Preheat oven to 350°. Place the first six ingredients in a food processor; cover and pulse until finely chopped. Add oil, pepper and salt; cover and process until blended. Rub over roast. Place on a rack in a large roasting pan.

2. Bake, uncovered, 1¾-2¼ hours or until meat reaches desired doneness (for medium-rare, a thermometer should read 135°; medium, 140°; medium-well, 145°).

3. Remove roast to a platter and keep warm; let stand 15 minutes before slicing.

4. Meanwhile, in a small saucepan, bring broth and wine to a boil; cook until liquid is reduced to 1 cup. Remove from heat; stir in butter and salt. Slice roast; serve with sauce.

Per 8 oz.: 338 cal., 19g fat (7g sat. fat), 92mg chol., 612mg sod., 4g carb. (1g sugars, 0 fiber), 31g pro.

Made this recipe a couple of months ago, and loved it! Will be making it again for New Year's. The herbs really give it just the right flavor without overpowering the beef.

RKEKLUND TASTEOFHOME.COM

HOLIDAY GREEN BEANS

HOLIDAY GREEN BEANS

(PICTURED ON P. 402)

My mom's recipe for these green beans had five stars drawn on it. I would have to agree. Made with fresh ingredients, this dish is worthy of a celebration.

—Marcia Shires, San Antonio, TX

Prep: 45 min. • **Bake:** 10 min.
Makes: 16 servings

- 2 cups (16 oz.) sour cream
- 2 tsp. sugar
- 1 tsp. salt
- ½ tsp. dill weed
- 1 lb. bacon strips, cut into 1-in. pieces
- 2 lbs. fresh green beans, cut into 1½-in. pieces (6 cups)
- 1 lb. medium fresh mushrooms, quartered
- 6 green onions, chopped
- 1 cup slivered almonds, optional
- 4 garlic cloves, minced
- 2 cups onion and garlic salad croutons
- 1½ cups shredded Monterey Jack cheese

1. Preheat oven to 350°. In a small bowl, combine sour cream, sugar, salt and dill weed. In a 6-qt. stockpot, cook the bacon over medium heat until crisp, stirring occasionally.

2. Meanwhile, in a large saucepan, bring 6 cups water to a boil. Add the beans in batches; cook, uncovered, 2-3 minutes or just until crisp-tender. Drain.

3. Remove bacon with a slotted spoon; drain on paper towels. Discard drippings, reserving 6 Tbsp. in pan. Add mushrooms, onions and, if desired, slivered almonds to drippings; cook and stir over medium heat 4-6 minutes or until mushrooms are tender. Add garlic; cook and stir 1 minute longer. Remove from heat; stir in beans, bacon and croutons. Stir in sour cream mixture. Transfer to an ungreased 13x9-in. baking dish. Sprinkle with the cheese. Bake for 10-15 minutes or until cheese is melted.

Per ¾ cup: 246 cal., 19g fat (9g sat. fat), 32mg chol., 468mg sod., 11g carb. (3g sugars, 2g fiber), 9g pro.

TUSCAN SAUSAGE & BEAN DIP

(PICTURED ON P. 55)

This is a spinoff of a Mexican dip I had once. The original was good, but since I was going through an I'm-so-over-Mexican-dip phase, I decided to switch it up. Take it to a holiday party—I'll bet you no one else will bring anything like it!

—Mandy Rivers, Lexington, SC

Prep: 25 min. • **Bake:** 20 min.
Makes: 16 servings

- 1 lb. bulk hot Italian sausage
- 1 medium onion, finely chopped
- 4 garlic cloves, minced
- ½ cup dry white wine or chicken broth
- ½ tsp. dried oregano
- ¼ tsp. salt
- ¼ tsp. dried thyme
- 1 pkg. (8 oz.) cream cheese, softened
- 1 pkg. (6 oz.) fresh baby spinach, coarsely chopped
- 1 can (15 oz.) cannellini beans, rinsed and drained
- 1 cup chopped seeded tomatoes
- 1 cup shredded part-skim mozzarella cheese
- ½ cup shredded Parmesan cheese
- Assorted crackers or toasted French bread baguette slices

1. Preheat oven to 375°. In a large skillet, cook sausage, onion and garlic over medium heat until sausage is no longer pink, breaking up sausage into crumbles; drain. Stir in wine, oregano, salt and thyme. Bring to a boil; cook until liquid is almost evaporated.

2. Add cream cheese; stir until melted. Stir in spinach, beans and tomatoes; cook and stir until spinach is wilted. Transfer to a greased 8-in. square baking dish; if using an ovenproof skillet, leave in skillet. Sprinkle with cheeses.

3. Bake until bubbly, 20-25 minutes. Serve with crackers.

Per ¼ cup: 200 cal., 14g fat (7g sat. fat), 41mg chol., 434mg sod., 7g carb. (2g sugars, 2g fiber), 10g pro.

RED VELVET PEPPERMINT THUMBPRINTS

I love the flavor of red velvet in both cookies and cakes. In this pretty thumbprint cookie, I added my favorite holiday ingredient: peppermint. It's a fun seasonal twist!
—Priscilla Yee, Concord, CA

Prep: 30 min.
Bake: 10 min./batch + cooling
Makes: about 4 dozen

- 1 cup butter, softened
- 1 cup sugar
- 1 large egg
- 4 tsp. red food coloring
- 1 tsp. peppermint extract
- 2½ cups all-purpose flour
- 3 Tbsp. baking cocoa
- 1 tsp. baking powder
- ¼ tsp. salt
- 2 cups white baking chips
- 2 tsp. canola oil
- ¼ cup crushed peppermint candies

1. Preheat oven to 350°. In a large bowl, cream butter and sugar until light and fluffy. Beat in the egg, food coloring and extract. In another bowl, whisk flour, cocoa, baking powder and salt; gradually beat into creamed mixture.
2. Shape dough into 1-in. balls. Place 1 in. apart on ungreased baking sheets. Press a deep indentation in center of each with the end of a wooden spoon handle.
3. Bake 9-11 minutes or until set. Remove from pans to wire racks to cool completely.
4. In a microwave, melt the baking chips with oil; stir until smooth. Spoon a scant teaspoon filling into each cookie. Drizzle tops with remaining mixture. Sprinkle with peppermint candies. Let stand until set.
Per cookie: 118 cal., 7g fat (4g sat. fat), 16mg chol., 63mg sod., 14g carb. (9g sugars, 0 fiber), 1g pro.

CHOCOLATE-STRAWBERRY PRETZEL COOKIES

CHOCOLATE-STRAWBERRY PRETZEL COOKIES

Every year I try to come up with a new recipe for my cookie tray, and this one has become a favorite. Who would ever guess how good pretzels are in cookies?
—Isabel Minunni, Poughkeepsie, NY

Prep: 30 min. + chilling
Bake: 10 min./batch + cooling
Makes: about 1 dozen sandwich cookies

- 1 cup unsalted butter, softened
- ½ cup sugar
- 2 large eggs
- 1½ cups finely ground pretzels (about 6 oz.)
- 1 cup all-purpose flour
- 1 tsp. baking powder
- ⅔ cup semisweet chocolate chips, melted
- ⅓ cup seedless strawberry jam
- Confectioners' sugar

1. In a large bowl, cream butter and sugar until light and fluffy. Add eggs, one at a time, beating well after each addition. In another bowl, mix ground pretzels, flour and baking powder; gradually beat into creamed mixture. Divide dough in half. Shape each into a disk; wrap in plastic. Refrigerate until firm enough to roll, about 1 hour.
2. Preheat oven to 350°. On a lightly floured surface, roll each portion of dough to ¼-in. thickness. Cut dough with a floured 3½-in. tree-shaped cookie cutter. Using a floured 1¾-in. tree-shaped cookie cutter, cut out centers of half of the cookies. Place solid and window cookies about 1 in. apart on ungreased baking sheets.
3. Bake 8-10 minutes or until edges are light brown. Remove from pans to wire racks to cool completely.
4. Spread melted chocolate onto bottoms of the solid cookies; let stand until firm. Spread jam over cooled chocolate; top with window cookies. Dust lightly with confectioners' sugar.
Freeze option Freeze undecorated cookies in freezer containers. To use, thaw in covered containers and decorate as directed.
Per sandwich cookie: 245 cal., 15g fat (9g sat. fat), 54mg chol., 164mg sod., 28g carb. (14g sugars, 1g fiber), 3g pro.

SNOW ANGEL COOKIES

Angel cookies swirled with heavenly frosting make the perfect holiday treat.
—*Carolyn Moseley, Dayton, OH*

Prep: 40 min. + chilling
Bake: 15 min./batch + cooling
Makes: about 5 dozen

- 1 cup butter, softened
- 1 cup granulated sugar
- 1½ tsp. vanilla extract
- 2 large eggs
- 3½ cups all-purpose flour
- 1 tsp. ground cinnamon
- ½ tsp. baking powder
- ½ tsp. salt
- ¼ tsp. ground nutmeg
- ¼ tsp. ground cloves

FROSTING

- 9 cups confectioners' sugar
- ¾ cup shortening
- ½ cup lemon juice
- 4 to 6 Tbsp. water
- Coarse sugar, optional

1. In a large bowl, beat the butter, sugar and vanilla until blended. Beat in eggs, one at a time. In another bowl, whisk the flour, cinnamon, baking powder, salt, nutmeg and cloves; gradually beat into creamed mixture.

2. Divide dough in half. Shape each into a disk; wrap in plastic. Refrigerate 1 hour or until firm enough to roll.

3. Preheat oven to 350°. On a lightly floured surface, roll each portion of dough to ⅛-in. thickness. Cut dough with a floured 4-in. angel-shaped cookie cutter. Place cookies 1 in. apart on ungreased baking sheets.

4. Bake 12-14 minutes or until the edges begin to brown. Remove from pans to wire racks to cool completely.

5. For frosting, in a large bowl, beat the confectioners' sugar, shortening, lemon juice and enough water to reach a spreading consistency. Spread or pipe over cookies; sprinkle with coarse sugar.

Per cookie: 162 cal., 6g fat (3g sat. fat), 14mg chol., 53mg sod., 27g carb. (21g sugars, 0 fiber), 1g pro.

BUTTER COOKIES

These classic cookies will melt in your mouth. They're favorites of my nephews, who love the tender texture and creamy frosting. Kids can help decorate, too.
—Ruth Griggs, South Hill, VA

Prep: 25 min. • **Bake:** 10 min./batch
Makes: about 6½ dozen

- 1 cup butter, softened
- ¾ cup sugar
- 1 large egg
- ½ tsp. vanilla extract
- 2½ cups all-purpose flour
- 1 tsp. baking powder
- ¼ tsp. salt

FROSTING

- ½ cup butter, softened
- 4 cups confectioners' sugar
- 1 tsp. vanilla extract
- 3 to 4 Tbsp. 2% milk
- Red food coloring, optional

1. Preheat oven to 375°. Cream butter and sugar until light and fluffy. Beat in egg and vanilla. In another bowl, whisk flour, baking powder and salt; gradually beat into creamed mixture.
2. Using a cookie press fitted with a heart disk, press dough 1 in. apart onto ungreased baking sheets. Bake until set but not brown, 6-8 minutes. Cool on wire racks.
3. Beat butter, confectioners' sugar, vanilla and enough milk to reach a spreading consistency. If desired, tint with food coloring. Decorate cookies as desired.
Per cookie: 157 cal., 7g fat (4g sat. fat), 24mg chol., 99mg sod., 22g carb. (15g sugars, 0 fiber), 1g pro.

Between the cookies, roses, Valentine's card and extra desserts, love was certainly in the air when we took this photo in 1997.

GENERAL RECIPE INDEX

This handy index lists recipes by food category, major ingredient and cooking method, so you can easily locate the dish that suits your needs.

ALPHABETICAL RECIPE INDEX

This index lists every recipe in alphabetical order so you can easily find all of your favorites.

P. 106

P. 328

P. 172